Authority and social work:
concept and use

Authority and social work: concept and use

edited by SHANKAR A. YELAJA

University of Toronto Press

©University of Toronto Press 1971

Printed in Canada by

University of Toronto Press

Toronto and Buffalo

ISBN 0-8020-1712-6 (cloth)

ISBN 0-8020-2048-8 (paper)

To my father

ANNARAO M. YELAJA

a dedicated teacher,

scholar and humanist

Contributors

CHESTER I. BARNARD was the first President of the New Jersey Telephone Company, President of the Rockefeller Foundation, and President of the National Science Foundation. He died in 1961.

SAUL BERNSTEIN is Professor of Social Work at the Boston University School of Social Work, Boston, Massachusetts.

ARTHUR K. COUSE is Executive Assistant at the John Howard Society of Ontario.

JACOB CHWAST is Consultant for Educational Alliance, New York, New York.

HAROLD ESTERSON is Director of Mental Health Services at Manhattanville Community Centers, New York, and Director of Group Therapy Guidance Center, New Rochelle, New York.

ARTHUR E. FINK is a Professor at the School of Social Work, the University of North Carolina, Chapel Hill, North Carolina.

CARL J. FRIEDRICH is Eaton Professor of the Science of Government at Harvard University, Cambridge, Massachusetts.

ERICH FROMM is a well-known author and philosopher. Dr. Fromm is Head of the Department of Psychoanalysis of the Medical School of the National University of Mexico since 1955. Anjunct Professor of Psychology at New York University, he has lectured at Columbia, Yale, and Michigan State Universities. He is author of several best sellers, two books, *The Revolution of Hope* and *The Crisis of Psychoanalysis* have recently been published.

DALE G. HARDMAN is Associate Professor of Sociology at Wisconsin State University, Oshkosh, Wisconsin.

SALLY KNISELY, who holds a Doctor of Education degree from the Teachers' College, Columbia University, has been in private practice in child psychology for the past 12 years in New York and Connecticut.

EDWIN F. KOEPP is Director and Chief Psychiatric Social Worker at the Brookings Area Guidance Centre, Brookings, South Dakota.

JOSEPH S. MILLER was a psychiatrist and psychoanalyst in New York and a graduate of the William Alanson White Institute. He died in 1960.

LLOYD E. OHLIN is a Professor of Criminology at the School of Law, Harvard University, Cambridge, Massachusetts.

BERNICE ORCHARD is a Professor at the University of Tennessee, Nashville, Tennessee.

DONNELL M. PAPPENFORT is a member of the faculty of the School of Social Work, Columbia University. Dr. Pappenfort is now with the Center for Urban Studies, Museum of Science and Industry, Chicago, Illinois.

HERMAN PIVEN was teaching at John Jay College of Criminal Justice, New York City, in 1969.

ROBERT V. PRESTHUS is a Professor at the School of Public Administration, Cornell University, Ithaca, New York.

FRITZ REDL is a Professor at Wayne State University School of Social Work, Detroit, Michigan.

ELIZABETH DE SCHWEINITZ is Consultant for In-Service Training, Board of Public Welfare, District of Columbia.

KARL DE SCHWEINITZ is Director of the Committee on Education and Social Services, American Council on Education, Washington, DC.

YVES R. SIMON is a distinguished Frenchman, scholar, teacher and philosopher. Professor Simon, although probably best known for his clarification of fundamental issues of political philosophy and for his studies on the differentiation and correlation of science and philosophy, was also praised as a logician and a metaphysician. He taught at Notre Dame (1938–1948), and at the Committee on Social Thought of the University of Chicago from 1948 to his death in 1961.

ELLIOT STUDT is Director of the Parole Action Study Center for the Study of Law and Society at the University of California, Berkeley, California.

EDITH M. TUFTS is a Professor at the School of Social Work, Catholic University, Washington, DC.

EDNA WASSER is Professor of Social Work at the University of Washington School of Social Work, Seattle, Washington.

IRVING WEISMAN is a Professor at the School of Social Work, Hunter College, New York, New York.

DAVID WINEMAN is a Professor at the School of Social Work at Wayne State University, Detroit, Michigan.

Contents

Acknowledgments

As I look back upon the many months and years involved in preparing and completing this book, I am amazed at the number of persons on whom I relied for assistance and without whose co-operation this book probably would not have seen the light of day. It gives me great pleasure to acknowledge their contributions and thank them for their parts in this book.

One man who contributed to my understanding of the concepts of freedom and authority through innumerable hours of "brainstorming sessions" is the late Professor Emeritus Roland J. Artigues, University of Pennsylvania, School of Social Work. His sad demise has left me with a void in my professional life which is difficult indeed to fill. He epitomized in a true sense the concept of "Indian Guru" to me. In professional social work practice, my colleagues at the Philadelphia Society to Protect Children, especially Miss Jean Goddard, Miss Julia Ann Bishop, and Mr. James Delsordo helped me to come to grips with constructive and positive use of authority in social work practice.

When the idea of this book was first conceived, I approached Dr. Norman Wagner, Director of Graduate Studies and University Research at the Waterloo Lutheran University. Dr. Wagner's wise counsel and guidance in working with the press and exploring a financial grant to meet part of the expenses were a real strength to my work on the book. I am thankful to the Administration of the Waterloo Lutheran University for a research grant. The faculty colleagues at the Graduate School of Social Work provided moral support and occasional consultative help on many ideas. The excellent library resources of the Waterloo Lutheran University were indispensable to my research. The library staff was most co-operative throughout my numerous inquiries. Mrs. Judy Miller and Mr. William Pond assisted in library research.

If there has been a buffer between me and insanity in the process of typing, retyping, and helping to make sense of my own handwriting, it has been served by that efficient office title known as secretary. Miss Lucille E. Binkle did most of the typing, which was not only efficient but creative. Miss Joan Pickering worked on some sections of the manuscript. The support and editorial assistance of Mr. Jan Schreiber and Mrs. W. K. Klepac of the University of Toronto Press were excellent.

One of the most gratifying aspects of this project was the numerous letters I received from authors whose articles are included in the book. The authors were most helpful in appreciating and commenting on the organization and basic framework of this book. The editors of *Social Casework, Social Work, Child Welfare, Crime and Delinquency*, and *Jewish Communal Service* were particularly helpful.

To this long list of acknowledgments must be added the contribution of my family without whose support and sharing of the burden in a multitude of ways the task could not have been successful.

To all, my deepest gratitude

Shankar A. Yelaja

Introduction

Nearly seven years ago, when I was working as a social worker in a children's protection agency in a large metropolitan centre of the United States, I became immensely interested in the concept of authority. As a child-protection worker my caseload consisted primarily of parents who neglected or abused their children. For the first time in my life I felt and experienced some of the most brutal and inhuman forms of treatment children can receive from their parents. Yet, contradictory as it may seem, my main function and goal was to help these parents to improve their "standards of child care" so that the quality of family life could be preserved and enhanced wherever possible. Most of the neglecting and abusive parents neither asked for nor consciously wanted help. They resisted the authority of a social agency that intervened in their lives, invading their freedom as parents. Inevitably I was caught in the value dilemma of imposing help where it was not asked for; preserving the quality of family life when all the subjective evidence would warrant a contrary decision, that is, removal of the children from the home; and accepting the neglecting and abusive parents as human beings, when unconsciously perhaps I wanted them to face retribution for their acts. Caught in this triad of opposing feelings, I began the search for the concept of authority and how it can be used as a positive dynamic in the helping process. This book characterizes the beginning of one phase in the process of my thinking and belief in authority as an inherently significant aspect of the social work profession and its positive contribution to the realization of the profession's basic values, objectives, and goals.

Authority is inherent in every social worker–client relationship. Because it is inherent in social work, and its presence is real, both the worker and client must come to grips with it, if it is to serve as a dynamic in helping clients. Authority stems both from the structure in which the social worker has a role and from the profession, which has certified his competence. The authority inherent in the social worker naturally differs from one service programme to another, ranging according to the client need that is being met, the sanctioning system involved in the authorization of service, and the role definition of the worker.

If authority is present in every form of social work relationship, why is it that most social workers are uncomfortable in their feelings about authority, let alone about using authority in a helpful manner in social work practice? It is perhaps a fair assumption that most social workers attempt to "soft pedal" their feelings towards authority, pretending that it does not exist, or that, even if it does exist, it can be handled without serious problems for both the worker and the client. Social workers' natural response to authority is to deny its existence in the hope that denial will be more helpful to clients than will acknowledgment and use in practice.

Social workers' concern for and commitment to client self-determination, freedom of choice, the inherent dignity of man, and full and willing client participation in the helping process tends to place authority as inimical to basic social work values and goals. The use of authority in social work practice naturally creates value dilemmas, because most of the social work values appear to be in conflict with authority. It is, therefore, not unusual to witness a segment of professional thinking that argues that social workers should get out of the business of dealing with "involuntary clients." Social work help should be offered only to those who ask for it. But this is a very simple solution to a complex problem. For one thing, social work literature has dealt with values only vaguely and abstractly, or with a scope too vast to be applicable at the practical level. Unless the implications and consequences of values for practice are carefully drawn, values fail to provide a useful frame for professional action. Moreover, the social worker often must adapt to the values of his client rather than impose his own personal values or those of the profession. This adaptation opens the way for the constructive use of authority. Furthermore, a profession has its mandate from society that sanctions and certifies its competence to deal with problems. Helping "involuntary clients" to adjust with social reality is one of these mandates. By abdicating professional responsibility for helping involuntary clients, social workers are in danger of losing their societal mandate as well as their own commitment to the broad goals of human welfare.

Most of the problems enumerated here appear to stem from social workers' ignorance of what authority is and is not. Coupled with the ignorance of the meaning of authority are one's own personal feelings and attitudes towards authority, which tend to reinforce a negative conception of authority as being antithetical to the democratic values and way of life. One of the ways in which this cycle of lack of knowledge, self-understanding, and self-awareness about authority can be broken down is to develop one's own intellectual awareness regarding authority. Hopefully, an intellectual awareness will lead to self-awareness and self-understanding about authority and its function as a dynamic in professional social work practice.

Related to the central concern of developing the social worker's understanding of authority is another concern, which arose out of my role as a social work educator. The concept of authority is both nebulous and complex. As a teacher, I have found it quite difficult to explain to students this concept with the degree of objectivity that is essential to its understanding. It is especially difficult to explain the positive implications of authority in social work practice. Social science literature on the subject is voluminous, but it lacks a coherent form of organization that is both meaningful and interesting to students. This particular concern is shared by many social work educators and colleagues in North America. By bringing together writings of different social scientists and social workers on the subject of authority, it was felt that students would be better able to understand the concept.

In the Council on Social Work Education curriculum study on education for social work in the correctional fields, authority is noted as a core concept in the correctional field. This study considered that social science concepts are of particular importance in preparing social workers to understand the correctional caseload and to work within the correctional agency. Among the social science concepts included were those of deviance, structure, role, *authority*, and subculture. One of the significant recommendations arising out of the study was the need to analyze the concept of authority from the standpoints of its knowledge base, attitudinal values, and skills in order to come to grips with "authority as a dynamic in service relationships." Yet, as I began to survey the social work literature, it became obvious that literature on authority in social work, including the correctional fields was sadly lacking. That there is no single volume on the subject is evidence of a serious gap in the development of social work literature. It was therefore felt that by collecting scattered writings on authority in social work under one cover, an important contribution to social work literature would be made.

A further reason for preparing this collection stemmed from a research interest. I wanted out of curiosity to explore the diverse literature on the concept of authority as it was dealt with in organizational theory, human behaviour, sociology, ethics, and philosophy. I was also interested in discovering the social work practitioners' knowledge and "practice wisdom" on how authority can be used positively and constructively in the helping process. I was aware that articles had been written on the use of authority in settings such as correction, delinquency, child neglect, and child abuse, because the use of authority has posed critical problems in rehabilitation of clients in those settings, but I did not know how extensive the coverage might be. The search for literature on the use of authority in social work brought many interesting surprises, thereby enhancing my belief in the notion of "serendipity." It was quite revealing, for instance, to find the use of authority in residential treatment centres for emotionally disturbed children, adoption, work with old-age clients, and mentally ill patients. The present research served to locate gaps in the literature and to point out significant areas in which qualitative literature on authority would be desirable. A brief discussion on this point appears in the introduction to the final section of this book.

The central framework of organization of this book consists of two distinct but interrelated sections. In the first, parts I and II, an analysis of the concept of authority is made with the help of social and behavioural science literature. In the second, parts III–V, the conceptual understanding is related to social work practice. The first section, to put it more simply, consists of a theoretical knowledge, whereas the second section looks at the implications of theoretical knowledge for social work practice.

The basic theoretical orientation of this book lies in the application of social and behavioural science concepts to social work practice. The interdependence of social and behavioural science with social work is no longer a cliché but a necessity arising out of practical realities. The social and behavioural sciences, with their prime emphasis on theory building and knowledge development, have a lot to offer to social work. By the same token, social work, with its major emphasis on practice and the application of knowledge to the alleviation of human sufferings of various kinds, has much to contribute to the social and behavioural sciences in their search and exploration of appropriate theories and knowledge. Both social work and social science have one common goal, which is contribution to the development of human resources.

Such an interdependence, in large measure, has tended to blur the distinction between "pure" and "applied" social sciences. As both social scientists and social work practitioners raise the question "knowledge for what?" the plausible answers to this question reaffirm the mutual inter-dependency of social sciences and social work.

Increased interdependence of the social and behavioural sciences with social work has its problems. Today new theories and concepts from the social and behavioural sciences are being poured into the mainstream of social work knowledge and practice at a phenomenal rate. If a social worker is to meaningfully integrate these new theories into his practice, he must exercise some caution as to both conceptual and empirical validity of new knowledge and their potential use for social work practice. An important functional distinction exists between the social and behavioural scientists and a social work practitioner. The heart of the distinction lies in the difference between the function of an academic discipline and the function of a professional discipline. The underlying function of the academic discipline, as of all science, is to acquire and disseminate knowledge. The task of developing means for applying the knowledge in practice belongs to the professional discipline. The objective of the humanitarian professions is to help people, and the acquisition of knowledge must be tested against this end.

Social work practitioners must, therefore, take a rather pragmatic view of new knowledge: how can it be useful in improving their professional services to client systems? But are there any guidelines available in selecting relevant social science theory and knowledge? In the organization of this book, some attempt is made to present various facets of theories on authority systematically, with a careful sifting of these for possible application to social work practice. If social and behavioural science theories and knowledge can be tested against the "practice wisdom" of social workers, at least this would be a beginning step towards a more meaningful and functional interdependence of social science and social work practice.

In social work, a large reservoir of knowledge consists of what one would call a "practice wisdom" – the structure of ideas that is based on acceptability by social workers. Social work practice today, to a large extent, has its knowledge base in conventional wisdom rather than in empirically tested and developed theories. One of the obvious problems in utilizing "practice wisdom" is that it exists in a highly scattered form needing to be collated and systematically organized for consumption by social workers. Social work is essentially an "artistic process of helping people"; its scientific nature is largely limited to evaluation of this process. That "practice wisdom" can serve as a basis for social-work practice can hardly be disputed.

In searching for essays and in selecting these for the first section of this book, an effort was made to cover diverse areas of knowledge and social and behavioural science disciplines. The primary goal was to explore the concept of authority, its meaning, and its theoretical formulations in a variety of disciplines in order to study the universalities and differences inherent in the concept. A secondary goal was to provide a philosophical undergirding to the concept of authority so that it would help readers to understand the concept within a philosophical context. Such an effort is obviously beset with many problems. Selecting essays with as much coherence and cohesion as possible and with a minimum overlapping was a major problem. Then, too, various authors writing on authority had developed the concept and its meaning from their own disciplines and orientations. Cutting across a common theme out of the varying orientations meant that one had necessarily to adopt a framework for analysis. In the first part such a framework includes looking at the inherent meaning of authority from its various attributes such as freedom, reason, discretion, and ethical values. These attributes were then mirrored against a philosophical essay. In the second part, theories on authority are explored and an attempt is made to provide raw data and material, again from an interdisciplinary stance, for formulation of a theory. The disciplines covered in the articles are sociology, organization theory, behavioural theory, and social work. One of the interesting features of these articles is that all five articles point out several hypotheses for further exploration rather than a definitive statement on the theory of authority. Empirical studies on authority in organizational settings have used some of the hypotheses presented by Weber and Barnard.

In searching for articles on the use of authority in social work practice, an effort was made to survey all the professional journals that include articles of importance and relevance to social work practitioners as well as social work journals published in North America. A considerable amount of data that is unpublished but equally important on this subject is not covered in the scope of this survey of the literature.

Selection of articles on the use of authority in social work was based on the following criteria: the chosen article must bring out new ideas or skills in creative use of authority in social work practice; it must have been written by a social worker with practical experience; although the article might deal with the use of authority in specific social work practice settings, the observations must be such that they should have generic applicability and importance to other settings and social agencies as well; and it should relate to some extent to the theoretical framework set forth in the first section of the book. The last point is important to emphasize, because a reader would be able to enhance his understanding about the article written by social work practitioners within the theoretical framework on authority and thereby gain insights into further implications for practice. Hopefully, it would also enable a reader to evaluate theories on authority and their practical worth.

Selecting a framework for organizing the wide range of material on the use of authority in social work was difficult indeed. Initially, the objective was to select articles that cut across a wide range of social work practice settings, rather than specific fields or agency settings in which the problems and issues in the use of authority have been identified. Naturally, there was a preponderance of articles on the use of authority in correctional agencies or agencies with some formal authority vested in them by law. Although there was a greater degree of choice for articles dealing with correctional agencies, the choice was quite restricted in selecting articles for other types of agencies. The range of social work fields includes child protection, child placement, residential treatment of emotionally disturbed children, correctional administration, and rehabilitation. Both public and private social agencies are represented in the choice of articles. Social casework and group work are the two methods primarily identified in the articles on the use of authority in social work practice.

A certain theme of organization began to take shape following the initial selection of articles for the collection. Since there is a predominance of articles dealing with the use of authority in social work practice, these were divided into three major parts: the concept of authority in social work; basic issues involved in the use of authority in social work; and the use of authority in different social work practice settings.

It is recognized that this book is not the final word on the conceptual analysis of authority and its applications to social work practice. Quite to the contrary, it is hoped that social workers will devote more serious efforts and energy to selecting socio-behavioural concepts for their application to social work, for this writer shares a basic conviction that the ultimate worth of a helping profession like social work is judged on the basis of its practice – service to client systems. If this book has any contribution to make, it is toward finding better ways and means of implementing the social work profession's ideal for "service to clients above all."

PART I

Philosophical concepts of authority

INTRODUCTION

There is a feeling of uneasiness and apprehension about authority in our society today. Authority in any form is seen as in direct conflict with our most cherished values of life, liberty, justice and truth. Why the need for authority if society is basically founded upon the notion of "good" for all? The necessity for authority in a society is under attack mainly for two reasons. First, authority cannot exist unless an individual has given up part of his freedom. Individuals, therefore, seem to be subjected to authority from choice. If individuals, then, do not choose to give up their freedom, authority is meaningless. It is perhaps true to say that man is basically a "self-interested" organism. The concept of "enlightened self-interest" is an acknowledgment and recognition of some definite limits (in the form of authority) on the pursuit of freedom. Second, the negative attitudes towards authority stem from past experiences. History is a witness to the fact that authority can be abusive and dangerous, especially if it is entrusted to certain types of individuals. Authority for these individuals becomes an involuntary force with which they can command others. A philosophical understanding and perspective of authority is necessary and helpful if one is to develop a rational basis for integrating the meaning of authority as a normal maturational process of life. It would perhaps be easier to reject all forms of authority, if one were to follow the thesis that man is basically a freedom-loving creature whose adherence to any limits is fraught with rejection. Yet one wonders how long a society could function without the limits of authority. It is true that all of us are basically "good human beings" and, therefore, will respect others. If one were to follow this statement to its ultimate, then it would seem that we do not particularly need traffic lights because we would obey each others rights of way while driving on highways and byways. But look at the chaos and confusion caused by even a temporary breakdown in traffic lights in our modern transportation system.

The four articles chosen in this part revolve around a common theme and yet provide a differential philosophical perspective for understanding the concept of authority. The common theme is the necessity for authority in order for society to perform efficiently and effectively its multitudinous functions. The conclusion is that authority based on reason is "good for the society." This theme is considered within a differential philosophical framework by Simon, Fromm, Friedrich, and Yelaja.

According to Simon, arguments derived from justice, life, truth, and order constitute a powerful prejudice against authority. "But the real problem," says Simon, "is not whether authority will wither away: no doubt it will always play an important part in human affairs, the problem is whether human deficiencies alone cause authority to be necessary."

Simon proposes the theory of analyzing authority into a plurality of functions, suggesting that "an analytical study of functions is perhaps all that is needed to ascertain the relation of authority to justice, to life, to truth, and to order." If the relation between authority and these cherished values were successfully clarified, a meaningful dialogue of the philosophers on the fundamental problems of society would be provided for.

Fromm develops a philosophical theory of authority based on ethical factors. He makes a clear and useful distinction between rational and irrational authority on the basis of its source. Rational authority, he believes, "not only permits but requires constant scrutiny and criticism of those subjected to it. It is always temporary, its acceptance depending upon its performance. The source of irrational authority, on the other hand, is always power over people." Fromm also distinguishes between authoritarian and humanistic ethics by two criteria, one formal, the other material. Formally, authoritarian ethics deny man's capacity to know what is good or bad; the norm giver is always an authority transcending the individual. Such a system is based not on reason and knowledge but on awe of authority and on the subject's feeling of weakness and dependence. Humanistic ethics are based on the principle that only man himself, and not an authority transcending him, can determine the criteria of virtue and sin. Materially, it is based on the principle that "good" is what is good for man and "evil" what is detrimental to man, the sole criterion of ethical value being man's welfare.

Friedrich attempts to answer the question: Does authority have no basis in reason? He proposes that authority and reason are closely linked; indeed, that authority rests upon the ability to issue communications that are capable of reasoned elaboration. A relation between discretion and the rational aspect of authority is also noted. Friedrich's philosophical proposition can be summarized as "only when what is commanded and maintained can thus be reasoned upon and defended is authority secure." Why should I agree or obey? needs to be stated in a manner worthy of acceptance in the eyes of those who give as well as receive orders.

The inherent conflict and tension between freedom and authority and an analysis of the basic source of this conflict forms the substance of Yelaja's essay. Using formal organization as a framework for analyzing the conflict between freedom and authority, he argues that man's basic instinct is self-interest (freedom) and the conflict will remain as long as he cannot reconcile his self-interest with the "common good" (authority). A rational balance between freedom and authority is possible only to the extent that an individual can yield his "inner self" to societal demands, which may be at variance with individual self-interest at times.

These essays, although written from different perspectives and points of view, seem to address themselves to the common attributes of authority, which are freedom, reason, discretion, and ethical values. For social workers, it would be helpful to look at both the common attributes and different philosophical approaches to the study of authority. Such an approach seems to be an indispensible aid in developing a rational basis for understanding authority and its positive function in helping people.

1
The bad name of authority

The issue of authority has such a bad reputation that a philosopher cannot discuss it without exposing himself to suspicion and malice. Yet
authority is present in all phases of social life. The skill of anarchist
thinkers may lend verisimilitude to systems marked by extensive dependence upon good will, tolerance, mutual understanding, persuasion and
consent. But, within these pictures of smoothly operating institutions,
authority is unmistakably present, or, if it is not, verisimilitude disappears
and what is left is a lifeless mimicry of social relations. Why is it that men
distrust so intensely a thing without which they cannot, by all evidences,
live and act together?

As a matter of common experience, subjection to authority causes
much discomfort and mortification; it involves the permanent foundation
of an ever threatening, if not ever present, distress. But reluctance to bear
such distress does not sufficiently account for the bad name of authority.
Over and above this obvious reluctance, aversion to authority derives
energy from sublime sources. Its really formidable power originates in the
loftiest inclinations of the human soul. The case would be relatively simple
and easy to deal with if the enemies of authority were only pride and pas-
sion. The fact is that authority is reputed to conflict with justice, life,
truth and order.

AUTHORITY IN SEEMING CONFLICT WITH JUSTICE

The common way to secure a good or service is to surrender a good or
service held equal in value. In a society where such method generally

Reprinted by permission of the University of Notre Dame Press, Notre Dame,
Indiana, from Yves R. Simon, *A General Theory of Authority* (Indiana: University
of Notre Dame Press), 1962, pp. 13–22.

obtains the services of plumbers and carpenters, as well as those of physicians and lawyers, are purchased at unpleasantly high cost. No wonder that some people feel a nostalgia for circumstances where an upper position gives a right to an abundance of facilities. Prices and wages forcibly kept low do not balance the goods and services procured. The exchange is unequal; more exactly, the transaction has only in part the character of an exchange; part of the service rendered is a tribute describable as the privilege of authority and disquietingly reminiscent of the stated sums which used to be paid periodically to the pirates of Barbary. The notion of authority thus comes to be associated with that of an exchange disrupted by sheer might.

AUTHORITY IN SEEMING CONFLICT WITH LIFE

Actions ordered by authority originate outside the agent; they bear a mark of externality in contrast with the spontaneousness which characterizes the operations of nature and life.[1] Suppose that the things procured are altogether good: the fact that they are procured by authority still denies them the cherished perfection of proceeding from within. A man can behave well either because he is told to do so or by his own inclination. Good behaviour obtained by commandment and obedience is still held defective inasmuch as it lacks spontaneity, life, voluntariness, liberty. The ideal subject of authoritarian rule would display all the submissiveness and determinateness of a machine. Other things being equal, a state of affairs brought about vitally is preferable to a state of affairs brought about mechanically. It may even be argued that the lesser results obtained through vital processes are more valuable than greater results obtained by curbing the forces of life. Authority boasts of unique ability to assure peace: but the peace it procures is that of death. – *They make a solitude, and call it peace* (Tacitus). Even when the effects intended are in line with nature, the way in which authority brings them about involves a sort of violence.

Authority becomes more detestable as the things subjected to its methods increase in dignity and pertain more directly to what is vital and spiritual in man. If, in order to cut down the rate of accidents, it is held expedient that street traffic be governed in machine-like fashion by the agents of an irresistible power, so let it be. The sacrifice of some spon-

1 / "That alone was right which was done of one's own inner conviction and mere motion, that was lifeless and evil which was done out of obedience to any external authority." F. Pollock, Introduction to William K. Cliffords' *Lectures and Essays* (London: MacMillan, 1901), vol. I, 44.

taneity at the wheel of a car is not a very serious one. But when a power pretends to shape the moral personality of citizens, their beliefs, their tastes and their loves, the time for anger has come. Authority, if needed at all, should be relegated to the domains where lifelessness is least destructive. If, through the mechanization of less important functions, it helps to liberate the higher forms of life, so much the better. But keep it away from things noble and spiritual, and do not attempt to force a soul into this enemy of life.

AUTHORITY IN SEEMING CONFLICT WITH TRUTH

Among the lofty things that authority is reputed to threaten is the respect of our minds for truth. The anger commonly aroused by the notion that authority might supersede the power of truth is a metaphysical sentiment of great significance. We all have some experience of situations in which a problem of truth happens to be unjustifiably answered by submission to authority. Thus, it often happens that in international disputes incompatible versions of the same event are held by diverse governments; to spare ourselves the pangs of anxiety, the labors of research, and sometimes the humiliation of having been wrong, we may make it a rule that our assent will go to the version officially held by the government which is ours. A similar situation is common in the conflict of political parties and in dialogues between schools of thought. Our daily life is constantly troubled by vexing questions, ideological, ethical, political, esthetic, and factual, to which we cannot remain indifferent, to which we must give some sort of answer, and which involve such obscurities that an answer in terms of objective determination is very hard to reach. But most of the time these questions admit of cheap, easy, pacifying, and heartening answers if we make it a set rule to repeat what authority has said. The lovers of truth easily come to suspect that the whole system of authority is a pragmatic device, designed to spare weak souls the hardship of finding truth and abiding by it.

No doubt, grounds for suspecting an antagonistic relation between authority and truth are as old as human reason and human testimony. However, such suspicion assumed a more determinate form and a greater power when, some time in the eighteenth century, the ideal of a social science built after the pattern of physics got hold of minds and imaginations. The essentials of this epoch-making adventure can be summed up as follows: Western men had become aware that their control over physical nature was immensely increased whenever scientific propositions replaced common experience as the theoretical basis of their action. As far as physical nature is concerned, wonders can be worked by arts grounded in scientific formulas. Why should it be impossible to do for society what is being done so successfully in the realm of physical nature? Why should it be impossible to work out a social science patterned after physics, and like physics objective, impersonal, free from anthropomorphic bias, free from value judgments, exact, rigorous, indifferent to national or personal whims and preferences, necessary, and irresistible? From such a science a rational art would be derived, and the proper conduct of societies would be insured by the impersonal decisions of enlightened reason. In the construct of a society ruled by the power of social science, authority plays no part. This construct helps us to understand why authority plays such an overwhelming part in societies ignorant of social science. We are wondering about the proper way to attain a certain goal and, because of our inability to demonstrate scientifically which way is the proper one, we would deliberate indefinitely did we not agree to follow the decisions of authority. These may not be the best possible ones, but they are still preferable to indefinitely protracted irresolution. The case is like that of Descartes' travelers, lost in the midst of a forest.[2] By moving constantly in the same direction, they will reach a place which may not be the best but where they will certainly be better off than in the midst of a forest. Not knowing which way to take, but realizing that movement in any clear direction is better than unending idleness, we let authority decide which we shall take, and we admire its ability to substitute definite action for endless deliberation. In the enthusiastic visions of early social science, such a state of affairs constitutes, according to an expression used by Karl Marx in a different connection, the prehistory of society. Genuinely human history begins when the travelers in the forest are provided by science with rational, objective, definite, and demonstrated methods of knowing which way to take in order to reach the place where they want to go. For the most audacious, social science would not only solve the conditional problem of selecting the way on the basis of an established intention of the goal; it would resolve, just as well, the problem of the goal to be intended. Authority would no longer have anything to do either with regard to the means or with regard to the end. It has a role to play as long as common action, by reason of ignorance, remains subject to looseness, flexibility, uncertainty. But as soon as mature reason, i.e., reason perfected by science, proposes definite forms of action according to truth, the method of authority becomes sheer deception. Of this method of deception, what can be the purpose if not just the advantage of the men or classes in power?

2 / *Discourse on Method,* Third Part.

AUTHORITY IN SEEMING CONFLICT WITH ORDER

The principle of authority has often been challenged by the spirit of disorder. It is a common belief that order inevitably implies suppressions, restrictions, curtailments, and violent destruction; hence the notion that any excess of order impairs life and that unorganized spontaneity must be defended and promoted for the sake of life itself. The conflict between life and authority, outlined in the foregoing, often appears as a particular case of a deeper conflict between life and order. Romanticism is famous for its rebels, enamoured of the most ebullient phases of life, and inebriated with the spring-like character of vital activity. Clearly, insofar as an opposition can be construed between understanding and nature, the phases of life to which the romantic revolt is dedicated belong to the realm of nature rather than to that of understanding. Life, as exalted by the romantic revolt, resembles prime matter in the description of St. Augustine:[3] in a first approximation, it seems to be a tempestuous stream of weird forms; but, as intuition grows in intensity, the forms disappear and no longer hinder the glory of a thing which is mobility, storm and drive, creativeness and unpredictability. In such a system of passionate intuitions, disorder, whether this name is used or not, assumes an appearance akin to that of life itself. The romantic rebel fights authority precisely because he sees in it a factor of order.

Yet it also happens that a spirit of dedication to order brings about a particular form of opposition to authority. The rules which create order in mankind are either laws or contractual arrangements. Authority may conflict with both. Indeed, laws are counted among the works of authority. But it should also be remarked that the more a law is universal, natural and impersonal, the more it has the character of a law, whereas the distinctive features of authority are more intensely present in the particular and the contingent law than in the universal and necessary one, in the decree than in the law, in the decree regulating matters strictly determined with regard to here and now than in the decree concerned with somewhat general cases, and in the command marked by the personality of a leader than in an anonymous and impersonal ordinance. Briefly: whereas the law is attracted by an ideal of rational impersonality, acts of authority tend toward a state of concreteness involving the personalities of men, and all the contingencies to which human wills are subject. Considered in its contrast with law, authority seems to be connected with human arbitrariness, by all means the worst enemy of order. As to the contractual settlement, it is essentially a rule of exchange, consequently an equalitarian

3 / *Confessions,* Bk. xii, 6.6.

rule. Order obtains in exchange relations when, regardless of all the ways in which the exchanging parties may be unequal, a free discussion has procured a sound approximation to definite equality between the exchanged values. When there is no problem except that of determining what value is equal to what value, any act of authority is a disruption of order.

HYPOTHESIS: AUTHORITY EMBRACES A COMPLEX OF FUNCTIONS

Arguments derived from justice, life, truth, and order constitute a powerful prejudice against authority. In spite of this, anarchy is rarely or never upheld with qualified consistency. In the pedagogy of Rousseau, there is a set purpose to let the child be guided by natural necessity rather than by human command, and to let him learn from the experience of physical facts rather than by obedience. "Keep the child solely dependent on things; you will have followed the order of Nature in the process of his upbringing. Never oppose to his unreasonable wishes any but physical obstacles or punishments resulting from the actions themselves – he will remember these punishments in similar situations. It is enough to prevent him from doing evil without forbidding him to do it. ..."[4] Remarkably, the theory that the method of authority is a poor substitute for the pedagogical power of nature has been accepted, in varying degree of enthusiasm or reluctance, by all schools of pedagogy and has demonstrated lasting power. Yet the authority of parents and tutors is present throughout pedagogical theories, even when it is passed over in silence. Childhood is the domain where the suppression of all authority is obviously impossible. The most radical constructs of anarchy, as soon as they rise above the level of idle rhetoric, must admit of qualifications so far as the immature part of mankind is concerned. Anti-authoritarian theorists, with few exceptions if any, do not mean that authority should disappear or that it can ever cease to be a factor of major importance in human affairs. What the thinkers opposed to authority generally mean is that authority can never be vindicated except by such deficiencies as are found in children, in the feeble-minded, the emotionally unstable, the criminally inclined, the illiterate, and the historically primitive. The real problem is not whether authority must wither away: no doubt, it will always play an all-important part in human affairs. *The problem is whether deficiencies alone cause authority to be necessary.* It is obvious, indeed, that in many cases the need for authority originates in some defect and disappears when sufficiency is attained. But the commonly associated negation, viz., that authority never

4 / *Emile,* II. Amsterdam, Jean Neualme, 1762.

originates in the positive qualities of man and society, is by no means obvious and should not be received uncritically. The supposition that authority, in certain cases and domains, is made necessary not by deficiencies but by nature – this supposition is not evidently absurd. To hold, in some aprioristic way, that it does not deserve examination would merely evince wishful thinking of the least scientific kind. The truth may well be that authority has several functions, some of which would be relative to deficient states of affairs and others to features of perfection.

We propose to try the theory that authority must be analyzed into a plurality of functions. But attitudes ignore analyses and commonly lump together heterogeneous aspects never considered in their distinct intelligibility. An analytical study of functions is perhaps all that is needed to ascertain the relation of authority to justice, to life, to truth, and to order. If the relation between authority and these cherished values was successfully clarified, unexpected reconciliations would take place, and improved circumstances would be provided for the dialogue of the philosophers on the fundamental problems of society.

ERICH FROMM

2
The ethics of authority

Once Susia prayed to God: "Lord, I love you so much, but I do not fear you enough. Lord, I love you so much, but I do not fear you enough. Let me stand in awe of you as one of your angels, who are penetrated by your awe-filled name."

And God heard his prayer, and His name penetrated the hidden heart of Susia, as it comes to pass with the angels. But at that Susia crawled under the bed like a little dog, and animal fear shook him until he howled: "Lord, let me love you like Susia again."

And God heard him this time also.[1]

HUMANISTIC VS. AUTHORITARIAN ETHICS

If we do not abandon, as ethical relativism does, the search for objectively valid norms of conduct, what criteria for such norms can we find? The kind of criteria depends on the type of ethical system the norms of which we study. By necessity the criteria in authoritarian ethics are fundamentally different from those in humanistic ethics.

In authoritarian ethics an authority states what is good for man and lays down the laws and norms of conduct; in humanistic ethics man himself is both the norm giver and the subject of the norms, their formal source or regulative agency and their subject matter.

The use of the term "authoritarian" makes it necessary to clarify the

Reprinted by permission of the author, Holt, Rinehart and Winston, Inc., and Routledge & Kegan Paul, Ltd., London, England, from *Man for Himself* by Erich Fromm. Copyright 1947 by Erich Fromm. The original title of this chapter was "Humanistic Ethics: The Applied Science of the Art of Living."

1 / *In Time and Eternity, A Jewish Reader*, edited by Nathan N. Glatzer (New York: Schocken Books, 1946).

concept of authority. So much confusion exists with regard to this concept because it is widely believed that we are confronted with the alternative of having dictatorial, irrational authority or of having no authority at all. This alternative, however, is fallacious. The real problem is what *kind* of authority we are to have. When we speak of authority do we mean rational or irrational authority? *Rational authority* has its source in *competence*. The person whose authority is respected functions competently in the task with which he is entrusted by those who conferred it upon him. He need not intimidate them nor arouse their admiration by magic qualities; as long as and to the extent to which he is competently helping, instead of exploiting, his authority is based on rational grounds and does not call for irrational awe. Rational authority not only permits but requires constant scrutiny and criticism of those subjected to it; it is always temporary, its acceptance depending on its performance. The source of *irrational authority,* on the other hand, is always power over people. This power can be physical or mental, it can be realistic or only relative in terms of the anxiety and helplessness of the person submitting to this authority. Power on the one side, fear on the other, are always the buttresses on which irrational authority is built. Criticism of the authority is not only not required but forbidden. Rational authority is based upon the equality of both authority and subject, which differ only with respect to the degree of knowledge or skill in a particular field. Irrational authority is by its very nature based upon inequality, implying difference in value. In the use of the term "authoritarian ethics" reference is made to irrational authority, following the current use of "authoritarian" as synonymous with totalitarian and antidemocratic systems. The reader will soon recognize that humanistic ethics is not incompatible with rational authority.

Authoritarian ethics can be distinguished from humanistic ethics by two criteria, one formal, the other material. Formally, authoritarian ethics denies man's capacity to know what is good or bad; the norm giver is always an authority transcending the individual. Such a system is based not on reason and knowledge but on awe of the authority and on the subject's feeling of weakness and dependence; the surrender of decision making to the authority results from the latter's magic power; its decisions can not and must not be questioned. *Materially*, or according to content, authoritarian ethics answers the question of what is good or bad primarily in terms of the interests of the authority, not the interests of the subject; it is exploitative, although the subject may derive considerable benefits, psychic or material, from it.

Both the formal and the material aspects of authoritarian ethics are apparent in the genesis of ethical judgment in the child and of unreflective value judgment in the average adult. The foundations of our ability to differentiate between good and evil are laid in childhood; first with regard to physiological functions and then with regard to more complex matters of behavior. The child acquires a sense of distinguishing between good and bad before he learns the difference by reasoning. His value judgments are formed as a result of the friendly or unfriendly reactions of the significant people in his life. In view of his complete dependence on the care and love of the adult, it is not surprising that an approving or disapproving expression on the mother's face is sufficient to "teach" the child the difference between good and bad. In school and in society similar factors operate. "Good" is that for which one is praised; "bad," that for which one is frowned upon or punished by social authorities or by the majority of one's fellow men. Indeed, the fear of disapproval and the need for approval seem to be the most powerful and almost exclusive motivation for ethical judgment. This intense emotional pressure prevents the child, and later the adult, from asking critically whether "good" in a judgment means good for him or for the authority. The alternatives in this respect become obvious if we consider value judgments with reference to things. If I say that one car is "better" than another, it is self-evident that one car is called "better" because it serves me better than another car; good or bad refers to the usefulness the thing has for *me*. If the owner of a dog considers the dog to be "good," he refers to certain qualities of the dog which to him are useful; as, for instance, that he fulfills the owner's need for a watch dog, a hunting dog or an affectionate pet. *A thing is called good if it is good for the person who uses it.* With reference to man, the same criterion of value can be used. The employer considers an employee to be good if he is of advantage to him. The teacher may call a pupil good if he is obedient, does not cause trouble, and is a credit to him. In much the same way a child may be called good if he is docile and obedient. The "good" child may be frightened, and insecure, wanting only to please his parents by submitting to their will, while the "bad" child may have a will of his own and genuine interests but ones which do not please the parents.

Obviously, the formal and material aspects of authoritarian ethics are inseparable. Unless the authority wanted to exploit the subject, it would not need to rule by virtue of awe and emotional submissiveness; it could encourage rational judgment and criticism — thus taking the risk of being found incompetent. But because its own interests are at stake the authority ordains *obedience to be the main virtue and disobedience to be the main sin.* The unforgivable sin in authoritarian ethics is rebellion, the questioning of the authority's right to establish norms and of its axiom that the norms established by the authority are in the best interest of the subjects.

Even if a person sins, his acceptance of punishment and his feeling of guilt restore him to "goodness" because he thus expresses his acceptance of the authority's superiority.

The Old Testament, in its account of the beginnings of man's history, gives an illustration of authoritarian ethics. The sin of Adam and Eve is not explained in terms of the act itself; eating from the tree of knowledge of good and evil was not bad *per se*; in fact, both the Jewish and the Christian religions agree that the ability to differentiate between good and evil is a basic virtue. The sin was disobedience, the challenge to the authority of God, who was afraid that man, having already "become as one of Us, to know good and evil," could "put forth his hand and take also of the tree of life and live forever."

Humanistic ethics, in contrast to authoritarian ethics, may likewise be distinguished by formal and material criteria. *Formally*, it is based on the principle that only man himself can determine the criterion for virtue and sin, and not an authority transcending him. *Materially*, it is based on the principle that "good" is what is good for man and "evil" what is detrimental to man; *the sole criterion of ethical value being man's welfare*.

The difference between humanistic and authoritarian ethics is illustrated in the different meanings attached to the word "virtue." Aristotle uses "virtue" to mean "excellence" – excellence of the activity by which the potentialities peculiar to man are realized. "Virtue" is used, e.g., by Paracelsus as synonymous with the individual characteristics of each thing – that is, its peculiarity. A stone or a flower each has its virtue, its combination of specific qualities. Man's virtue, likewise, is that precise set of qualities which is characteristic of the human species, while each person's virtue is his unique individuality. He is "virtuous" if he unfolds his "virtue." In contrast, "virtue" in the modern sense is a concept of authoritarian ethics. To be virtuous signifies self-denial and obedience, suppression of individuality rather than its fullest realization.

Humanistic ethics is anthropocentric; not, of course, in the sense that man is the center of the universe but in the sense that his value judgments, like all other judgments and even perceptions, are rooted in the peculiarities of his existence and are meaningful only with reference to it; man, indeed, is the "measure of all things." The humanistic position is that there is nothing higher and nothing more dignified than human existence. Against this position it has been argued that it is in the very nature of ethical behavior to be related to something *transcending* man, and hence that a system which recognizes man and his interest alone cannot be truly moral, that its object would be merely the isolated, egotistical individual.

This argument, usually offered in order to disprove man's ability – and right – to postulate and to judge the norms valid for his life, is based on a fallacy, for the principle that good is what is *good for man* does not imply that man's nature is such that egotism or isolation are good for him. It does not mean that man's purpose can be fulfilled in a state of unrelatedness to the world outside him. In fact, as many advocates of humanistic ethics have suggested, it is one of the characteristics of human nature that man finds his fulfillment and happiness only in relatedness to and solidarity with his fellow men. However, to love one's neighbor is not a phenomenon *transcending* man; it is something inherent in and *radiating from* him. Love is not a higher power which descends upon man nor a duty which is imposed upon him; it is his own power by which he relates himself to the world and makes it truly his.

CARL J. FRIEDRICH

3

Authority, reason, and discretion

Ever since the eighteenth-century revolt against the established authorities in church and state, there has been a marked tendency among freedom-loving intellectuals to view "authority" with a jaundiced eye, if not to denounce it. When Charles S. Peirce wrote a generation ago that "when the method of authority prevailed, the truth meant little more than the Catholic faith,"[1] he was echoing this intellectual sentiment. Conservatives have maintained that the implication here is that what Peirce called "the method of authority" was some kind of unreasoning superstition, some foolishness which must be superseded by the clear voice of "reason." When the Jacobins erected altars to the Goddess of Reason, they had proudly assumed that they were abandoning authority for reason. Little did they realize how authoritative was their outlook, and how much depended upon their authority for their particular reasoning to prevail.

In reaction, conservatives since Bonald and de Maistre have made a fetish of authority beyond all reason. The ringing phrases in which de Maistre denounced the rationalism of the enlightenment center upon the

Reprinted with permission of the author and The American Society for Political and Legal Philosophy from Carl J. Friedrich, *Authority* (Cambridge, Mass.: Harvard University Press), 1958, pp. 28–48.

An earlier attempt at a formulation of the position of this study may be found in an article, "Loyalty and Authority," in *Confluence* (1954), vol. III, pp. 307ff. Cf. Miss Hannah Arendt's challenging article, "Was ist Autorität?" reprinted from an unspecified journal (1955), and Francis G. Wilson's "The Prelude to Authority," in *The American Political Science Review*, 31:12ff. (1937); see also George S. Langrod, "Liberty and Authority," ch. XIV of *Freedom and Authority in Our Time*, ed. Lyman Bryson, Louis Finkelstein, R. M. MacIver, and Richard McKeon (1953); and Sebastian de Grazia, "Authority and Rationality," *Philosophy*, 27 (1952). See also footnote 20, below.

1 / Charles S. Peirce, "How to Make Our Ideas Clear" as reprinted in *Love, Chance and Logic* (1923), p. 55.

issue of authority against reason. He would claim infallibility for the pope in the same phrase in which he would vindicate an unqualified monarchical sovereignty.[2] Because reasoning, *raisonnement*, can lead to the dissolution of all social order, to anarchy and terror, men ought to and are in fact ready to subject themselves to authority without asking the "reasons why." Similar sentiments are frequently expressed in contemporary American conservatism.

But are reasoning and authority so antithetical? Does authority have no basis in reason? The following analysis seeks to elucidate the proposition that authority and reason are closely linked, indeed that authority rests upon the ability to issue communications which are capable of reasoned elaboration.

In common usage, authority is often confused with power or taken to be a synonym of power. In more learned discourse, authority has been defined as a particular kind of power, such as "formal power" or "rightful power." It has been spoken of in relation to persons, as well as to other entities, such as law or the dictionary. The problem of what makes people "accept" authority, by obeying commands or believing a message, has given rise to a variety of interpretations of authority. Authority has been juxtaposed to freedom, or to force, or to reason. It has been praised and condemned in all contexts, and as a result, the word has been incorporated in a pejorative adjective, "authoritarian," and linked as a general characteristic to "personality" as an objectionable and eradicable trait. In most of these discussions, both on the popular and the learned level, it has been assumed that authority is a peculiar something that can be possessed, and gained or lost, as the case may be. Against such views it has been argued through the ages that there is only power based on some sort of constraint, and that authority is merely a make-belief, based upon religious faith at best.

It is illuminating to cast a glance at the Roman antecedents from which the word "authority" is derived. *Auctoritas* is, according to Mommsen,[3] not readily definable in its original meaning. It has predominantly the

2 / "L'infaillibilité dans l'ordre spirituel, et la souveraineté dans l'ordre temporel, sont deux mots parfaitement synonymes." *Du Pape*, Book I, ch. I.

3 / Theodor Mommsen, *Römisches Staatsrecht* (2nd ed., 1888), III, 1033ff. I should like to call attention in this connection to the fact that Apollo was the "augmenter." When one considers the symbolism of Apollo as the God of the Sun, of reason and moderation, this serves as a most revealing symbolic *datum*. Cf. W. K. C. Guthrie, *The Greeks and Their Gods* (1950), pp. 183ff. Guthrie writes of "Apollo's primary aspect, his championship of law and order, ... limit, moderation, obedience to authority, and condemning excess in all its forms" (p. 203). There also are the precepts which this augmenter represented.

sense related to the verb from which it is derived: *augere*, to augment. *Auctoritas* thus supplements a mere act of the will by adding reasons to it. Such augmentation and confirmation are the results of deliberation by the "old ones." The *patrum auctoritas* is, for that reason, more than advice, yet less than a command. It is, as Mommsen comments, advice which cannot be properly disregarded, such as the expert gives to the layman, the leader in Parliament to his followers. This augmentation or implementation and confirmation had in ancient Rome, as did indeed authority elsewhere, religious overtones. While it was not intended to set limits to the free decision of the community, it was intended to prevent violations of what was sacred in the established order of things. It was believed that because such violations were a crime (*nefas*) against the divine order, they might jeopardize the divine blessing. Thus, the preservation of good auspices probably was the basic idea underlying the *patrum auctoritas*, the authority of the fathers, that is to say, of the Senate. It was a matter of adding wisdom to will, a knowledge of values shared and traditions hallowed, to whatever the people wanted to do. (Later on, the *auctoritas* became a more general notion, and something of what our modern word "author," meaning a maker or originator, suggests.)

Why bother with these ancient verbal connotations? Because they suggest the role of reasoning, they thereby help to get clearly into focus what is probably the central fact to which a great many of the situations refer in which the word "authority" is employed. When there are good reasons for doing or believing something, such action or thought acquires a quality which is otherwise lacking. This has been overlooked by that rather numerous group of writers and philosophers who thought they could build law upon power alone. The power of him who willed something was, they thought, what gave someone's decision authority. Hobbes, as well as Rousseau and many others, thought that the sovereign will was the source of all law.[4] Much Anglo-American legal tradition has, by contrast, retained the older notion – a notion that can be traced back through the Middle Ages to the Stoics – that reason, and more especially Coke's "artificial reason of the law" are of decisive importance in providing law with the necessary authority.[5] It is this view which assigns to the judge such a central position in a legal system: he, as a man "learned in the law,"

4 / Hobbes, *Leviathan*, ch. x, vi–viii; Rousseau, *Contrat Social*, book II. For Hobbes the key of "authority" is "the right of doing any act."

5 / Sir Edward Coke, *Reports*, VIII, Bonham's case; see C. J. Friedrich, *Philosophy of Law in Political and Historical Perspective* (University of Chicago Press, 1958), ch. x. Cf. also C. D. Brown, *The Lion and the Throne – The Life and Times of Sir Edward Coke 1552–1634* (1957), pp. 302ff.

is conceived as lending the statutory "decisions" of an elected legislature an additional quality, by relating them to the basic principles of the law and thus making them authoritative. Only by fitting the willed statutory law into such a broader framework of "reason" does it become fully right, that is to say, authoritative.

In his forthright little study on political verbiage, T. D. Weldon makes an effort at clearing away some of the thick underbrush that has grown up around the word "authority." He remarks that until recent times, no clear distinction has been drawn between power and authority, and that it is "too simple to identify 'authority' with 'force rightly or justly applied.' " He differentiates four kinds of authority, ranging from pure force to unquestioning confidence, and hence asserts that "force exercised or capable of being exercised with the general approval of those concerned is what is normally meant by 'authority.' " Thus, if the followers *want* wickedness, they will obey a wicked authority.[6] And yet, at the start of his analysis, Weldon had pointed out that authority somehow is related to the fact that he who possesses it could produce reasons, if challenged. Such was the case of the Roman Senate, such is the case of the modern judge. To say, as Weldon does, that "the proper use of force is always authoritative" is quite inadmissible, unless this statement is made into a tautology by giving to the adjective "proper" the meaning of "reasonable," in the sense of possessing adequate reasons for him to whom the force is applied. What is more, Weldon himself seems to know this, for he tells us that when people begin to ask the question, "Why should I obey X," X is on the way to losing his authority.

This last observation deserves further exploration. For when such a question is raised, a number of answers may be given. One answer would be in terms of hierarchy and status – because he is your king or your father. Another might be in terms of religion and faith – because God has commanded you to do so. A third would be in terms of interest and advantage – because he may make you his heir and successor. A fourth would be in terms of personal emotions and loyalties – because he loves you and you are devoted to him. A fifth would be in terms of law – because article so-and-so of the civil code requires you to do it. Such a recital, though incomplete, suggests some of the values and beliefs involved in reasoning upon authority, and at the same time, it gives a first hint of the fluid, indeed the fugitive quality of power based on authority. However, these five answers do not enable us really to get at the distinctive phenomenon which the augmentation and confirmation of will by some sort of reasoning accomplishes. The escape into the psychological concomitants

6/T. D. Weldon, *The Vocabulary of Politics* (Pelican Books, 1953), pp. 50–56.

of this datum of political experience suggests that a crucial aspect belonging to its ontological core has not yet been laid bare.[7]

We have, in the previous paragraph, spoken of authority in terms of obedience. This is very commonly done; indeed, in action-related situations, obedience is the predominant aspect. But there is another phase of authority which is paramount in such situations as those involving the teacher, the scholar, and the dictionary. As to the last, some very interesting special problems are presented by the authority of nonpersonal entities, such as dictionaries, laws, and the like. It might be argued that one could bracket these entities and their "authority," because their authority may be traced back to the human "authors" who created them. There is, furthermore, often a question as to who were the makers: the fathers at Philadelphia, or the long line of judges who adorned the Supreme and other courts, or yet the presidents and congressmen. From a certain standpoint, it may even be said that the Constitution as it exists today is the work of the entire American people. The problem of the "authority" of impersonal entities will, I believe, become more comprehensible, once the analysis of the rational component of authority has been further advanced.

Leaving aside, then, the authority of such impersonal entities, we return to the situation of the teacher, the scholar, the doctor, or the lawyer. Here authority seems to be related to the fact that the person wielding authority possesses superior knowledge or insight. Frequently – for instance, among scholars accepting each other's authority – the authority of X rests upon the fact that he could give extended reasons for the opinions he expounds.[8] It is not essential for such authority, however, that these opinions are conclusively demonstrable; indeed only where they are not thus demonstrable, the phenomenon of authority in the strict sense is involved. In any case, the authority of the teacher, the scholar, the doctor, and the lawyer is infused with a rational element, and the belief in it includes the belief in superior "reasoning." It is challenged on the part of those who accept it, by asking, not, why should I obey? but, why should I agree?

Before I proceed with this analysis, it might be well to turn to a kind of primordial authority which has been particularly controversial in our time, namely parental authority. In the course of each child's development, the

7 / The close relation between the psychological and the nominalist misinterpretation of phenomena like authority is strikingly illustrated in the approach of Max Weber, who, confusing authority with legitimacy, misses one of the key aspects of authority, by minimizing its rational aspect.

8 / This aspect of the matter is strikingly illuminated by the role that agreement upon methods of work and modes of demonstration plays among scientists. For an elaboration of this factor, as far as science is concerned, see my paper, "Political Philosophy and Political Science," in *Approaches to the Study of Politics* (Northwestern University Press), 1958.

growth of authority may be studied and experienced. It might be remarked in passing that it is in this sphere that misunderstandings about the nature of authority have been most frequent. Along with the teacher-pupil relationship, the parental relationship has been jeopardized by ideas that in the last generation have played havoc with genuine community in the name of "progress."[9] And yet there was much good in these youth movements and "progressivisms" of our younger days; it was really the manner of stating the issue, rather than the criticism of outmoded patterns of living, that was at fault. In a nutshell, it might be said that these movements challenged "authority" as such, when they should have asked for the replacement of outworn and unreal authority by genuine authority. What this means, I should like to illustrate by the parental problem. In the beginning, the child is helplessly dependent and in the power of the parents. Indeed, their power is absolute force to such a degree that the legislator has seen fit to step in and regulate by law, to control and limit, the unlimited power of the parents, at least to some extent. But this absolute power does not continue, as the child grows. A wise parent will increasingly prefer to explain what needs to be done and to be believed, to give reasons, thus replacing subjection by understanding. He will respond to the questions, "why?" and "wherefore?" and seek to develop in the child an understanding of, a participation in, the *reasons* which animate the parent in asking for obedience as well as for agreement. It is in this process that a new relationship, different from that of power and force, comes into being, and it is this relationship which I should like to designate as authority. Such authority rests upon the fact that the child increasingly gains insight into parental orders and regulations, into parental opinions and beliefs. The child learns to relate both to basic values, and thereby comes to share these values with his parents. Such insight anticipates the insight into the regulations and opinions of the larger community, the church, the school, and eventually the polity. What is important is to realize that all such discourse provides for participation of the child. By coming to understand these regulations and beliefs, the child is helped, so to speak, to shape them into proper possessions, to make them his own. Thus discipline is transformed into self-discipline. It may well happen and often does in fact happen, that this process takes place only partially and incompletely. Power and force continue to play their role, often to the point where they create dangerous tensions and frustration about which modern

9 / This particular pitfall was the crux of the more radical extravaganza committed in the name of progressive education some years ago. See, for a statement of the opposing position, my paper, "This Progressive Education" in *The Atlantic Monthly*, 154:421ff. (October 1934), which became a stormy petrel of controversy for a while, but was never really refuted.

psychology and psychoanalysis have taught many revealing lessons. For, if
the power of parents is wielded without such growing participation and insight on the part of the child, then either the community of the family is
destroyed by the rebellion of the child, or the child's personality is destroyed by the imposition of meaningless opinions, rules, and regulations.
It is this latter situation which has been the focal point of attack by many
thoughtful critics who have written about the "authoritarian personality"
and "authoritarian family relations," when actually what they mean is
better termed "totalitarian personality," and "totalitarian family."[10] But I
do not care, to speak with Locke, about the words, as long as the matter be
clearly understood. What seems to me significant about this well-known
development within the family is that the phenomenon of authority is associated with "reasoning." And by reasoning I do not mean the absolute
rationality alleged to be possessed by mathematics and logic, that is to say,
the reasoning which calls no value judgments into play, but rather the
reasoning which relates actions to opinions and beliefs, and opinions and
beliefs to values, however defined.[11]

It has, I hope, become apparent that I not only reject the use of the word
"authority" for the purpose of designating any kind of power, but that
when I speak of authority, I wish to say that the communications of a
person possessing it exhibit a very particular kind of relationship to reason
and reasoning. Such communications, whether opinions or commands, are
not demonstrated through rational discourse, but they possess the *potentiality of reasoned elaboration* – they are "worthy of acceptance."[12] Seen
in this perspective, authority is a *quality* of communication, rather than of
persons, and when we speak of the authority of a person, we are using a
shorthand expression to indicate that he possesses the capacity to issue
authoritative communications. And furthermore, when we say X possesses authority, we thereby propose to suggest that the communications
which X addresses to A, B, and C are based upon reasoning that has
meaning not only to X, but also to A, B, and C, in the sense of being

10 / See Theodor W. Adorno, *et al., The Authoritarian Personality* (1951),
especially the section written by Adorno himself. See also the discussion on the issue
with Else Brunswick, a contributor to *Totalitarianism*, ed. Carl J. Friedrich (1953),
pp. 171ff, and 274f.

11 / Cf., for example, Raymond Polin, *La Création des Valeurs* (1945; 2nd ed.,
1952), *passim.*

12 / This suggestive term was proposed by Morton White in a discussion of the
group mentioned in footnote 20. It makes it clear that authority in its reasoning
dimension is primarily a quality of the bearer of authority and of his communications, rather than those subject to it. But while it helps to express the thought I am
concerned with, it does not sufficiently stress the rational component to suffice for
this purpose.

related to knowledge which they all possess, or to opinions, beliefs, and values which they all share. But we are not concerned with the problem of persuasion; it is not a matter of X's ability to "influence" the thinking or acting of the others, though this usually is involved in the situation. What matters is that this capacity to issue communications which may be elaborated by reasoning is a decisive phenomenon in a great many social and more particularly political relationships. We should like to call it authority, but, whatever it is called, this potentiality of reasoned elaboration would appear to play a vital role in situations which involve authority. Perhaps one should be content to call it the "rational factor" in authority.

As far as the opinions, beliefs, and values involved in such reasoned elaboration are concerned, they may be one or many, readily identifiable or highly speculative and abstract. One value, such as truth or justice or health, may predominate, or there may be an infinitely complex array of values[13] such as is represented by a culture or a way of life.[14] What matters is that some propositions, whether judgments or commands, can be elaborated by suitable reasoning in terms of these values, opinions, or beliefs, while others cannot, or only imperfectly. The capacity of men to speak in meaningful terms, to say the things which may be thus elaborated, varies enormously. This capacity, I think, is implied when we speak of some of them as authorities.

Now it is important that this "reasoning" is not necessarily, nor even usually, employed in fact, though it may be hinted at or suggested by symbols. But it is important that the "potentiality of reasoned elaboration" of the communication exists. In other words, not the psychological concomitant of a *belief* in the capacity of the authority for such reasoned elaboration is decisive, but the actual existence of such a capacity. This does not mean that there could not arise situations wherein the capacity was erroneously believed to exist. Such errors are a common occurrence in relations among men. But such situations are properly and meaningfully described as involving "false" or "faked" authority. Genuine author-

13 / I do not use the term "system" here, nor in related contexts, although this is now frequently done, because the term should be avoided, unless the actual presence of a system can be demonstrated – which is rarely the case. On system analysis, cf. Ludwig von Bertalanffy, "Problems of General System Theory" in *General System Theory – A New Approach to the Unity of Science, from Human Biology* (1951).

14 / I have no objection to anyone wishing to employ the term "authority" for designating some other social phenomenon, such as "rightful power" or "legitimate power" or yet "power based on esteem or respect." But I do insist that in that case some other term will have to be suggested or invented for designating the social reality which I am describing and have labeled "authority," believing this to be its specific meaning.

ity, on the other hand, requires that the capacity actually is present. The respect, esteem, or other psychological concomitants, while undoubtedly present as well, are not a distinctive feature of authority. Power, wealth, and a host of other qualities likewise occasion these psychological reactions.

It is evident that the capacity to communicate authoritatively, that is, to be able to enlarge upon what is being communicated in terms meaningful to those who are being addressed, has a vital relation to the phenomena of power. Indeed, there can be no question but that this capacity always gives some power to him who possesses authority, and therefore authority is one of the sources of power. But just as the dagger by which I can kill a man and thus force him to surrender his purse is in any strict sense not power but the source of it, so likewise authority is *not* power, but it may cause it. This explains the undoubted fact that has been the occasion of much political comment, namely the continuance of power without authority, as well as the continuance of authority without power. Nero exercised power without authority, while the Senate of his time possessed authority yet little or no power. In precise terminology, which would speak of authority only when thinking of communications, this is readily comprehensible.[15]

The phenomenon which we have thus identified as a crucial aspect of authority explains why authority is a necessary part of all human relationships and communities. Such relationships are unmanageable without authority, because communication would become impossibly cumbersome. Wife and husband, no less than government and citizen, could not carry on for long if all the reasoning involved in saying what they have to say to each other would have to be stated or reproduced each time a communication were to be made. It is enough that the potentiality of such reasoning, the relating of actions to opinions, and of opinions to values, exists and is readily recognized. Indeed, in complementary relationships, such as that of husband and wife in contemporary American society, or that of fellow scholars or colleagues in related professional pursuits, there occurs what might be called the phenomenon of mutual authority. What I mean by "mutual" authority is that each of the persons in such a relationship is an authority to the other, but in divergent fields of work. This phenomenon is nearly incomprehensible when the relationship is merely seen in terms of power in its various forms.[16]

15 / Harold Lasswell and Abraham Caplan, by contrast, having defined authority as "formal power" (see *Power and Society*, 1950, pp. 133ff.), leave this kind of situation in the dark. For how does it help to describe the situation in which the Senate found itself as "formal power"?

16 / This proposition provides the clue to the nature of political authority under

The foregoing analysis also helps in understanding better the peculiarly fluid quality of power based on authority. Since opinions, values, and beliefs are continually changing, in response to changes in the environment and to creative innovations, whether of a political, aesthetic, or religious nature, it is quite possible, indeed a recurrent experience, that a person may lose his power based on authority, not because the commands he gives or the opinions he utters are less "authoritative" in the sense that they may be elaborated by reasoning, but because such reasoning is related to opinions, beliefs, and values that have lost their validity. When one, in such situations, says that a man has "lost his authority," this is really a shorthand expression; he has lost power because his authority, or rather the authority of his communications, is disintegrating, because this rational component which is crucial is deteriorating.

Another perplexing situation that becomes clearer, it is hoped, as a result of the analysis attempted here is the role of authority in totalitarian societies. If authority is interpreted as some kind of power, whether "formal," or "legal" or "rightful," the role of authority in totalitarian systems remains controversial and indeed obscure. Some say, with reference to a totalitarian regime, if they identify themselves with it and its rulers, that the authority of the ruler is very great. Others, identifying themselves with the subject elements of the population who are coerced into obedience, insist that there is no authority or very little in such a totalitarian society. The rational aspect of authority which we identified as the potentiality for reasoned elaboration of communications, whether they be commands or opinions or beliefs, makes it possible to understand these societies better. In contrast to constitutional societies where authority is diffuse and pluralistic, since authoritative communications issue from many centers of authority, such as churches, schools, trade unions, parties, all kinds of associations, as well as the government, authority in totalitarian societies is strikingly polarized and intensified at the center of the totalitarian movement. Thus the authority of a Lenin, a Stalin, or a Hitler when confronting his followers is very much greater than that of a democratic leader, while at the same time his authority in confronting

democratic conditions. Only the mutual respect of the citizens can give meaning to the acceptance of majority decisions, and the difficulty of mass democracy of the great urban concentrations of the present day must be seen as springing from this dissolution of the neighborhood and the disappearance of the respect associated with it. See my *The New Image of the Common Man* (1941 and later) for an exploration of the problems involved here. The contrast to present-day conditions can be seen in such processes as the New England town meeting; for this see John Gould, *New England Town Meeting* (1940), which, while a bit romantic, conveys well the point of mutuality of which I am speaking.

the rest of the society is very much weaker. To put it another way, governmental authority is both enlarged and reduced: enlarged, when one considers the followers, reduced, when one considers the rest of the people. Authority is not being centralized, or as the National Socialists called it, *gleichgeschaltet,* but it is being concentrated at the center of such a society. The explanation, in terms of our analysis, is not far to seek. The opinions and the commands of a Stalin or a Hitler, oriented to the regime's ideology, to the values and beliefs embodied in *Das Kapital* or *Mein Kampf,* could as a rule be elaborated by extensive reasoning.[17] It is important to bear in mind that such reasoning may well appear wholly "irrational" to anyone outside the particular belief and value system.[18]

Still another phenomenon, and one of paramount importance to democratic constitutional government which our theory of authority is able to elucidate, is that of discretion. Authority interpreted as involving the potential reasoning in interpersonal communications, that is to say as the capacity for reasoned elaboration, provides the clue to the problem of why discretion is both indispensable and manageable in all political and legal systems. In what follows, I shall concentrate on the phenomenon of discretion in constitutional democracies, that is, governments according to law made with popular participation.

It is worth remembering that John Locke discusses the problem of discretion when he comes to consider the prerogative. "This power to act according to discretion for the public good, without the prescription of the law and sometimes even against it, is that which is called prerogative," he writes in the *Second Essay* (160). And further that "the good of society requires that several things should be left to the discretion of him that has the executive power" (*Second Essay,* 159). There is an interesting similarity between Locke's approach and the Chinese tradition of "tsung-tung" or legitimate authority; no authority can be legitimate that fails to fulfill the function for which it was created – the public good.

Discretion may be defined in various ways, but what is always involved

17 / The recent tergiversations of Khrushchev in trying to explain his adherence to the objectives and purposes of Stalin, while rejecting some of his methods, seemed to me a striking illustration of the point here made: by attaching himself to the "reasoning" of Stalin in terms of the communist ideology, he evidently sought to preserve, and if possible, to strengthen his authority, at the same time reducing that of Stalin, whom he shows to have done things which *he could not have justified by reasoned elaboration.* Hence the juxtaposing of Lenin to Stalin.

18 / This instance is particularly worthy of attention, because Hitler's position appears to any outsider to have been that of utter madness. His conduct was not only irrational, but contrary to all common sense and reason. But reason in the general sense and "reasoning" in the sense here suggested, namely, relating to values, opinions, and briefs, are not the same thing.

is (1) the notion that a choice between several alternatives can, indeed must, be made; and (2) the notion that such a choice is not to be made arbitrarily, wantonly, or carelessly, but in accordance with the requirements of the situation.[19] There is the further notion (usually) that discretion ought to come into play within the framework of rules, implementing them, carrying them through, elaborating them. Thus a court, when using discretion in imposing a penalty, is acting within the framework of the rules of the penal law according to which the criminal has been adjudged guilty, and an administrative body, in fixing a rate, is acting within the framework of the rules of, say, the law of public utilities which fixes the way such utilities should be operated, after defining them and so forth. When a court or a commission or an administrative official acts in accordance with such general standards as "reasonableness" or "good morals," it is supposed to be doing this within the range of rules established by the law.[20]

To put it another way, discretion comes into play whenever no rules (or principles) can be, or have been, formulated, while at the same time, mere whim cannot be allowed. For a concrete example, one might turn to the choice of personnel. A legislative body or other principal may give fairly elaborate rules and establish precise regulations for the selection of personnel, as is done in civil service legislation. There always will remain, in many instances, an element of discretionary choice. The candidates may all be of a certain age, may all have a certain education and experience, come from certain localities, and possess a variety of other specified traits. There will often be candidates who are identical in all these respects, yet a choice has to be made between them. The selection board may have to decide whether to prefer a man from Yale or from Harvard, they may have to assess the precise meaning of words used in letters of recommendation, and so forth. The law will, therefore, give specified persons "discretion" to select the candidate. In doing so, the expectation will be that the person or persons given discretion will use it "to the best of their

19 / The author wishes here to acknowledge his general indebtedness to an informal discussion group of Harvard faculty members, mostly from the Law School, who met during 1956–1957 and explored the general problems of the "rule versus discretion" as a problem of legal philosophy. The group owed its existence to the initiative of Lon Fuller.

20 / Here we are face to face with the problem of the general clauses which are carried to such disastrous lengths in totalitarian (as indeed in many autocratic) regimes. A German jurist, J. W. Hedermann, stressed the dangers of such a "flight" in the German judicial decisions preceding Hitler's advent to power in his book *Die Flucht in die Generalklauseln* (1933); but the issue is much more pointedly developed by Fritz von Hippel, in *Die Perversion von Rechtsordnungen* (1955), giving many concrete illustrations of how such general clauses (and some not so general) may be carried beyond the limits allowed by the system. These are instances of the abuse of discretion.

ability." What this means is that they will give careful thought to all the factors involved. They may, to stay with our illustration, evaluate the writers of the letters of recommendation, considering their reliability, their past record of assessing men's ability, and other factors. They may consider that there are already several Harvard men in the organization and that there should be some diversity; or they may, reversely, consider that experience with Yale men has been so good that preference should be given to another Yale man.

At the same time, it will be generally assumed that a person vested with power to exercise discretion will be able to give reasons for what he has done. This aspect is particularly evident where a superior gives a subordinate discretion. He will ordinarily assume that the subordinate will use good sense, experience, stick to established precedent, and so on. But he will also expect the subordinate to be able to "explain," if for any reason he finds that the decision made ought to be subjected to review. The superior will rarely be satisfied with an explanation such as "I just felt that way" or "my instinct told me this was the right man," let alone an explanation which would say "I liked his face" or "she had such a lovely voice."

If one inspects such "reasoned elaboration" or inquires into what is expected under such a heading, he finds that the reasoning involved is both "instrumental" and "valuational," or to put it another way, it proceeds to argue both in terms of means and ends. The personnel man may suggest that the person chosen believes in democracy, or he may insist that the man rejected is possibly a believer in socialism or a fellow traveler. He may say that the candidate is steady and a good family man, or reversely that he is a drunkard and a bachelor. But besides such value judgments, there may be instrumental judgments, dwelling upon the man's ability, his knowledge of foreign languages, or what have you. The discretion as used is, in other words, tied to the opinions, values, and beliefs shared by members of the organization, as well as to the tasks to be performed.

It is by now becoming apparent why discretion is so valuable and indeed also why it is so inescapable an aspect of not only all government and administration, but all human relationships. Philosophers have since time immemorial dwelt upon the fact that rules can never cope with the infinite variety and detail of the concrete situations. To cope with the resulting inadequacy of all law, they have at times sought to find persons of exceptional wisdom, to identify as it were a natural elite of persons who would be so wise as to be able to exercise limitless discretion. Plato went perhaps further than any other thinker in this respect, at least the younger Plato of the *Republic*. Nor is it easy to argue against him, once the crucial concession is made that such men can be found by some reliable method. Plato himself took refuge in the hope of some kind of providential coincidence by which the philosopher and the holder of absolute power are brought together. Most of the rest of us have rejected his notion of the philosopher-king, precisely because the problem which he minimized, namely how to find the persons worthy of being entrusted with so much discretion, seems to be the most difficult.[21] For in the choice of personnel, as our humble illustration suggested, some of the most persistent discretionary problems present themselves. But though one rejects Plato's notion of a natural elite, and most of what goes with it, the fact remains that precisely where the novel, the unprecedented situation arises, calling for creative innovation and invention, all rules and regulations break down and discretion comes to the fore. And when such discretion is used in such a way as to benefit society, when, as the ancient verbiage has it, the "general good" is served, then government and administration are most universally acclaimed. Eisenhower deciding to cross the channel, Congress deciding to grant Puerto Rico commonwealth status, Truman deciding to act in Korea – these are recent instances of the exercise of discretion in dramatic situations calling for creative initiative, and utterly removed from the possibility of being handled by precedent or established rule.

Whenever discretion is thus used, whenever the factors relevant to a decision are obviously numerous and at least in part unforeseeable, it will seem to most men that an attempt to limit such discretion by pre-established rule or regulation would be unwise and in its consequences probably unjust.[22] But it appears similarly unwise and unjust to entrust such discretionary power to persons not qualified to exercise good judgment, that is to say, not acting in such a way that their reasoning could afterwards be examined and found defensible. At this point, we are con-

21 / Cf. Plato, *Republic*, especially at 473d. Aristotle, dubious of this doctrine, has an approach to the problem of discretion which is more nearly in keeping with our views, especially in connection with his doctrine of *epieikeia*. Cf. my *Philosophie des Rechts* (1954), ch. II. Note the sage comment of Kant on this doctrine of the limitless discretion of the philosopher-king: "It is not to be expected that kings philosophize or that philosophers become kings, nor is it to be desired because the possession of power corrupts the free judgment of reason inevitably." See my *The Philosophy of Kant* (1949), p. 456, and *Inevitable Peace* (1948), *passim*. The passage on the royal lie, or "noble falsehood" as A. D. Lindsay translates it, is found in *Republic*, 414.

22 / This point was especially emphasized by Henry Hart, in the discussions referred to in footnote 20. The argument has been elaborated from time to time by various authors. The political thought of writers like Machiavelli and Hegel is dominated by this problem, and its range overemphasized by them. Much of the literature of the New Deal in one way or another carries this implication. It is equally true of British labour thought. For the latter, see the scholarly work of W. A. Robson, especially his *Justice and Administrative Law* (3rd ed., 1951).

fronting the vital relationship of discretion to responsibility. Irresponsible discretion is not what is ordinarily wanted. But what constitutes "responsible discretion"? Essentially it is discretion which is exercised with due regard to all the considerations that enter into the situation. This will usually mean that the person exercising such discretion is duly qualified. He will seem to act responsibly when he acts in accordance with the full knowledge of the particular science, art, craft, or operation involved in the situation calling for discretion. That is why the selection of personnel appears as the core of the problem of how to arrange for the exercise of discretion. (It is, incidentally, the sound residue in Plato's notion of the philosopher-king.) And that is why administrative responsibility turns to such a large extent upon evaluation of the performance in terms of objective standards prevalent in a particular field of work and the sense of workmanship connected with it.[23]

At this point, the relation of discretion to the rational aspect of authority we have stressed becomes almost self-evident. When a person possesses the capacity to act in such a way that his communications concerning his actions possess by implication the potentiality of being supported by effective reasoning, he would appear to be eminently suited to occupy a position of discretionary power. To put this proposition in terms of our previous analysis, it follows that the exercise of discretionary power presupposes the possession of authority. Whenever a person possesses authority, in the sense in which we have here been employing the term, he is capable of using discretion. The fact that his decisions, commands, or other communications could be reinforced by reasoned elaboration relating them to established values and beliefs will lend his acts that "authority" without which discretion becomes arbitrary abuse of power.

If what has just been said is correct, it explains why authority is so often seen in the perspective of its psychological penumbra. For it is important, if authority is to be the source of power, that is, if the potentiality for reasoned elaboration is to manifest itself by people being willing to "go along" without such reasoned elaboration, that those subject to the command, or expected to conform in opinion or belief, recognize this potentiality. It is this undoubted fact which has led many to mistake the respect, esteem or admiration involved for the very nature of authority. Actually, as already mentioned, these psychological concomitants are unsatisfactory if made the sole or primary criterion for identifying the nature of authority, because they occur in other comparable situations. For example, power

23 / Cf. *Constitutional Government and Democracy* (1951), ch. XIX, and *The New Belief in the Common Man* (1941), ch. VI, "Responsibility and the Sense of Workmanship."

generates esteem, and wealth respect, and holiness admiration, so that if these psychological concomitants are made the heart of the matter, authority tends to be confused with any or all of these.

At this point, it might be well to explore further the difficulties resulting from making authority antithetical to reason and truth. There is some ground for this kind of antithesis on an elementary level; for as we saw earlier, authority as defined by us does not come into play when the communication rests upon self-evidence, or the rigid rationality of demonstrable truth. But truth has a wider connotation and embraces many kinds of existential situations.[24] Incidentally, truth is one of the key values to which authority in many contexts is vitally linked. It is the sharing of this value which allows scholars to accept each other's authority, where they would not accept that of a journalist or a preacher. We might add that theology is a striking instance of reasoned elaboration of a patently transcendental system of belief. Ecclesiastical authority is vitally related to it. Thus the Catholic faith is just one of numerous possible grounds for reasoned elaboration. Every body of thought – pragmatism and skepticism as well as "the faith" – must build upon some unexplained major premises. Actually, the great *Summa* of Thomas Aquinas is one of the most ambitious efforts at reasoned elaboration ever attempted by the mind of man, and it stands to reason that those who share with Thomas Aquinas his basic opinions, beliefs, and value judgments should look upon anyone who is fairly conversant with his thought as possessed of a certain authority. The case is really not very different when the authority is rooted in a full knowledge of Karl Marx or John Dewey.

But, we are told by thoughtful men, most of the people who accept authority, whether of the church or of the government, have no idea of these elaborate reasonings, would not understand them if they heard them, and do not care to learn about them. This may well be true, up to a point, as it is when we consult a doctor or engineer, but I submit that it is the potentiality of such reasoned elaboration that matters. The communications are intrinsically "worthy of acceptance." Much institutionalized authority is maintained without the persons involved being able to elaborate. Here are the points where the "interlarding" of authority and power

24 / Cf. Karl Jaspers, *Von der Wahrheit* (1947), where incidentally a position concerning authority is developed which has some points of contact with that here stated, at least in general. Cf. especially pp. 862ff., where an authority which reason "grasps" (*ergreift*) is contrasted with an authority that is "catholic," and hence transcendent and absolute. Jaspers' notion that such authority may be "grasped" and thus mastered by "reason" underestimates the amount of reason involved in catholic authority, on one hand and the "power of reason" in mastering authority, on the other.

is more frequent. Hence these institutionalized situations are the most fertile source of the confusion between authority and power. For there is always a considerable number of people around who are obeying, believing, or conforming, because they submit to power in its various forms, including physical violence, but talk about it as obeying authority. Far be it from me to insist that all obedience and other kinds of conformity are the result of authority, since I incline toward the view that this is the error involved in the views on authority I am questioning – views which confound authority with power. All I really insist upon is that the potentiality for reasoned elaboration of communications, that is, the potentiality of supporting communications by valuational and instrumental reasoning, since it usually elicits belief, provides a potent ground for maintaining conformity in matters of action, opinion, and belief where a community exists. It is a fundamental aspect of social and more particularly of political relations. Without it no community or society can function, because no discretionary power can for long be exercised, and hence all creative, innovating, inventive activity would cease. It seems to me that this fundamental potentiality of reasoned elaboration is the differentiating characteristic of what men have talked about since the days of the *auctoritas* of the fathers of the Roman Senate, when they have spoken of authority as contrasted with power. It is related to truth as much as to any other value about which men can and do reason. It is related to freedom, because without it there can be no discretion, and without discretion there can be no freedom, in private or public life. It is the result of the fact that man, endowed with reason, is yet a finite being, whose reason is likewise finite and enclosed within definite limits. An extravagant belief in human reason is apt to lead (as it has led in the past) to extravagant claims on behalf of authority. But the reach of authority is forever confined to the reach of reasoning. There can be no absolute, no total authority, because there does not exist any absolute truth or total reason. The belief in such absolute truth is associated with a claim to absolute authority transcending the analysis here given, as faith transcends science.

What then is "false" authority? It is that phantom which recurs in human society when men issue communications as authoritative which are believed to allow for reasoned elaboration when actually they do not. That is why the psychological interpretation of authority leads astray; for people may well *believe* that communications could be effectively elaborated and are therefore worthy of acceptance when no such potentiality exists. The falseness of such authority is revealed the moment the pretended potentiality has to be actualized. There is nothing subtle or surprising in these observations: "genuine" and "false" are terms which customarily refer to the possibility that the appearance may be deceptive. In a remarkable study on the influence of authority in matters of opinion, a nineteenth-century liberal concluded that "in the present state of the civilized world, the progress of society will depend in part upon legislative improvements, and upon those measures which a government can command or influence; but it will depend still more upon the substitution of competent for incompetent guides of public opinion; upon the continued extension of their influence; and upon the consequent organization of a sound authority in all the departments of theory and practice."[25] Cast into the less hopeful mood of our skeptical age, one might say instead that the maintenance of a measure of civilized existence depends upon the continued operation of authority as outlined in this essay. As long as we can maintain a measure of authority, that is to say, as long as those who wield power recognize their responsibility for discretionary acts in the sense of an obligation to retain the regard for the potentiality of reasoned elaboration, a constitutional order can be maintained. Once this regard is lost — and it may be lost by man at large no longer accepting reason as a guide — the night of meaningless violence is upon us. In conclusion, I should like to quote a little-known passage from an *Address to the King* by Edmund Burke which was written at the time certain members of parliament who had opposed the measures of the government in the contest between Britain and the American colonies thought of seceding from that venerable body. "We have been too early instructed, and too long habituated to believe, that the only firm seat of all authority is in the minds, affections, and interests of the people, to change our opinions ... for the convenience of a mere temporary arrangement of state."[26] Only when what is commanded and maintained can be thus reasoned upon and defended is authority secure. Only then can the five answers given above to the question, "why should I agree or obey?" be stated in a manner worthy of acceptance in the eyes of those who gave as well as those who receive them.

25 / See George Cornwall Lewis, *An Essay on the Influence of Authority in Matters of Opinion* (London, 1849). Lewis, in a striking sentence, lends support to the position here developed: "He who believes upon authority, entertains the opinion simply because it is entertained by a *person* who appears to him *likely to think correctly on the subject.*" He defines the "principle of authority" as that of "adopting the belief of others, on a matter of opinion, without reference to the particular grounds on which that belief may rest" (pp. 6–7), where the stress is on the *particular*.

26 / Edmund Burke, *Works* (Boston, 1839), vol. v, p. 135.

SHANKAR A. YELAJA

4
Freedom and authority

In one of the public housing projects, the housing authorities gave notice to a resident to vacate the housing quarters because his housekeeping was found to be below the "minimal standards of acceptable living." When the resident appeared before the housing manager to find out the details of the notice, he found that the housing authorities had visited his house several times upon numerous complaints from neighbours and had found the complaints justified. The housekeeping standards were such that a serious concern regarding public health and safety had arisen. This resident questioned the order, saying that it was an intrusion on his personal freedom and that he has every right to live the way he likes. His contention was that he could not be evicted, on the grounds of poor housekeeping, which is solely a private matter, and on the grounds that publichousing authorities by visiting his house had invaded his privacy. Furthermore, the housing authorities should have heard his side of the story before serving an eviction notice. The conflict in this situation is obvious. The manager had a hard time explaining the housing regulations and how his poor housekeeping impinges on the freedom of others. The basic issue in this incident, I submit, is a conflict between the boundaries of freedom and the limits of authority. I have every reason to believe that this conflict occurs in almost every sphere of our life activities, whenever we question the arbitrary or even non-arbitrary limits imposed upon our personal freedom.

Consider, for example, the present form of youth rebellion against the so-called "establishment" in North American society, which is undergoing a value crisis without parallel in its history. The younger people are "dropping out," and are expressing non-conformity to many aspects of social institutions. The trends in universities perhaps tend to dramatize the changing moods of youth and their non-conforming attitude towards a form of authority that imposes controls on their behaviour. When students take over an administration building, they are defining their own terms and meaning of freedom. This action is a rejection of authority and a confirmation, perhaps, of what free students are capable of doing under certain circumstances. The rejection and non-conformity of youths in North American society symbolize in yet another way an inherent conflict between freedom and authority.

Let me turn to an example from a special agency and its professionals, because they also are prone to conflicting notions of freedom and authority. The instance relates to one of the highly organized and complex bureaucratic social agencies. This agency had a system of time control over its professional and other staff, who were expected to record their arrival and departure times so that the office would know where the staff members were in case of emergency or for a routine check on the activities of the staff. Despite the time-control sheet, it was repeatedly found that the agency staff, especially those members whose jobs included field work out in the district, did not record their times of arrival and departure from the office. Although the agency clarified the rationale behind time control, the staff members managed to operate without it. Finally, the agency decided to impose strict limits on its members' time accounting, only to realize that it had invited more trouble.

The implications of this conflict between freedom and authority, in fact, pervade almost every aspect of our life. But we have hardly considered why this conflict occurs and whether there is a way to reconcile these two seemingly different but most important factors of our society. The purpose of this paper is limited to seeking to identify the nature of the conflict between freedom and authority, but within the framework of a formal organization. The discussion should provide at least part of the answer, so that we can become more aware of the conflict and how it can be resolved. Since the administrative organization is part and parcel of a social organization, some of the remarks may very well apply to the concepts of freedom and authority and their functions in social organizations.

It would be useful to clarify the conceptual meaning of the terms freedom and authority by attempting their definition. The terms freedom and liberty are used interchangeably. Liberty has been as often the rallying cry of a selfish interest intent upon privilege for itself as it has been the basis of a demand which sought the realization of a good wider than that by which it was itself affected. "It is therefore not unfair to describe the medieval idea of liberty as a system of corporate privileges wrung or purchased from the dominant power and affecting the individual less as himself than as a member of some group in whom those privileges cohere."[1] "Liberty may be defined as the affirmation by an individual or group of his or its own essence. It seems to require the presence of three factors. It seeks in the first place a certain harmonious balance of personality; it requires on the negative side the absence of restraints upon the exercise of that affirmation; and it demands on the positive the organization of opportunities for the exercise of a continuous initiative. The problem of liberty has always been the prevention of those restraints, upon the one hand, that men at any given period are not prepared to tolerate and, upon the other, the organization of those opportunities the denial of which results in that sense of frustration which when widely felt leads to imminent or actual disorder."[2]

Within the framework of the above definition, two things become clear about liberty. One is that, whereas its large limits may have a fairly permanent character, its particular content is always changing with the conditions of time and place. To one age the demand for liberty may express itself in an insistence upon religious toleration, to another political enfranchisement may be its essential expression. In modern times recognition and enforcement of the civil rights of minority groups has been a rallying cry of people advocating social justice. Liberty is, therefore, always inherent in a social process and is unintelligible apart from it. Second, liberty must be conceived, if its philosophy is to be an adequate one, as related to law. Liberty can never be absolute; some restraints are inevitable, some opportunities must be denied, simply because men have to live with one another. So closely interwoven is the network of our relationships that it would be impossible to define a sphere of conduct within which freedom of action can be sanctioned as liberty.

The task of defining objectively the concept of freedom is fraught with value problems, but a definition by Muller can help us to look at the concept. According to Muller, freedom means "the condition of being able to choose and to carry out purposes."[3] This definition has three immediate implications: "(1) the primary dictionary meaning − the absence of external constraints; (2) practicable purposes, or an actual ability with available means; and (3) a power of *conscious choice*, between significant, known alternatives ... In simple words, a man is free in so far as he can do something or choose not to do it, can make up his own mind, can say yes or no to any given question or command, can decide for him-

1 / Harold J. Laski, "Liberty," *Encyclopedia of The Social Sciences* (New York: The MacMillan Company), 1933, p. 442.

2 / *Ibid.*, p. 444.

3 / Herbert J. Muller, *Issues of Freedom: Paradoxes and Promises* (New York: Harper & Brothers, Publishers), 1960, p. 5.

self the matter of duty ... but all these statements must, of course, be qualified."[4] The notion of liberty and freedom cannot be separated from the concept of authority. "Since freedom and liberty have to be reconciled with social process, they have to find terms upon which to live with authority."[5]

Authority is always a function of concrete human situations. It operates in situations in which a person, fulfilling some purpose or end, requires guidance from a source outside of himself. "His need defines a field of conduct or belief in which help is required. He grants obedience to another person, to a group, or to a method or rule, with a claim to be able to assist him in mediating this field of conduct or belief, as a condition of the grant of such assistance. Any operating relationship of this sort is an authority relationship ... ."[6] However, one of the crucial issues in the authority relationship is, does it involve elements of coercion? Some political scientists have argued that the essence of authority is ultimately force or power. Horace Kallen in his essay on Coercion[7] argues that coercion obtains whenever the action or thought of one individual or group is compelled or restrained by another through some form of physical or moral compulsion. Kallen defines authority as "the sanctioned exercise of indirect coercion ... The coercer is credited with the power to impose feared penalties and his authority holds good only so long as his credit is good."[8] There appears to be a close relationship between authority and power. Authority is a manifestation of power and is meaningful only to the extent that it is sanctioned and institutionalized. In the exercise of authority legitimation plays a crucial role. Legitimation may be acquired through a variety of sources including legal sanction, traditional acceptance, charismatic leadership, and voluntary consent. To sum up the discussion on the definition of authority it may be defined as (1) a property of a person or office, especially the right to issue orders; (2) a relationship between two offices, one superior and the other subordinate, such that both incumbents perceive the relationship as legitimate; (3) a quality of a communication by virtue of which it is accepted ..."[9]

4 / *Ibid.*, p. 6.
5 / Laski, p. 444.
6 / Kenneth D. Benne, *A Conception of Authority: An Introductory Study* (New York: Teachers College, Bureau of Publications, Columbia University), 1943, p. 2.
7 / Horace M. Kallen, "Coercion," *Encyclopedia of the Social Sciences* (New York: The MacMillan Company), 1933, pp. 617–619.
8 / *Ibid.*, p. 618.
9 / Robert L. Peabody, "Authority," *International Encyclopedia of the Social Sciences* (New York: The MacMillan Company and the Free Press), 1968, Volume I, p. 473.

The definition of authority in a formal organization has much in common with the above definitions. However, various organization theorists have looked at the concept of authority in formal organizations from different vantage points. Barnard defines authority as "the character of a communication (order) in a formal organization by virtue of which it is accepted by a contributor to or 'member' of the organization as governing the action he contributes; that is, as governing or determining what he does or is not to do so far as the organization is concerned."[10] According to this definition, authority involves two aspects. First, the subjective, the accepting of a communication as authoritative, and second, the objective, the character in the communication by virtue of which it is accepted. The essence of the definition provided by Barnard seems to be that authority lies with the person to whom it is addressed, and does not reside in "persons of authority." It is the willingness to be influenced, whatever the origin of the willingness, that determines the authority or power. In effect, authority can be recognized only by its effects on the person who accepts it. Simon, who uses the basic theory of Barnard and sees authority as existing when behaviour promises of another are accepted as a basis for decision, develops more fully the relation between motivation and sanctioning systems.[11] The thesis of Simon is based on the premise that when authority is employed to enforce responsibility, sanctions will probably play an important part in the process.

The conceptual understanding of the terms freedom and authority evidently suggests that they are not antithetical but complementary and interdependent. In order to exercise certain privileges, liberties, or freedoms, one must give up something and accept rationally-defined limits imposed by the society. In an administrative organization, the freedom and authority, ideologically speaking, are also complementary, provided that the individual member of an organization has accepted the authority and is willing to exercise his rights for freedom within the jurisdiction or by the formal authority over him.

The question still remains – why is there a conflict then between freedom and authority? I believe part of the answer lies in the fact that man by very nature is more concerned with his self-interest and, therefore, higher freedom than with conformity to the limits of authority. Hobbs rightly remarked that man by very instinct is selfish and, therefore, his self-interest comes first.

10 / Chester I. Barnard, *The Functions of the Executive*, p. 49 above.
11 / Herbert A. Simon, *Administrative Behavior* (New York: MacMillan Company), 1957, p. 34.

If one were to arrange human needs and drives for "self actualization"[12] in a hierarchical order, self-interest (and preservation) as a natural human drive would be on the top of that order. Self-interest, however, does not mean that an individual is all wrapped up in himself and that he wants to pursue his self-interest without due regard to others. In self-actualizing persons there is a rational process involved in the pursuit of self-interest, which can be encapsulated as collective freedom, that is to say, all members are free to pursue their self-interests within certain limits defined by the "common good." A rational self-interest must come to grips with the conception of the "common good" and be able to evaluate the extent to which self-interest and the "common good" are complementary and not antithetical to each other, as well as the ways in which the pursuit and fulfilment of self-interest can contribute to the "common good" of a society.

The conflict between freedom and authority can take place when self-interest is above and beyond the conception and practice of the "common good." In a formal organization, the "common good" is represented by the inherent goals of the organization. The optimal success in reaching the organizational goals is a function of two factors. One is the extent to which individual members of that organization are willing to give up their self-interest or are able to define self-interest in conjunction with common goals, and the second is the extent to which there is a consensus on the viability of organizational goals.

The functions carried by an individual member in a formal organization can be identified as one piece of the total job of the agency. But a member may not accept authority or controls exercised by a formal organization to an equal degree in all parts of his job. Barnard[13] differentiates between three parts of an individual's job on the basis of the employee's perception of the authority. He introduces the term "zone of indifference" to identify that area within which each individual is willing to accept controls "without conscious questioning." There are two other areas: "a zone of neutrality" in which the acceptor makes a decision as to whether he will or will not be influenced and "a zone of unacceptability"

12 / Self-actualization is defined in various ways by different psychologists, but a solid core of agreement is perceptible. All definitions accept or imply, (a) acceptance and expression of the inner core or self, i.e., actualization of these latent capacities, and potentialities, "full functioning," availability of the human and personal essence, and (b) minimal presence of ill health, neurosis, psychosis, or loss or diminution of the basic human and personal capacities. For a detailed conceptual analysis of the self-actualizing process, see Abraham H. Maslow, *Toward A Psychology of Being* (New York: D. Van Nostrand Company, Inc.), 1962, pp. 177–200.

13 / Pp. 53 above.

in which he refuses to recognize the authority of the agent and, therefore, rejects any form of authority. According to the previous definition of authority by Barnard, since the authority depends upon the individual by whom it is felt, his willingness to accept it or not is the crucial factor. Barnard in effect stressed the "psychology of authority" that is important in the process of carrying out organizational functions. It is in the "zone of unacceptability" that the conflict between freedom and authority is most obvious. The examples presented in the beginning of this paper clearly fall in this category.

Thus, it seems that the controls that are necessary to strike a rational balance between authority and freedom must necessarily emanate from the inner "self." Unless the self of the individual member of a formal organization has recognized the need for establishing controls from within the "self" and has thus been able to attempt to reach a rational self-interest, the conflict between freedom and authority can hardly be resolved. The "inner self" must through a process of rational thinking yield to outside controls as being helpful both to the self and to the formal organization.

The key to conflict management between freedom and authority can, therefore, be found in self-realization. To illustrate, in the first example of poor housekeeping, the resident cannot conform to acceptable standards set by the housing authority unless he can bring his notion of freedom (to "live as he likes") under conscious control and evaluate how pursuit of his freedom would impinge on the freedom of others in the housing project. Authority and freedom in the final analysis are subjective notions and their integration depends upon individual orientation.

Kenneth Pray said, "Freedom is a relative term; there is no absolute freedom in this world and there ought not to be. None of us has absolute individual freedom; none of us believes in it, none of us would know what to do with it if we had it. Some structure of authority, defining and enforcing the necessary limits upon individual personal responsibility and conduct, as a condition of social cooperation, is an indispensable basis of any kind of life in any society."[14]

Implicit in my discussion on freedom and authority thus far there is an assumption made that needs further clarification. Freedom within the confines of this paper is equated with the pursuit of rational self-interest and authority is seen as representing the "common good." In a formal organization it is perhaps relatively easy to define and understand the

14 / Kenneth L. M. Pray, "Casework Paves the Way in Preparation for Freedom," in *Social Work in a Revolutionary Age* (Philadelphia: University of Pennsylvania Press), 1949, p. 214.

conception of the "common good" as it relates to organizational goals, but what about societal "common good"? Who defines the "common good" for a society? And what are the normative standards of the "common good"? Is it realistic to expect an objective and rational definition of the "common good"? Or is it purely a function of social and political power? These are some of the questions that must be raised and analyzed in order to relate the thesis of my paper to the concepts of freedom and authority as they relate to the function of a society. In the recent past we witnessed the rise of military dictators and authoritarian personalities who were capable of defining the "common good" for society as they saw fit and appropriate. The result was a more severe and serious conflict between freedom and authority rather than a resolution. How can society protect itself from the rise of dictators assuming totalitarian responsibility for defining the "common good"? Questions such as this are perhaps easier to raise than to answer. But they must be answered in order to resolve the conflict between freedom and authority.

PART II

Formulations of theories about authority

The five articles included in this part are meant to explore theoretical underpinnings and knowledge of authority with a view to formulation of a theory of authority. Surveying the social and behavioural science literature, there appear to be many articles on the subject. Political scientists, for example, have explored the concept of authority as it relates to political institutions within a society. The field of psychology, especially experimental psychology perhaps, makes the largest contribution to theories of authority, with attempts to explain the phenomena of the "authoritarian personality" and behavioural characteristics and processes involved in compliance to authority. Sociologists likewise have searched and researched the concept of authority in their attempts to build a certain typology of authority. To this reservoir of knowledge is added an emerging concern of social scientists who are interested in studying authority in an organizational context. To select a few theories out of the vast literature was, therefore, no small task. The following five articles were selected primarily to provide a range and an overview of theories on authority, distinct in their theoretical underpinnings. Emphasis is placed on the fact that these five theories by no means exhaust all theories on authority. To the contrary, these tend to serve as "pathways to further theoretical understanding of authority." Also each of the five theories represents a distinct contribution to the body of our knowledge. Most of the research carried on in social and behavioural sciences, for example, has used Max Weber's typology of authority as a point of departure. By the same token Barnard's theory on authority has been widely used in studies on organizational behaviour. A further concern in selecting these articles was that each of the five authors should represent a different discipline. It was hoped that an interdisciplinary theoretical exploration of authority would be helpful for social workers in their understanding and formulation of a theory of authority as one of the foundations in social work practice.

Barnard's theory of authority is based on the following major constellations of ideas. Authority, according to Barnard, "lies with the persons to whom it is addressed, and does not reside in 'persons of authority' or those who issue these orders." Four conditions must simultaneously exist in order for a person to accept a communication as authoritative. These are (1) that he can and does understand the communication, (2) that at the time of decision he believes that it is consistent with the purpose of the organization, (3) that it is compatible with his personal interest as a whole, and (4) that he is able mentally and physically to comply with it. In formulating this theory, Barnard has introduced a new idea, "zone of indifference," which means that "in each individual there exists an area within which orders are acceptable without conscious questioning of their authority."

Why are theories on bureaucratic authority in formal organization selected for this book? Most social workers (with the exception of those in private practice) function in formal organizations – public and private. Social agencies, where most social workers are employed, meet the criteria of a formal organization, which include division of labour, specialization and hierarchy, authority and responsibility, routinization of activity, formal and informal relationships, and process of decision-making. Because social workers function in formal organizations, it would be helpful to them if a theory of authority were to be explored and understood within a formal organization. It is recognized that the role and functional responsibilities of social workers are shaped also by other factors in a formal organization. Since authority is singled out as a major concern, theories on authority help to explain the general functioning of formal organizations. Specific application of these to social agencies is not attempted but is generally assumed.

Organizational theory today contains two sharply different views of systems of bureaucratic authority. In one, developed most fully by Barnard, they are communications processes. In his conception, neither legitimacy nor hierarchy plays a particularly central role. Both occur, but individual self-interest rather than shared moral commitments provides the main motivations. In the other, which has its source in the writings of Max Weber, systems of bureaucratic authority are power structures operating in a quasi-judicial fashion: rational values legitimate them, trained experts run them, and the principle of hierarchy, prescribing a positive relation between the rank of a unit and its power, defines their shape. Whereas the outstanding elements in Weber's conception of bureaucratic authority are power, hierarchy and legitimacy, in Barnard's conception these are decision-making, communication, and rational self-interest. Weber's conception of authority presents an image of a pyramid; Barnard's on the other hand, suggests a wheel, with lines of communication as so many spokes radiating from the few persons at the organization's centre, who make the decisions, to the many along the rim, who finally carry out the decisions.

A composite view of authority begins to emerge when one analyzes the similarities in Barnard's and Weber's conceptions of bureaucratic authority. These can be summarized as follows:

1 Authority is a form of interaction: one person issuing a command and a second complying with it.

2   A role relationship is authoritative to the degree that it exhibits a stable distribution of commanding actions to one role and reciprocal complying actions to the other.

3   Authority involves a complex structure of relations. Three principal classes of participants are included in the structure: a ruling group from which general orders are issued, an administrative staff which interprets and transmits the orders, and "subjects," that is, those who only comply.

4   An authority system is only an abstract aspect of some concrete social system. It is embedded in some kind of a group, at least in part. The members of the group share various values and norms, among which are the values that justify the existence or non-existence of authority systems.

5   In principle, any form of group may provide values legitimizing an authority structure. Bureaucratic systems of authority occur in the context of groups having a certain type of value system and a certain type of organization and are themselves in turn characterized by certain distinctive structural features.

6   Bureaucratic authority always operates relative to a given set of rules and produces compliance with them; its systematic exercise is specifically unidirectional: and the measure of its effectiveness is the degree of compliance with the group's formal rules or with the administrated interpretations of them.

Current studies of formal organization tend to fall into two categories, those in which the authority system is viewed as a power structure and those in which it is viewed as a communication process, a division that essentially reflects different philosophical strands in viewing the functions of authority. That social workers need to understand and appreciate the difference in these points of view is recognized. Although the similarities are highlighted, readers can easily ascertain the differences between Weber's and Barnard's conceptions of authority.

Presthus' article, "Authority in Organizations," is an attempt to bridge the differences between the conceptions of Weber and Barnard. Authority, according to Presthus, is defined as "a transactional process, characterized by active, reciprocal interrelationships in which the values, training, and perceptions of members play a crucial role in defining and validating the authority of organizational leaders." The process of validating authority may be called legitimation, which rests upon four bases, including technical expertise, formal role or position in the organization's hierarchy, rapport of leaders to meet individual needs for recognition, security, etc., and finally, legitimation through a generalized deference towards authority. Interestingly enough, Presthus' definition of authority is closer to Barnard's than to Weber's, but its operation within a formal organization tends to follow the lines of Weber's thinking.

The article by Tufts is included in the section mainly because it captures a new dimension of authority. Yet this dimension – "psychological authority" – is perhaps the most crucial for social workers in their use of authority as part of the helping process. The psychological dimension of authority is seen as an interpersonal relation in which one person (or group) exercises influence over the (social) behaviour of another person (or group) who does not fully accept the reasoning that relates values to actions, but in which both parties know that this influence is being exercised; its intent is known and, hence, recognized for what it is.

Hardman's "bread and butter theory" of authority in social casework can be best described as a "middle range" type of theory – applicable to limited ranges of social work rather than to an "integrated" conceptual structure covering all theories. Hardman's theoretical formulation can be stated as follows. The use of authority is not antagonistic to the principles of "good social work" or counselling. Furthermore, the actual employment of authority itself – its skilful use – can be a powerful therapeutic tool in social service. Based on this theoretical framework, Hardman has developed eight postulates ranging in abstraction from general to specific. A general level of abstraction, for instance, is that "authority is inherent in all cultures, and that a society free of authority does not and cannot exist." A level of specificity is seen in the postulate, "an outstanding service that a worker can render to a client with authority conflict is to provide a new and differential and therapeutic experience with authority." An empirical analysis of the worker-client relationship and the authority factors present in that relationship would be the next step, if one were to test Hardman's "bread and butter theory."

The five articles included in the following section are meant to explore a wide range of theoretical knowledge on authority. The omission of other theories is perhaps due to the fact that these would tend to overlap. Any one formulation of the theory of authority is deliberately avoided. A reader would hopefully integrate his own theory of authority based on different theories presented in the section.

CHESTER I. BARNARD

5

The theory of authority

THE SOURCE OF AUTHORITY

If it is true that all complex organizations consist of aggregations of unit organizations and have grown only from unit organizations, we may reasonably postulate that, whatever the nature of authority, it is inherent in the simple organization unit; and that a correct theory of authority must be consistent with what is essentially true of these unit organizations. We shall, therefore, regard the observations which we can make of the actual conditions as at first a source for discovering what is essential in elementary and simple organizations.

I

Now a most significant fact of general observation relative to authority is the extent to which it is ineffective in specific instances. It is so ineffective that the violation of authority is accepted as a matter of course and its implications are not considered. It is true that we are sometimes appalled at the extent of major criminal activities; but we pass over very lightly the universal violations, particularly of sumptuary laws, which are as "valid" as any others. Even clauses of constitutions and statutes carrying them "into effect," such as the Eighteenth Amendment, are violated in whole-sale degrees.

Violation of law is not, however, peculiar to our own country. I observed recently in a totalitarian state under a dictator, where personal liberty is supposed to be at a minimum and arbitrary authority at a maxi-

Reprinted by permission of the Harvard University Press, Cambridge, Mass., from Chester I. Barnard, *The Functions of the Executive* (Cambridge, Mass.: Harvard University Press), 1956, pp. 161–84.

mum, many violations of positive law or edict, some of them open and on a wide scale; and I was reliably informed of others.

Nor is this condition peculiar to the authority of the state. It is likewise true of the authority of churches. The Ten Commandments and the prescriptions and prohibitions of religious authority are repeatedly violated by those who profess to acknowledge their formal authority.

These observations do not mean that all citizens are lawless and defy authority; nor that all Christians are godless or their conduct unaffected by the tenets of their faith. It is obvious that to a large extent citizens are governed; and that the conduct of Christians is substantially qualified by the prescriptions of their churches. What is implied is merely that which specific laws will be obeyed or disobeyed by the individual citizen are decided by him under the specific conditions pertinent. This is what we mean when we refer to individual responsibility. It implies that which prescriptions of the church will be disobeyed by the individual are determined by him at a given time and place. This is what we mean by moral responsibility.

It may be thought that ineffectiveness of authority in specific cases is chiefly exemplified in matters of state and church, but not in those of smaller organizations which are more closely knit or more concretely managed. But this is not true. It is surprising how much that in theory is authoritative, in the best of organizations in practice lacks authority — or, in plain language, how generally orders are disobeyed. For many years the writer has been interested to observe this fact, not only in organizations with which he was directly connected, but in many others. In all of them, armies, navies, universities, penal institutions, hospitals, relief organizations, corporations, the same conditions prevail — dead laws, regulations, rules, which no one dares bury but which are not obeyed; obvious disobedience carefully disregarded; vital practices and major institutions for which there is no authority, like the Democratic and Republican parties, not known to the Constitution.

II

We may leave the secondary stages of this analysis for later consideration. What we derive from it is an approximate definition of authority for our purpose: Authority is the character of a communication (order) in a formal organization by virtue of which it is accepted by a contributor to or "member" of the organization as governing the action he contributes; that is, as governing or determining what he does or is not to do so far as the organization is concerned. According to this definition, authority involves two aspects: first, the subjective, the personal, the *accepting* of a communication as authoritative, the aspects which I shall present in this section; and, second, the objective aspect – the character in the communication by virtue of which it is accepted – which I present in the second section, "The System of Coördination."

If a directive communication is accepted by one to whom it is addressed, its authority for him is confirmed or established. It is admitted as the basis of action. Disobedience of such a communication is a denial of its authority for him. Therefore, under this definition the decision as to whether an order has authority or not lies with the persons to whom it is addressed, and does not reside in "persons of authority" or those who issue these orders.

This is so contrary to the view widely held by informed persons of many ranks and professions, and so contradictory to legalistic conceptions, and will seem to many so opposed to common experience, that it will be well at the outset to quote two opinions of persons in a position to merit respectful attention. It is not the intention to "argue from authorities"; but before attacking the subject it is desirable at least to recognize that prevalent notions are not universally held. Says Roberto Michels in the monograph "Authority" in the *Encyclopaedia of the Social Sciences*,[1] "Whether authority is of personal or institutional origin it is created and maintained by public opinion, which in its turn is conditioned by sentiment, affection, reverence or fatalism. Even when authority rests on mere physical coercion it is *accepted*[2] by those ruled, although the acceptance may be due to a fear of force."

Again, Major General James G. Harbord, of long and distinguished military experience, and since his retirement from the Army a notable business executive, says on page 259 of his *The American Army in France*:[3]

A democratic President had forgotten that the greatest of all democracies is an Army. Discipline and morale influence the inarticulate vote that is instantly taken by masses of men when the order comes to move forward – a variant of the crowd psychology that inclines it to follow a leader, but the Army does not move forward until the motion has "carried." "Unanimous consent" only follows cooperation between the *individual* man in the ranks.

These opinions are to the effect that even though physical force is involved, and even under the extreme condition of battle, when the regime is nearly absolute, authority nevertheless rests upon the acceptance or

1 / New York: Macmillan.
2 / Italics mine.
3 / Boston: Little, Brown and Co., 1936.

consent of individuals. Evidently such conceptions, if justified, deeply affect an appropriate understanding of organization and especially of the character of the executive functions.

Our definition of authority, like General Harbord's democracy in an army, no doubt will appear to many whose eyes are fixed only on enduring organizations to be a platform of chaos. And so it is – exactly so in the preponderance of attempted organizations. They fail because they can maintain no authority, that is, they cannot secure sufficient contributions of personal efforts to be effective or cannot induce them on terms that are efficient. In the last analysis the authority fails because the individuals in sufficient numbers regard the burden involved in accepting necessary orders as changing the balance of advantage against their interest, and they withdraw or withhold the indispensable contributions.

III

We must not rest our definition, however, on general opinion. The necessity of the assent of the individual to establish authority *for him* is inescapable. A person can and will accept a communication as authoritative only when four conditions simultaneously obtain: (*a*) he can and does understand the communication; (*b*) *at the time of his decision*, he believes that it is not inconsistent with the purpose of the organization; (*c*) *at the time of his decision*, he believes it to be compatible with his personal interest as a whole; and (*d*) he is able mentally and physically to comply with it.

(*a*) A communication that cannot be understood *can* have no authority. An order issued, for example, in a language not intelligible to the recipient is no order at all – no one would so regard it. Now, many orders are exceedingly difficult to understand. They are often necessarily stated in general terms, and the persons who issued them could not themselves apply them under many conditions. Until interpreted they have no meaning. The recipient either must disregard them or merely do anything in the hope that that is compliance.

Hence, a considerable part of administrative work consists in the interpretation and reinterpretation of orders in their application to concrete circumstances that were not or could not be taken into account initially.

(*b*) A communication believed by the recipient to be incompatible with the purpose of the organization, as he understands it, could not be accepted. Action would be frustrated by cross purposes. The most common practical example is that involved in conflicts of orders. They are not rare. An intelligent person will deny the authority of that one which contradicts the purpose of the effort as *he* understands it. In extreme cases many individuals would be virtually paralyzed by conflicting orders. They would be literally unable to comply – for example, an employee of a water system ordered to blow up an essential pump, or soldiers ordered to shoot their own comrades. I suppose all experienced executives know that when it is necessary to issue orders that will appear to the recipients to be contrary to the main purpose, especially as exemplified in prior habitual practice, it is usually necessary and always advisable, if practicable, to explain or demonstrate why the appearance of conflict is an illusion. Otherwise the orders are likely not to be executed, or to be executed inadequately.

(c) If a communication is believed to involve a burden that destroys the net advantage of connection with the organization, there no longer would remain a net inducement to the individual to contribute to it. The existence of a net inducement is the only reason for accepting *any* order as having authority. Hence, if such an order is received it must be disobeyed (evaded in the more usual cases) as utterly inconsistent with personal motives that are the basis of accepting any orders at all. Cases of voluntary resignation from all sorts of organizations are common for this sole reason. Malingering and intentional lack of dependability are the more usual methods.

(d) If a person is unable to comply with an order, obviously it must be disobeyed, or, better, disregarded. To order a man who cannot swim to swim a river is a sufficient case. Such extreme cases are not frequent, but they occur. The more usual case is to order a man to do things only a little beyond his capacity; but a little impossible is still impossible.

IV

Naturally the reader will ask: How is it possible to secure such important and enduring coöperation as we observe if in principle and in fact the determination of authority lies with the subordinate individual? It is possible because the decisions of individuals occur under the following conditions: (a) orders that are deliberately issued in enduring organizations usually comply with the four conditions mentioned above; (b) there exists a "zone of indifference" in each individual within which orders are acceptable without conscious questioning of their authority; (c) the interests of the persons who contribute to an organization as a group result in the exercise of an influence on the subject, or on the attitude of the individual, that maintains a certain stability of this zone of indifference.

(a) There is no principle of executive conduct better established in good organizations than that orders will not be issued that cannot or will not be obeyed. Executives and most persons of experience who have thought about it know that to do so destroys authority, discipline, and morale.[4] For reasons to be stated shortly, this principle cannot ordinarily be formally admitted, or at least cannot be professed. When it appears necessary to issue orders which are initially or apparently unacceptable, either careful preliminary education, or persuasive efforts, or the prior offering of effective inducements will be made, so that the issue will not be raised, the denial of authority will not occur, and orders will be obeyed. It is generally recognized that those who least understand this fact — newly appointed minor or "first line" executives — are often guilty of "disorganizing" their groups for this reason, as do experienced executives who lose self-control or become unbalanced by a delusion of power or for some other reason. Inexperienced persons take literally the current notions of authority and are then said "not to know how to use authority" or "to abuse authority." Their superiors often profess the same beliefs about authority in the abstract, but their successful practice is easily observed to be inconsistent with their professions.

(b) The phrase "zone of indifference" may be explained as follows: If all the orders for actions reasonably practicable be arranged in the order of their acceptability to the person affected, it may be conceived that there

4 / Barring relatively few individual cases, when the attitude of the individual indicates in advance likelihood of disobedience (either before or after connection with the organization), the connection is terminated or refused before the formal question arises.

It seems advisable to add a caution here against interpreting the exposition in terms of "democracy," whether in governmental, religious, or industrial organizations. The dogmatic assertion that "democracy" or "democratic methods" are (or are not) in accordance with the principles here discussed is not tenable. As will be more evident after the consideration of objective authority, the issues involved are much too complex and subtle to be taken into account in *any* formal scheme. Under many conditions in the political, religious, and industrial fields, democratic processes create artificial questions of more or less logical character, in place of the real questions, which are matters of feeling and appropriateness and of informal organization. By oversimplification of issues this may destroy objective authority. No doubt in many situations formal democratic processes may be an important element in the maintenance of authority, i.e., of organization cohesion, but may in other situations be disruptive, and probably never could be, in themselves, sufficient. On the other hand the solidarity of some coöperative systems (General Harbord's army, for example) under many conditions may be unexcelled, though requiring formally autocratic processes.

Moreover, it should never be forgotten that authority in the aggregate arises from *all* the contributors to a coöperative system, and that the weighting to be attributed to the attitude of individuals varies. It is often forgotten that in industrial (or political) organizations measures which are acceptable at the bottom may be quite unacceptable to the substantial proportion of contributors who are executives, and who will no more perform their essential functions than will others, if the conditions are, to them, impossible. The point to be emphasized is that the maintenance of the contributions necessary to the endurance of an organization requires the authority of *all* essential contributors.

are a number which are clearly unacceptable, that is, which certainly will not be obeyed; there is another group somewhat more or less on the neutral line, that is, either barely acceptable or barely unacceptable; and a third group unquestionably acceptable. This last group lies within the "zone of indifference." The person affected will accept orders lying within this zone and is relatively indifferent as to what the order is so far as the question of authority is concerned. Such an order lies within the range that in a general way was anticipated at time of undertaking the connection with the organization. For example, if a soldier enlists, whether voluntarily or not, in an army in which the men are ordinarily moved about within a certain broad region, it is a matter of indifference whether the order be to go to A or B, C or D, and so on; and goings to A, B, C, D, etc., are in the zone of indifference.

The zone of indifference will be wider or narrower depending upon the degree to which the inducements exceed the burdens and sacrifices which determine the individual's adhesion to the organization. It follows that the range of orders that will be accepted will be very limited among those who are barely induced to contribute to the system.

(c) Since the efficiency of organization is affected by the degree to which individuals assent to orders, denying the authority of an organization communication is a threat to the interests of all individuals who derive a net advantage from their connection with the organization, unless the orders are unacceptable to them also. Accordingly, at any given time there is among most of the contributors an active personal interest in the maintenance of the authority of all orders which to them are within the zone of indifference. The maintenance of this interest is largely a function of informal organization. Its expression goes under the names of "public opinion," "organization opinion," "feeling in the ranks," "group attitude," etc. Thus the common sense of the community informally arrived at affects the attitude of individuals, and makes them, as individuals, loath to question authority that is within or near the zone of indifference. The formal statement of this common sense is the fiction that authority comes down from above, from the general to the particular. This fiction merely establishes a presumption among individuals in favor of the acceptability of orders from superiors, enabling them to avoid making issues of such orders without incurring a sense of personal subserviency or a loss of personal or individual status with their fellows.

Thus the contributors are willing to maintain the authority of communications because, where care is taken to see that only acceptable communications in general are issued, most of them fall within the zone of personal indifference; and because communal sense influences the motives of most contributors most of the time. The practical instrument of this sense is the fiction of superior authority, which makes it possible normally to treat a personal question impersonally.

The fiction[5] of superior authority is necessary for two main reasons:

(1) It is the process by which the individual delegates upward, or to the organization, responsibility for what is an organization decision – an action which is depersonalized by the fact of its coördinate character. This means that if an instruction is disregarded, an executive's risk of being wrong must be accepted, a risk that the individual cannot and usually will not take unless in fact his position is at least as good as that of another with respect to correct appraisal of the relevant situation. Most persons are disposed to grant authority because they dislike the personal responsibility which they otherwise accept, especially when they are not in a good position to accept it. The practical difficulties in the operation of organization seldom lie in the excessive desire of individuals to assume responsibility for the organization action of themselves or others, but rather lie in the reluctance to take responsibility for their own actions in organization.

(2) The fiction gives impersonal notice that what is at stake is the good of the organization. If objective authority is flouted for arbitrary or merely temperamental reasons, if, in other words, there is deliberate attempt to twist an organization requirement to personal advantage, rather than properly to safeguard a substantial personal interest, then there is a deliberate attack on the organization itself. To remain outside an organization is not necessarily to be more than not friendly or not interested. To fail in an obligation intentionally is an act of hostility. This no organization can permit; and it must respond with punitive action if it can, even to the point of incarcerating or executing the culprit. This is rather generally the case where a person has agreed in advance in general what he will do. Leaving an organization in the lurch is not often tolerable.

The correctness of what has been said above will perhaps appear most probable from a consideration of the difference between executive action in emergency and that under "normal" conditions. In times of war the disciplinary atmosphere of an army is intensified – it is rather obvious to all that its success and the safety of its members are dependent upon it. In other organizations, abruptness of command is not only tolerated in times of emergency, but expected, and the lack of it often would actually be demoralizing. It is the sense of the justification which lies in the obvious situation which regulates the exercise of the veto by the final authority

5 / The word "fiction" is used because from the standpoint of logical construction it merely explains overt acts. Either as a superior officer or as a subordinate, however, I know nothing that I actually regard as more "real" than "authority."

which lies at the bottom. This is a commonplace of executive experience, though it is not a commonplace of conversation about it.[6]

THE SYSTEM OF COÖRDINATION

Up to this point we have devoted our attention to the subjective aspect of authority. The executive, however, is predominantly occupied not with this subjective aspect, which is fundamental, but with the objective character of a communication which induces acceptance.

I

Authority has been defined in part as a "character of a communication in a formal organization." A "superior" is not in our view an authority nor does he have authority strictly speaking; nor is a communication authoritative except when it is an effort or action of organization. This is what we mean when we say that individuals are able to exercise authority only when they are acting "officially," a principle well established in law, and generally in secular and religious practice. Hence the importance ascribed to time, place, dress, ceremony, and authentication of a communication to establish its official character. These practices confirm the statement that authority relates to a communication "in a formal organization." There often occur occasions of compulsive power of individuals and of hostile groups; but authority is always concerned with something *within* a definitely organized system. Current usage conforms to the definition in this respect. The word "authority" is seldom employed except where formal organization connection is stated or implied (unless, of course, the reference is obviously figurative).

These circumstances arise from the fact that the character of authority in organization communications lies in the *potentiality of assent* of those to whom they are sent. Hence, they are only sent to contributors or "members" of the organization. Since all authoritative communications are official and relate only to organization action, they have no meaning

---

6 / It will be of interest to quote a statement which has appeared since these lines were written, in a pamphlet entitled "Business – Well on the Firing Line" (No. 9 in the series "What Helps Business Helps You," in *Nation's Business*). It reads in part: "Laws don't create Teamplay. It is not called into play by law. For every written rule there are a thousand unwritten rules by which the course of business is guided, which govern the millions of daily transactions of which business consists. These rules are not applied from the top down, by arbitrary authority. They grow out of actual practice – from the bottom up. They are based upon mutual understanding and compromise, the desire to achieve common ends and further the common good. They are observed *voluntarily*, because they have the backing of experience and common sense."

to those whose actions are not included within the coöperative system. This is clearly in accord with the common understanding. The laws of one country have no authority for citizens of another, except under special circumstances. Employers do not issue directions to employees of other organizations. Officials would appear incompetent who issued orders to those outside their jurisdiction.

A communication has the presumption of authority when it originates at sources of organization information – a communications center – better than individual sources. It loses this presumption, however, if not within the scope or field of this center. The presumption is also lost if the communication shows an absence of adjustment to the actual situation which confronts the recipient of it.

Thus men impute authority to communications from superior positions, provided they are reasonably consistent with advantages of scope and perspective that are credited to those positions. This authority is to a considerable extent independent of the personal ability of the incumbent of the position. It is often recognized that though the incumbent may be of limited personal ability his advice may be superior solely by reason of the advantage of position. This is the *authority of position.*

But it is obvious that some men have superior ability. Their knowledge and understanding regardless of position command respect. Men impute authority to what they say in an organization for this reason only. This is the *authority of leadership.* When the authority of leadership is combined with the authority of position, men who have an established connection with an organization generally will grant authority, accepting orders far outside the zone of indifference. The confidence engendered may even make compliance an inducement in itself.

Nevertheless, the determination of authority remains with the individual. Let these "positions" of authority in fact show ineptness, ignorance of conditions, failure to communicate what ought to be said, or let leadership fail (chiefly by its concrete action) to recognize implicitly its dependence upon the essential character of the relationship of the individual to the organization, and the authority if tested disappears.

This objective authority is only maintained if the positions or leaders continue to be adequately informed. In very rare cases persons possessing great knowledge, insight, or skill have this adequate information without occupying executive positions. What they say ought to be done or ought not to be done will be accepted. But this is usually personal advice at the risk of the taker. Such persons have influence rather than authority. In most cases genuine leaders who give advice concerning organized efforts are required to accept positions of responsibility; for knowledge of the applicability of their special knowledge or judgment to concrete *organization* action, not to abstract problems, is essential to the worth of what they say as a basis of organization authority. In other words, they have an organization personality, as distinguished from their individual personality,[7] commensurate with the influence of their leadership. The common way to state this is that there cannot be authority without corresponding responsibility. A more exact expression would be that objective authority cannot be imputed to persons in organization positions unless subjectively they are dominated by the organization as respects their decisions.

It may be said, then, that the maintenance of objective authority adequate to support the fiction of superior authority and able to make the zone of indifference an actuality depends upon the operation of the system of communication in the organization. The function of this system is to supply adequate information to the positions of authority and adequate facilities for the issuance of orders. To do so it requires commensurate capacities in those able to be leaders. High positions that are not so supported have weak authority, as do strong men in minor positions.

Thus authority depends upon a coöperative personal attitude of individuals on the one hand; and the system of communication in the organization on the other. Without the latter, the former cannot be maintained. The most devoted adherents of an organization will quit it, if its system results in inadequate, contradictory, inept orders, so that they cannot know who is who, what is what, or have the sense of effective coördination.

This system of communication, or its maintenance, is a primary or essential continuing problem of a formal organization. Every other practical question of effectiveness or efficiency – that is, of the factors of survival – depends upon it. In technical language the system of communication of which we are now speaking is often known as the "lines of authority."

II

It has already been shown[8] that the requirements of communication determine the size of unit organizations, the grouping of units, the grouping of groups of unit organizations. We may now consider the controlling factors in the character of the communication system as a system of objective authority.

(*a*) The first is that *channels of communication should be definitely known.* The language in which this principle is ordinarily stated is, "The lines of authority must be definitely established." The method of doing so is by making official appointments known; by assigning each individual to

7 / See Chapter VII, p. 88.
8 / Chapter VIII, "The Structure of Complex Formal Organizations," beginning at p. 106.

his position; by general announcements; by organization charts; by educational effort, and most of all by habituation, that is, by securing as much permanence of system as is practicable. Emphasis is laid either upon the position, or upon the persons; but usually the fixing of authority is made both to positions and, less emphatically, to persons.

(b) Next, we may say that *objective authority requires a definite formal channel of communication to every member of an organization.* In ordinary language this means "everyone must report to someone" (communication in one direction) and "everyone must be subordinate to someone" (communication in the other direction). In other words, in formal organizations everyone must have definite formal relationship to the organization.[9]

(c) Another factor is that *the line of communication must be as direct or short as possible.* This may be explained as follows: Substantially all formal communication is verbal (written or oral). Language as a vehicle of communication is limited and susceptible of misunderstanding. Much communication is necessarily without preparation. Even communications that are carefully prepared require interpretation. Moreover, communications are likely to be in more general terms the more general – that is, the higher – the position. It follows that something may be lost or added by transmission at each stage of the process, especially when communication is oral, or when at each stage there is combination of several communications. Moreover, when communications go from high positions down they often must be made more specific as they proceed; and when in the reverse direction, usually more general. In addition, the speed of communication, other things equal, will be less the greater the number of centers through which it passes. Accordingly, the shorter the line the greater the speed and the less the error.

How important this factor is may be indicated by the remarkable fact that in great complex organizations the number of levels of communication is not much larger than in smaller organizations. In most organizations consisting of the services of one or two hundred men the levels of communication will be from three to five. In the Army the levels are: President, (Secretary of War), General, Major-General, Brigadier-General, Colonel, Major, Captain, Lieutenant, Sergeant, men – that is, nine or ten. In the Bell Telephone System, with over 300,000 working members, the number is eight to ten.[10] A similar shortness of the line of communication is

9 / In some types of organizations it is not unusual, however, for one person to report to and to be subordinate to two or three "superiors," in which case the functions of the superiors are defined and are mutually exclusive in principle.

10 / Disregarding the corporate aspects of the organization, and not including board of directors.

noteworthy in the Catholic Church viewed from the administrative stand-point.

Many organization practices or inventions are used to accomplish this end, depending upon the purpose and technical conditions. Briefly, these methods are: The use of expanded executive organizations at each stage; the use of the staff department (technical, expert, advisory); the division of executive work into functional bureaus; and processes of delegating responsibility with automatic coördination through regular conference procedures, committees for special temporary functions, etc.

(d) Another factor is that, in principle, *the complete line of communication should usually be used*. By this is meant that a communication from the head of an organization to the bottom should pass through every stage of the line of authority. This is due to the necessity of avoiding conflicting communications (in either direction) which might (and would) occur if there were any "jumping of the line" of organization. It is also necessary because of the need of interpretation, and to maintain responsibility.[11]

(e) Again, the *competence of the persons serving as communication centers, that is, officers, supervisory heads, must be adequate*. The competence required is that of more and more *general* ability with reference to the work of the entire organization the more central the office of communication and the larger the organization. For the function of the center of communication in an organization is to translate incoming communications concerning external conditions, the progress of activity, successes, failures, difficulties, dangers, into outgoing communications in terms of new activities, preparatory steps, etc., all shaped according to the ultimate as well as the immediate purposes to be served. There is accordingly required more or less mastery of the technologies involved, of the capabilities of the personnel, of the informal organization situation, of the character and status of the subsidiary organizations, of the principles of action relative to purpose, of the interpretation of environmental factors, and a power of discrimination between communications that can possess authority because they are recognizably compatible with *all* the pertinent conditions and those which will not possess authority because they will not or cannot be accepted.

It is a fact, I think, that we hardly nowadays expect individual personal ability adequate to positional requirements of communication in modern large-scale organization. The limitations of individuals as respects

11 / These by no means exhaust the considerations. The necessity of maintaining personal prestige of executives as an *inducement to them* to function is on the whole an important additional reason.

time and energy alone preclude such personal ability, and the complexity of the technologies or other special knowledge involved make it impossible. For these reasons each major center of communication is itself organized, sometimes quite elaborately. The immediate staff of the executive (commanding officer), consisting of deputies, or chief clerks, or adjutants, or auxiliaries with their assistants, constitute an executive unit of organization only one member of which is perhaps an "executive," that is, occupies the *position* of authority; and the technical matters are assigned to staff departments or organizations of experts. Such staff departments often are partly "field" departments in the sense that they directly investigate or secure information on facts or conditions external to the organizations; but in major part in most cases they digest and translate information from the field, and prepare the plans, orders, etc., for transmission. In this capacity they are advisory or adjutant to the executives. In practice, however, these assistants have the function of semi-formal advice under regulated conditions to the organizations as a whole. In this way, both the formal channels and the informal organization are supplemented by intermediate processes.

In some cases the executive (either chief or some subordinate executive) may be not a person but a board, a legislature, a committee. I know of no important organizations, except some churches and some absolute governments in which the highest objective authority is not lodged in an *organized* executive group, that is, a "highest" unit of organization.

(*f*) Again, *the line of communication should not be interrupted during the time when the organization is to function.* Many organizations (factories, stores) function intermittently, being closed or substantially so during the night, Sundays, etc. Others, such as army, police, railroad systems, telephone systems, never cease to operate. During the times when organizations are at work, in principle the line of authority must never be broken; and practically this is almost, if not quite, literally true in many cases. This is one of the reasons which may be given for the great importance attached to hereditary succession in states, and for the elaborate provision that is made in most organizations (except possibly small "personal" organizations) for the temporary filling of offices automatically during incapacity or absence of incumbents. These provisions emphasize the non-personal and communication character of organization authority, as does the persistent emphasis upon the *office* rather than the *man* that is a matter of indoctrination of many organizations, especially those in which "discipline" is an important feature.

The necessity for this is not merely that specific communications cannot otherwise be attended to. It is at least equally that the *informal* organization disintegrates very quickly if the formal "line of authority" is broken. In organization parlance, "politics" runs riot. Thus, if an office were vacant, but the fact were not known, an organization might function for a considerable time without serious disturbance, except in emergency. But if known, it would quickly become disorganized.

(g) The final factor I shall mention is that *every communication should be authenticated*. This means that the person communicating must be known actually to occupy the "position of authority" concerned; that the position includes the type of communication concerned – that is, it is "within its authority"; and that it actually is an authorized communication from this office. The process of authentication in all three respects varies in different organizations under different conditions and for different positions. The practice is undergoing rapid changes in the modern technique, but the principles remain the same. Ceremonials of investiture, inaugurations, swearing-in, general orders of appointment, induction, and introduction, are all essentially appropriate methods of making known who actually fills a position and what the position includes as authority. In order that these *positions* may function it is often necessary that the filling of them should be dramatized, an essential process to the creation of authority *at the bottom*, where only it can be fundamentally – that is, it is essential to inculcate the "sense of organization." This is merely stating that it is essential to "organization loyalty and solidarity" as it may be otherwise expressed. Dignifying the superior position is an important method of dignifying *all* connection with organization, a fact which has been well learned in both religious and political organizations where great attention to the subjective aspects of "membership" is the rule.

This statement of the principles of communication systems of organizations from the viewpoint of the maintenance of objective authority has necessarily been in terms of complex organizations, since in a simple unit organization the concrete applications of these principles are fused. The principles are with difficulty isolated under simple conditions. Thus, as a matter of course, in unit organizations the channels of communication are known, indeed usually obvious; they are definite; they are the shortest possible; the only lines of authority are complete lines; there is little question of authentication. The doubtful points in unit organization are the competence of the leader, never to be taken for granted even in simple organizations; and whether he is functioning when the organization is in operation. Yet as a whole the adequately balanced maintenance of these aspects of simple leadership is the basis of objective authority in the unit organization, as the maintenance of the more formal and observable manifestations of the same aspects is the basis of authority in the complex organizations.

RECONCILIATION WITH LEGALISTIC CONCEPTIONS

Legalistic conceptions of authority, at least somewhat different from those we have presented, seem to have support in the relations between superior and subsidiary organizations. A corporate organization, for example, is subject to the law of the state. Is not this a case where authority actually does come down from the top, from the superior organizations? Only in exactly the same sense that individuals accept objective authority, as we have described it. A subsidiary or dependent organization must accept law to give law its authority. Units of organization, integrated complexes of organization, and dependent organizations, make and must make the subjective decision of authority just as individuals do. A corporation may and often does quit if it cannot obey the law and still have a net reason for existence. It is no more able to carry out an unintelligible law than an individual, it can no more do the impossible than an individual, it will show the same inability to conform to conflicting laws as the individual. The only difference between subsidiary, or dependent, unit and group organizations and individuals is that the denial of authority can be made directly by the individual, and either directly or indirectly by the unit, group, or dependent or subsidiary complex. When it is direct, the effect of the law or order upon the organization as a whole is in point; when it is indirect the effect is on the individuals of whose efforts the whole is made up. Thus no complex can carry out a superior order if its members (either unit organizations or individuals) will not enable it to do so. For example, to order by law working conditions which will not be accepted by individual employees, even though the employer is willing, is futile; its authority is in fact denied. The employees quit, then the organization ends.

But in the final analysis the differences are not important, except occasionally in the concrete case. The subsidiary organization in point of fact derives most of its authority for most of its action from its own "members" individually. They may quit if they do not accept the orders, no matter what the "ultimate" authority; and no absolute or external authority can compel the necessary effort beyond a minimum insufficient to maintain efficient or effective organization performance. An important effect of the ascription of legalistic origin of a part of the formal authority of subsidiary and independent organizations has been its obscuring of the nature of the real authority that governs the greater part of the coöperative effort of such organizations.

There is, however, a considerable quantitative difference in the factor of informal organization, that is, the factor of public opinion, general sentiment. This is not a difference of principle, but merely one of the relationship of the size of the informal organization relative to the individual or formal group. A strong individual can resist the domination of opinion if it is confined to a small number; but rarely if there is in question the opinion of an overwhelming number, actively and hostilely expressed. Now the size of any subsidiary organization is small compared with the informal organization that permeates the State; and this wide informal organization will usually support "law and order" regardless of merits if the question at issue is minor from its point of view. The pressure on the subjective attitude of individuals or on that of subsidiary or dependent organizations is strong ordinarily to induce acceptance of law in an "orderly" society.

But this informal support of objective authority of the State depends upon essentially the same principles as in the case of ordinary organizations. Inappropriateness of law and of government administration, lack of understanding of the ultimate basis of authority, indifference to the motives governing individual support, untimely or impossible legislation, as is well known destroy "respect for law and order," that is, destroy objective political authority. In democracies the normal reaction is to change law and administration through political action. But when majorities are unable to understand that authority rests fundamentally upon the consent of minorities as well as of majorities, or when the system is autocratic or absolute, the liquidation of attempted tyranny is through revolution or civil war. Authority lies always with him to whom it applies. Coercion creates a contrary illusion; but the use of force *ipso facto* destroys the authority postulated. It creates a new authority, a new situation, a new objective, which is granted when the force is accepted. Many men have destroyed all authority as to themselves by dying rather than yielding.

At first thought it may seem that the element of communication in organization is only in part related to authority; but more thorough consideration leads to the understanding that communication, authority, specialization, and purpose are all aspects comprehended in coördination. All communication relates to the formulation of purpose and the transmission of coördinating prescriptions for action and so rests upon the ability to communicate with those willing to coöperate.

Authority is another name for the willingness and capacity of individuals to submit to the necessities of coöperative systems. Authority arises from the technological and social limitations of coöperative systems on the one hand, and of individuals on the other. Hence the status of authority in a society is the measure both of the development of individuals and of the technological and social conditions of the society.

MAX WEBER

6
The type of authority

THE BASIS OF LEGITIMACY

The definition, conditions, and types of imperative control
"Imperative co-ordination" was defined as the probability that certain specific commands (or all commands) from a given source will be obeyed by a given group of persons. It thus does not include every mode of exercising "power" or "influence" over other persons. The motives of obedience to commands in this sense can rest on considerations varying over a wide range from case to case; all the way from simple habituation to the most purely rational calculation of advantage. A criterion of every true relation of imperative control, however, is a certain minimum of voluntary submission; thus an interest (based on ulterior motives or genuine acceptance) in obedience.

Not every case of imperative co-ordination makes use of economic means; *still less* does it always have economic objectives. But normally (not always) the imperative co-ordination of the action of a considerable number of men requires control of a staff of persons. It is necessary, that is, that there should be a relatively high probability that the action of a definite, supposedly reliable group of persons will be primarily oriented to the execution of the supreme authority's general policy and specific commands.

The members of the administrative staff may be bound to obedience to their superior (or superiors) by custom, by affectual ties, by a purely material complex of interests, or by ideal (*wertrational*) motives. *Purely material interests* and calculations of advantage as the basis of solidarity between the chief and his administrative staff result, in this as in other connexions, in a relatively unstable situation. Normally other elements, affectual and ideal, supplement such interests. In certain exceptional, temporary cases the former may be alone decisive. In everyday routine life these relationships, like others, are governed by custom and in addition, material calculation of advantage. But these factors, custom and personal advantage, purely affectual or ideal motives of solidarity, do not, even taken together, form a sufficiently reliable basis for a system of imperative co-ordination. In addition there is normally a further element, the belief in legitimacy.

It is an induction from experience that no system of authority voluntarily limits itself to the appeal to material or affectual or ideal motives as a basis for guaranteeing its continuance. In addition every such system attempts to establish and to cultivate the belief in its "legitimacy." But according to the kind of legitimacy which is claimed, the type of obedience, the kind of administrative staff developed to guarantee it, and the mode of exercising authority, will all differ fundamentally. Equally fundamental is the variation in effect. Hence, it is useful to classify the types of authority according to the kind of claim to legitimacy typically made by each. In doing this it is best to start from modern and therefore more familiar examples.

1 The choice of this rather than some other basis of classification can only be justified by its results. The fact that certain other typical criteria of variation are thereby neglected for the time being and can only be introduced at a later stage is not a decisive difficulty. The "legitimacy" of a system of authority has far more than a merely "ideal" significance, if only because it has very definite relations to the legitimacy of property.

2 Not every "claim" which is protected by custom or by law should be spoken of as involving a relation of authority. Otherwise the worker, in his claim for fulfilment of the wage contract, would be exercising "authority" over his employer because his claim can, on occasion, be enforced by order of a court. Actually his formal status is that of party to a contractual relationship with his employer, in which he has certain "rights" to receive payments. At the same time, the concept of a relation of authority naturally does not exclude the possibility that it has originated in a formally free contract. This is true of the authority of the employer over the worker as manifested in the former's rules and instructions re-

garding the work process; and also of the authority of a feudal lord over a vassal who has freely entered into the relation of fealty. That subjection to military discipline is formally "involuntary" while that to the discipline of the factory is voluntary does not alter the fact that the latter is also a case of subjection to authority. The position of a bureaucratic official is also entered into by contract and can be freely resigned, and even the status of "subject" can often be freely entered into and (in certain circumstances) freely repudiated. Only in the limiting case of the slave is formal subjection to authority absolutely involuntary.

Another case, in some respects related, is that of economic "power" based on monopolistic position; that is, in this case, the possibility of "dictating" the terms of exchange to contractual partners. This will not, taken by itself, be considered to constitute "authority" any more than any other kind of "influence" which is derived from some kind of superiority, as by virtue of erotic attractiveness, skill in sport or in discussion. Even if a big bank is in a position to force other banks into a cartel arrangement, this will not alone be sufficient to justify calling it a relation of imperative co-ordination. But if there is an immediate relation of command and obedience such that the management of the first bank can give orders to the others with the claim that they shall, and the probability that they will, be obeyed purely as such regardless of particular content, and if their carrying out is supervised, it is another matter. Naturally, here as everywhere the transitions are gradual; there are all sorts of intermediate steps between mere indebtedness and debt slavery. Even the position of a "salon" can come very close to the borderline of authoritarian domination and yet not necessarily constitute a system of authority. Sharp differentiation in concrete fact is often impossible, but this makes clarity in the analytical distinctions all the more important.

3 Naturally, the legitimacy of a system of authority may be treated sociologically only as the probability that to a relevant degree the appropriate attitudes will exist, and the corresponding practical conduct ensue. It is by no means true that every case of submissiveness to persons in positions of power is primarily (or even at all) oriented to this belief. Loyalty may be hypocritically simulated by individuals or by whole groups on purely opportunistic grounds, or carried out in practice for reasons of material self-interest. Or people may submit from individual weakness and helplessness because there is no acceptable alternative. But these considerations are not decisive for the classification of types of imperative co-ordination. What is important is the fact that in a given case the particular claim to legitimacy is to a significant degree and ac-

cording to its type treated as "valid"; that this fact confirms the position
of the persons claiming authority and that it helps to determine the choice
of means of its exercise.

Furthermore a system of imperative co-ordination may – as often
occurs in practice – be so completely assured of dominance, on the
one hand by the obvious community of interests between the chief and his
administrative staff as opposed to the subjects (bodyguards, Pretorians,
"red" or "white" guards), on the other hand by the helplessness of the
latter, that it can afford to drop even the pretence of a claim to legitimacy.
But even then the mode of legitimation of the relation between chief and
his staff may vary widely according to the type of basis of the relation of
authority between them, and, as will be shown, this variation is highly
significant for the structure of imperative co-ordination.

4 "Obedience" will be taken to mean that the action of the person
obeying follows in essentials such a course that the content of the command may be taken to have become the basis of action for its own sake.
Furthermore, the fact that it is so taken is referable only to the formal
obligation, without regard to the actor's own attitude to the value or lack
of value of the content of the command as such.

5 Subjectively, the causal sequence may vary, especially as between
"submission" and "sympathetic agreement." This distinction is not, however, significant for the present classification of types of authority.

6 The scope of determination of social relationships and cultural
phenomena by authority and imperative co-ordination is considerably
broader than appears at first sight. For instance, the authority exercised
in the school has much to do with the determination of the forms of
speech and of written language which are regarded as orthodox. The
official languages of autonomous political units, hence of their ruling
groups, have often become in this sense orthodox forms of speech and
writing and have even led to the formation of separate "nations" (for
instance, the separation of Holland from Germany). The authority of
parents and of the school, however, extends far beyond the determination
of such cultural patterns which are perhaps only apparently formal, to the
formation of the character of the young, and hence of human beings
generally.

7 The fact that the chief and his administrative staff often appear
formally as servants or agents of those they rule, naturally does nothing
whatever to disprove the authoritarian character of the relationship. There
will be occasion later to speak of the substantive features of so-called
"democracy." But a certain minimum of assured power to issue com-

mands, thus of "authority," must be provided for in nearly every conceivable case.

The three pure types of legitimate authority
There are three pure types of legitimate authority. The validity of their claims to legitimacy may be based on:
1 Rational grounds – resting on a belief in the "legality" of patterns of normative rules and the right of those elevated to authority under such rules to issue commands (legal authority).
2 Traditional grounds – resting on an established belief in the sanctity of immemorial traditions and the legitimacy of the status of those exercising authority under them (traditional authority); or finally,
3 Charismatic grounds – resting on devotion to the specific and exceptional sanctity, heroism or exemplary character of an individual person, and of the normative patterns or order revealed or ordained by him (charismatic authority).

In the case of legal authority, obedience is owed to the legally established impersonal order. It extends to the persons exercising the authority of office under it only by virtue of the formal legality of their commands and only within the scope of authority of the office. In the case of traditional authority, obedience is owed to the *person* of the chief who occupies the traditionally sanctioned position of authority and who is (within its sphere) bound by tradition. But here the obligation of obedience is not based on the impersonal order, but is a matter of personal loyalty within the area of accustomed obligations. In the case of charismatic authority, it is the charismatically qualified leader as such who is obeyed by virtue of personal trust in him and his revelation, his heroism or his exemplary qualities so far as they fall within the scope of the individual's belief in his charisma.
1 The usefulness of the above classification can only be judged by its results in promoting systematic analysis. The concept of "charisma" (the "gift of grace") is taken from the vocabulary of early Christianity. For the Christian religious organization, Rudolf Sohm, in his *Kirchenrecht*, was the first to clarify the substance of the concept, even though he did not use the same terminology. Others (for instance, Hollin, *Enthusiasmus und Bussgewalt*) have clarified certain important consequences of it. It is thus nothing new.
2 The fact that none of these three ideal types, the elucidation of which will occupy the following pages, is usually to be found in historical cases in "pure" form, is naturally not a valid objection to attempting their con-

ceptual formulation in the sharpest possible form. In this respect the present case is no different from many others. Later on the transformation of pure charisma by the process of routinization will be discussed and thereby the relevance of the concept to the understanding of empirical systems of authority considerably increased. But even so it may be said of every empirically historical phenomenon of authority that it is not likely to be "as an open book." Analysis in terms of sociological types has, after all, as compared with purely empirical historical investigation, certain advantages which should not be minimized. That is, it can in the particular case of a concrete form of authority determine what conforms to or approximates such types as "charisma," "hereditary charisma," "the charisma of office," "patriarchy," "bureaucracy," the authority of status groups [Ständische], and in doing so it can work with relatively unambiguous concepts. But the idea that the whole of concrete historical reality can be exhausted in the conceptual scheme about to be developed is as far from the author's thoughts as anything could be.

LEGAL AUTHORITY WITH A BUREAUCRATIC ADMINISTRATIVE STAFF

Legal Authority: the pure type with employment of a bureaucratic administrative staff
The effectiveness of legal authority rests on the acceptance of the validity of the following mutually inter-dependent ideas.
1 That any given legal norm may be established by agreement or by imposition, on grounds of expediency or rational values or both, with a claim to obedience at least on the part of the members of the corporate group. This is, however, usually extended to include all persons within the sphere of authority or of power in question – which in the case of territorial bodies is the territorial area – who stand in certain social relationships or carry out forms of social action which in the order governing the corporate group have been declared to be relevant.
2 That every body of law consists essentially in a consistent system of abstract rules which have normally been intentionally established. Furthermore, administration of law is held to consist in the application of these rules to particular cases; the administrative process in the rational pursuit of the interests which are specified in the order governing the corporate group within the limits laid down by legal precepts and following principles which are capable of generalized formulation and are approved in the order governing the group, or at least not disapproved in it.
3 That thus the typical person in authority occupies an "office." In the

action associated with his status, including the commands he issues to others, he is subject to an impersonal order to which his actions are oriented. This is true not only for persons exercising legal authority who are in the usual sense "officials," but, for instance, for the elected president of a state.

4 That the person who obeys authority does so, as it is usually stated, only in his capacity as a "member" of the corporate group and what he obeys is only "the law." He may in this connexion be the member of an association, of a territorial commune, of a church, or a citizen of a state.

5 In conformity with point 3, it is held that the members of the corporate group, in so far as they obey a person in authority, do not owe this obedience to him as an individual, but to the impersonal order. Hence, it follows that there is an obligation to obedience only within the sphere of the rationally delimited authority which, in terms of the order, has been conferred upon him.

The following may thus be said to be the fundamental categories of rational legal authority: –

(1) A continuous organization of official functions bound by rules.

(2) A specified sphere of competence. This involves (a) a sphere of obligations to perform functions which has been marked off as part of a systematic division of labour. (b) The provision of the incumbent with the necessary authority to carry out these functions. (c) That the necessary means of compulsion are clearly defined and their use is subject to definite conditions. A unit exercising authority which is organized in this way will be called an "administrative organ" [Behörde].

There are administrative organs in this sense in large-scale private organizations, in parties and armies, as well as in the state and the church. An elected president, a cabinet of ministers, or a body of elected representatives also in this sense constitute administrative organs. This is not, however, the place to discuss these concepts. Not every administrative organ is provided with compulsory powers. But this distinction is not important for present purposes.

(3) The organization of offices follows the principle of hierarchy; that is, each lower office is under the control and supervision of a higher one. There is a right of appeal and of statement of grievances from the lower to the higher. Hierarchies differ in respect to whether and in what case complaints can lead to a ruling from an authority at various points higher in the scale, and as to whether changes are imposed from higher up or the responsibility for such changes is left to the lower office, the conduct of which was the subject of complaint.

(4) The rules which regulate the conduct of an office may be technical

rules or norms. In both cases, if their application is to be fully rational, specialized training is necessary. It is thus normally true that only a person who has demonstrated an adequate technical training is qualified to be a member of the administrative staff of such an organized group, and hence only such persons are eligible for appointment to official positions. The administrative staff of a rational corporate group thus typically consists of "officials," whether the organization be devoted to political, religious, economic – in particular, capitalistic – or other ends.

(5) In the rational type it is a matter of principle that the members of the administrative staff should be completely separated from ownership of the means of production or administration. Officials, employees, and workers attached to the administrative staff do not themselves own the non-human means of production and administration. These are rather provided for their use in kind or in money, and the official is obligated to render an accounting of their use. There exists, furthermore, in principle complete separation of the property belonging to the organization, which is controlled within the sphere of office, and the personal property of the official, which is available for his own private uses. There is a corresponding separation of the place in which official functions are carried out, the "office" in the sense of premises, from living quarters.

(6) In the rational type case, there is also a complete absence of appropriation of his official position by the incumbent. Where "rights" to an office exist, as in the case of judges, and recently of an increasing proportion of officials and even of workers, they do not normally serve the purpose of appropriation by the official, but of securing the purely objective and independent character of the conduct of the office so that it is oriented only to the relevant norms.

(7) Administrative acts, decisions, and rules are formulated and recorded in writing, even in cases where oral discussion is the rule or is even mandatory. This applies at least to preliminary discussions and proposals, to final decisions, and to all sorts of orders and rules. The combination of written documents and a continuous organization of official functions constitutes the "office" which is the central focus of all types of modern corporate action.

(8) Legal authority can be exercised in a wide variety of different forms which will be distinguished and discussed later. The following analysis will be deliberately confined for the most part to the aspect of imperative coordination in the structure of the administrative staff. It will consist of an analysis in terms of ideal types of officialdom or "bureaucracy."

In the above outline no mention has been made of the kind of supreme head appropriate to a system of legal authority. This is a consequence of certain considerations which can only be made entirely understandable at a later stage in the analysis. There are very important types of rational imperative co-ordination which, with respect to the ultimate source of authority, belong to other categories. This is true of the hereditary charismatic type, as illustrated by hereditary monarchy and of the pure charismatic type of a president chosen by plebiscite. Other cases involve rational elements at important points, but are made up of a combination of bureaucratic and charismatic components, as is true of the cabinet form of government. Still others are subject to the authority of the chief of other corporate groups, whether their character be charismatic or bureaucratic; thus the formal head of a government department under a parliamentary regime may be a minister who occupies his position because of his authority in a party. The type of rational, legal administrative staff is capable of application in all kinds of situations and contexts. It is the most important mechanism for the administration of everyday profane affairs. For in that sphere, the exercise of authority and, more broadly, imperative co-ordination, consists precisely in administration.

The purest type of exercise of legal authority is that which employs a bureaucratic administrative staff. Only the supreme chief of the organization occupies his position of authority by virtue of appropriation, of election, or of having been designated for the succession. But even *his* authority consists in a sphere of legal "competence." The whole administrative staff under the supreme authority then consists, in the purest type, of individual officials who are appointed and function according to the following criteria:

(1) They are personally free and subject to authority only with respect to their impersonal official obligations.

(2) They are organized in a clearly defined hierarchy of offices.

(3) Each office has a clearly defined sphere of competence in the legal sense.

(4) The office is filled by a free contractual relationship. Thus, in principle, there is free selection.

(5) Candidates are selected on the basis of technical qualifications. In the most rational case, this is tested by examination or guaranteed by diplomas certifying technical training, or both. They are *appointed*, not elected.

(6) They are remunerated by fixed salaries in money, for the most part with a right to pensions. Only under certain circumstances does the employing authority, especially in private organizations, have a right to terminate the appointment, but the official is always free to resign. The salary scale is primarily graded according to rank in the hierarchy; but in addi-

tion to this criterion, the responsibility of the position and the requirements of the incumbent's social status may be taken into account.

(7) The office is treated as the sole, or at least the primary, occupation
of the incumbent.

(8) It constitutes a career. There is a system of "promotion" according
to seniority or to achievement, or both. Promotion is dependent on the
judgment of superiors.

(9) The official works entirely separated from ownership of the means
of administration and without appropriation of his position.

(10) He is subject to strict and systematic discipline and control in
the conduct of the office.

This type of organization is in principle applicable with equal facility
to a wide variety of different fields. It may be applied in profit-making
business or in charitable organizations, or in any number of other types
of private enterprises serving ideal or material ends. It is equally applicable
to political and to religious organizations. With varying degrees of approximation to a pure type, its historical existence can be demonstrated in
all fields.

1 For example, this type of bureaucracy is found in private clinics, as well
as in endowed hospitals or the hospitals maintained by religious orders.
Bureaucratic organization has played a major role in the Catholic Church.
It is well illustrated by the administrative role of the priesthood [*Kaplano-
kratie*] in the modern church, which has expropriated almost all of the
old church benefices, which were in former days to a large extent subject
to private appropriation. It is also illustrated by the conception of the
universal Episcopate, which is thought of as formally constituting a universal legal competence in religious matters. Similarly, the doctrine of
Papal infallibility is thought of as in fact involving a universal competence,
but only one which functions "ex cathedra" in the sphere of the office, thus
implying the typical distinction between the sphere of office and that of the
private affairs of the incumbent. The same phenomena are found in the
large-scale capitalistic enterprise; and the larger it is, the greater their role.
And this is not less true of political parties, which will be discussed separ-
ately. Finally, the modern army is essentially a bureaucratic organization
administered by that peculiar type of military functionary, the "officer."

2 Bureaucratic authority is carried out in its purest form where it is most
clearly dominated by the principle of appointment. There is no such thing
as a hierarchy of elected officials in the same sense as there is a hierarchical
organization of appointed officials. In the first place, election makes it
impossible to attain a stringency of discipline even approaching that in
the appointed type. For it is open to a subordinate official to compete for

elective honours on the same terms as his superiors, and his prospects are not dependent on the superior's judgment.

3 Appointment by free contract, which makes free selection possible, is essential to modern bureaucracy. Where there is a hierarchical organization with impersonal spheres of competence, but occupied by unfree officials – like slaves or dependents, who, however, function in a formally bureaucratic manner – the term "patrimonial bureaucracy" will be used.

4 The role of technical qualifications in bureaucratic organizations is continually increasing. Even an official in a party or a trade-union organization is in need of specialized knowledge, though it is usually of an empirical character, developed by experience, rather than by formal training. In the modern state, the only "offices" for which no technical qualifications are required are those of ministers and presidents. This only goes to prove that they are "officials" only in a formal sense, and not substantively, as is true of the managing director or president of a large business corporation. There is no question but that the "position" of the capitalistic entrepreneur is as definitely appropriated as is that of a monarch. Thus, at the top of a bureaucratic organization, there is necessarily an element which is at least not purely bureaucratic. The category of bureaucracy is one applying only to the exercise of control by means of a particular kind of administrative staff.

5 The bureaucratic official normally receives a fixed salary. By contrast, sources of income which are privately appropriated will be called "benefices" [*Pfründen*]. Bureaucratic salaries are also normally paid in money. Though this is not essential to the concept of bureaucracy, it is the arrangement which best fits the pure type. Payments in kind are apt to have the character of benefices, and the receipt of a benefice normally implies the appropriation of opportunities for earnings and of positions. There are, however, gradual transitions in this field with many intermediate types. Appropriation by virtue of leasing or sale of offices or the pledge of income from office are phenomena foreign to the pure type of bureaucracy.

6 "Offices" which do not constitute the incumbent's principal occupation, in particular "honorary" offices, belong in other categories. The typical "bureaucratic" official occupies the office as his principal occupation.

7 With respect to the separation of the official from ownership of the means of administration, the situation is essentially the same in the field of public administration and in private bureaucratic organizations, such as the large-scale capitalistic enterprise.

8 Collegial bodies at the present time are rapidly decreasing in importance in favour of types of organization which are in fact, and for the most part formally as well, subject to the authority of a single head. For instance, the

collegial "governments" in Prussia have long since given way to the mono-cratic "district president" [*Regierungs präsident*]. The decisive factor in this development has been the need for rapid, clear decisions, free of the necessity of compromise between different opinions and also free of shift-ing majorities.

9 The modern army officer is a type of appointed official who is clearly marked off by certain class distinctions. In this respect such officers differ radically from elected military leaders, from charismatic condottieri, from the type of officers who recruit and lead mercenary armies as a capitalistic enterprise, and, finally, from the incumbents of commissions which have been purchased. There may be gradual transitions between these types. The patrimonial "retainer," who is separated from the means of carrying out his function, and the proprietor of a mercenary army for capitalistic purposes have, along with the private capitalistic entrepreneur, been pion-eers in the organization of the modern type of bureaucracy.

ROBERT V. PRESTHUS

7
Authority in organizations

In a sense the study of organization is a search for conceptual tools to
help us understand the complexities of organizational behavior with its
many personal and structural variations. When such tools are linked to
perceptive questions, gains become possible. The concept of authority
seems a useful tool because it asks and suggests answers as to how the
organization achieves its ends. How are the energies of its members
directed along desired channels? Why do individuals accept authority?
In order to gain their larger objectives, organizations must rely upon certain instruments of motivation and constraint. This can be recognized
without denying the existence and propriety of the idiosyncratic goals
of their members. Authority is a crucial element in this equation, particularly if it is defined broadly to include conceptions of reward and reciprocity. This suggests a transactional theory of authority relations between
organizational leaders and their followers.[1]

This conception is similar but not identical with equilibrium theory
which explains participation as the result of a rough balance between the
individual's contributions to the organization and the psychic and economic compensations he receives in return. The transactional view assumes that compliance with authority is in some way rewarding to the
individual, and that he plays an active role in defining and accepting au-

Reprinted by permission of Prentice-Hall, Inc., from Sidney Mailick (ed.),
Concepts and Issues in Administrative Behaviour (Englewood Cliffs, N.J.: Prentice-
Hall), 1962, pp. 122–35.

1 / This conception of authority is similar to Barnard's "permissive" thesis in
which authority is made good by the "acceptance" of those exposed to it. However,
it incorporates greater limitations on the individual's influence over organizational
elites, and it attempts to set down more precisely the conditions under which authority will be accepted. See Chester I. Barnard, *Functions of the Executive* (Cambridge:
Harvard University Press, 1938).

thority, not merely in some idealistic sense but in operational terms. Organizational behavior thus becomes a form of bargaining or exchange. A similar process characterizes equilibrium theory. However, the latter implies that the organization and the individual independently decide what kinds of concessions they are willing to make in sharing their authority or in determining the work bargain. A kind of collective bargaining occurs, in a traditional economic context. The transactional concept, however, is essentially personal and psychological. It regards the individual as being intrinsically involved in the authority process through *interpersonal relations*. One can have equilibrium in an organization without having this kind of reciprocity among individuals at different levels in the hierarchy.

SOME DEFINITIONS

Authority can be defined as the capacity to evoke compliance in others on the basis of formal position and of any psychological inducements, rewards, or sanctions that may accompany formal position. The capacity to evoke compliance without relying upon formal role or the sanctions at its disposal may be called *influence*. When formal position is not necessarily involved, but when extensive sanctions are available, we are concerned with *power*. The definitions turn upon formal position or role because this point of reference best suits the conditions of large-scale organization. The sanctioned control of organized resources through formal position is probably the major source of power in modern society. Authority, power, and influence are usually interlaced in operating situations. However, the definitions attempt to focus on the conception of organizing as a system in which interpersonal relations are structured in terms of the prescribed authority of the actors. Even so-called "informal organization" becomes structured in a similar way, as William F .Whyte and others have shown.[2]

The transactional concept to be developed here rests upon two propositions about authority in organizations: that the authority process is reciprocal, and that it is mediated by four types of legitimation. These propositions have the advantage of being active while at the same time they permit us to specify the conditions under which authority operates and the bases upon which it is accepted by members of the organization.

THE RECIPROCAL NATURE OF AUTHORITY

The idea of reciprocity stems in part from the theory of perception, which tells us that reality is not some fixed, monistic entity existing independent

2 / Whyte, *Street Corner Society*, revised (Chicago: University of Chicago Press, 1958). Whyte's appendix on the research methods used in this study is fascinating reading for those interested in field research.

of time and space, but instead that all sense phenomena are defined in terms of individual judgments. Reality becomes relative; one man's Picasso is another man's poison. In this sense interpersonal relations are highly individualized, a product of the values which the actors bring to a given situation. This process is clearly seen in communication where the way that B defines the cues he has received from A determine their *meaning* for him and his reply. How close B comes to A's intended meaning is a function of chance, shared values, and the precision with which they express themselves. In sum, objective situations are structured by the varying means that individuals impute to them; this in turn is a reflection of their own personality.

A similar process occurs in organizations when authority operates. Thus authority is not some static, immutable quality that some people have while others do not, but instead is a subtle *interrelationship* whose operational consequences are influenced by everyone concerned. The process is reciprocal because the anticipated reactions of all actors become a datum in the behavior of each. A gaming process occurs in which each actor asks himself, "If I do this, what will X's reaction be, and in turn, what will my response to his assumed reaction be?"

In organization, one's perceptions of the authority enjoyed by others, as well as by himself, is thus a critical variable. Experimental evidence supports this conclusion. As Lippitt found:

1 In groups a real consensus upon who is powerful tends to occur;
2 A group member is more likely to accept direct attempts to influence him from a person he defines as powerful;
3 The average group member will tend to initiate deferential, approval-seeking behavior toward higher power choices.[3]

We may conclude that the highly-structured authority system of the typical big organization increases the probability of such reactions to authority. This proposition will be developed further after the process of validating authority is considered.

THE LEGITIMATION PROCESS

The process by which authority is validated may be called legitimation.[4] This term usually occurs in connection with *socialization*, a process by

3 / R. Lippitt, N. Polansky, and S. Rosen, "The Dynamics of Power," 5 *Human Relations* (1952), pp. 44–50; for another empirical study, see Robert L. Peabody, "Perceptions of Organizational Authority: A Comparative Analysis" 6 *Administrative Science Quarterly* (March 1962).

4 / The idea of legitimation and the conception of authority used here reflects mainly Weber's influence. See *From Max Weber: Essays in Sociology*, trans. and ed. by H. H. Gerth and C. W. Mills (New York: Oxford University Press, 1946), pp. 294–329.

which the individual is integrated into a society or a group by virtue of accepting its norms and values. The act of accepting such values is called *legitimation*. This concept is useful in several ways. It helps us differentiate *authority* and *power*, since the former typically stems from one's hierarchical position, whereas the latter is a condition that exists without any necessary reference to formal role and may be imposed without the acceptance of those over whom it is exercised. In politics, for example, real power is sometimes held by anonymous private groups or individuals who manipulate those holding formal positions of authority in the political system.

The concept of legitimation also enables us to give a more precise and sophisticated answer to the critical question: How does authority make good its claims? It permits us to tie theoretical conceptions of the authority process to observable behavior. When this is done, we find that authority has several bases of legitimation, and indeed, that an executive's reliance upon his formal role for legitimation of his leadership is usually a confession of weakness. Authority seems more likely to be a contingent grant, received initially as part of formal position, but which requires continual nourishment from other kinds of legitimation as well.

Legitimation also stresses the importance of the social context in which authority is expressed; it emphasizes the specific conditions that affect acceptance, including the mission and traditions of the organization, the substantive question involved, the relative influence of the actors in a given situation, and the behavioral alternatives that each may elect. Although this conditional aspect of authority is developed below, an experiment may be cited here.[5] The study was designed to test the proposition that an individual's responses to a structured authority situation are an index of his general reactions to authority. Personality tests were given 54 male university students to determine their attitudes toward authority; both thematic apperception tests and the Berkeley ethnocentrism scale were used. Next, the students were asked to begin a simple task, with the instruction that they could stop whenever they wished. However, when the student did stop, the researcher would immediately ask, "Don't you want to do some more?", thus creating a situation in which the student was obliged to say that he did want to continue (which seemed to be what the researcher wanted) or to refuse to go on with the task.

A comparison of the two general types revealed by the personality and ethnocentrism tests and the responses to the experimental situation indicated that students who continued the task had a general tendency to

5 / J. Block and J. Block, "An Interpersonal Experiment on Reactions to Authority," 5 *Human Relations* (1952), pp. 91–98.

accept authority. Those who refused were characteristically independent in authority situations. The consequences of such generalized attitudes toward authority for organizational behavior will be considered more fully below.

The legitimation concept of authority is explicit in Barnard's conclusion that authority can rarely be imposed from above; rather, that it becomes viable only through the acceptance of those exposed to it.[6] However, the *specific conditions* under which authority will be accepted or rejected remain to be isolated by careful research. Superficially, we can assume that in highly-disciplined organizations such as the Marine Corps, the legitimation process becomes virtually automatic, a function of the Corps' traditions, its volunteer character, and the intense feelings of commitment among its members. Turning to the other end of the continuum, the university or the research organization, the legitimation process becomes diffused and unstructured, reflecting an environment in which professional bases of legitimation compete strongly with hierarchical ones.[7]

These examples suggest that the legitimation process varies widely among different kinds of organizations. Moreover, the values of the observer further complicate the analysis. As Simon concludes, "Authority that is viewed as legitimate is not felt as coercion or manipulation, either by the man who exercises it or by the man who accepts it. Hence, the scientist who wishes to deal with issues of manipulation that are sometimes raised in human relations research must be aware of his own attitudes of legitimacy. ... If he regards the area of legitimate authority as narrow, many practices will appear to him coercive or manipulative that would not seem so with a broader criterion of legitimacy."[8]

FOUR BASES OF LEGITIMATION

Several bases of legitimation will be suggested, including technical expertise, formal role, rapport, and legitimation through a generalized deference to authority. The first three may be regarded as essentially rational and

6 / Barnard, *op. cit.*, pp. 163–169.

7 / N. Kaplan, "The Role of the Research Administrator," 4 *Administrative Science Quarterly* (June 1959), pp. 20–42; for an excellent analysis of the effects on authority of different types of organization, see A. Etzioni, "Authority Structure and Organizational Effectiveness," 4 *Administrative Science Quarterly* (June 1959), pp. 43–67.

8 / "Authority" in C. Arensberg (ed.), *Research in Industrial Human Relations* (New York: Harper & Bros., 1957), p. 106; Simon posits four bases of "acceptance"; confidence (technical skill), sanctions, social approval, and legitimacy. The latter "refers to the tendency of people to do what they ought to do." Thus "legitimacy" is used in a more restricted sense than here. *Ibid.*, pp. 103–118.

sociological, resting mainly upon institutionalized norms and objective qualities of skill and position. The fourth basis engages psychological mechanisms, and from one point of view, seems non-rational in that it stems from individual needs for group approval and security, and the unrealistic perceptions of authority that often accompany such needs. My purpose here, it should be said, is not an exhaustive analysis of each basis of legitimation, but rather an exploratory outline which may be useful in conceptualizing authority in an operational context.

Legitimation by Expertise

For a variety of historical and cultural reasons, technical skill and professional attitudes are perhaps the most pervasive criteria for validating authority in the United States. An interesting philosophical basis for this legitimation is the ideal of equality of opportunity which in its attempts to overcome ethnic and religious discrimination has enthroned the standard of personal competence as the only moral basis for selection. While the protectionism of professional groups and the self-consciousness of religious and ethnic groups sometimes distort this ideal, the general expectation and the demand for impartiality have had widespread consequences, including fair-employment practices laws.

Allied with this normative claim has been a philosophy of pragmatism which cuts through subjective bases for evaluating men and organizations to ask: Can they do the job? In some fields the competitive demands of the market virtually force organizations to recruit on an objective basis to secure and to retain eminence in their field. In the United States, of course, the adoption of pragmatic criteria was made relatively easy by the absence of a rigid class system and considerable mobility across such class lines as did exist. Thus such problems as that of the British civil service in the nineteenth century, which became a sinecure for disinherited sons of the landed aristocracy, were avoided. On the other hand, political demands for patronage have often meant the violation of the expertise criterion in our public service.[9]

Over a period of time the emphasis upon technical skill was reinforced by the variety of talents required in an industrializing society. As Durkheim shows, specialization feeds upon itself.[10] As the educational system sought to meet market demands, and to strengthen its own bargaining

9 / For a review of patronage and related problems in our public service, see John M. Pfiffner and Robert V. Presthus, *Public Administration* (fourth ed., New York: Ronald Press Co., 1960), chaps. 16–18.

10 / *The Division of Labor in Society* (Glencoe, Ill.: The Free Press, 1952), pp. 267–270.

position, job training became the major object of both high school and university programs. In turn the expanding job market validated the proliferation of courses as each specialized field strained to make itself "professional," i.e., to build a body of discrete knowledge, skills, and values that enabled it to serve the public and in the process to control the market for its members through licensing, and so on. Thus the role of fulfilling and rationalizing the demands of the skill market was shared by the educational system and professional associations, reinforcing expertise as a basis for legitimation. Generally, this pragmatic orientation provided successfully the skills needed in a bureaucratic society. This achievement has become more recognized in the light of United States technical assistance programs in poorer countries whose educational systems, whatever their other gains, have not generally provided the skills and the values required for economic development.[11]

Legitimation by Formal Role

Like other bases of legitimation, formal position in a hierarchy is probably intermixed with other legitimations in practical situations. Nevertheless, for analytical purposes it can be separated. There are also some indications that formal role is becoming more significant as a result of certain organizational developments ... . In big organizations, authority is structured to insure control by limiting information, centralizing initiative, restricting access to decision making centers, and generally limiting the behavioral alternatives of members. Formal allocations of authority are also reinforced by various psychological inducements to obey in the form of status symbols, rewards, and sanctions. Such differential allocations of status, income, and authority have important objectives and consequences other than as personal rewards for loyal and effective service. They provide a battery of cues or signals for the entire organization; they provide the framework for personal transactions; they mediate appropriate behavior and dramatize its consequences. In brief, such signals function as a mechanism for defining and reinforcing authority.

These structural and psychological instruments seem peculiarly effective in legitimating formal role or hierarchical position as a basis for organizational authority. Here again, of course, the traditions and the mission of the organization are important conditioning factors. Business organizations exhibit a high potential for validating authority mainly in terms of hierarchy; military organizations are similar, although there is some evi-

11 / For an inquiry into this problem see Robert V. Presthus, "The Social Bases of Organization," 19 *Social Forces* (December 1959), pp. 103–109.

dence that technical expertise is assuming a larger role as warfare and weapons become more scientific and complex.[12] There is also some evidence that the size and differentiation characteristic of modern organizations are forcing a greater reliance upon legitimation by formal role, even in milieus such as research and higher education where legitimation by expertise has been traditional. The bureaucratization of research which attends the huge grants of government and the big foundations provides some evidence.[13] The aggrandizement of administration in universities and the political demands upon publically-supported universities and colleges for "other-directed" behavior are also germane.

Still, in most organizations a conflict usually exists between formal position and expertise as bases for authority. In organizations with many functional areas this conflict is aggravated because the generalist at the top can rarely be expert in more than one functional area. Thus he will be denied the legitimation of expertise by most professionals in the organization. He may also experience personal conflict betwen his generalist role and his identification with a functional area. Nevertheless, the generalist seems firmly in control. Certainly the fear in government that the technically-skilled bureaucrat will engulf his political master seems overdrawn. An analysis of the Dixon-Yates case suggests that political authority remains supreme in major policy decisions, and that the role of technical advice may sometimes be one of rationalizing policy decisions based upon ideological considerations.[14]

We can safely conclude, however, that the problem of authority and its legitimation is aggravated by the tendency of functional groups to validate authority on the basis of competence in their own fields, and thus to look to different reference groups as models for their own behavior. This condition has important consequences for loyalty to the organization, acceptance of its rules, and the major direction of professional energies. Gouldner has divided individuals into two role types, "cosmopolitans" and "locals," in terms of their major reference groups.[15] Cosmopolitans,

12/ Morris Janowitz, "Changes in Organizational Authority: The Military Establishment," 3 *Administrative Science Quarterly* (March, 1959), pp. 473–493. For a detailed analysis of the conflict between hierarchical and specialist authority, see Victor A. Thompson, *Modern Organization* (New York: Alfred A. Knopf, Inc., 1961).

13 / C. Wright Mills, *The Sociological Imagination* (New York: Oxford University Press, 1959); Dwight Macdonald, *The Ford Foundation* (New York, 1956).

14/ Robert V. Presthus and L. Vaughn Blankenship, "Dixon-Yates: A Study in Political Behavior" (1958, unpublished ms.).

15/ A. Gouldner, "Cosmopolitans and Locals: Toward an Analysis of Latent Social Roles," 2 *Administrative Science Quarterly* (December 1957–March 1958), pp. 281–306; 440–480.

as the term suggests, exhibit an outward orientation, with their major loyalty and energy directed toward national leaders in their profession and toward activities which will gain them eminence in their field. Locals, on the other hand, are oriented toward the organization with which they are associated; they express great loyalty toward it, honor its rules, justify its policies, and endorse its major values.

Legitimation by formal role is thus challenged by the conflicting demands and assumptions of the many groups that comprise large organizations. It should also be said that legitimation by expertise suffers from a similar conflict as *each* self-conscious group strives to make its own skills and values supreme. The resulting stalemate among the professionals creates a power vacuum which the generalist soon fills, again reinforcing the hierarchical basis of authority. In the main, modern organizations are characterized by hierarchical control, made possible by the elite's monopoly of the distribution of status and income rewards. As Michels has shown, other mechanisms underlying this control include the monopoly of information, initiative, and scarce values enjoyed by leaders; their extended tenure and the tactical skills which tenure insures; their control of procedural and judicial matters within the organization; the absence of any legitimate, internal opposition (the common one-party system) to the "official" policies enunciated by leaders; and their mastery over external relations with other elites.[16] In sum, the apparatus of formal authority remains crucial, despite the inroads of specialization, and, to a lesser extent, of democratic theory.

Legitimation by Rapport

Democratic values, the conflict between generalists and specialists, and, one suspects, the desire to rationalize human energies in the service of management, have combined to emphasize human relations in organizations. The impersonality and routinization of big organization also need to be blunted. This means that authority will often be legitimated on the basis of interpersonal skill and the work climate that executives and supervisors maintain. This process may be called legitimation by rapport. Essentially extra-bureaucratic, this rationale is highly personalized, a contemporary residue of Weber's charismatic basis of authority. Bureaucratization reinforces this mechanism by standardizing work conditions, pay, and career opportunities, with the result that subjective elements tend to become the major distinction among jobs. As a result, rational, technical, and hierarchical criteria of legitimation tend to be challenged by validation on the

16 / Robert Michels, *Political Parties: A Study of Oligarchical Tendencies in Modern Democracy* (Glencoe, Ill.: The Free Press, 1949).

ground that the boss is a warm person who has a real interest in people. Research supports this proposition. Evidence suggests that executives rarely fail for lack of technical skill, but rather for inadequate personal relations. More important, as French and Snyder have shown, the acceptance of authority is positively related to affection for the person exercising it:[17]

1 The amount of influence or authority that a leader attempts to exert increases with increased acceptance of him by the recipients;
2 The effectiveness of a leader's attempt to influence the group increases with increasing acceptance of him as a person;
3 The leader's effectiveness is even more strongly influenced by how much he is accepted relative to how much he accepts the follower.[18]

In the same study the leader's effectiveness was also found to increase with the increasing perception by the group that he was an expert in the area of influence concerned (legitimation by expertise). In a subsequent experiment, it was found that influence was positively related to the group's acceptance of the authority conferred by the leader's formal role. One practical implication of such generalizations is that the administrator must be aware of these several bases of legitimation of his authority; he must accommodate himself to the particular basis that an individual or a group seems most likely to use in validating his authority in a given situation.

Legitimation by a Generalized Deference to Authority
We now turn to a psychological analysis of the legitimation process. Here, the organization co-opts the deep-seated respect for authority inculcated in most individuals by socialization. This legitimation may be thought of as a general category, underlying the other bases outlined above. One is tempted to suggest that the others are often mere rationalizations for this more basic instrument. Since this form of legitimation meets individual needs for security and occasionally mediates distorted perceptions of authority, it seems to fall in the category of nonrational behavior, or at least, it is less rational than legitimations based upon objective indexes such as technical skill and formal position. However, definitions of rationality must rest upon an explicit statement of the objectives of any given behavior. If an individual derives security and less strained interpersonal relations from habitual submission to authority, his behavior is rational from this standpoint.

17 / J. R. P. French and R. Snyder, "Leadership and Interpersonal Power," in D. Cartwright (ed.), *Studies in Social Power* (Ann Arbor, 1959), Michigan University Research Center for Group Dynamics, Publication No. 6, pp. 118–149.
18 / *Ibid.*, pp. 147–48.

The analysis assumes that behavior in complex organizations may usefully be conceptualized as a series of reactions to authority.[19] Its theoretical framework is determined by Sullivan's view that personality is the result of an individual's characteristic mode of accommodating to authority figures over a long period of time. (It is important to note that Sullivan's theory is based upon two decades of clinical experience, involving literally thousands of cases.) His belief that anxiety-reduction is the basic mechanism in such accommodations is also central: "I believe it fairly safe to say that anybody and everybody devotes much of his lifetime and a great deal of his energy to ... avoiding more anxiety than he already has, and, if possible, to getting rid of some of this anxiety."[20]

Sullivan insists that anxiety is the major factor in learning: the child and the adult learn to trade approval and the reduction of anxiety for conformity with the perceived wishes of significant individuals. It would seem that such formulations about human behavior can validly be transferred to the authority-structured interpersonal context of big organizations. We thus assume that individual reactions to organizational authority are a form of learning. Moreover, as in all learning, the mechanisms of reward, perception, and reinforcement are operating. Complex organizations may be regarded as educational institutions whose patent systems of authority, status, and goals provide compelling stimuli for their members. Learning may be defined as a process of limiting alternatives and reinforcing behavior that internalizes appropriate choices. Essentially, actions that satisfy basic needs are reinforced because they reduce the unpleasant tension generated by the need. The reduction of anxiety by accepting organizational claims for loyalty, consistency, and obedience seems a powerful reinforcement.

These considerations suggest some limitations of Barnard's "permissive" concept of authority, which holds that subordinates play a major role in legitimating organizational authority. Basically, this concept seems to overstate the amount of discretion enjoyed by those who receive a superior's order. It probably underestimates the disparities in authority, influence, and power between any given individual and the organization's leaders. *But more important, it neglects the behavioral effect of a lifetime of socialization built upon the acceptance of authority and attending psychological gains.* If Sullivan is correct, the individual is trained from infancy onward to defer to the authority of parents, teachers, executives, and leaders of various kinds. He develops over a period of time a general-

19 / This analysis is more fully developed in Robert V. Presthus, *The Organizational Society* (New York: Alfred A. Knopf, Inc., 1962).

20 / Harry Stack Sullivan, "Tensions, Interperson and International," in H. Cantril (ed.), *Tensions that Cause Wars* (Urbana: University of Illinois Press, 1950), p. 95.

ized deference to authority, a "self-system" based upon satisfactory interpersonal accommodations and their rewards in security, approval, and influence.

This syndrome appears exceptionally compelling in the bureaucratic situation in which authority and the symbols that define it are rather sharply defined. Unlike many group associations, big organizations are "authoritative" milieus; influence is rarely the primary ingredient in interpersonal affairs. As Mills says, "Institutions [organizations] are sets of roles graded by authority."[21] If this is their essential quality, we can assume that legitimation by a generalized deference to authority will be common in large organizations.

This theory of behavior is reinforced by the fact that organizations comprise a "structured field," that is, a psychological field which facilitates learning because its stimuli are obvious and compelling, thereby easing perception and compliance with the behaviors suggested by such stimuli. Titles, income, accessibility, size and decor of office, secretarial buffers, and degree of supervision are among such organizational stimuli. They provide cues that define interpersonal relations, limit alternatives, and inhibit spontaneity. The extent to which authority and its indexes are institutionalized is suggested by the fact that whereas the individuals who occupy the formal roles may change, the *system* of authority relationships persists, reinforcing formal position as a legitimation.

Anxiety plays its part, too, because a moderate amount of anxiety often facilitates learning. Pavlov was among the first to note that anxious people acquire conditioned responses with unusual speed. Eysenck reports a study in which normal individuals required 25 repetitions of a nonsense syllable accompanied by a buzzer before a conditioned response was established, while anxiety neurotics required only 8 repetitions.[22] Research on the effects of different anxiety loadings on behavior would require further specification of organizational role types in terms of their reactions to authority. It seems reasonable to assume that a certain amount of anxiety is conducive to organizational socialization, while too heavy a load results in dysfunctional reactions to authority, e.g., resistance, rebellion, or awkward interpersonal accommodations.

The group character of organizations also affects the legitimation process. A safe generalization is that individuals tend to accept group judgments in return for the psychic satisfaction of being in the majority and

21 / C. Wright Mills, *The Sociological Imagination* (New York: Oxford, 1959), p. 30.
22 / H. J. Eysenck, *The Psychology of Politics* (London: Routledge & Kegan Paul, 1954), O. H. Mowrer, "Anxiety Reduction and Learning," 27 *Journal of Experimental Psychology* (1940), pp. 497–516.

winning the group's approval.[23] Organizations are composed of a congeries of groups and subhierarchies, each bound together by authority, mission, skill, and interest to form a microcosm of the larger system. Thus the conformity of any given individual is encouraged by psychological inducements and other sanctions that small groups have at their disposal, including approval, acceptance, rejection, and even kicks and blows when other inducements fail. Each group has its own authority structure in which its leaders enjoy considerable autonomy in intra-group relations, although they are often nonleaders when viewed from a larger perspective.[24] This devolution of authority and power has important consequences for legitimation. Discipline is insured since the life chances of those in each group are determined largely by representations made on their behalf by their immediate leaders. Organizational authority is transmitted downward by the subleaders, reinforcing their own authority and status by the received opportunity to demonstrate the loyalty and dispatch with which they carry out higher policy.

Conflict may occur here due to the built-in ambiguity of the leader's role, which demands that he simultaneously promote the larger goals of the organization yet maintain equilibrium in his own group by defending the "cosmopolitan" or extra-organizational objectives of its members. Again, he will sometimes be caught between the conflicting demands of hierarchy and technical skill; his own identification with a professional field may aggravate such conflicts, making it more difficult to meet the larger organizational claims implicit in his formal position. At other times conflicting goals or policies within the larger organization make role conflict almost certain. This problem is nicely demonstrated in prison administration where rehabilitation and custodial goals may be pursued in the same prison at the same time, resulting in role conflict among those responsible for dealing directly with the prisoners.[25] This example can be conceptualized as a problem in the legitimation of authority. Like the ambivalent leader mentioned above, the prison sociologist or psychologist is torn between the authority of professional rehabilitation values (i.e., expertise) and hierarchical authority which typically stresses custodial goals. Such theoretical versatility makes the authority concept a valuable tool both in organizational analysis and teaching.

23 / See for example, the classic experiments of Sherif and Asch, reported in M. Sherif, *Outline of Social Psychology* (New York: Harper & Bros., 1952) and S. E. Asch, *Social Psychology* (Englewood Cliffs, N.J.: Prentice-Hall, 1952).

24 / E. Stotland, "Peer Groups and Reactions to Power Figures," in D. Cartwright (ed.), *Studies in Social Power* (Ann Arbor: Institute for Social Research, Univ. of Mich., 1959), pp. 53–68; W. G. Bennis and H. A. Shepard, "A Theory of Group Development," 9 *Human Relations* (1956), pp. 415–437.

25 / D. R. Cressey, "Contradictory Directives in Complex Organizations," *ibid.*, pp. 1–19.

8

Psychological authority:
an operational definition for social work

Social workers for many years have recognized three kinds of authority that directly influence their effectiveness in helping clients with problems in social functioning. *Institutional authority* is that by which private or public social agencies are established, financed, and allowed to designate the services that they will provide, including selection of the type of clients that they may or shall accept. *Administrative authority* is the source of the delegation of responsibility to the social worker to carry out his role in accordance with the functions of the specific agency employing him. *Professional authority* is that which recognizes competence and skill of the social worker as *the authority*, and which requires him to act in accordance with the values ascribed by his profession.

Another kind of authority, *psychological authority*, however, has received less attention. On the one hand, there is confusion regarding the meaning of psychological authority and, on the other hand, there is so much concern with the possible misuse of authority in treatment, that the potentials for constructive use of authority in client-worker relationships often are overlooked in the literature of the profession.

This paper will point first to social work's intervention in the lives of hard-to-reach clients as an expression of authority that is related to the rights of the individual and to the responsibilities of the profession. The present efforts to provide a conceptual framework of authority in social work will be considered next – efforts that have not clarified the meaning of psychological authority. Understanding of the psychological aspects of authority can more readily be achieved by drawing upon the perceptions of authority revealed in the literature of the political and behavioral sciences, which have given attention to the meaning of authority and to its uses. The

From *Social Work Papers*, VIII: 1–8, 1961.

paper concludes by proposing an operational definition of psychological authority in social work.

AUTHORITY IN SOCIAL WORK LITERATURE

If the literature of social work correctly represents the common elements in practice – and this is debatable – the constructive use of authority in service to involuntary clients was of little concern to the profession during the past two decades. The fact that aggressive case work, "reaching out" to clients, has had the attention of the current literature would indicate that these are new and daring approaches in a profession whose primary purpose is to enable individuals to increase their social functioning by helping them to solve problems of social dysfunction.

Initiators of special projects, such as the New York City Youth Board, the St. Paul Family Centered Project, the Community Research Associates in San Mateo, and others, state or imply that they are applying the principles of practice by which the profession has long been guided, to newer knowledge about people and their problems. These principles include the individual's right to self determination so long as others do not suffer; the protection of the weak or ill or disadvantaged; the freedom of the individual to make choices that affect his own destiny; the capacity of a person to change; the importance of the family; and the obligations of the profession to serve in the interest of the client, and not for personal aggrandizement and power.

These projects, and discussions of them, have resulted in more thoughtful review of social work's rights and responsibilities in social treatment. For example, intervention in the lives of individuals or families can be viewed as an *obligation* of social work stemming from the *right* of the individual to be helped when he has a *need* for which social work would have provided service had the individual sought it.

The method of seeking out clients to involve them in solving their problems is not too different from that used in the early days of social work, but the understanding of individuals and of the dynamics of relationship as they affect methods, differs – as it should if knowledge and skills are not to remain static. *Professional authority* is retained through acceptance of the values upon which the principles of practice are based.

Apathetic, discouraged, or hostile clients do improve their social functioning when the social worker "reaches out" to them. Those who do not change, or who become worse, no longer are considered untreatable or impossible to treat; rather, the failures are thought to reflect inability of the profession to know, as yet, what help is needed and how to provide it, how to involve such individuals and their families in treatment, and how to modify the social environment in their behalf.

The *authority of expertness* – that is, professional authority – is retained, although with recognition that the expertness of the present can be increased in the future. And it is possible that there may be some individuals and their families who have been so damaged by stressful situations that help for them will require radical changes in our social customs.

But these reports of work with "hard to reach clients" do not attempt to provide a conceptual base for employing authority in social treatment. The writings of Elliot Studt have begun to sketch out the outlines of such a framework. She has focused attention on aspects of authority in social work, with special reference first to the field of corrections, and in later writings, on the dynamics of authority as they may apply to several fields of service.

In a cogent and provocative article, "An Outline for the Study of Social Authority Factors in Casework,"[1] Studt discusses authority relationships in the social agency, social authority in correctional agencies, the casework functions with offenders, and the problems in achieving psychological authority with these clients.

Studt, in this article, selected two definitions of authority: sociological as described by Lasswell and Kaplan, and psychological as described by Erich Fromm. The former[2] sees authority as power

assigned to a position, and exercised by the individual in the position as he participates in the making of decisions by others. It requires both the delegation of that power to the position according to legitimate means, and the acknowledgement by the individual toward whom the authority is exercised that such exercise of power is "just and proper."

Fromm's definition of psychological authority is "an interpersonal relation in which one person looks to another as somebody superior to him."[3] Studt points out that the client acknowledges that the caseworker is "superior to himself for the *purposes of the problem at hand*," and that not all the relationships in which Fromm's "authority" appear are also formally recognized and supported in the social structure.[4]

In a later article, Studt develops further her frame of reference by stating "... (social) authority is created when, in order to get the job done properly, a person in one position in an organization is authorized

1 / Elliot Studt, "An Outline for the Study of Social Authority Factors in Casework," *Social Casework*, Vol. 35, No. 6, June 1954, p. 232.
2 / *Ibid.*, p. 233.
3 / *Ibid.*, p. 233.
4 / *Ibid.*, p. 233.

to direct the role activities of a person in another position."[5] She states elsewhere in the same periodical that "I found it extremely complicated to try to conceptualize social authority and psychological influence under the single term 'authority.' "[6]

Studt's application of social (institutional) authority factors to social work organization and practice is acceptable with minor reservations, hence the complication between influence and authority mentioned by her warrants attention. The complication may be due in large part to the inadequacy of the definition she selected of psychological authority, a definition that describes professional authority, the authority of the expert, rather than psychological authority as it can occur in many contexts. Although, in social work practice, professional authority may be closely associated with psychological aspects of authority, the two differ. Yet the differences cannot be delineated until there is an operational definition of psychological authority. Aid in the development of such a definition can come from reviewing the perceptions of authority described in the writings of political scientists and behavioral scientists who have been studying the meaning of authority, kinds of authority, and the usefulness of authority to mankind.

AUTHORITY AND THE POLITICAL AND BEHAVIORAL SCIENCES

During the past few years, political and behavioral scientists have given increasing attention to the concept of authority, and to empirical tests of some aspects of its manifestations. At first glance, however, their writings confuse rather than clarify. For example, they present national authority, irrational authority, secular authority, founded authority, formal authority, legal authority, social authority, institutional authority, and psychological authority. Each is defined in part and compared to one or more of the other kinds of authority. There are discussions also of parental authority, or *the* authority, or authority *to*, authority *in*, or the authority *of*. These identify the locus and nexus of authority. Together they imply that authority is a concept at too high a level of abstraction to permit full discussion. But deeper perusal reveals some sparkling ideas and a few studies that illuminate the nature of authority.

Social work usually turns first either to psychiatry or to sociology in its search for meaning. With regard to authority, however, political science and philosophy are more appropriate sources.

5 / Elliot Studt, "Worker-Client Authority Relationships in Social Work," *Social Work*, Vol. 4, No. 1, January 1959, p. 18.
6 / Elliot Studt, "Letters," *Social Work*, Vol. 4, No. 1, January 1959, p. 124.

The word authority stems from the Latin word *auctoritas*, author, which in turn is derived from the Latin *augere*, to augment. According to the political scientists,[7] however, the original meaning of *auctoritas* is not easily definable. *Patrum auctoritas* referred to the old ones in the Roman senate who supplemented a mere act of will by adding reason to it. They gave advice that was not to be disregarded, for it was based on experience, values, and reason.

Authority would be more than advice and less than command, a confirmation as a result of deliberation.

Some political scientists describe authority as the power to require behavior for the common good, a power that may be forcibly applied. Others look upon authority as a means to direct behavior without resorting to force. These consider that authority is no longer present if force is required to secure compliance.

Individuals are seen as responding to authority for several reasons, because of the symbols of authority, the status or role of the one exercising authority, and his competence.[8] Discretionary decisions are made by individuals who have authority delegated to them because of the complexity of situations in which authority is exercised. The rightness or justness of the decisions may be questioned by the recipient; he may, nevertheless, conform because of fear or faith.

From political science and philosophy come additional ideas of importance to social work. Authority is essential not only for the welfare and security of the state or society. It is necessary also for the individual who gains security when authority prescribes the limits of acceptable behavior, and points out the choices available as well as the consequences to be expected from alternate courses of action.[9]

Viewed sociologically, authority is a fundamental part of the social functioning of any society; it is the institutional right to control actions or to regulate activities of persons or groups with reference to the public interest.[10] Authority is always goal directed.

Sociologists examining manifestations of authority in social organizations of various types, such as probation and parole departments, hospitals for the mentally ill, welfare agencies and the like, have shown how

7 / Carl J. Friedrich, "Authority, Reason, and Direction," *Authority*, Carl J. Friedrich, Ed. (Cambridge: Harvard University Press, 1958), pp. 28–48.

8 / Herbert J. Spiro, "Authority, Values, and Policy," *Authority*, Carl J. Friedrich, Ed. (Cambridge: Harvard University Press, 1958), pp. 49–57.

9 / David Easton, "The Perception of Authority and Political Change," *Authority*, Carl J. Friedrich, Ed. (Cambridge: Harvard University Press, 1958), pp. 170–196.

10 / Talcott Parsons, "Authority, Legitimation, and Social Action," *Authority*, Carl J. Friedrich, Ed. (Cambridge: Harvard University Press, 1958), pp. 197–221.

the *structure* and *values* in a system influence the manner in which responsible authority is exercised by persons in specific roles in the organization.
Conflict between role expectations and opportunity to function in accordance with those expectations has been described as conflict within systems
of authority, sometimes between levels of the same kind of authority, and
sometimes between administrative and professional authority practices,[11]
or among different professions.

From sociologists studying delinquency have come speculation and research about lower class value systems that "authorize" behavior unlike
that legally prescribed, and about the norms of conduct to which members
of this class subscribe as a way of life. Normlessness or anomie is said to
characterize those groups that have given up the struggle to achieve a
status that is denied them.[12] The main stream of sociological speculation,
however, considers conflict between middle class and lower class values
as of prime importance in explaining the fact that most juvenile delinquents and adult offenders, that is, those having "trouble with authority,"
come from the lower economic classes. Stressed in both theories – norm
acceptance or norm conflict – is the importance of *values* and *structure*
as guides in role performance of the individual (or group) and in his
acceptance or rejection of social behavior expected by the larger society.

Psychologists have been studying the kinds of individuals who enjoy or
dislike the exercises of authority, and they have examined also the meaning of authority to individuals in many types of situations of employment
and of status. They have focused attention on the rigidity of some prejudiced individuals, labeled the authoritarian personality,[13] and have suggested that only through structured authority can such persons accept
guidance in behavior. Psychologists have experimented also with the uses
of immediate rewards and delay in gratification as ways of facilitating
children's persistence in learning – a tempting examination that may lead
to better understanding of the use of reward and penalty as stimuli for
learning acceptable social behavior.

Cultural anthropologists have shown that all cultures, in order to carry
out minimal coordination of essential activities, have limitations on the
pattern of behavior of members, selecting some behavior that is permitted

11 / Lloyd E. Ohlin, Herman Piven, and Donnell M. Pappenfort, "Major Dilemmas of the Social Worker in Probation and Parole," *N.P.P.A. Journal*, Vol. 2, No. 3,
July 1956, pp. 211–225.

12 / Robert K. Merton, "Social Structure and Anomie," *Social Perspectives on
Behavior*, Herman D. Stein and Richard A. Cloward, Eds. (Glencoe, Illinois: The
Free Press, 1958), pp. 517–537.

13 / T. W. Adorno, Elsie Frankel-Brunswick, Daniel J. Levinson, and R. Nevitt
Sanford, *The Authoritarian Personality* (New York: Harper & Brothers, 1950).

and ruling out or suppressing others.[14] The means for permitting or suppressing action differ from culture to culture, and reflect the *value system* upon which the culture is based. Yet in all cultures, there are methods by which the individual is guided by a "framework for experience and action"[15] – authority – so that he learns how or how far his culture can help him. Authority also may assuage guilt.

Research into the basic psychology and biology of behavior discloses that animals learn adaptive behavior through responses to stimuli that originate from outside – from the environment. In his interesting book, *Aggression*,[16] John Paul Scott summarizes the results from animal experiments, including some with the human animal, as to the means by which adaptive behavior is learned and modified. If the findings can be applied to individuals, explanations of motivation to aggression (precisely defined as initiating an attack – fighting, physical or verbal) can be reinforced through success in response and can be modified by success in inhibiting the original type of response. Yet, it appears that, without continuing to practice the type of response learned last, the animal, when it again receives the stimulus, reverts to the original type of response. Success in inhibitory response appears to be more easily lost than success in the response first learned.

Although Scott does not discuss authority directly, the place of the experimenter as the one who applies the stimulus and who "teaches" the appropriateness of response, is obvious.

Out of all this interest in authority in society and for the individual on the part of the allied fields, authority emerges as necessary in any culture or society. Authority provides security, guidance, and instruction to persons; through the influence of authority, social behavior is learned, alternate courses of actions are recognized, and the results or consequences of actions can be understood. Values, behavior, and reasoning are interrelated; the person who exercises authority understands this interrelatedness, but the one who is influenced by authority does not fully accept, and may not comprehend, the way in which values are related to choices between behavior which is or is not permitted. A person may respond to authority because of fear of the consequences if he does not modify his actions, or he may respond because he trusts the authority-bearer and therefore is willing to be influenced by him. Authority is a special kind of influence that is more than advice and less than command.

14 / E. Adamson Hoebel, "Authority in Primitive Societies," *Authority*, Carl J. Friedrich, Ed. (Cambridge: Harvard University Press, 1958).

15 / Dorothy Lee, *Culture and Freedom* (Englewood Cliffs, New Jersey: Prentice-Hall, Inc., 1959).

16 / John Paul Scott, *Aggression* (Chicago: University of Chicago Press, 1958).

With this review of literature from allied fields attention is again turned to the psychological aspects of authority that may be present in worker-client relationships. To ascertain whether or not this kind of authority is present in social treatment, it is important to state an operational definition of psychological authority.

PSYCHOLOGICAL AUTHORITY DEFINED

Authority, in its psychological aspects, is an interpersonal relation in which one person (or group) exercises influence over the social behavior of another person (or group) who does not fully accept the *reasoning* that relates *values* to *actions*, but in which both parties know that this influence is being exercised; its intent is known, and hence recognized for what it is.[17]

If social workers, like political and social scientists, perceive authority as one very important means by which persons learn acceptable social behavior and are enabled to use a relationship with another to achieve better social functioning, there will be less avoidance of authority in treatment with some clients who may not know the limits of acceptable behavior or who have a value system that is in marked contrast to that of the larger society. It may be that there are more persons who require some use of authority in treatment than heretofore has been realized. Perhaps the intitial stages of treatment show more use of psychological authority than do later stages. It may be that group workers use psychological aspects to authority more frequently than do caseworkers. These speculations can only be verified by using an operational definition of psychological aspects of authority and testing its application in social work practice. This is a test that we hope our readers will make. If the definition is useful, another plank can be added to the conceptual framework of authority and social work.

17 / I am indebted to David Easton, *op. cit.*, p. 179, for some of the ideas expressed in this definition, although their application to social treatment is solely my responsibility.

9

Authority in casework –
a bread-and-butter theory

Some years ago some of my family got together to build a house for my father. We were pretty well prepared for this, since in the family we had a carpenter, a roofer, a sheet metal man, a social worker, and a bootlegger.

We met at the building lot on the appointed day and said, "Okay, Dad, what kind of a house do you want?" Well, he thought he'd like a sort of meatloaf shape with large rooms; windows about this wide (indicating with his hands) and about this high from the floor. He wanted an old-fashioned fruit pantry about so wide, with shelves about this high, and so on through the house.

So we set to work. However, it soon became evident that no two of us were building the same house, and we had soon wasted half a day. We finally went back to Dad in desperation and said: "We simply can't get anywhere until we can see what it is we are trying to do. It's absolutely impossible to work without a *plan*."

On that day I learned something about carpentry, and also about social service: you must have a plan to know what you're doing.

In the social sciences we call such a plan a theory, or philosophy, or frame of reference. It is such a plan – a plan for authority in casework – that I should like to acquaint you with.

The value of a theory, says Guthrie,[1] is to facilitate communication between people. Unlike Guthrie's theory this plan is not designed for laboratory testing. It is a plan for practitioners – a bread-and-butter theory.

Reprinted from *National Probation and Parole Journal*, v: 249–55, July 1959, by permission of the National Council on Crime and Delinquency.

Presented at the National Conference on Social Welfare, May 13, 1958.

1 / E. R. Guthrie, Ch. II in J. McV. Hunt, *Personality and the Behavior Disorders*, New York, Ronald Press, 1944.

LIMITATIONS

A plan for a house or for a social service faces certain restrictions:
1 It must conform to the setting. I can't have an eight-foot basement where there is a six-foot water table, for instance. During the war years we employed a conscientious objector in the receiving cottage of our institution. One day a husky boy pounced on another caretaker and began a tussle to get his keys. Our CO took one look, ran to the door, unlocked and flung it open, and the boy ran away. My plan, then, must be compatible with agency policies, rules, and standards.
2 My plan must comply with my unique personality requirements – my needs, goals, standards, and culture. If I am thirty inches wide, then twenty-four inch doors won't do. I'd get stuck. If my experience tells me that aggression is learned and my theory holds that aggression is innate, I will get stuck whenever I deal with aggression
3 My plan must have an internal consistency. A friend of mine built a house with a bedroom which you entered through the bathroom. If you awakened some morning and found someone taking a bath, you could either wait for him to finish, or you could climb out of the window. It lacked internal consistency. A Rankian instructor I knew would not allow her students to use her first name. "In the world of reality," she said, "one may not call administrators by their given names. I will therefore help you to learn to adapt to this reality by daily practice in class." On graduation day she gave a social for her students. When a student addressed her as Miss Y she replied: "Charlie, you may now call me Jane." You may or may not like this rationale, but I would like you to observe that it has an internal consistency which is a thing of beauty. The Rogerians consistently and repeatedly insist that a client make his own decisions and assume his own responsibilities. Above everything else I believe they have achieved internal consistency.

If I seem to belabor this point, it is because social workers in the correctional field have lacked internal consistency. It is toward achieving this end that this paper is presented.

FOUNDATION

Like most houses, our plan calls for a foundation. The foundation upon which this house must stand or fall is this:
The use of authority is not antagonistic to the principles of good social work or counseling. Further, the actual employment of authority itself – its skillful use and manipulation – can be a powerful therapeutic tool in social service.

Contrast this, for instance, with Scheidlinger:[2] "This [authority] would be very undesirable as it would change the child's concept of the therapist as a warm, accepting, and nonpunitive person." Use of authority, then, makes one cold, rejecting, and punitive. Or consider a halfway station between these two views – Williamson and Foley:[3] "Disciplinary counseling may prove to be less effective than other types of counseling, because of the necessary coercive conditions under which it must take place." An apologetic approach to authority, at best.

Now note that I did not limit this assertion to the correctional field. This was not an oversight. "Positive Aspects of Authoritative Casework" would have been a misleading title for this paper because I do not believe there are two kinds of casework – authoritative and nonauthoritative. Every public welfare worker, school worker, child guidance worker, marriage counselor, and probation or parole officer must learn to say "These are our rules; this is our policy. These are the limits within which you may operate." When we reach the point of having agencies without policy, then, but not until then, may we have social service without authority.

FRAMEWORK

We must have a framework for our house:

Postulate I: *Authority is inherent in all cultures. A society free of authority does not and cannot exist.*

In any Utopia we will find a need for traffic lights, stop signs, and Form 1040.[4] Two corollaries of this are: (1) One of the dimensions of socialization, and consequently of adjustment, is an individual's ability to adapt to authority. (2) Any measure of antisocial tendencies is largely a measure of the individual's resistance to authority.

If I were asked to name a half-dozen common conflicts which a social worker encounters, I would name dependency, separation and rejection, sex, status, and authority. (The sixth choice is yours.) I would guess that welfare workers most often encounter dependency conflict; child welfare workers, separation and rejection; marriage counselors, a high ratio of sex conflict. In the correctional field no conflict appears more frequently or intensely than conflict around authority.

Postulate II: *In a democratic society, all authority is derived or delegated authority. No person may exercise control or coercion over another except as this authority is delegated to him by society.*

2 / S. Scheidlinger, Chap. II in S. R. Slavson, *The Practice of Group Therapy*, New York, International Universities Press, 1947.

3 / E. G. Williamson and J. D. Foley, *Counseling and Discipline*, New York, McGraw-Hill, 1949.

4 / Form 1040 is the United States tax-return form.

What about parent-child rights, you say. Consider: If I attempt to turn back history and assume the right to sell or trade my child, for instance, I will shortly have one of these probation officers knocking on my door. Further, the moment that any social agency assumes any authority not specifically delegated to it, it's in trouble. Which is exactly why we have executive boards. I may exercise only such authority, then, as society delegates to me, whether I am a parent, probation officer, or playground director.

NEED FOR AUTHORITY

Postulate III: *Every person entertains both positive and negative feelings toward authority.*

At our correctional school we inherited several hundred wooden pallets from war surplus – large flat wooden racks. The boys from one cottage learned they could nail six or eight of these together to make a little shanty; permission was granted and soon we had a young shanty town springing up. I went to have a look at this budding young Utopia, and each boy took me to see the progress on his particular shack.

But before *any* individual shanty was finished, they stopped work on their own construction and jointly and cooperatively completed one large civic structure – the one and only social endeavour in their community. What do you suppose this was? I fancy that you will *not* guess it was a school or a church or a library. A beer joint, perhaps? A casino or bawdy house or some such den of iniquity? No, they built a jail. They built it first and they built it best. One boy proudly demonstrated its virtues by locking himself in for me. Now only three days before, this boy was in my office telling me: "You wanna know what'd make me real happy? A whole squadron of Russian bombers come flying over this place and drop about a million tons of bombs on it. I'd sit up there on that hill and watch the bricks fly and the smoke boil up and I'd just laugh and laugh." Furthermore, a month or two prior to this we were tearing out some old lockup cells. Every boy in the institution wanted a chance to wield a sledge hammer and knock down a few walls. And motivated! If social workers attacked their problems with the zeal of those kids with the sledge hammers, I'm sure we could solve the problems of the world in a few months. Yet these same lads, so eager to smash any symbol of authority or restraint, were a few weeks later building a jailhouse. Why? We do not adequately describe authority conflict by saying they have resistance to authority. They also have some strong positive feelings: a need to be controlled, a need for a checkrein on their wild impulses – a need for authority. Ambivalence can operate here as well as in love relations.

Postulate IV: *As in other casework roles, the aim of casework in authority is to help a client understand and accept these conflicted feelings, and to learn new ways of controlling and expressing them.*

Dr. Schulze relates the story of a young social work student who entered the boys' dormitory in an institution and found a small boy in a tantrum, smashing the furniture to kindling. Her reaction was not unlike our conscientious objector's; she flung her hands in the air, screamed, and ran out. Because these workers were unable to come to grips with the problem of authority, these children were not helped to face or rechannel their conflicted feelings. On the contrary, their pathological behavior is reinforced when they learn they can control adults therewith.

ANY RELATION CAN BE THERAPEUTIC

Postulate V: *Any interpersonal experience can be made therapeutic or nontherapeutic, helpful or harmful, by the way it is handled.*

In the January '58 issue of *Social Work*,[5] Zimmerman maintains that a school social worker cannot be a truant officer. Yes, a social worker can be a parole officer or an intrusive case worker, he admits, but not a truant officer. Why? Because school social work "is based upon a basic tenet of service." Service, then, is inconsistent with use of a truant officer's authority.

Now I have just said – and I'm stuck with it – that *any* interpersonal experience can be made helpful or harmful, according to its handling. First I must define my term "helpful" or "therapeutic": Any time that I help a client achieve a self-enhancing experience, so that he is better prepared to achieve other such experiences, this is therapeutic. Further, any time that I help a client to face a traumatic experience so that he is better prepared to face similar subsequent experiences, this is therapeutic. Facing negative as well as achieving positive experience, then, is therapeutic.

Is this a new definition? I ask you to reflect on your caseloads. In how many cases must you help the client make the best of a bad situation rather than eliminate the problem? How often must a client learn to live with a handicap, with an alcoholic husband, or with a neurosis? Are we nontherapeutic when we attempt these things?

Let's carry this postulate to the ultimate. *Any* interpersonal relationship would include death. Let's say I am warden of a prison, and as such it is my job to put another human being to death. The degree to which my work is therapeutic is the degree to which I can reduce the trauma of the situation. I understand that the period between conviction and execution

5/P.95.

is a little more than one year. I imagine that our prisoner will want something to keep his mind occupied during these long days. I believe he may want someone to talk to professionally, to ventilate some feelings. I will try to provide this. He may want to make his peace with God, I will try to provide him with a clergyman. I am sure he will want to see friends and family during this interim. I once stood by while a young murderer said his last goodbyes to his family, a few hours before his execution. There is no question in my mind that this helped reduce the trauma of the situation – in short, that it was therapeutic. Is his total experience with me less traumatic than if he were in unskilled hands? Is my work, then, therapeutic by this definition?

Some highly pertinent inferences can be drawn from this definition. I will not attempt a job that someone else can do better; neither will I send someone else to do a job that I can do better. For instance, if I have a violator to be picked up, I don't send a cop to do the job. I do it myself. There was a time when I didn't believe this. I recall I once issued a pickup order on a juvenile parole violator and after his arrest I went to visit him in jail. The arresting officer had slapped him around considerably, called him various names, manhandled his mother, and otherwise abused his family. I said I was sorry he had had such a rough experience, but that he had to be brought in. He replied angrily: "Yeh, I know that. But you coulda come and got me yourself." Yes, I could have. Why didn't I? I could find volumes to rationalize my not going – filled with such phrases as "incompatible, inconsistent, and antithetical." But note that the boy did not think it inconsistent for his caseworker to come after him. What seemed to him inconsistent was that his friend and caseworker should send a sadistic cop to maul him and his family around. I kept saying to myself: "This is for the boy's good – I must preserve our relationship." But this was not the *real* reason I didn't go after him. The real reason was that it was not therapeutic for Hardman. Whose needs, then, was I filling? How well did I preserve our relationship?

AUTHORITY – A TOOL

This leads us to Postulate VI: *The degree to which a worker can be helpful to a client with authority conflict is a function of (1) the degree to which the worker understands and accepts his own feelings around authority, and (2) the skill with which he uses his delegated authority.*

Again I assert that this dictum is not peculiar to correction. Last year I attended a case conference on a military post. It was the consensus of the staff that the client had symptoms which indicated referral to the

Neuro-psychiatric Clinic. The next question: how to get him there? We had the authority, if necessary, to send him over under military police escort, though no one anticipated this. The psychologist suggested: "Call his sergeant and let him make the referral. We'll let the sergeant be the bastard that sent him." (He was unwittingly paraphrasing Shakespeare: Some sergeants are born bastards, some achieve bastardy, and some have bastardy thrust upon 'em.)

Now let's apply our dictum that we don't send someone else to do a job that we can do better. Why? Would the sergeant likely increase or decrease the man's anxiety about referral? Make the clinic's job harder or easier? Make the man more or less likely to bolt and go AWOL? What is the probability that the client will learn from the sergeant, from the other noncoms, the clinic, or even from us, by some slip, that this was *our* idea? In my experience it is 50–50. Will this enhance our relationship? If we thought referral would help him, the client says, why didn't we refer him ourselves? If we thought it wouldn't, why did we send him?

Now suppose we *do* decide to refer him ourselves. "Private Z," we say, "we would like to get some expert opinion in your case. We would like you to see Dr. X, a psychiatrist at the base hospital. [Now note the next line.] What do you think about this?"

This was a good interview until that last line. Suppose he says, "I think the idea stinks." Or more likely, just: "Do I have a choice?" No, he doesn't. If we should let him choose not to go and he commits an act of violence, we are responsible. Then why ask him? Are we not, in effect, throwing him a few crumbs of spurious autonomy from our table? Our client, like most, entertains an impoverished self concept. Does it enhance his self concept to throw him crumbs? Would he not be more likely to feel like a worthwhile, mature person if we honestly and openly shared with him exactly where we stood and where he stood? When, at a later date, I insist that the client be responsible for his decisions, will he consider how I passed my responsibility on to the sergeant? Is this good teaching? Good correction? Good casework? Yet I will wager that the records of any social agency will reveal a hundred examples of such casework. Why do we do it? Why pass the buck to the sergeant? Why pretend that we don't hold and use authority when we do? Because we believe that he who executes authority becomes a bastard. In short, we suffer from the same illness as our client.

All of which introduces Postulate VII: *Authority need not be associated with hostility, punishment, or rejection, except as these traits inhere in the personality of the worker. Authority can be identified with love, acceptance, and understanding.*

A few summers ago I worked in a cerebral palsy camp. When we opened our swimming pool the director announced to the campers: "We are very sorry, but we can't allow you to swim alone. The Red Cross has a very strict rule against it." Now this was not a Red Cross camp. We had no affiliation with this organization. Yet we felt compelled to find some scapegoat to hang our authority on. Why? Because it's mean, punitive, and rejecting to use authority. But must it be so? Consider this approach to swimming rules: "We don't want you to swim without a counselor in the pool because we are concerned about you and don't want you to get drowned." I hold that this same approach is equally applicable to probation and parole, to school attendance work, to disciplinary counseling, or to protective agencies.

And lastly, Postulate VIII: *An outstanding – perhaps the greatest – service that a worker can render to a client with authority conflict is to provide a new and differential and therapeutic experience with authority.* Some of the aspects of this new relationship are:

1 Whenever I use authority, I will use it openly and honestly. Whenever I do anything to or for or about a client, I will tell him so. This means that I will never make a referral, recommendation, or report about a client without sharing this with him.

2 I will fully execute that authority, but *only* that authority delegated to me by the administrative agency. By following this dictum I avoid overuse or underuse of authority.

3 I will make crystal clear in structuring with a client where my authority begins and ends. This will eliminate a vast amount of testing.

4 I will further clarify which decisions are mine to make and which the client must make. If agency policy includes increasing client responsibility (by such means as preparole honor cottage living, for instance), I will clarify each successive transfer of responsibility to the client.

5 I will steadfastly resist all of the client's efforts to alter my decisions by threats, tantrums, seduction, illness, etc. I will just as steadfastly defend his right to make his decisions and stand by them.

6 I will scrupulously insist that my client assume and face the responsibilities impinging on his decisions. And I will just as scrupulously stand by the responsibility for my decisions.

7 The exercise of authority will always be managed with empathy for and understanding of the client's total needs as a person – a person always worthy of my interest, respect, and affection.

Mullahy[6] quotes Harry Stack Sullivan as saying: "Restraints, above everything else, bring about the evolution of the self dynamism." Is it

6 / P. Mullahy, *Oedipus: Myth and Complex*, New York, Hermitage, 1948.

possible that it is rather the *balance and interaction* of authority and autonomy which engenders maturation and socialization? In either case – if either of these be true, or only partly true – then authority is a major dimension in the process of social adjustment. I therefore submit that for a person with antisocial traits to experience a fresh and wholesome relationship with authority is as truly therapeutic as for a dependent person to experience independence or an inadequate person to experience adequacy.

PART III

The concept of authority in social work

INTRODUCTION

One of the major theses underlying the theme of this book is that the social worker's creative use of authority in helping clients is dependent in part on his understanding of the meaning of authority and the place of authority in a social agency and the profession. In the five articles included in this section, an attempt is made to unravel the configuration of authority in and its meaning to the profession, the agency, and the worker. There are at least four major themes permeating these articles. One is that, despite the differences between social agencies, authority inheres in the role and function of social workers and these can be identified as social authority factors in all agencies. The second is that the nature and function of the social agency has its influence on the kinds of authority invested with workers. The third is that in worker-client authority relationships, the client's perceptions of authority often determine whether authority will or will not be helpful. The last is that there appears to be no "personality set" of social workers in relation to their attitudes towards authority.

The social agency serves as a base for social work practice. It is an organization fashioned to express the interests and will of a society or some groups in that society for the welfare of its members. The social agency, therefore, is a social institution designed to express societal interest and concern for provision of services. The social worker's identification with the purpose and functions of the social agency is an important component of the structure of social welfare services. The social worker has the obligation, as a professional social worker, not only to use his knowledge and skill in the administration of the service as it presently exists, but also to make his professional experience, knowledge, and skill available in responsible ways to society's review of (1) its purpose in establishing and maintaining the agency and (2) the effectiveness of programme, policy, and agency structure for its realization. The social agency is a living organism and like any other organism is capable of change and development.

The social worker is an employee of the social agency, but also he is a representative of his profession. There is some debate as to where his basic source of accountability and responsibility should lie, in agency or profession, or both. Regardless of this debate, the fact remains that both the agency and the profession have an impact on the social worker, especially in determining the authority factors.

Elliot Studt's article, "An Outline for Study of Social Authority Factors in Casework," analyzes authority factors inherent in social casework. Every casework relationship starts with a formal authority relationship. The authority of the caseworker has its sanction from the agency, which is in turn a delegation of "societal authority" to help people. But in any social agency the formal authority relationship must become a relationship of "psychological authority," if the client is to be helped. It may be said that, in the casework relationship, whenever the psychological aspects of the authority relation develop strongly, the formal, social authority aspects, although still present and effective, become secondary; and the casework process emerges as a particular, highly skilled form of the exercise of influence.

Elizabeth and Karl de Schweinitz make an important distinction between "constituted" and "inherent" authority within the context of the protective function of a public-welfare agency. The basic source and sanctioning system of "constitutional authority" are derived from a status, or hierarchical position in a society or an organization. This kind of authority can be best described as "authority of the office." "Inherent authority" on the other hand, is wisdom, understanding of others, experience, etc., leading to judgments that less experienced, less learned persons are willing to follow. There is no compulsion involved in "inherent" authority, except that which tends to make us follow authority. In formulating their conception of "inherent" authority, the de Schweinitzes are perhaps following Weber's conception of "charismatic personality" as a source of inherent authority, although they broaden their conception to include a variety of factors not necessarily considered by Weber. Using the conceptual framework of "constituted and inherent authority," the de Schweinitzes trace the historical movement of protection of children as a public responsibility, and emphasize that in history "constituted" authority – power to remove the child from home under public laws – came first. In the complex society of today, dependence on "constituted" authority for protection of children is hardly a viable approach. The social agency that carries a mandate for protection of children must incorporate in its function a meaning of "inherent" authority, if it has to adhere to a philosophy and practice that takes into consideration rights and interests of both children and their parents.

Couse's article deals with authority within a private agency, the John Howard Society of Ontario, which provides "preparatory services in penal institutions prior to release as well as after care services" to those who served a prison term. While public social agencies are legitimatized through legal and judicial processes, private social agencies derive their legitimation from community support. Interested citizens and local groups create and support voluntary, private agencies because of a certain degree of conviction and commitment to the desirability of a social welfare service. Interestingly enough, the private agency's effective functioning – rehabilitation of criminal offenders – according to Couse "is to a large extent dependent on "inherent" authority and not on "constituted" authority," with the social worker assuming a position of very real authority himself. The social worker's authority is derived from his specialized knowledge, professional integrity and competence, and a real concern for the rehabilitation of criminal offenders.

Studt in her second article formulates a "generic approach to authority in social work." Does authority enter into all social worker–client relationships and, if so, in what ways? Since authority arises from the structural arrangements by which people are organized to do a job, Studt hypothesizes that there is probably a wide range of patterns for authority relationships in various social welfare organizations where social workers are employed. In order to understand authority as a dynamic in professional practice, it would be necessary to examine various kinds of social work practice in the framework of analysis developed in her article.

Koepp's article is unique in that it explores the attitudes of social work professionals towards authoritarianism, a phenomenon that has received hardly any significant attention in social work literature. Using an experimental research design. Koepp attempts to test several hypotheses about personality differences that are commonly assumed to exist between social work students and their grouping on the basis of desired area of professional employment, religious affiliation, and amount of prior experience in social work. The study findings seem to indicate that social work students preferring to work in corrections were no more authoritarian than their counterparts interested in other employment areas, such as psychiatric social work, child welfare, and social group work. However, the findings seem to indicate a slightly differential trend for social group work students, who were significantly more authoritarian than students in corrections, child welfare, and psychiatric social work. Implications arising out of Koepp's study are important to consider, for these will have bearing on both the selection of social work students in terms of their attitudinal values towards authority and their preparation in professional education for social work.

ELLIOT STUDT

10

An outline for study of social authority
factors in casework

In a recent class in advanced casework, where a parole case was under
study, the students formulated alternative propositions about the nature
of casework in an authoritative setting. Several students believed that the
correct formulation would be, "Casework services are provided in spite
of the authority which the caseworker must exercise by the nature of his
job." Others suggested that it would be more accurate to say, "Casework
services are given in and through the exercise of the authority inherent in
the job." In a recent article, "The Function of Contact in Psychotherapy
with Offenders,"[1] the authors make the point that the psychotherapist who
is not part of the legal structure must establish with the offender this separation from legal structure in order to achieve a therapeutic relationship.
These are random illustrations of the variety of current ideas about
authority and helping which are assumed by many caseworkers to imply
that professional help to offenders, directed toward change of attitudes
and behavior, is best offered outside the "authoritative agency."[2]

Reprinted with permission of the Family Service Association of America, New
York, from *Social Casework*, xxxv, 231–8, June 1954.
1 / By Melitta Schmideberg, M.D., and Jack Sokol, in SOCIAL CASEWORK, Vol.
xxxiv, No. 9 (1953), pp. 385–392.
2 / Both S. A. Szurek and Erich Fromm have defined the word "authoritarian" in
such a way that the term "authoritative" would seem more appropriate for application to social agencies. S. A. Szurek ("Emotional Factors in the Use of Authority,"
in Ethel L. Ginsburg, ed., *Public Health Is People*, Commonwealth Fund, New
York, 1950, pp. 212–213) uses the term "authoritative" when the authority relationship is "democratic" or legitimate, and is exercised for the welfare of the subordinate;
and applies the term "authoritarian" to situations that involve "coercive power" or
the exploitation of the subordinate individual by the dominant individual. See also
Erich Fromm, *Escape from Freedom*, Farrar and Rinehart, New York, 1941, pp.
164–165, for a similar distinction between "rational authority" and the "inhibiting
authority" characteristic of the "authoritarian personality."

Since most of the literature dealing with psychological treatment of offenders has been written by persons outside the formal legal structure, or adjunctive to it, there has been little professional examination of the problems and skills of the caseworker who does carry direct legal responsibility for the offender. Up to this point, the profession has, in general, disposed of questions concerning authority in the casework process by using two propositions: (1) that casework is practiced most freely and satisfyingly in a setting where authority plays the least "handicapping" role; and (2) that in any case where authority factors enter into the relationship, a comfortable attitude on the part of the caseworker toward authority is, in general, all that is required to achieve skilful use of such authority factors. Since there are elements of authority in every agency that offers social services, a more precise development of theory concerning the relationships between helping and authority might be considered a useful contribution to the total body of casework theory.

Discussion of authority factors in the casework process is frequently unclear because the word "authority" itself is left undefined. Two definitions of authority from related disciplines may be clarifying: one referring to the sociological base from which stem formal authority structures; the other formulating the psychological factors that enter into all authority relationships.

A useful definition of authority, derived from sociological analysis, is found in *Power and Society*, by Lasswell and Kaplan,[3] where a series of definitions of the significant words "influence," "power," and "authority" is offered. According to this formulation, *influence* is the generic term, defined as "value position and potential," and its exercise "consists in affecting the policies of others than the self." *Power* is only one – but one of the most important – of the operative values on which influence relations are based. It is defined as "participation in the making of decisions," with emphasis on the fact that power is that form of influence relation which involves effective control over the policy of others. *Authority* is defined as "formal power," "expected and legitimate," or that use of power which has been legitimized in the institutional structure of society.

These authors recognize that a psychological factor enters into all operations by persons within such formal structure:

Authority is thus the expected and legitimate possession of power ... To say that a person has authority is to say not that he actually has power but that the political formula assigns him power, and that those who adhere to the

3 / Harold D. Lasswell and Abraham Kaplan, *Power and Society*, Yale University Press, New Haven, 1950. See pp. 71, 75, 133.

formula expect him to have power and regard his exercise of it as just and proper ... Thus ascription of authority always involves a reference to persons accepting it as such ... Authority is in this sense "subjective"; its existence depends on someone's think-so ...[4]

Thus, authority, for the purpose of sociological analysis, is power assigned to a position, and exercised by the individual in that position as he participates in the making of decisions by others. It requires both the delegation of that power to the position according to legitimate means, and the acknowledgment by the individual toward whom the authority is exercised that such exercise of power is "just and proper."

AUTHORITY RELATIONSHIPS IN THE SOCIAL AGENCY

Translating these sociological definitions into terms that may be useful in understanding authority relationships in social agencies, we find that power over community resources has been delegated to social agencies to which persons in need of such resources turn; and that authority within the agencies has been assigned to personnel known as caseworkers, who are therefore able to participate effectively in the decisions of clients through the exercise of this formal and legitimate power. Many agencies employ for these positions of authority only those individuals who have, following a period of professional preparation, demonstrated skill and responsibility in the exercise of influence in the lives of those in need. In such instances the authority of expertness, formally recognized through the professional structure of education and experience, coincides with the authority delegated to the position in the agency and is the basis for selection of persons to fill these positions. Every agency, private or public, professionally staffed or not, represents the community-sponsored organization of resources and the resulting delegation of authority to official persons who administer these resources to clients, and who thus exercise formally sanctioned influence over the lives of others.

Since casework involves not only the distribution of community resources through socially recognized channels but also the use of interpersonal relations in order to help clients use such resources, we need, for the purposes of social work theory, a psychological definition of authority as well as one drawn from sociological analysis. Erich Fromm has defined authority as "an interpersonal relation in which one person looks upon another as somebody superior to him."[5] It is this acknowledged superiority of one over the other which always appears in a psychological

4 / *Ibid.*, p. 133.
5 / Fromm, *op. cit.*, p. 164.

authority relationship – for example, in the teacher-student relationship – that Fromm selects as "the condition for the helping of the person subjected to the authority."[6] All the authority relations included in the definition by Lasswell and Kaplan involve this psychological factor to a certain extent; not all the relationships in which Fromm's "authority" appears are also formally recognized and supported in social structure. However, most of the authority relationships with which social workers deal, such as parent-child, teacher-student, and caseworker-client relationships, are socially recognized and operate within a framework of institutionalized authority relationships.

Social work has long recognized the fact that helping by means of the casework relationship depends upon the acknowledgment by the client that the caseworker is superior to himself for the *purposes of the problem at hand*, and so is able to help. Out of unsatisfying experiences with the impotence of formal authority alone to effect significant changes in the lives of human beings, caseworkers developed the doctrine of the crucial importance of the *voluntary* request for help, since the client, by this act, gives the caseworker the right to help. A formal authority relationship has always been able to secure certain external conformities in behavior depending on the client's need to secure services. But a more meaningful influence relationship is achieved only when the client genuinely joins with the caseworker in dealing with a commonly acknowledged problem, and gives to the caseworker temporary leadership responsibilities in this process. The caseworker accepts the temporary dependency implied in this relationship and attempts to encourage in the client whatever capacities for solving the problem exist within him. In this process the particular authority relationship moves toward dissolution as the client becomes stronger and more able to deal independently with his situation.

An analysis of authority factors in casework, therefore, reveals both social and psychological aspects. Every casework relationship starts with a formal authority relationship. The caseworker is unknown to the client, but is brought together with him by reason of the caseworker's position in an agency to which has been delegated the community's power to help. In each case, and in any social agency, the formal authority relationship must become a relationship of psychological authority if the client is to be helped. It may be said that, in the casework relationship, whenever the psychological aspects of the authority relation develop strongly, the formal, social authority aspects, although still present and effective, become secondary; and the casework process emerges as a particular, highly skilled form of the exercise of influence.

6 / *Ibid.*, p. 165.

It is possible to order all the social services within which casework is appropriately practiced along a continuum that suggests the specific patterning of the social and psychological authority relationships in each. Variations in patterns along the continuum depend on three interrelated variables: the source of the reality pressures bringing the client to the agency; the extent of responsibility for dealing with the problem assumed by the community; and the difficulty with which the caseworker establishes the psychological authority essential for helping.

At one end of this continuum are found such services as the private family agency and the outpatient psychiatric clinic. In these agencies, the source of pressure that brings the client for help tends to be the psychological suffering caused by stress of problems and maladjustments. The authority of the caseworker depends primarily on professional expertness that is recognized both by the agency in employing him and by the client in seeking this particular kind of help. The casework relationship begins with a degree of psychological readiness on the part of the client to acknowledge the helping authority of the caseworker. In such agencies the client generally remains within the relationship only if he experiences help.

In agencies such as Travelers Aid societies and medical social service departments, the stress that brings the client for help is often related to external emergencies which bother him but which he seldom perceives as suffering produced by an inner problem. In such agencies the client's acceptance of authority rests heavily on his experience of a reality situation in which he lacks the ability to help himself. In the medical agency the authority of the doctor, who is given great prestige in our society, may influence the patient to perceive the caseworker also as an authority person capable of helping him.

The stress of economic need, a particularly severe external reality pressure, is the effective cause that brings the client to the public welfare agency. In response to this kind of need the community has established public agencies within which the power of the community to relieve need is delegated by law to officials who administer the eligibility requirements in providing services. A century ago, clients receiving such help were assigned a semi-wardship status in relation to the community, with certain restrictions, such as denial of the right to vote to persons on the relief rolls, and community assumption of the right to make disposition of children whose parents could not support them. Such widespread authority over the lives of the economically dependent is no longer part of our public assistance programs, although in relation to the economic aspects of the client's life the authority is unmistakable. A further extension of explicit authority exercised by the community over a particular aspect of the client's life is seen in the public health services, from which individuals with certain illnesses, such as venereal diseases and tuberculosis, must accept medical services and the concomitant restrictions whether they desire them or not.

A more comprehensive assertion of community authority in relation to the life of the client is observed in those agencies in which the client is a ward of the state. In many child welfare services the caseworker is responsible for overseeing and approving all the basic life provisions for such wards. The protective care provided for the mentally deficient and mentally ill wards of the community asserts the right and duty of the community both to provide for and to control certain individuals who may be dangerous to themselves or to others. In these agencies the client enters the casework relationship without voluntary request and is held within it by means of the social authority delegated to the caseworker. Securing the client's acceptance of the caseworker's psychological as well as social authority is necessary in these situations and may be easy or difficult depending on many factors.

In the correctional agencies of the community the authority laid upon the agency includes not only responsibility to care for persons who have been made wards of the state by reason of criminal behavior, but also the responsibility to protect the community from further destructive behavior. The workers in such agencies become "supervisors" of legally determined offenders, participating in legal, quasi-parental relationships with persons who have been assigned a restricted and minority type of status in society. These workers are expected both to administer the restrictions assigned by the community to offenders and to help the offenders modify attitudes and behavior in the direction of "adjustment." In this relationship the client participates without regard to his desire and often against his will. He is held in the relationship by a legal obligation, regardless of real need or psychological readiness. In such casework relationships the task of turning the formal authority relationship into a psychologically useful influence relationship is difficult but is of primary importance. Since in this form of casework service the effect of social authority factors on the casework process is particularly clear, an examination of the problems met in such casework, and the skills to be developed in relation to these problems, may offer clues to the therapeutic use of such authority in any setting.

SOCIAL AUTHORITY IN CORRECTIONAL AGENCIES

The social authority relationships in the correctional agency are established by law. The legally determined offender is assigned a restricted supervised status with associated obligations which must be fulfilled if he is to return to normal status in the community. Agencies are created to administer these restrictions and to provide services that will help the offender avoid further delinquent actions. The personnel of these agencies accept legal responsibility to "supervise" the general life adjustment of these wards of the community. Probation and parole officers are those government employees who accept this legal responsibility for supervision over offenders who are permitted to remain in the community. It is obvious, therefore, that it is not possible to speak of the practice of case-work by the probation and parole officer "in spite of his exercise of control." Either he can give help within the framework of his agency's assigned function, or he is not properly termed a caseworker.

If a job such as probation or parole is to be studied as casework, it is clear that the services offered in the discharge of its primary functions must be related to the needs of those who are served. Although the restricted status assigned to the offender, with the associated supervision, is legally determined by the community in reaction to an offense, it is often only a formal acknowledgment of a real need in the client for someone outside himself to assume more responsibility for him than is provided for in the normal, unrestricted status accorded a free member of the community.

On the basis of our knowledge of human growth we readily accept the principle that authority, in the sense of loving, effective participation by the more mature and responsible individual in the decisions of the less mature, is essential at all stages of development, particularly at the early, formative stages and in times of unusual stress. Clients who come to the correctional agency have usually experienced special stress and are often persons who, by personality structure, are poorly fitted to handle stressful situations. The correctional case load is largely composed of persons who cannot easily tolerate tension and who have low thresholds for its discharge, who are singularly inept in manipulating their available resources for the purpose of getting normal satisfactions, and who are only tenuously related to the normal group structure of society. The correctional caseworker observes continually in his work his client's ability to damage his own life through producing emergencies, engaging in guerrilla warfare with all representatives of authority, and alternating between acted-out expressions of hostility and dependency. For a large number of these persons the provision of a supervisory individual in their lives seems to be a particularly appropriate response to the needs they are expressing.

Scientific study of the personality types that appear most frequently in correctional agency case loads has been sporadic and is not yet fully developed. Characteristically, these persons do not themselves seek help and so have usually not been reached by those treatment services where individualized study is a usual function. Many of them are known only to the correctional agencies, which are chronically understaffed and limited in resources for research. It is clear, however, that proportionally few classically neurotic individuals and few who are clearly psychotic are to be found in case loads composed of caught and convicted offenders. The central core of the case load consists of those individuals who are variously classified as "acting-out personalities," "delinquent personalities," "anti-social characters," or psychopaths. Much more needs to be understood about the personality needs represented by such persons and the treatment skills that are required. In general we do know that these individuals tend to be persons who need external help in maintaining socially acceptable behavior as well as in mobilizing resources to deal with their problems. Like children, they tend to require in their lives some sponsoring person who has a legal right to provide these necessary services for them. Like children, also, many of them can use a period of supported dependency for their continued growth.

In the correctional case load, even those individuals whose personalities may be relatively well organized need certain services best provided by one who represents the authority of the community. For instance, most offenders require some help in adjusting to the experience of being labeled an offender. The experiences that offenders undergo in arrest, detention, and court hearing often intensify their tendency to withdraw from participation in the normal community, and so separate them still further from the normal group controls provided by the community. The community, perhaps unconsciously recognizing the potential danger to mental health in hostile separation from community life, has created in probation or parole a formal relationship between the offender and its representative, thus keeping him within the reach of influence and providing a bridge to reacceptance on both sides. Also, many legally determined offenders, simply by reason of their restricted status, require, as do many persons in minority status, some mediating person in authority who can effectively mobilize community support for them. Since persons of all kinds and with every sort of need are to be found in correctional case loads, much depends on the caseworker's ability to individualize these persons and their needs and to exercise authority accordingly. The correctional caseworker is responsible for determining the degree of seriousness of the individual offender's problems, how strong the supporting control structure needs to be, and what kinds of social and personal treatment are required. Thus the probation or parole officer, like any other caseworker, makes an individualized approach to persons in his case load in rendering a basic community service that is provided for a designated category of persons with problems.

CASEWORK FUNCTIONS WITH OFFENDERS

Making a differential diagnosis of needs and personalities is part of every caseworker's task. The probation or parole officer, however, has certain casework functions that seem particularly dependent upon his legal authority over the offender for their successful discharge: (1) holding the client within a relationship from which he cannot legally withdraw and within which the problems leading to delinquent behavior can be identified and tackled; (2) helping the client digest emotionally the experience of having been classed as an offender; (3) assuming sponsoring responsibility for the client in the re-establishment of normal relationships with the community.

In discharging these three responsibilities, the probation or parole caseworker is attempting to heal a broken social relationship between the offender and his community for the benefit of both. These tasks can be accomplished only by a person who has clear legal responsibility for the welfare of the client, and who is accepted as a responsible authority by both the client and the community.

If we accept the propositions that the services provided in legal supervision of the offender are designed to meet some urgent needs that he is evidencing in his behavior; that certain services cannot be given to him without the legal framework implied in such supervision; and that these services can be properly individualized within the legal requirements; then it is appropriate to study the casework skills by which help is given within such a framework. The social authority factors arising out of such a framework will be seen to affect the casework process and will modify the skills by which help is given. Following is a tentative list of all the skill problems met by the professional caseworker who seeks to give psychological help within the supervisory structure of probation or parole.

PROBLEMS IN ACHIEVING PSYCHOLOGICAL AUTHORITY

1 *Dealing with the characteristic negative transference attitudes which the offender brings to his first contact with the new person in authority and which affect the process of establishing a helping relationship.* These attitudes are, of course, primarily derived from early parental experiences, but in offenders they are found to be distorted and exaggerated by more

recent experiences with other representatives of community authority such as police, jailers, judges, and custody personnel in institutions. The offender's expectations of his new "supervisor" tend to be overwhelmingly negative, while his defenses against entering into a relationship with a person so perceived are strong, ranging from rigid control to fawning conformity. Perhaps the greatest hazard of work with the offender is the ease with which his readiness to perceive the caseworker as hostile, destructive, and magically powerful, and his resulting defense against relationship, render ineffective the worker's efforts to understand and to help.

Everything that Dr. Schmideberg has said[7] about the positive, direct action required on the part of the psychotherapist to establish, in the first interview, a reality relationship that will make communication and helping possible, is equally important for the caseworker who has supervisory responsibility for the client. The difference lies in the fact that the correctional agency caseworker, in making clear his position, will be explicit about just what legal functions he does carry in regard to the client's life. Beyond this difference he will be as active as the psychotherapist in evidencing knowledge of the offender's experiences and culture, in taking initiative to establish a relationship in which feeling can be expressed and to demonstrate that he is a person who can be trusted.

Important professional questions requiring study in connection with this problem include: What are the skills required to establish with the necessary speed this positive reality relationship? Are there individuals who, because of unusually severe difficulties with authority persons, are unable to relate on any basis except a formal one with the caseworker who is responsible for supervising them? If there are such individuals, how can they be recognized and steered to other services for treatment? What are the appropriate treatment goals for the relationship that it is possible to establish between the offender and the social authority figure in his life?

2 *Avoiding a distorted initial psychosocial diagnostic formulation; modifications in the client's behavior due to his experiences with law enforcement and correctional processes immediately preceding his first meeting with the supervising caseworker often occur.* This is a corollary of the first problem but emphasizes the effect of such experiences on psychosocial diagnosis. At whatever stage in the correctional process the caseworker begins with his client, he will find that the experiences preceding this relationship will have had effect not only on the feelings expressed by the client but also on his behavior and ways of relating. For instance, the parole officer may well find that, during the first six weeks to three months

7 / *Op. cit.*, p. 388.

of parole, the client's symptom picture be so much affected by the preceding period spent in the institution that beginning hypotheses concerning the nature of the client's personality will have to be modified as he becomes "free" psychologically as well as physically. In study of this problem, not only will characteristic distortions of the psychosocial picture resulting from certain kinds of experiences become clear, but the diagnostic value of these for understanding the client's patterns of dealing with authority will be demonstrated.

3 *Handling the increased dependency manifestations in the client's behavior resulting from his quasi-minority status.* This status has been assigned to him and stimulates what may be already severe dependency needs. These dependency strivings are particularly evident in the relationship with his "supervisor."

4 *Relating himself to the varied authorities institutionalized in his agency judicial, administrative, and treatment – which he must represent to the client.* In working with an individual client, the caseworker may be administering concurrently the orders of the court, the limitations of agency procedures, and the recommendations of the consulting psychiatrist. In the correctional agency, both judicial and administrative authorities set particularly stringent controls on the treatment process because of the weight of responsibility toward the community. As a caseworker, he needs to be able to differentiate with the client between the controls which govern them both and the areas in which he and the client have discretion in developing treatment plans. His own relationship with the authorities inherent in his agency will affect his ability to communicate comfortably with his client as a person in authority.

5 *Using legal procedures and the framework of restrictions as supports for treatment goals and as the content of a socially re-educative process with the client.* This point refers to the little understood skills involved in such formal processes as writing petitions in such a way that they contribute to the client's acceptance of reality; using the probation investigation so that at the end of the process the client has a better appreciation of his problem; structuring the court hearing experience in such a manner as to maximize its contribution to emotional education; handling parole rules so that they function in a way that brings significant questions for discussion into the relationship with the caseworker.

6 *Working with family members and community agencies from the vantage point of a person in authority in the client's life.* This use of one's position of authority in the client's life for the purpose of encouraging support from other persons, is a use of authority to which probation and parole officers must give much attention. The effect of his restricted status on the

offender's relationships, and the skills of an added figure in authority in dealing with the normally constituted authorities in the offender's life, need further elucidation as a part of our theory concerning the effect of social authority on casework processes.

Throughout his work with the offender, the caseworker in the correctional agency will be concerned to use his socially delegated authority to support and educate his client. While accepting his formal position of authority and using its structure for therapeutic purposes, he will also recognize that formal authority alone never accomplished the casework goal of freeing human beings for richer life. He will, therefore, not deny his position of authority; he will use it in many helpful ways; but he will also seek to build within its framework an experience of psychological authority which will result in a true influence relationship. In studying how an influence relationship may be built within the framework of formal authority, the above listing of points in the basic casework process, where some modification of skill in achieving a position of psychological authority occurs as a result of social authority factors, will be found useful. Since a formal framework of authority exists in all casework relationships, analysis of skill adjustments required in the correctional setting may offer meaningful suggestions about the use of social authority factors wherever they appear.

ELIZABETH DE SCHWEINITZ

KARL DE SCHWEINITZ

11

The place of authority in the protective
function of the public welfare agency

Authority is not one but two things, two separate principles so intimately related that they appear as one and indeed become one. It is with an analysis of this phenomenon that we commence our discussion of the place of authority in the protective function. For this analysis we turn to Porter R. Lee, speaking in 1923 at a meeting of the National Conference of Social Work.

"There is a kind of authority," said Mr. Lee, "that goes with status. The president, the king, the priest, the teacher, the manager, the parent, the policeman carry authority regardless of the qualifications of the person who holds the office. Whatever the source of such authority, it is recognized generally and traditionally receives respect. This is constituted authority, if we may spread a bit the strict meaning of this phrase. It is the authority of the office. ...

"Constituted authority, however, is not the only type which human beings follow. The guide, counselor, and friend is usually an authority, but he does not derive his authority from his status. Rather, he derives his status from his authority. Civilization has become so complex that no man can be an authority with respect to all matters that are vital in his life. In politics, in finance, in health, in recreation, in religion, in philosophy, in his vocation, he needs outside assistance. Anyone whose judgment in any one of these fields he respects may be to him an authority. Authority in this sense is not constituted. It is rather inherent in the wisdom and understanding of the individual. Inherent authority is the authority of experience and learning, leading to judgments which less experienced, less learned persons are willing to follow. Inherent authority is the authority of those whose lead we follow without any compulsion to do so."[1]

Reprinted by permission of the Child Welfare League of America, New York, from *Child Welfare*, XLIII: 286–91, 315, June 1964.
1 / Porter R. Lee, "Changes in Social Thought and Standards Which Affect the

CHANGING ATTITUDES TOWARD USE OF AUTHORITY

In the history of the movement to protect children, constituted authority came first. It was based on the power to remove the child from the home, a power conferred by statute, by charter, and by public opinion. In its emphasis upon separation, it was a typical illustration of that anomaly of the nineteenth century – a preaching at all times of the sanctity of family life, but, in practice, a taking of the child from its parents on the slightest occasion. The first society to protect children from cruelty started when the institutional emphasis was at its peak. In 1875, there was little in the mind of the community, the court, the agency, or its representatives that regarded with reservation the action of the state in breaking up the home whether the cause was poverty or a comparatively minor deviation from what was considered to be proper behavior.

In those days, constituted authority could operate with only the slightest admixture of inherent authority. The agent of the protective organization could say "either, or" with an assurance that was seldom shadowed by any doubts of his own or of his supporting public. He commanded, admonished, reproached, threatened. He had a constituted authority that was strengthened by the fact that the court, like his agency, sensed the approval by the community of a policy that, with little hesitation, took the child from the home.

Then came the twentieth century, with its Children's Charter, its mother's pensions, its Social Security Act. Its beginning decades, which moralists have accused of undermining the family, have done more than all their predecessors to provide economic and social measures that can be used to conserve the spiritual values of the home. At the same time, the uses to which the constituted authority of the protective agency has been put and the ways in which it has been employed have changed, and there has come a growing appreciation of the importance of an inherent authority in its representative.

Today, public opinion no longer supports a wholesale use of the power to take children from their parents. Sometimes the law goes too far to the other extreme and is not specific enough in this respect. Thus, the statute authorizing protective measures in the District of Columbia includes no mention of the duty to initiate action to remove the child when its home is not suitable. The protective agency operates in this respect under a legal interpretation, not under a direct mandate. In general, the social worker now lacks that assurance from the community or within himself that previously he derived from the emphasis upon removal.

Family," in *Proceedings of the National Conference of Social Work* (Chicago: The University of Chicago Press, 1923), p. 289.

THE WORKER'S RESPONSIBILITY

The situational and psychological limitations of which the worker is increasingly aware are familiar to us all. The court, in deciding upon the recommendation to take the child, follows both the profession and the community in feeling that the burden of proof is upon the social worker who advocates such action. Facilities to implement a plan for removal are insufficient in number and in quality. So long as a home retains even partial values, it is better than a good institution and better than growing up under foster care. There is the problem of different standards within the same community. What is dirt to one person is little more than sweet disorder to another. How bad must physical conditions be to outweigh the values of an emotional setting that offers a measure of satisfaction to the child? Again, undesirable actions in an individual are only part of a total behavior. The mother may persist in leaving the child alone, but in other respects she seems to take reasonably good care of him. The boy tampers with buses in the park, but he is only 7 years old. The social worker is thus constantly confronted with the relativity of the situations and of the behavior that takes him to the family.

Against this is the absolute character of the action to remove, which he may initiate. The behavior may be partial, but the ultimate measure employed is total. The situation is not unlike the one that arises in the grant-in-aid programs of Federal or state governments. The Federal agency has the responsibility of assuring the Congress that the participating state is maintaining a proper administration, but administration is a succession of particular actions. It is one detail after another. In contrast, the ultimate recourse of constituted authority is complete and sweeping – the discontinuance of the grant. Similarly in the protective function, it is all or nothing. Either the child is taken or he is left where he is. There seems, in this respect, to be no halfway measure, nothing that can be appropriately balanced against a special item of undesirable behavior in the relationship between parents and children.

These limitations, which, in the main, derive from the basic change in attitude toward the family and in the development of our understanding of human personality, have shifted the base of the constituted authority of the agency and have modified the concept of the protective function. Constituted authority to a large extent now centers in the duty to investigate; in the power of the representative of the agency "to be there." It is a power that the protective agency exercises solely in its own discretion. It is a self-contained authority. Therefore, it has an absolute quality as contrasted with the reservations and restrictions that limit the power to remove.

THE PARENTS' LOSS OF INDEPENDENCE

The power to be there bears with terrible weight upon the parents with whom it is exercised. Investigation that enters into the relationship of parents with children would be difficult to endure even if it were an isolated procedure, but when the protective worker finds that the complaint is justified, that the life in the home jeopardizes the welfare of the child, he must continue to investigate; he must take from the parents what every man cherishes most of all, his right to live in privacy within his own walls. An official with an authority derived from the sanction of the community, whether his organization be public or voluntary, now has the power to impose himself upon the life of the family. The parents have lost their independence. They are no longer free. Even the actual removal of the child may not be so hard to bear as an alien presence in the home. The placement may come as a relief after the sense of restriction caused by the realization of the power of someone else "to be there."

Often the most oppressive feature of this power is the way it impinges upon the lesser details of life. We quote from the report of a worker who on a recent visit to a family found the mother not at home:

The three children – Mary, 10; Louise, 5; and Barbara 3 – were together in the one room the family occupies on the second floor. ... The worker asked Mary if she expected her mother back soon. She said yes ... and asked the worker to sit down. ... Barbara was sitting up in the middle of the bed. ... The worker remarked that she thought all three girls' dresses were attractive.

She then noticed that Barbara had no panties on, because her dress came up as she slid off the bed. Mary noted the worker's observation and said that Barbara and Louise had wet their panties. She pointed to coat hangers on the wall where she had hung the panties to dry after washing them out. Obviously, in order to please worker, she gave Louise the one pair of clean panties left to put on. Louise objected, saying her mother would not want her to. ... Mary then explained that her mother had in mind waiting to the last minute to put the clean panties on Louise before taking her to the clinic so that the clinic would approve.

The presence of the worker in and of itself had changed the plans of the family in this respect, and the worker had not said a word – she had only noticed.

She discussed a child care center with Mary, telling her about the swimming pool there. But Mary said her mother did not want her to go swimming – another item of difference. Then the worker talked to Mary about school. The worker wished Mary could go to school every day so she could catch up with the other children of her age.

Here is the real issue. The protective situation centers in school attendance. But it is another point of control.

Mrs. R came into the room hurriedly and said to Mary, "Why did you let
her" (i.e., the worker) "stay here? You knew I had to take Louise to the
clinic." And to worker, "What do you keep coming here for? It does not do
any good." The worker said she was sorry she felt that way, but she had really
come to let Mrs. R know she faced a serious charge that would involve court
action, and our agency would like to assist her in solving this problem, if
possible. The worker had intimated in a former interview that court action
would be taken if Mary was not kept in school.

Mrs. R then went on in a very irritated manner to accuse our agency. If
charges were brought, she did not care what we did; we had to prove things in
court. She was doing all right. After all, we just paid her rent and a little more,
but we were not going to run her family.

In the multiple-function agency from which this record is taken, the
assistance worker in this interview takes on the additional role of protection. The pressure on the mother is the greater, and it serves only to
emphasize the feeling of restraint and loss of freedom that goes with the
fact that the worker is there.

This power has always been a factor in protective work. The difference
today is in our greater appreciation of its psychological effect and in a
lesser reliance upon the principle of removal. This shift in emphasis has
been paralleled by a change in the concept of the protective function. In
the first days of the SPCC, enforcement was usually concentrated in one
organization, and most other activities that had to do with the family were
handled through other agencies. With the increase in psychological understanding came a realization that more than threat and compulsion was
needed if children were to have the kind of physical care and the sort of
social relationships that they require from their parents. A new approach
was made to the problem. Ample illustration of this approach will be
found in law or in administrative policy. In the District of Columbia, for
example, the statutory duties of the Board of Public Welfare include, as
expressed in one and the same clause, an obligation "to investigate the
circumstances affecting children handicapped by dependency, neglect or
mental defect, or who may be in danger of becoming delinquent and to
provide such services for the care and protection of such children as will
assist in conserving satisfactory home life."[2] In effect, the representative
of the protective agency says to the parents, "This must change; can I
help?" More than a constituted authority is required by this paradoxical

2 / Public Law 397, Seventy-seventh Congress, Section 1, Subsection 1.

combination of command and offer. Inherent authority, hitherto merely a desirable factor in the protective job, is now a necessity. The question, "Can I help?" can be followed by the answer "Yes," only if the parents sense more than the authority of office in the individual who has entered their home. The use of "can" instead of "may" is significant. Permission to help is not enough. The parents must want to effect change and must want to use the representative of the agency in doing this. The real question is not whether the social worker *may* help, but whether he *can* help. Whether he can depends upon the personal qualities and the professional discipline that combine to establish his inherent authority and upon the parents' appreciation of that authority as something that can be of constructive service to them and that they want to use in offering a new life to their children. "Can I help?" The social worker can help only if the parents decide that he can.

THE NATURE OF INHERENT AUTHORITY

What, then, is the nature of the inherent authority that has come to play a decisive part in the protective function? It may be said to include four major elements.

1 *An understanding of the law; of the administrative policies of the organization; of the attitude of the court; of the standards in health, housing, and similar areas that the constituted agencies in those fields support, and the resources they offer; and an appreciation of what in family life the community believes should be maintained.* One can know law, policies, and institutional standards. The degree to which one can count upon the quality of judicial action will vary in every jurisdiction, but experience offers the social worker an indication of what he may expect. The community is not one but many. Opinion is usually divided, but one can perceive what the general trends are and the direction in which the civic leadership is heading. Thus, they are, in this factor of understanding, specifics about which one can be certainly informed and imponderables that one can only estimate. A knowledge of the certain and an awareness of the variable can contribute to their possessor a kind of security that helps to establish his inherent authority.

2 *The capacity to ascertain and evaluate facts.* Does the complaint on its face justify investigation? The social worker must weigh the evidence and decide. If an investigation is necessary, and usually it is, he must be able to get at the essence of the matter. A neighbor or a separated husband says that a mother swears horribly at her children or that they are out on the streets late at night. The situation may be more serious in the mind of

the complainant than it is in fact; on the other hand, there may be under-lying conditions that, if discovered, would warrant intervention by the agency. The information that the social worker seeks must be relevant. To inquire – as one worker recently did – about whether the parents had a marriage license, when the issue was truancy, was confusing to the family and did not advance the solution of the problem. The worker must also be able to perceive what opportunities to get at the heart of the matter people offer him in what they say – to see that his response to the mother who in desperation says that her son must be crazy should not be so much inquiry about whether there have been mentally ill relatives in the family as about what it is in the boy's behavior that has caused her to make this comment.

3 *A recognition and an acceptance of one's constituted authority.* It is not easy to occupy a role that includes compulsion and the power to restrict the freedom of another person. We want other individuals to like us; at least we want a comfortable relation with them. Except for excursions into the sadistic, which vary in their frequency and severity with most people – and, let us hope, are minimal to the point of absence in the social worker – the urge, where one feels the isolation of authority, is to want to make friends in a kind of propitiatory spirit. The representative of the protective agency must recognize the implications of his status and main-tain that impersonal, considerate, professional expression of himself that avoids the punitive on the one hand and the ingratiating on the other. He must know the boundaries of his authority and be able to live within them, appreciating where his responsibilities begin and end.

4. *The capacity to distinguish what is possible from what is not possible, and to deal with the individual and with the community on that basis.* What are the parents capable of doing? If they have not in themselves that which can, with help, cope with the situation, it is only frustrating to cause them to commence what they cannot complete. We are swinging back from the extreme position of feeling that placement is a confession of failure and coming to recognize that, for a variety of problems, there must also be many forms of treatment and that foster family and institu-tion each has its specific contributions to make.

WORKER'S RELATIONSHIP WITH PARENTS

Much more difficult in the protective job is the necessity for facing condi-tions that are unsatisfactory but not so bad as to warrant the removal of the children. To quote Helen Witmer: "The idea dies hard (in both pro-fessional and lay circles) that, once in the hands of a social worker, a client can be led to desire what somebody else deems best for him."[3] The protective agency will find families in which, desire or no desire, nothing can be effected. Not only is it hard for the representative of the organization to accept this and to discontinue activity; it is even harder for the complainant or the succession of complainants. "Something must be done," they feel and say. To deal with persons in the varying states of mind with which they thus come to the agency – exasperation, or vindictiveness, or lofty self-satisfied morality – requires all that inherent authority can provide. One must not be defensive; one must not cut people short; one must not overexplain; one must not divulge information about the person complained against; one must indicate appreciation and understanding, but with a recognition that the mere saying of these words is not necessarily convincing. Here is an area of the job that has had some special study and attention and warrants even more.

Transcending and permeating the elements that enter into an inherent authority is a professional self-discipline – the ability to act responsibly and appropriately in relation to the protective purpose; with an understanding and an awareness of the other person – parent or child; and with regard for, and in relation to, whatever strength that person has to offer, whether the child remains in the home or is taken away.

Any discussion of authority, constituted and inherent, in the protective function inevitably runs the danger of an exclusive preoccupation with the status and activity of the social worker. We must avoid falling into the error that Cotton Mather made in 1699 in his little book, *A Family Well Ordered, or An Essay to Render Parents and Children Happy in One Another*. He had addressed to the fathers 36 out of the 37 pages devoted to a discussion of the duty of parents to their children, before he recalled the importance of another member of the household, and added: "Let it be remembered that the fathers are not the only parents obliged thus to pursue the salvation of their children. You that are mothers have not a little to do for the souls of your children."

Let us remember that when the social worker says "This must change; can I help?" and the answer is "Yes," his purpose may be the protection of the child, but the object of his service is the parents. It is their authority, constituted in part, but mostly and primarily inherent, that must be the means of achieving "a family well ordered" and "parents and children happy in one another." If the answer is "No," for the present at least, and the child must be removed, his parents may still be his most important re-

3 / Helen Leland Witmer, *Social Work* (New York: Rinehart & Company, 1942), p. 190.

lationship, and a good deal of the quality of this may be destroyed by the social worker who does not recognize the parents' place in the child's life or who does not consciously seek to conserve the parents' inherent as well as their constituted authority.

PRESERVATION OF PARENT-CHILD RELATIONSHIP

The person who, in seeking a career with a protective agency, advances as a qualification the fact that he likes to work with children has given an insufficient reason. He must want to work with adults, specifically with parents. He must understand children, and he must be aware of the problem the child is facing; but so long as he is engaged in offering help, his basic activities must be directed to the parents.

Everything that he does, from the first step to the last, must be undertaken with regard for its influence upon the relationship between parents and child. If the constituted authority of the father and the mother in this relationship is jeopardized – and the circumstances that summoned the agency may have already caused it considerable damage – then the chances of success with the child have been greatly reduced. The affections of children may transcend every other consideration. As one young woman was overheard to say, "Parents are peculiar, but you love them." To assume, however, that filial attachment will overcome the effect of a disregard of the parent by the social worker is to open the way to failure. This danger is accentuated when the representative of the agency establishes his initial or continuing relationship with the child.

For example, the representative of a protective agency is asked to intervene because a boy has run away from home and is afraid to go home because he will be whipped. He is not yet 9 years old. The social worker begins by interviewing the child in the house of detention. She then takes him to his own home and on the way buys him candy. She has not yet seen the parents. Has she in this taken the dominant role? Has she invaded the constituted authority of father and mother? Will she become the one to whom the boy will turn? Has she taken something from the parents?

Contrast this method beginning with that of another worker assigned to the same family following a subsequent running away. Her first contact is with the mother at home; her second with the boy in the detention institution; her third with both parents in her office. Here the constituted authority of the parents is respected and here also the mutual responsibility of both parents is recognized. The previous worker had done just the reverse. Not only had she established her primary relationship with the boy, but in her first interview she took over from the parents the decision of how they would deal with him. To the father, she said that the boy was afraid of him and asked him not to whip him or to allude to the runaway. To the mother, she said that the boy must not go to school in the shoes he was wearing, that the mother must take him to and from school and not allow him to go out alone.

There was no discussion of the situation. She told the parents what to do and assigned to each his or her task. The parents followed the letter of her instructions but, almost inevitably, only the letter. The boy ran away again; the father blamed the mother; the mother, the father; and the social worker reproached them both.

To talk over pros and cons and to work through the problem with the parents is, obviously, better than any amount of admonition and advice, whereas to censure has the effect of transferring the responsibility from the father and the mother to the social worker, and of widening the gap between the parents and their children.

Though the child is the *objective*, the father and the mother are the *objects* of protective activity. Whether the action is to remove the child, whether it is to ascertain if change is necessary or if change has taken place, or whether it is to offer service when the answer is "Yes" to the question, "Can I help?" the place of the parent as parent should be recognized. Everything that the social worker does should be undertaken with this in mind. That means to intervene only when intervention is unavoidable and to continue that intervention only as long as the necessity for compulsion continues or until the child can be placed, or as long as the parents can use the help that stems from an inherent authority. And that authority must recognize and support the parents' desire and their capacity to play their appropriate part in the life of the child.

"Authority," reads the sentence at the head of a National Conference program, "frequently verging on the authoritarian, is implicit in the client-worker relationship, though perhaps in a minor degree." We hope that an authoritarian authority does not enter at all into the client-worker relationship, but authority in the protective function is not minor. It is what initiates the contact; it is what insists upon change. To think that it ever ceases to be present is to be unwilling to accept the implications of the protective role.

Cotton Mather, writing in his *Family Well Ordered*, as a parent to parents, said:

"Our authority should be so tempered with kindness, and meekness and loving tenderness that our children may fear us with delight."

Words do not mean now what they meant in 1699, and so the two social workers who speak to you through this paper will translate Dr. Mather into the language of today: Let us so temper the constituted with the inherent that the burden of authority carried by the worker and the weight of authority felt by the parent will be easier to bear – and that the child may receive in protection and, let us hope, in happiness the most that is possible in this most difficult of situations.

12

Power and authority in treatment –
a private agency point of view

Discussions of the proper place of power and authority, as these may be used in treating the criminal offender, must not ignore the extensive literature on these subjects and the wide divergence of opinion and theory expressed both within and between the professions studying or working in the correctional field. Nor can these discussions exclude the related problems of freedom and the responsibility which goes with freedom.

In a recent paper[1] on the dilemmas presented to the helping professions by the issues of freedom and responsibility. Rollo May discusses the inadequacy of both the "exaggerated freedom solution" and "the identification of therapy and counselling with the moral and social controls of society." Erich Fromm in his "Escape from Freedom" argued that modern man may be fearful of freedom and of the individuality he has achieved and that segments of the population have shown a clear drive to submit to or to be dominated by outside and "irrational" authority.[2] The late Dr. Robert Lindner, who had direct experience with offenders, expressed the same kind of concern when he took the social agencies to task for supporting the "Eleventh Commandment" – "You Must Adjust."[3]

On the other hand, from professionals who have had a good deal of practical experience in the correctional fields, we hear rather different views expressed. In a project report of the curriculum study for the Coun-

Reprinted by permission of the Canadian Association of Social Workers, Ottawa, from *The Social Worker*, XXXI: 18–26, January-February 1963.

1 / Rollo May, "Freedom and Responsibility Reexamined." Paper read Apr. 18, 1962 at meeting of the American College Personnel Association, Chicago. Copyright 1962 by Teachers College, Columbia University.
2 / Erich Fromm, *Escape from Freedom*. New York: (Rinehart & Co.), 1941.
3 / Robert Lindner, *Must You Conform*. New York: (Rinehart & Co.), 1956.

cil on Social Work Education, Elliot Studt says, "the professional social worker must integrate treatment and control functions in one professional role if he is to be a competent practitioner in correctional service."[4]

Schmideberg insists, "The aim of psychotherapy is to sensitize the offender to social pressure, to develop a normal attitude toward punishment, and to teach him to foresee consequences and be motivated rationally by such foresight. The aim is to adjust him to the legal framework, not to take the framework away."[5]

My observations about the use of authority are based largely on experiences within a private agency and are therefore highly subjective and limited to that experience. These views must also be seen in the context of the agency's history, development and purposes.

The current focus of the social work services in the John Howard Society of Ontario (like its counterparts in other Canadian Provinces) is related in an important way to the comparatively slow development of public correctional services in Canada. The non-institutional correctional services in particular are in their early stages of development, with the National Parole Service now only a few years old.

Traditionally, Canadian prisoners have been released at the expiry of their sentence as free agents in the community. This is still the case with roughly 80% of the inmate population. The historical fact that governments have taken little legislative responsibility for the ex-inmate was one stimulus for socially conscious citizens in many communities to assume this responsibility. As a consequence, groups of citizens in industrial centres formed voluntary after-care societies to meet the obvious needs of the released offender.

The John Howard Society of Ontario as a private social work agency now provides preparatory services in penal institutions prior to release as well as after-care services. These services are supported primarily by Community Chests and United Funds and in a secondary fashion by government funds. Last year in thirteen industrial communities in Ontario, for example, on combined budgets of close to a quarter of a million dollars, the John Howard Society of Ontario, through social work staff and volunteers, provided service to over 2,300 ex-inmates.

Significant in the development of agency attitudes to the use of authority are the broad correctional framework within which the agency operates and its experience with ex-offenders.

4 / Elliot Studt, "Education for Social Workers in the Correctional Field." Council on Social Work Education, New York, 1959.
5 / Melitta Schmideberg, "The Offender's Attitude Toward Punishment," *Journal of Criminal Law, Criminology and Police Science*, v (3), 1960.

As a private social work agency it has developed a unique partnership with the government by integrating its services closely with institutions and parole authorities. Out of lengthy experience with ex-inmates asking for service voluntarily its workers are impressed with the failure of the majority of these ex-offenders to sustain voluntary helping relationships to the point where basic problems are really resolved. On the other hand, the staff find that a more socially useful service is rendered with parolees placed under agency supervision by parole authorities. It is in this latter service that the agency has had its most concrete experience with the use of authority and all that this implies.

Thirty years ago the John Howard Society of Ontario described itself as a "Prisoner's Aid Society." It would appear that the concern then focused primarily on the man, to provide tangible help and job placement to him as a socially isolated, disadvantaged and stigmatized ex-prisoner. Within the past ten years, the term "correctional after-care agency" is more frequently chosen to describe the agency. This reflects a shift in service to one in which after-care services are closely integrated with institutional programs and correctional treatment is continued as the ex-prisoner faces the demands and pressures of the free community. The focus is not on the offender in isolation but upon him as an individual seeking to become a member of the community once more.

It might fairly be said that as penal conditions and community attitudes toward the offender have improved the agency has become less concerned with "protecting the client" and increasingly concerned with discovering ways and means of helping him to invest more of himself in coming to grips with his broad social situation and emotional problems. The use of limits, the setting of expectations, the exercising of control and the carrying out of various authority roles are some of the basic skills considered necessary for social workers in this setting.

The John Howard Society of Ontario takes the position that authority is inherent in and inseparable from its structure and the service it provides to human beings. Private social agencies are all authorized by the communities which create and support them. Citizens forming Boards of Directors lay down policies and practices of service on behalf of the communities which in turn hold them accountable. Social workers have authority delegated to them to administer these services in a responsible fashion within prescribed limits, by approved methods and in line with agency goals.

Within this organizational authority the social worker assumes a position of very real authority himself – an authority created by his peculiar knowledge and skills, his responsibility to make decisions about giving or denying service and to set specific conditions and requirements for service in line with general policies and purposes.

The kind of authority used within the after-care agency, as in the public probation and parole services, will hinge very greatly upon the personality, integrity and competence of the service staff. Sensitivity of the social worker to his interaction with and influence on clients in this respect and to the hazards and problems involved is a measure of his professional competence. Authority in our Agency will be expressed in formal and informal terms, giving or denying, in controls, limits, intervention, expectations and protections. Social workers in our Agency would reject, I am certain, an authority which relies on coercion or threats, an "authority" described by one social philosopher as one for which "no good reason for obedience to it can be given other than the fact that it has the power to make itself obeyed."[6]

When social workers in the John Howard Society of Ontario assume a parole supervisory role, their authority includes surveillance which by definition means close observation. This surveillance involves the evaluation of the parolee's behaviour through personal, family or community contacts. This is a realistic checking and control function. It is obviously different from the surveillance conducted by police, which in practice appears to range from shadowing and questioning to the apprehension of suspects.

One ideal aim of this Agency is to provide a continuity of interchange with a person in authority so that the ex-offender has the maximum opportunity to learn from this experience to handle the demands and responsibilities of broader society where he has the capacity for such learning. It is, as Ellit Studt says, "an exercise of influence,"[4] an experience in living which cannot ignore the minimal expectations of the community.

It is apparent that the quality of authority may differ from agency to agency, in either the public or private field, depending upon the legal status of the client and the kind of formal authority which lies within the agency. Basically, however, it is our view that the difference in the authority that rests with public or private agencies is only a matter of degree. If it is truly the goal of the private agency to enable improved social functioning of the ex-prisoner in the free community, its methods cannot isolate its clients from the values of the community or protect the offender from experiencing the pressures of the community's basic rules.

6 / Charles Frankel, "Social Philosophy and the Professional Education of Social Workers," *The Social Service Review*, xxxiii (4), December 1959.

"B" was a strong aggressive man. In his late twenties, with fifteen years of institutional experience behind him. His tremendous energy and good work skills made his initial adjustment appear outstanding. Everything was done in a rush without much planning and with negligible patience when frustrated.

"B" called one evening, swearing, fuming and castigating "the cop who tagged my old car with a $20.00 parking fine." "They are out to get me. Will you pay the fine or get it fixed for me?"

The social worker suggested to "B" that he come to the office to discuss this matter. He let him ventilate his wrath some more and then insisted that he look at his statement "They are out to get me." He helped him accept the fact that he would have to pay his own parking fine like any other citizen who parked his car in a rush hour zone.

The social worker in this situation recognized that the ex-prisoner was having great difficulty accepting "Square John" rules. However, it would have served no useful purpose to pay the fine and to help him avoid his basic responsibility for his own behaviour.

At times it would appear that the authority inherent in the correctional after-care agency is more difficult to handle than it would be in a public agency. Service policies in this private agency are written in rather broad terms, leaving a good deal to the discretion of the social worker for individual judgment. Without rather precise regulations there may be a tendency to greater conflict for the social worker who has to analyze motivation rapidly and decide, sometimes under unusual pressure from the ex-inmate, if the meeting of his request will, on a long term basis, help or hinder him.

"M" was a particularly demanding, impulsive, intense man who had great difficulty relating to anyone out of the prison culture. His agency service previously was characterized by permissiveness in the meeting of his tangible demands. Within the situation he developed a warmth and trust for one social worker but had great difficulty tolerating others. He saw help coming from the individual as a person rather than through the agency.

Having to meet a new person was exceedingly difficult for him. His demand for tangible help was unrealistic and excessive. He said he was broke, he needed help to get a start with room and food and he had spent his fairly liberal prison gratuity paying off some debts. The worker said that he would be glad to talk to him further about his request, if he could get some receipts for the debts which he had paid. "M" simply could not tolerate this condition. He threatened the worker and stormed out of the office saying that it was not his practice to get receipts from anybody.

The next time that "M" came from the penitentiary seeking service the experience was reviewed with him and service was interpreted as conditional on similar sorts of expectations. Although it was not an easy relationship, "M" was able to tolerate conditions more readily and subsequently to make significant and responsible steps to solve many of his own problems.

The social worker with a voluntary client in this instance had the authority to meet tangible needs but only if, in his judgment, the community's funds were spent constructively. This conscious use of his authority to set conditions, in the face of a reaction against his authority, ultimately led to a productive use of service and, we think, a rather new experience for this particular offender.

One of the other areas where the limits and controls are used positively in the period of transition from institutional jurisdiction to fuller freedom is in our insistence that the offender go through the process of obtaining from the community what is rightfully his. Whether or not the legally defined offender perceives the voluntary correctional agency as less authoritarian is a moot question in our mind. We are not at all sure that he finds it more comfortable, as a voluntary client, to express feeling about public and legally constituted authority. The fact is that he often expresses these feelings. His mistrust of authority – of the system – is quite clear. Often, as a colleague describes it, "he is still in the institution" and fighting it.

His plea to a "more benign authority" like a private agency to meet those needs which are normally met by legislative right through public agencies cannot be accepted. The offender must be helped in the community to face the discomfort of applying for such things as medical treatment and public assistance. The important thing is to help him to go through the experience and to help him examine a number of alternatives to solving problems.

With the parolee under the supervision of our agency, the constituted authority lies with the Regional Representative of the parole authority. The parolee is released under the authority of this public servant with several conditions to his parole agreement. One basic condition is that he accept the "supervision and assistance" of the John Howard Society. This relationship entails regular reporting by the agency to the parole authority on progress, changes in behaviour and violation of conditions. It allows the supervisor wide flexibility in the requirements he might set for the parolee, especially in the frequency and nature of the face-to-face contacts. In our opinion the restrictions are reasonable, they allow for individualized controls, the testing of social capacity and changes in control when these are indicated.

This type of authority around client behaviour permits the worker and the client to know precisely the framework in which they will operate. It provides, in other words, "something to chew on."

"J" has had a unique history with parental figures. His father was brutal, his mother most permissive to the point of encouraging his juvenile crime. On his last sentence to penitentiary, a particularly long one, there were petitions to increase the severity of the sentence. The gap between this inmate and the administrative authority widened. Hostility was focussed and intensified with every custodial officer on duty. "J's" charge sheet had entries in the hundreds, sometimes for serious charges like assault but more frequently for small infractions of the rules. Some of the rules seemed unreasonable and it is not surprising that "J" had irrational outbursts at times. He came to expect unreasonableness and capriciousness in most of the people who were in control over him. He learned to be quite a manipulator.

In his first contact with the supervisor he assured the supervisor that he had heard a lot of nice things about him and terminated the conversation nervously by saying, "You and I will get along fine – as long as I have my own way."

His first interview was a short one. Both the supervisor and the client were intensely uncomfortable. The parolee wished to control the supervisor by terminating the interview, using the excuse that someone was waiting for him.

The supervisor allowed the interview to terminate but early the next day asked "J" to return for a further interview. Quickly and directly he made reference to the initial interview and the fact that he thought it was essential to set out some clearly understood expectations now upon which future contact would be based. He did no exploration of past relationships. He simply made the statement that the parolee was probably unhappy about this need to set out expectations but he knew that "J" was a man who responded best when reasonable rules were set. "J" asked how the worker knew so much about him. The supervisor replied that he had taken the trouble to talk to many institutional people about him because of his interest in seeing him make a successful readjustment. "J" made no further comment at that time.

In subsequent interviews he tested the worker frequently with requests which appeared to be premature in the light of his recent discharge. He was able to accept refusal of this type of request, to look at the alternatives and the reasons for the refusals. Some hostility was still expressed at different times but the limits were clearly understood. "J" subsequently maintained a daily contact for a period of months although this was never set as a requirement.

As contrasted with the voluntary relationship with the ex-offender, the authority delegated to us in parole supervision provides a continuity in the after-care period in which negative reactions to restrictions can be experienced and examined as these happen. We feel that this gives us a better opportunity to understand these reactions and to handle such stresses as the facts of life.

On the other hand, the authority of the worker in the parole situation can provide a framework in which the ex-offender must stay to face his pattern of solving problems and to learn new methods of meeting problems.

"N" was a passive, solitary restless 23-year-old. A serious childhood illness took him out of contact with his father and he lived under the protective wing of an indulgent and excessively permissive mother. The mother's death led to "N" leaving the home to lead a nomadic existence in the sub-culture of the racetrack where he was only required to develop superficial relationships with people.

The goal of the supervisor was to determine whether "N" could move back into normal family relationships. He worked persistently over an eight month period in weekly interviews with "N' and in interpretative interviews with "N's" older brothers, his employer and his foreman. He combined consistent support for "N" with consistent limits and expectations that "N" try to stay in the situation rather than to seek his associations in the racetrack field.

It was necessary for him to insist on the keeping of appointments, to examine "N's" rationalizations closely and to tighten up controls as he saw depression and deterioration set in.

When it became clear that "N" could only tolerate personal relationships in which expectations and demands were not too high the supervisor was able to reduce his controls and to allow him to develop relationships less demanding than those of his family but more demanding than the racetrack sub-culture.

In a voluntary relationship this young man undoubtedly would have withdrawn and broken contact immediately. In a routine monthly check-in on parole supervision it is also unlikely that he would have faced his problem or shared them with the supervisor.

In this agency we are gathering a body of experience in the use of authority in contacts with important members of the offender's family unit, if he has been fortunate enough to have maintained these kinds of relationships. A clear attempt is made prior to offering supervision on behalf of the parolee to interpret both to the potential parolee and his family the kinds of limits within which the parolee must function. Permission is sought for regular contact and communication with the wife or other significant family members, in addition to the contact required of the parolee. It is our experience that total family attitudes about authority are often distorted and to work with the parolee while ignoring his family unit can bring about a few significant gains.

Similarly, if the offender agrees to allow this kind of contact, a constructive service can be provided to support wives or parents or other individuals to understand and to choose the kinds of limits which they would want to place on the offender's behaviour, with or without outside controls.

"S" had an extensive history of excessive drinking, with blackouts and amnesia for events as early as age 18. During a prolonged drinking bout he was responsible for the death of a casual acquaintance.

His return to the community on a very lengthy parole was conditional among other things upon abstention from intoxicants. He adapted well to community responsibility and controlled his drinking for a few months after release. It was natural, in the face of this evidence, to relax supervision, to encourage independence and freer decision making.

A few months after discharge "S" voluntarily revealed his first drinking bout. To the supervisor it was a symptom which required closer evaluation and controls on his behaviour. It seemed to indicate the kind of relationship with a parolee which facilitated this type of revelation "in spite of authority." This later proved to be a fallacious assumption.

The worker chose to involve "S's" wife, with his permission, in an attempt to understand the problem. She was obviously fearful and the more fearful she became the more passive was her adjustment.

As she became aware of the nature of alcoholism she began to fear the arbitrary decisions of formal authority. The desire to retain her husband was stronger than the desire to help him. She assisted him in concealing further drinking bouts, expecting these to mean automatic revocation of the parole. Only when "S's" social adjustment in work and recreation deteriorated did his wife's anxiety drive her to reveal the true picture and to seek help from the same authority figure.

Because of parallels between current and pre-conviction behaviour the supervisor consciously took the role of formal authority and very firmly indicated that his behaviour would have to be more closely and regularly checked and that "S's" behavioural changes would have to be reported to the parole authority. This support and firmness appeared to give "S's" wife sufficient strength to begin to assert herself in the marriage relationship. She recognized that she could not delegate all decisions to her husband, particularly when he showed lack of capacity. She began for the first time perhaps to see herself as an important person in the family unit.

This kind of communication with a person in authority reduced the tendency to gloss over or to conceal behavioural changes. Ultimately it provided the opportunity for both the man and his wife to recognize the seriousness of the problem and to seek help with it as a family.

The conscious use of authority is only one measure of bringing about positive changes in some offenders. Its use does present problems to the client, to the agency and to the social worker. In part the problems are related to the quality of experiences which the offender has had, with all authority figures from childhood on and with particular emphasis on the experiences within the correctional process which are within easy recall. Still other problems will depend on the clarity with which the agency states its policies and chooses its overall goals. Further obstacles lie in the life experiences and attitudes of the social worker, how adequately his training has fitted him to accept the challenge of authority and the need to impose controls as one means of influencing human behaviour.

It is the experience of this agency that such controlled use of authority is most effective with clients who express little guilt, whose behaviour has been influenced markedly by the sub-culture of prison and whose conflict with authority is on an open and conscious basis. It is equally applicable to another group of clients whose tendency has been to submit abjectly to authority in the past. As we gain experience with its use we will be more selective. We do know that it contributes to growth in many individuals. We see a number of individuals seeking limits and continuing on from relationships formed under parole supervision to completely voluntary relationships.

To deny the reality of authority in all relationships is unrealistic. To neglect it as a dynamic in the life of the offender is to ignore his needs. To move beyond the formal authority of his position to create a "relationship of psychological authority"[4] is the challenge for the social worker. To achieve the "rational" authority described by Erich Fromm is an accord with the philosophical assumptions of the social work profession.

Rational Authority – like a genuine ideal – represents the aims of growth and expansion of the individual. It is, therefore, in principle never in conflict with the individual and his real, and not his pathological, aims.[2]

(Paper presented at the American Correctional Association in Philadelphia)

13

Worker-client authority relationships
in social work

A framework for study of the social worker's authority toward the client was not necessary when the profession was saying that casework could not be "done" from an authority position. Nor was it pressing so long as authority was considered to be a factor in only one kind of service, *i.e.*, corrections, or in only a few special situations, the "authoritative settings." But recently the profession has been noting that all social workers use authority in some way or other. The public welfare worker acts with authority when he determines eligibility; the group worker uses authority in refusing to permit certain behavior in the clubroom; the child welfare worker is authoritative in selecting a foster home; the school social worker represents the authority of the state in insisting with child and family that he must attend school; the therapist in the clinic exercises authority in setting the conditions for treatment. While we recognize that there is a commonness in all these actions, we are not sure it is in reality the same thing for a family worker to say to a voluntary client, "This is the way we will work together," as it is for a probation officer to say to an offender, "There are certain things you cannot do. If you do them we will have to report back to the court." If it is true that authority appears in all helping relationships, then we should agree about what authority is. We need also to understand its dynamics in action and how its exercise varies from setting to setting.

STRUCTURE WITHIN WHICH AUTHORITY OCCURS

In all the examples of authority actions by social workers toward clients listed in the preceding paragraph, the social worker is engaged in defining

Reprinted by permission of the National Association of Social Workers and the author from *Social Work*, IV: 18–28, January 1959.

certain aspects of the client role which must be accepted by the client if he is to participate in the service. Our task in this paper is to propose a framework for examination of such actions. First let us look at the nature of authority in general and the social conditions which create authority relationships.

Authority appears as a relationship between persons only in an organization of human beings to accomplish a task. Authority is not the power of a bully to control the actions of a weaker person, since authority is always legitimized power. It is not the influence of one friend over the decisions of another, since authority is a special form of influence occurring only when one person has certain official responsibilities toward the behavior of another. Rather, authority is created when, in order to get the job done properly, a person in one position in an organization is authorized to direct the role activities of a person in another position.

In using this definition of authority we should note that the authority of one person toward another does not extend beyond the responsibilities of the relationship between the two positions. The "directing" referred to should be understood in the sense of "giving direction to." It calls for relatively few authority actions as such and depends for effectiveness in large measure on other forms of influence. Most authority actions are simply a matter of making explicit, in a particular behavioral context, the role definitions governing the subordinate position.

The positions to which authority is delegated are links in a hierarchical chain of relationships in task-oriented social organizations. These chains of relationship connect broad social authorization of the task with the activities of the person at the bottom who is doing a primary unit of the task. We can think of the operation of these chains of relationships as the sanctioning process by which authority actions at each intermediate position are directed, limited, and made socially responsible.

The sanctioning of authority involves both the delegation of responsibility for certain decisions and actions to each position in the chain and the acceptance of the rightfulness of the authority by the persons toward whom it is exercised. The dynamics of authority actions can only be understood by keeping in mind the essential two-way process of delegation and acceptance by which authority is sanctioned.

The length and complexity of the chain of relationships which implement this sanctioning process vary greatly among human organizations depending on the nature of the social task to be accomplished. Because the family is the basic unit in our society for the socialization of children, there are few formal steps (such as legal marriage) inserted between the community's authorization of parental responsibilities in the basic law and the authority actions of the particular parent. On the other hand, when the political unit has taken responsibility for meeting economic need, many complex links appear in the sanctioning system by which the authorization of federal funds for public assistance is translated into action toward an individual applicant in the local welfare office. Still another form of sanctioning organization is observed in provisions for medical services in our society, with two sanctioning systems – the professional and the legal – operating jointly to authorize an individual doctor to practice medicine.

When one examines the positions to be filled in a given sanctioning system, one observes that all of them are assigned certain responsibilities in relation to the total task. Certain of these positions are filled by persons who contribute to the task by influencing the activities of others. Persons in the positions at the bottom of the chain of sanctioning relationships do not discharge their responsibilities through other people but are assigned units of the basic task in relation to which they make decisions and take action. It is at this final level that the basic task of the organization is achieved.[1]

In a factory this final unit of responsibility consists of the materials and tools which the individual manages in order to produce his share of the product. In such an organization all the personnel required to achieve the task are employed and the organization owns the product of their work. There is, however, a different pattern of relationships in those change-producing social organizations which are responsible for developing, educating, socializing, and helping people. The product of these organizations is a kind of human functioning whose benefits accrue to the people involved and to the community at large. The basic work of such tasks is not done by those who are employed by the organization but by those who are being helped or educated. Thus the child in school is the one who does the learning which is the goal of the educational institution, while the teacher contributes to this task by guiding the child in his role as student. Similarly in the social agencies, it is not the social worker who does the basic task for which the organization is created. It is the client who gets well, achieves rehabilitation, maximizes his functioning, and makes constructive use of resources or the goal of the service is not achieved. This fact points to a significant characteristic of the social agency as a change-producing organization. For such organizations the basic task is achieved through the operation of persons in a role group who are never employed by the agency but who become members of the organiza-

---

1 / I am indebted to Elliot Jacques, *The Changing Culture of the Factory* (New York: The Dryden Press, Inc., 1952), pp. 249–297, for several concepts in this analysis of authority actions.

tion for shorter or longer periods of time in order to benefit from participation in the agency's task. Each client has a position in the organization during his period of need. This position passes through phases from intake to termination as the client moves toward the goal of more independent functioning. Thus the client of a social agency temporarily becomes a functioning member of the social organization and, while he is a client, is subject to its sanctioning system and participates in its authority relationships. To the social worker is delegated the authority to direct the client's role behavior through its various phases so that the goal for which he and the organization came together can be achieved.

DYNAMICS OF AUTHORITY ACTIONS

If such a definition of authority is to be useful in understanding authority relationships in social work, we should be able to observe the central concepts of the definition in reality situations. According to our definition any given authority event would reveal a social organization, two related positions, and two persons in the positions which are interacting to produce a particular outcome. Let us look at a simple authority action to see if our conceptual formulation is adequate and illuminating in the effort to understand practical reality.

The authority event used below as an example is not a social worker-client authority action, but is drawn from a change-producing organization. It has more than one kind of usefulness for our purposes: it is somewhat more simple than a social worker-client action; and since it is based in an institution it is easier to perceive the client as "a member of the organization." Furthermore, since this is a strict authority situation, it is useful for examining the question of latitude for choice among actions as the authority structure becomes more specific in its definition. As we analyze this action, we should take care to be sure that social organization, two positions, and two persons can actually be observed interacting. If they are all here, then we will have to take each of these concepts into account in any further analysis.

The scene is a young men's reformatory and the action takes place in a mess hall, where the men are lining up with trays along a counter. As reported to the interviewer by one of the inmates, the action went this way: "I nearly got a discipline charge last week. I felt I was going to blow up. I had to take it out on something and I didn't want to get into a fight. I tried to steal an extra piece of cake as I went through the line. Luckily the officer who saw me knew me. He told me to put it back and passed it off as a joke.

Let us look first at the authorizing social organization and the particular authority position. This is a reformatory with a treatment orientation. In the generalized groups occupied by persons in this institution we note that two reciprocal roles have been established – that of officer and that of inmate – each with rather clearly outlined rights, duties, and obligations toward the other. The particular position which we are noting – in which any of a number of officers might have been stationed – is that of a mess hall supervisor with general responsibility for assuring a fair distribution of food to all inmates. Some of the means by which the responsibility of this position is to be discharged have been specified, while others are permitted and still others are proscribed. Thus the mess hall supervisor may give a discipline charge to a rule violator but he is forbidden to hit him. In the verbal realm he has wide latitude for possible action all the way from a stern rebuke to letting the incident go without comment. The general expectations of the sanctioning social organization as to what is acceptable performance in this position clearly affects the outcome of this authority action. For instance, the outcome would have been different if administration required that a discipline charge be written for every such rule violation; or if the officer perceived administration as rewarding officers who sent in many such charges; and still different if inmate and officer had learned from experience that administration did not back up its officers when such charges were written.

Even in this quite strictly defined authority position we note the decisions which were made by the particular officer who took part in the action, and how much he contributed to the final outcome. The officer might have chosen to discharge his responsibility by giving a provocatively hostile rebuke which could have triggered off the explosion which the inmate was trying to control. If, on the other hand, the officer had chosen to let the incident go by without comment he might unwittingly have confirmed in the inmate a pattern of using this means for the outlet of aggression. What the officer did choose to do was bring the violation to the inmate's attention in a pleasant fashion. The action he chose limited the area in which the young man could discharge his explosive feelings, both by making it impossible to steal cake and by refusing to let this incident become a focus for all the inmate's wrath against authority.

The position in which the inmate was operating is more complicated and difficult to describe. In the first place, the organization has defined for him a generalized role – that of inmate – which is pervasive throughout the activities of his life in the institution. The expectations of the inmate role emphasize conforming behavior toward a number of persons, each of whom is in a somewhat different supervisory position over him. At the same time, by reason of his role, he is also a member of an inmate population. The culture of this population brings pressure to bear on him for conforming to values which are contrary to the expectations of the organization. When the inmate gets caught in the group in an effort to defeat institutional rules, the incident is crucial for his relationship with the organization and with his peers and is particularly difficult for him when the officer acts in a contemptuous or essentially debasing fashion. Thus the role of the inmate is an inherently conflictual one and behavior in any given episode will be affected by the interplay of antagonistic expectations.

Finally, the outcome of this particular authority action was also affected by the person in the inmate role. He was a person who was chronically sensitive to authority actions and particularly so at this moment. However, in spite of his sense of imminent explosion from within, he was able to accept the action of the officer and be influenced by it, perhaps because of some sense that the officer viewed him as an individual. Another person in his state of mind might by his general attitude have so affected the officer's behavior that there would have been the kind of rebuke which triggers explosive action.

It is evident from this example that we will need to examine the social organization in which the authority action occurs, the two positions which are related by authority, and the two persons in these positions in order to understand what goes on in any given authority event. Let us see what we know in general about these components of an authority relationship in social work. In this examination we should be ready for the possible emergence of another essential concept, since social work operation is more complex than the example we have just analyzed.

AUTHORITY IN SOCIAL WORK

The organization of the service agency
The organization of any agency reflects the social task for which it is responsible. The task of the service agency employing social workers is that of meeting crucial needs in the lives of individual human beings, needs which are of high enough incidence in a given society to require organization to meet them. This is a task area of marked social and personal sensitivity. It impinges deeply on the values which govern the interrelationships of people – affecting homes, happiness, welfare and integrity. Since persons in serious need are also sometimes socially dangerous, protection of the community as well as of the individual sometimes becomes an explicit part of the task. Furthermore, the magnitude of

the task, when many individuals in a society experience needs that can only be met through social organization, calls for extensive mobilization of financial resources and professional personnel.

Given a social task which includes meeting widely experienced individual needs, protecting the community, and supporting values, we can expect to find in the social services a complex organization involving a number of sanctioning systems. Each of these systems is required to provide certain resources in money or skills and to implement the support of certain values. At least three sanctioning systems operate simultaneously in the organization of the social services: the legal which establishes the basic structure of services and rights; the administrative which is responsible for getting the job done; and the professional which is concerned with competence and values. Some services are also responsible to a fourth sanctioning system, the religious, by which certain additional values are protected. Each of these systems has its characteristic decision-making patterns, governing values and reference groups. All of them affect the design of the social worker's authority position, and set up certain expectations about performance in it.

These sanctioning systems are organizationally related to each other in different ways in different service agencies, depending on the particular social need to be met by the agency. For instance, a private family agency with its voluntary case load is governed, relatively remotely, by the legal system through a legislative act authorizing incorporation for certain purposes. In this sort of agency the professional and administrative systems have tended to become identical so there is minimal complication and little cross-checking by various sanctioning systems. Compare this with the field of mental health where the case load includes a wide range of voluntary and involuntary clients. In this field several professions together take responsibility for the service with ultimate authority in both the administrative and professional systems lodged in the medical profession. Also in this field the legal sanctioning system is more active, licensing medical practitioners, establishing certain public services, and making decisions about those clients who must be hospitalized involuntarily. Then compare either of these fields with that of corrections where all clients have demonstrated some potentiality for danger to society. In this field, the legal sanctioning system makes decisions about every client; all the professions (each of which is sanctioned by its characteristic system) are involved in service; and administrative processes have certain responsibilities such as custody which, though often organizationally separated from treatment, affect the professional processes.

One way of understanding differences among fields of social service is to observe the interrelations of sanctioning systems which are deemed necessary to authorize the activities of each service. It seems evident that the greater the authority of the agency to act in relation to involuntary clients, and the more serious the potential danger to society from client behavior, the more complex is the organization of the sanctioning systems required to provide the necessary resources and to protect the values affected by the service.

An important result of the fact that there are several sanctioning systems in social work organization is the emergence of the decision-making team as a significant step in the exercise of social work authority. This is the additional concept which we anticipated. Most social services are provided through the joint operation of a number of personnel each of whom may represent a different sanctioning system. These personnel may be stationed in the same agency with the worker; or may represent other agencies necessary to the service required by the particular case. Each member of this decision-making team (of which the clinical team is only one example) has a differently defined responsibility, yet the areas of responsibility overlap; and the service which ultimately gets to the client in the one-to-one or one-to-group relationship is affected by the shared decision-making of this team. The way the social worker's role is defined within this team affects the nature of the decisions which will be reached in its deliberations; and these decisions limit and direct the social worker's exercise of authority in decision-making with the client. The more complex the organization of sanctioning systems necessary for giving the particular service, the more complex will be the authority relationships in the team, and the more probable that difficulties at this point will have an unfortunate effect on the worker's use of authority with the client.

The clients and positions for the client
The social worker's authority position is an individualizing link between the social resources provided by the organization and the client with his needs. Therefore, it would be useful at this point to modify the order of our outline and examine the necessities of the client's position as he enters into membership in the service organization before we look at the authority position of the social worker.

One of the significant characteristics of the client group is its vulnerability to the exercise of authority. Individuals would not be clients if they were not at least temporarily handicapped in taking responsibility for some aspect of their personal lives.[2] In such situations they are particularly de-

2 / This formulation does not sufficiently take into account the nature of need brought by members of many groups served by group workers. This whole

pendent on the authority person who can link them to the social and psychological resources which are necessary to repair damage and to reinstate their ability to manage for themselves. They are impelled to seek help because of internal or external difficulties which matter to them, and the resources to which they can turn are usually limited. In this perspective social work tends to deal with a "captive case load," and the opportunities for well-intentioned misuse of this power position are numerous.

In a democratic society we can expect to find certain important safeguards built into the processes which authorize intervention by authority persons in such vulnerable lives. Some of these are built into the definition of the client position. The stipulation that the request for help shall be voluntary is one of these. The professional emphasis on the client's right to self-determination within the limits of reality is another. In certain services we find legal protections for the rights of clients such as provisions that financial assistance shall be granted when eligibility is demonstrated, and procedures for appeal from disadvantageous decisions. Social concern that the persons in authority toward needy people shall have been tested and tried through an educational process which insures their trustworthiness for this responsibility also stems from recognition of the vulnerability of persons in the client role. Another characteristic of the group of persons who appear in the client role is the very wide variation among clients in ability to take responsibility for themselves. Some have the strengths necessary for self-management in all essential areas. Some are limited in their ability for independent management in only one area. There are others, however, who are not only seriously limited in ability to take responsibility for themselves but are also socially dangerous and unwilling to seek help in modifying their situations. Some, found particularly in correctional case loads, are supported by their group relationships in a strong antagonism to any intervention which would modify their social functioning.

As a result of these facts about persons in client positions one would expect to find in the social services a graded series of definitions of the client role which reflect the different abilities of individuals to take responsibility for themselves. At one end of the range the client position is designed to allow for self-determination in all areas of personal functioning. Such positions are usually found in private family agencies and in outpatient psychiatric clinics. There are intermediate positions in which the role definition of client calls for submitting one or more aspects of personal

---

statement is in process of formulation and presents a number of theoretical problems requiring further testing against the realities of various kinds of social work practice.

functioning to shared decision-making with the worker, such as the economic area in public assistance, parent-child communication in foster home care, and the management of illness in the medical services. At the other end of the range would be positions for clients who enter the role involuntarily and are assigned to work with authority persons in relation to extended areas of personal functioning. Such positions are found in agencies dealing with parental neglect, in many institutions, and in correctional services. All social agency case loads fit within this continuum, with variously designed positions for clients which reflect the nature of the need, the ability of the client to take responsibility for his own life, and the potential danger to society in his behavior.

Finally, client motivation to accept and use authority constructively in the accomplishment of life tasks varies over a wide range. Our concern as a profession that the request for help be voluntary stems in part from the fact that such a request is an explicit sanction from the client for the worker's use of authority. Yet there are many client situations where the combined needs of the individual and his community require social work services even when the client is not able or willing to make a verbal request for help. We have seen that authority does not become effective except as the person toward whom it is exercised sanctions its use and acts in accord with the intention of the authority person. The profession must therefore be concerned with the possibility of motivating involuntary clients to make constructive use of authority relationships; and with the skills by which this is accomplished. In accepting such a responsibility we will continue to given attention to the safeguards which prevent the use of extended authority except as individual and social need warrant such intervention and the proper authorization has been made.

The social worker's authority position and the persons in it
We have said that authority appears as an aspect of human relationships in social organizations where a person in one position is responsible for directing the role performance of a person in another position. Under this definition the social worker's position carries authority for directing the client's use of his position in the organization toward the achievement of the goals for which client and service come together. The authority allocated to the worker's position will be restricted or extended depending on the kind of responsibility assumed by his agency for the personal functioning of the client. At the same time the social worker's authority will be delimited by the operation of the decision-making team with which he shares responsibility for the service. Thus in one sense the worker's position seems to be that of a middle man in the authority system.

He brings information to the decision-making team, participates in its deliberations, and administers decisions made at this organizational level. In work with the client he encourages the client in making his own decisions.

It is important, however, not to ignore the decisions which the social worker makes independently as he chooses among the alternative behaviors possible to him. There is in fact an extremely wide latitude of decision-making which is necessarily left in the hands of the social worker as he deals with clients, whether he is determining the number and frequency of interviews, establishing eligibility, selecting a foster home, or evaluating a violation of probation. No matter how stringent and detailed the authority structure within which the worker operates, his primary assignment is to individualize the provisions by which the social service is given. In the most strict authority structure, therefore, he has authority to select among the available alternatives in terms of the individual with whom he is working. Such decisions are often made at the moment of action and are based on information to which only he has access. In this activity the worker has at his disposal a wide range of means by which one person may influence another; in addition, what he does with the client is relatively unobserved.[3] In the light of these facts about his function, the authority position of the social worker is necessarily designed to allow for flexible exercise of extensive power to influence others while insuring responsible action governed by the purposes of the service and the needs of the clients.

One of the attributes of the person in authority which significantly affects the outcome of authority actions is the way he feels about his position. Elliot Jacques has pointed out that the person in the authority position also sanctions his exercise of authority when he is clear about what is required of him, competent to undertake the task, and able to resolve the ambivalences which are stimulated by the exercise of authority.[4] When the person in authority is uneasy about his assignment, he tends to take refuge in abdication from or over-assertion of the authority for which he is legitimately responsible. Either of these adjustments interferes with his effectiveness in the total task. Since the social work profession has in general been uncertain about the place of authority in the dynamics of helping, it can be expected that many practitioners experience uneasiness in social work positions which call for an extended use of authority.[5]

3 / Lloyd E. Ohlin, "Conformity in American Society Today," *Social Work*, Vol. 3, No. 2 (April 1958), pp. 60–61.

4 / Jacques, *op. cit.*, pp. 275–291.

5 / Lloyd E. Ohlin, Herman Piven, and Donell M. Pappenfort, "Major Dilemmas of the Social Worker in Probation and Parole," in Herman D. Stein and

It is clear that positions in which this amount of power to influence the lives of others is sanctioned should be filled with persons who can make these decisions competently and in the interest of the client. Such positions call for mature, disciplined workers who are capable of relatively independent functioning. They need the realistic knowledge of life and the personal strength necessary to make decisions, to exercise authority responsibly, and to stand as toughly flexible members of the decision-making team. They also need educational preparation for analyzing and understanding the dynamics of authority in the total social work task.

Thus it would seem that authority relationships between social workers and clients are determined by the following facts:

Social workers and clients come together in a complex *organizational setting* in which a number of sanctioning systems combine to define the task and determine the allocation of authority.

Social workers act as members of *decision-making teams* whose decisions both limit and direct the social worker's exercise of authority with the client.

The *authority positions* in which social workers are placed require ability to share decisions at the team level; independent functioning at the level of primary responsibility; and ability to free the client for self-determination to the extent of his ability within the definition of his position.

The *positions for clients* are variously designed within the different social services, depending on variations among groups of clients in ability to use help responsibly. The authority of the worker is restricted or extended depending on the extent to which the personal life of the client is drawn within the definition of his position as client in that particular service.

The *persons in the client positions* vary extensively in their ability to use authority constructively. Since effective exercise of authority depends on its sanction and use by the person in the subordinate position, social workers are often faced with the necessity of helping individual clients relate positively to the authority which directs their role performance in the service.

The social worker as the *person in the authority position* needs to be clear as to the nature of the authority which is delegated to him, flexible in authority relations at the different levels of decision-making, and skillful in handling destructive responses to authority from the client.

Richard A. Cloward, eds., *Social Perspectives on Behavior* (Glencoe, Ill.: The Free Press, 1958), pp. 251–262.

TOWARD A GENERIC APPROACH TO AUTHORITY IN SOCIAL WORK

It would be useful to test this general description of authority relation-ships between social workers and clients in a number of different ways. On the one hand, it would be theoretically valuable to examine a number of different samples of social work practice to see how differences in social organization, in the design of worker and client positions, and in the per-sons who fill these positions are reflected in differences in the exercise of authority. What, for instance, are the professional problems and skills in the use of authority by the group worker, the public assistance worker, the caseworker in the child guidance clinic, the institutional caseworker, and the probation officer? What is the base which is common to all? What are the different emphases which flow from different structural provisions and orientations?

On the other hand, this outline could be useful in locating the source of problems in authority relations appearing in a particular service. Are the expectations of the organization clear or conflicting? Does the decision-making team operate effectively? Is the worker sure of the nature of his authority? What of the client position – does it harbor unsuspected con-flicts? What steps are taken to motivate clients to participate usefully in authority relationships?

Of the many questions which require further exploration, three occur to the writer as particularly significant for problems of practice.

Authority relationship and action

Professional use of an authority relationship for helping requires a care-ful distinction between authority relationship and authority action.[6] Not all actions of an authority person toward the person in the subordinate role are authority actions. The person in any authority position also uses many other means of influence, such as counsel, exploration of possibili-ties, supportive understanding, and training in skills. However, there tends to be a halo effect from an authority relationship which can lead the subordinate to perceive all actions of the authority person as authority actions.

We have long known that professional control of the helping process can be achieved through awareness of the psychological and social forces which enter into the helping relationship. If authority is a real factor in social work-client relationships, lack of attention to its operation could well result in a more diffuse and rigidly determining authority influence

6 / Herbert A. Simon, *Administrative Behavior* (New York: The Macmillan Co., 1957), pp. 125–128.

than is warranted by the facts or desirable for the client's freedom to act in his own behalf. It seems probable that clarification by the worker for himself and with the client as to the authority which is actually delegated to the worker's position can help to reduce the halo effect and limit the inappropriate or unaware use of authority by both worker and client.

Although increased awareness of the dynamics of authority in relationships can help to reduce undesirable effects of authority actions on helping, we still need more exploration about what happens to the helping relationship as the worker's responsibility for authority actions increases. As a profession we have been fearful that each increment of authority reduces the ability of the client to use the relationship for help. On the other hand, social workers in a number of services have reported that appropriate authority actions actually enhance the ability of the client to take responsibility for himself. It may well be that one of the major skills in the use of authority in helping involves the gradual substitution of other means of influence for the authority actions which are necessary in the initial phase of the relationship. Only further study of actual authority actions in the context of the helping relationships can resolve these questions.

Design of worker-client positions
It is evident that these two positions are reciprocal in that a change in one implies a change in the other; therefore it is useful to consider them together as a certain kind of role relationship. Up to this point in social work theory we have tended to use a "best" or "preferred" model for the professional worker-client relationship. This role model has been primarily drawn from experience in those services where the client makes a voluntary request for help and retains responsibility for all his life decisions. The authority of the worker in this model tends to be limited to the decisions which he makes in managing the helping process.

As we have given increased attention to social work positions in which the worker takes more initiative in motivating clients to want help and increased responsibility for decisions in the client's personal life, we have had some uneasiness about whether these positions falsify or debase the ideal role model which we have seen as essential to professional functioning. The foregoing analysis of authority relationships suggests a theoretical step which can open the way to more flexible examination of various kinds of practice. It may well be that the social worker-client relationship can occur within a variety of role designs which can be subsumed under a more highly generalized model. Within the basic definition of these reciprocal roles would be found a number of somewhat differently designed positions which take into account client need and the resulting distribution of decisions between worker and client.

We noted in our examination of an authority action in an institution that the design of the inmate role produced inherent but often unobserved strains in the inmate's relationship with authority, and that these strains could seriously interfere with the inmate's ability to work constructively with the authority person. It may well be that the prevailing role design for social worker-client relationships actually poses inherent and insuperable conflicts for individuals in certain social groups who need and could otherwise use our services.[7] If this is so it may be due to the fact that our current generalized role model includes decision-making patterns appropriate to certain social work positions but not to others, and that we need to formulate our ideal model at a higher level of generalization. This would open the way for professional experimentation with role design where need is evident.

We have already made a number of steps in the direction of this kind of a formulation. The profession made a significant adjustment to client perception of the client position when fee service was provided in private agencies in order to make it possible for persons from higher income groups to use our services. And some of the techniques in use with hard-to-reach families and groups represent efforts to design the details of the client position so that persons with lower-class cultural patterns can participate in the social task for which the agency is organized. Empirical evidence would suggest that two areas of social work practice which call for re-examination of role design are found in corrections and institutional work.

The decision-making team in the social services

Our analysis suggests still a third area which invites exploration. We have noted that the authority relationship between the worker and his client is affected by the operation of the decision-making team which is active in relation to a given case. Who makes what decisions and how decisions are shared among the representatives of the different sanctioning systems set a determining framework for the ultimate decision process as it occurs between the worker and the client.

Examples of how these differently constituted teams affect the exercise of authority by the worker were elaborated in a seminar of thirty persons who represented several different fields of social service. According to those present in this seminar, a serious authority problem in public

7 / *See* August B. Hollingshead and Frederick C. Redlich, *Social Class and Mental Illness* (New York: John Wiley & Sons, Inc., 1958), pp. 130–135, for a description of characteristic expectations of such groups.

welfare occurs in relating the decisions of different categorical aids to the service needs of a particular client. For mental hygiene services, on the other hand, authority problems appeared particularly crucial in the relationships among the different professions. In child welfare, authority problems were identified at the point of integrating services from public and private agencies or from legal and service agencies for the same client. In corrections, a special problem appeared when the social worker shared responsibility for decisions with police and judges.

In each of these fields of service, problems in making constructive use of authority with the client seemed to be exacerbated by unresolved authority problems at the level of the team which is responsible for service decisions. As the examples given above were reported, it was evident that these problems were not simply matters of poor relationships among persons but were rooted deeply in communication and action difficulties deriving from the fact that each team member was responsible to a different sanctioning system with its own definition of values, goals, and appropriate methods of action. Such problems are inherent in complex decision-making. They are of such importance to effective service that they indicate the need for careful professional attention to the various patterns by which different service teams make shared decision-making effective in service to the client.

SUMMARY

At the present level of development in social work theory it is no longer intellectually defensible to analyze the dynamics of authority for one field of service alone. A finding in one field that authority relationships are important in determining the nature of service leads us inevitably to ask: Does authority enter into all social worker-client relationships and, if so, in what ways? Since authority arises from the structural arrangements by which people are organized to do a job, it is probable that we will discover a range of patterns for authority relationships in the variously organized fields of service in which social workers are employed. A theoretical formulation about authority for the profession should include the concepts and principles which are common to use of authority by social workers wherever they work as well as the variables which determine differential adaptation of the generic theory within various fields of service. It is suggested that one way of making progress toward understanding authority as a dynamic in professional social work practice is to examine various kinds of social work practice in the framework of this analysis with special attention to problem areas.

14

Authoritarianism and social workers: a psychological study

Past research concerning the relationship between the selection of social work as a profession and the presence or absence of certain personality traits has dealt with social workers as a relatively homogeneous group of individuals. In this study, however, an attempt was made to examine social work students in terms of their expressed area of professional interest. The major objective of this research effort was to test empirically a hypothesis based on an assumption that is sometimes made by social workers concerning certain of their colleagues, *i.e.*, that social workers in the field of corrections tend to be more authoritarian than social workers in other areas. In addition, comparisons in terms of "authoritarianism"[1] were made of social work students grouped on the basis of religious affiliation and amount of prior experience in the social work field.

Although there has been much discussion about the "sort of person" who goes into social work, relatively few studies have been conducted. Three – by Lewis, Piotrowski, and Harrower and Cox – have been discussed by Anne Roe.[2] She reported that Lewis compared 50 women social workers with the norm groups on the Minnesota Multiphasic Personality Inventory and found them to be significantly higher on the depression and hysteria scales and significantly lower on masculinity, hypochondriasis, psychasthenia, and schizophrenia. The suggestion made

Reprinted with the permission of the National Association of Social Workers and the author. From *Social Work*, VIII: 37–43, January 1963.

This research was carried out on the campus of the Graduate School of Social Work at the University of Wisconsin – Milwaukee. Thanks are given to Dr. John Teter, Chairman of the University of Wisconsin – Milwaukee Graduate School of Social Work for giving his consent for social work students to be studied.

1 / See p. 38 for definition.

2 / *The Psychology of Occupations* (New York: John Wiley & Sons, 1954), pp. 173–174.

by Roe is that the low scores on these scales may reflect the social workers' unusual sophistication in psychopathology.

Piotrowski, who used 18 social work students of superior intelligence in a comparative study of the Rorschach, found that those who were studying social work because they wished to, rather than for other reasons (*e.g.*, outside pressures, marriage to a social worker), showed particularly greater interest in persons. However, contrary results were reported by Harrower and Cox, who studied a very small sample of 8 social workers and unexpectedly found them to be low in human movement responses, an assumed index of interest in other people.

More recently McCornack and Kidneigh sent the Strong Vocational Interest Blank to 700 men and 700 women randomly selected from the 1952 *Membership Directory* of the American Association of Social Workers. Approximately 87 percent of the total sample returned the questionnaires. "All subjects were full members of the AASW, had at least three years of full-time experience, were currently actively engaged in their profession, were less than 60 years of age, and resided in the continental United States." Results of the study indicated that both male and female social workers had "a strong liking for activities involving people, a strong liking for verbal activities," and tended to dislike "conservative" people. The men also showed a dislike for the physical sciences and athletic men, and the women a dislike of athletic women as well as of scientific, selling, and clerical activities.[3]

In another study, by Kidneigh and Lundberg, a total of 80 social work students entering graduate schools at the Universities of Iowa, Kansas, Minnesota, and Nebraska were compared with a total of 180 students beginning graduate studies in education, engineering, law, library science, nursing, and psychology at the University of Minnesota in the 1956–57 academic year. The authors reported that the social work students, by scoring lower on the Authoritarian Personality Social Attitudes Battery, were significantly more "liberal" than the other groups. According to Kidneigh and Lundberg these results correlate with the qualities valued by social work educators and the social work profession and "would include non-judgmental attitudes toward a client, meeting dependency without control, warm and understanding acceptance, and the lack of personal bias in the social worker." No significant difference was found between social work students with prior experience in the field and those without prior experience.[4]

3/ Robert McCornack and John C. Kidneigh, "The Vocational Interest Patterns of Social Workers," *Social Work Journal*, Vol. 35, No. 4 (October 1954), pp. 161–163.
4/ John C. Kidneigh and Horace W. Lundberg, "Are Social Work Students

THE AUTHORITARIAN PERSONALITY

As early as 1928 Gordon Allport was working with a test for measuring ascendance-submission personality traits, which concern a person's tendency to control or to be controlled by other people in social situations.[5] However, it was the appearance of *The Authoritarian Personality*, by Adorno *et al.*, in 1950 that provided the major stimulus for the abundance of research concerning the personality traits described as being authoritarian. According to these authors, the authoritarian personality is said to exist when an individual has:

... a particularly strong and rigid adherence to conventional values, ...
... a general tendency to look down on and to punish those who were believed to be violating conventional values.
... been forced to give up basic pleasures and to live under a system of rigid restraints, and who therefore feels put upon, [and] is likely not only to seek an object upon which he can "take it out" but also to be particularly annoyed at the idea that another person is "getting away with something."
... hostility that was originally aroused by and directed toward ingroup authorities [which becomes] displaced onto out-groups.[6]

The writers concluded that

... it is to be expected, therefore, that the conventionalist who cannot bring himself to utter any real criticism of accepted authority will have a desire to condemn, reject, and punish those who violate those values.[7]

In general agreement with these definitions, Christie and Jahoda considered the presence of authoritarianism to be demonstrated in individuals who are "punitive and condescending toward inferiors, unreceptive to scientific investigation, less sensitive to interpersonal relationships, and prone to attribute their own ideology to others."[8]

Different?" *Social Work*, Vol. 3, No. 3 (July 1958), pp. 57–61. According to Kidneigh and Lundberg, the battery was Levinson's selection and/or modification of items originally produced by the authors of *The Authoriation Personality*, for which *see* n. 6.

5 / Gordon Allport, "A Test for Ascendance-Submission," *Journal of Abnormal and Social Psychology*, Vol. 23 (July-September 1928), pp. 118–136.

6 / T. W. Adorno, Else Frenkel-Brunswik, D. J. Levinson, and R. N. Sanford, *The Authoritarian Personality* (New York: Harper & Brothers, 1950), pp. 227, 232, and 233.

7 / *Ibid.*, p. 233.

8 / Richard Christie, "Authoritarianism Re-examined," in *Studies in the Scope and Method of "The Authoritarian Personality,"* Richard Christie and Marie Jahoda, eds. (Glencoe, Ill.: The Free Press, 1954), p. 140.

The 66-item Form D of Rokeach's Dogmatism Scale, an assumed measure of authoritarianism, consists of statements designed to measure individual differences in the "openness" or "closedness" of belief systems. According to Rokeach, the extent to which a belief system is open or closed is jointly determined by two opposing sets of motives: (1) the need to know and (2) the need to defend against threat.[9]

Furthermore, if a person is in strong agreement with such statements it would indicate that he possesses one extreme of the particular characteristic being tapped; if he is in strong disagreement, it would indicate that he possesses the opposite extreme. Each statement was designed to transcend specific ideological positions in order to penetrate these characteristics. An example of the type of statements employed is: "Of all the different philosophies which exist in the world there is probably only one which is correct."

Rokeach contends that persons adhering *dogmatically* to such diverse viewpoints as capitalism and communism, Catholicism and anti-Catholicism, should all score together at one end of the open-closed continuum, and other persons having equally diverse but undogmatic views should all score together at the opposite end. Form D has a reported corrected reliability score of .91, which was obtained from a sample of 137 college students in England. This is a substantial index of reliability for a "personality scale" and means that persons taking the test respond to the items in a highly consistent fashion.

Having a reliable instrument, however, does not always insure validity, a concept that is extremely difficult to represent by a single number. Typically, we say that a test is valid when it measures what it is presumed to measure. Here we usually find ourselves on less sure ground. A general note of caution pertaining to "personality scales" has been sounded by Jackson and Messick, who pointed out that

stylistic determinants, such as acquiescence, overgeneralization, and a tendency to respond in a socially undesirable manner, as distinct from specific content, account for a large proportion of response variance on some personality scales, particularly the California F scale, the MMPI, and the California Psychological Inventory.[10]

9 / Milton Rokeach, *The Open and Closed Mind* (New York: Basic Books, 1960), pp. 73–80. These items were used with the permission of the author. The order of the items, however, was randomly determined in an attempt to prevent the effects of response set on items of similar content; they therefore were not presented in the same sequence in the study as set forth in Rokeach's book.

10 / Douglas N. Jackson and Samuel Messick, "Content and Style in Personality Assessment," *Psychological Bulletin*, Vol. 55, No. 4 (1958), p. 250.

Although the Fascism or F Scale as devised by Adorno *et al.* was generally accepted as the best measure of authoritarianism for nearly a decade, Rokeach has offered evidence to support the hypothesis that the Dogmatism or D Scale measures a general form of authoritarianism, whereas the F Scale measures a more specific form, related to the political sphere of one's belief system. He has pointed out that dogmatism scores are found with approximately equal frequency along all positions of the political continuum, while the F Scale correlates more highly with two measures of liberalism-conservatism, with the high F scores being more conservative. Rokeach concluded that "this finding once more supports the suspicion that the F Scale is measuring right authoritarianism."[11]

TEST PROCEDURE AND RESULTS

The 66-item Form D of the Dogmatism Scale was administered in group settings to 63 graduate and 53 undergraduate social work students who attended the University of Wisconsin during the academic year 1960–61. The graduate group comprised 42 males and 21 females with the modal age range falling between 26 and 30, the undergraduate group 18 males and 35 females within a modal age range of 21–25. Each of the 116 students filled out a biographical data sheet.

One week prior to administration of the scale, each instructor requested the participation of his students in a research project, informed them that the test results would in no way affect their course grades, a fact emphasized by the anonymity of the questionnaire, and encouraged the students to answer honestly. The same information was repeated on the day the scale was administered.

Special instructions for responding to the items of the scale were the same as those used by Rokeach and were taken from the F Scale. The tests were collected by passing an unmarked manila folder among the students, into which they were allowed to insert their tests. Almost all of the students completed the test within forty-five minutes.

The range of scores for any one item was -3 to $+3$, with the zero or neutral point being eliminated. Hence, the subjects were forced to either disagree or agree with the item in question but were unable to respond in a neutral fashion. For scoring purposes this scale of -3 to $+3$ was converted to a 1–7 scale by adding a constant of 4 to the score obtained on each item. The total score for a subject was obtained by adding the converted scores on each of the 66 items.

The following indicates which areas of social work employment were

11 / Rokeach, *op. cit.*, p. 121.

selected and by how many students: 28 in corrections, 28 in psychiatric social work, 22 in child welfare, and 9 in social group work. The remainder of the students selected the areas of administration, community organization, research, public assistance, medical and school social work; none of these areas, though, was selected by a sufficient number of students to be of use in making statistical comparisons.

Graduate status

It is important to point out, initially, that when the total graduate group was compared with the total undergraduate group no significant differences were found in authoritarianism as measured by the Dogmatism Scale. Consequently, it was decided to combine these two groups in order to make comparisons on an overall basis.

Preferred specialization

The results of the comparisons made between groups of social work students on the basis of their desired area of employment (Table 1) indicate that those interested in corrections were not more authoritarian than

TABLE 1

Comparisons of students grouped on the basis of desired area of employment in the social work profession

Group	Number	Group	Number	t
Graduate students	63	Undergraduate students	53	1.527
Corrections	28	Psychiatric social work	28	.648
Corrections	28	Child welfare	22	.507
Corrections	28	Group work	9	2.526*
Psychiatric social work	28	Child welfare	22	1.058
Psychiatric social work	28	Group work	9	2.516*
Child welfare	22	Group work	9	2.317*

Symbols refer to the level of significance of the difference between group means: * = $p < .05$; variances tested for homogeneity (Bartlett's Test).

students in the areas of psychiatric social work, child welfare, and social group work. In fact, when comparisons were made on an over-all basis, the students selecting social group work scored significantly higher on the Dogmatism Scale than those in corrections ($p < 0.05$), psychiatric social work ($p < 0.05$), and child welfare ($p < 0.05$). Comparisons made between students in corrections, psychiatric, and child welfare groups, within their respective graduate and undergraduate levels, also indicated no significant differences in authoritarianism among these groups. Thus, it seems clear that the common assumption made by social workers about their colleagues in the field of corrections is not supported by the data of this study.

This conclusion also appears to be anticipated by Studt, who reported in 1959 that the profession is becoming aware that all social workers use authority in some way. She stated,

The public welfare worker acts with authority when he determines eligibility; the group worker uses authority in refusing to permit certain behavior in the club room; the child welfare worker is authoritative in selecting a foster home; the school social worker represents the authority of the state in insisting with child and family that he must attend school; the therapist in the clinic exercises authority in setting the conditions for treatment.[12]

The fact that one uses authority during the performance of his job duties as a social worker in no way implies that this is a direct expression of an authoritarian personality. Thus, when a social worker legitimately works within the structure of his agency's policy or utilizes the casework technique of "limit-setting" this behavior certainly need not be construed as an authoritarian act. It is possible that confusion about the proper or legitimate use of authority has resulted in an increased tendency on the part of the social worker to seem himself as "permissive" and to view those working in penal or probationary settings as "authoritarian." It is also possible that the original assumption about those working in corrections was based on an observation made when correctional personnel were closely identified with the police and judicial systems and were not trained social workers.

As noted, the students selecting social group work were found to be significantly more authoritarian than students preferring to work in the corrections, psychiatric, and child welfare areas. This may indicate that group workers perceive the group setting as the best situation in which their own values may be extended, through such program activities as they believe will facilitate healthy group interaction. The intensity with which these aims are held may have resulted in higher dogmatism scores for the group workers. However, further research with larger numbers of group workers will have to be conducted in order to obtain additional data bearing on this hypothesis.

Religion

Results of the comparisons made between groups of social work students on the basis of their religious affiliation (Table 2) indicate that Catholic

12 / Elliot Studt, "Worker-Client Authority Relationships in Social Work," *Social Work*, Vol. 4, No. 1 (January 1959), p. 18.

TABLE 2

Comparisons of students grouped on the basis of
religious affiliation

Group	Number	Group	Number	t
Catholic	44	Protestant	55	1.631
Catholic	44	Jew	6	1.136
Catholic	44	None	7	1.961*
Protestant	55	Jew	6	.521
Protestant	55	None	7	1.247
Jew	6	None	7	.430

Symbols refer to the level of significance of the difference between group means: $* = p < .05$; variances tested for homogeneity (Bartlett's Test).

students scored higher on the Dogmatism Scale than Protestants, Jews, and students who professed no religious affiliation. On an overall basis, Catholic social work students scored significantly higher in authoritarianism than the students who stated they had no religion ($p < 0.05$); undergraduate Catholic students were significantly more authoritarian than undergraduate Protestant students ($p < 0.05$). These results are in close agreement with the findings of previous investigations on the relationship between religious affiliation and authoritarianism. Wrightsman *et al.*, Rokeach, and Brown and Bystryn found that Catholic students scored significantly higher than other college students on the F, E, Dogmatism, and Machiavellian Scales.[13] Rokeach's interpretation of these results may be paraphrased as follows: Members of the Catholic church are required to follow the church's doctrine closely and, as a result of the social pressures of reward and punishment over a period of time, the members learn to commit themselves in advance to the ingroup's ideology and learn to reject in advance the ideology of outgroups.[14]

Catholic undergraduate students also were found to be significantly more authoritarian than Catholic graduate students ($p < 0.05$). Similar results were reported by Brown and Bystryn, who found that Catholic freshmen were significantly more authoritarian than Catholic seniors as measured by the F Scale. They suggested that the seniors became more liberal as a result of their increased exposure to the college curriculum. In the present

13 / L. S. Wrightsman, R. W. Radloff, D. L. Horton, and M. Mercherikoff, "Presidential Voting Preferences and the Authoritarian Syndrome." A paper presented at the American Psychological Association Convention, Chicago, Ill. (September 3, 1960); Rokeach, *op. cit.*; D. R. Brown and D. Bystryn, "College Environment, Personality, and Social Ideology of Three Ethnic Groups," *Journal of Social Psychology*, Vol. 44 (1956), pp. 279–288.

14 / Rokeach, *op. cit.*, p. 118.

study, comparisons among undergraduate students showed that Catholics were significantly more authoritarian than Protestants, while comparisons ,among graduate students showed no significant differences between Catholics and Protestants. These findings suggest that differences between religious groups may disappear during the process of completing a four-year liberal arts education.

Prior experience
The results of the comparison between graduate social work students with prior experience in the field and those with no experience revealed no significant differences in authoritarianism.[15] This finding was in agreement with Kidneigh and Lundberg, who also found no significant differences in authoritarianism between social work students on the basis of amount of prior experience as measured by the Authoritarian Personality Social Attitudes Battery. Thus, on the basis of these two studies one may tentatively reject the assumption that work experience before entering graduate school is associated with authoritarian "rigidity." Perhaps the experienced student is not so "set in his ways" as to make it difficult for him to assimilate graduate social work education.

Considerably more research needs to be conducted on personality traits of social workers. Possibly an analysis of the items comprising the Dogmatism Scale might yield further information on differences between social work students that did not appear when comparisons were made on the basis of total scores. In addition, better matching of subjects on the basis of age, intelligence, and religion may also be important. In subsequent research it would be desirable to increase the total number of subjects and to include full-time social workers practicing in their respective fields. Finally, it might be interesting to study the relationship between traits and reasons for selecting social work as a profession, as well as the relationship between traits and effectiveness as a social worker.

15/The 34 graduate students with prior experience in the field had a group mean of 210.1 and the 29 graduate students with no prior experience a group mean of 198.2. This comparison yielded a t score of 1.282 with 61 degrees of freedom, which was not a statistically significant difference.

PART IV
Authority in social work: basic issues

INTRODUCTION

A crisis in the basic values of a society has a natural impact on the professions. The social work profession, perhaps like any other humanitarian profession, is undergoing a "value crisis" in which the traditionally accepted and cherished social work values are under attack by both the society and social work professionals. If the underlying purpose of all social work effort is to release human power for the creation of the kinds of society, social institutions, and social policy that make self-realization a reality, two values assume primary significance in such a purpose. These are: respect for the worth and dignity of every individual and concern that he has the opportunity to realize his potential as a fulfilled, socially contributive person. The other values, such as self-determination, responsibility, deviance control, protection, rehabilitation, acceptance of difference, right to participate in one's own destiny, individual duty, and societal responsibility for human betterment, are intermediary values which facilitate the two central values undergirding social work practice.

Does the use of authority in social work practice conflict with basic values and principles of social work? What conflicts and limitations arise when social workers carrying some form of authority are called upon to help their clients? What are the dilemmas of social workers in using authority? How can these conflicts be resolved, if at all? These and others are some of the major issues in the following section. An objective and logical analysis of these issues is important, for such an analysis would help social workers understand the concept of authority and grapple with its meaning. In the use of authority in social work practice these issues are unavoidable. The key lies perhaps in the degree to which social workers can understand and objectively assess various dimensions of these issues, a first step towards possible resolution. The ultimate goal is of course not to seek any mechanical or stereotype solution to the issues, for the nature of some of these issues is such that they cannot be resolved without a serious value conflict resulting in modifications or alterations in the value system. If, on the other hand, social workers can apprehend the issues with all their complexities and pursue these for deeper analysis, a personal resolution of these issues is possible, recognizing, however, that the nature of one's resolution may not necessarily result in a formula applicable to all social workers. It is to be hoped that this kind of personal resolution is the key to creative use of authority in social work practice.

The four articles selected in this section revolve around the major values and principles of the social work profession, namely, self-determination (freedom and ability of clients to make decisions affecting their lives), responsibility (for one's decisions and actions), belief in the unlimited capacity for growth in all clients, and a concern for the basic human rights of recipients of professional service. Each of the four articles in its own way raises issues relative to the basic social work values and principles. The main rationale in choosing the four articles was the quality of in-depth analysis of these issues. None of the articles claims to profess complete resolution of the issues. Rather, they stimulate the reader's continuous engagement in creative thinking on the issues raised.

Bernstein's article, "Self-Determination: King or Citizen in the Realm of Values?" is perhaps one of the classics in social work literature. This article can be noted for its two major contributions: in-depth analysis of the concept of self-determination as it applies to social work, and a re-affirmation that the social work profession can and must consider self-determination as "supremely important" for professional practice, notwithstanding the current value crisis within the profession. An attempt is made in this article to arrange "self-determination" in the hierarchy of value systems in any given situation. At least six steps are identified in the hierarchical order with human worth as a top value and self-determination at the bottom. A tentative conclusion is reached that self-determination is not the king value. In the process of helping clients, the central goal is to help them choose, affirm, and respect, a direction that is unique to them. Maximization of self-determination becomes an essential concern in social work help.

Wasser's article extends the discussion on self-determination further with additional discussion of other social work values, namely, responsibility and protection. The specific issues raised in the article include: who is to take responsibility for an older person when he has no relative or close associate able and willing to do so? What is the responsibility of the social work profession, the social agency, and the social worker in relation to the client who lacks or loses the capacity for self-determination in a crucial area of his functioning? Does assumption of responsibility by agency and worker under such circumstances require direction of the client and control of his affairs, even possible intervention by initiation of necessary legal proceedings? Can the social agency and the social worker in good conscience carry out social work treatment in such situations unless they are willing to exercise authority? And what makes for the "sound use of authority"? Implicit in this article is an assumption that certain value conflicts in the use of authority are inevitable for social workers. One way of resolving the conflicts is to be aware of the "ends of social work help." An emphasis is placed on the point that "the controlling, coercive aspect of authority in social work represents only the means which may be needed to achieve protection of the individual and of society."

The Weisman and Chwast article is a meaningful departure from the earlier two articles. A courageous and defensive stance is taken that in the implicit and explicit use of values, social workers are essentially imposing controls on the client. Social workers are challenged to re-examine the concepts of "diagnosis" and "treatment" that include incorporation of certain values. It is noted that a value focus and its implementation in the treatment process may provide the social worker with a foundation for helping clients build healthy internal controls. Such controls, when based on both the client's values and the societal values, permit a real expression of an individual's potentialities for growth. Needless to say, this particular stance raises further questions as to the ethical responsibility of the helping professions to their clients and the society.

The section concludes with yet another classical article in social work literature by Ohlin, Piven, and Pappenfort. Using the probation and parole setting as a framework for analysis, major dilemmas confronting social workers are delineated and discussed. The prison and correctional system may exemplify, better than any other organization, the dilemmas of social workers, because of dual and often contradictory goals of the organization. On the one hand, the prison system represents an instrument of social change, and, on the other, it is also an instrument of social welfare with its emphasis on reform and rehabilitation. Occupational dilemmas are inevitable for social workers whose professional orientations tend to fall in the latter category, which is often at variance with generally accepted standards and concepts of rehabilitation.

15

Self-determination: king or citizen
in the realm of values?

Probably some of the most poignant inner searching among social workers has been and is around self-determination, which may be regarded as a technique, a fact, a cultural assumption, or a value. Many and apparently diverse meanings are attached to this concept. There is the deeply rooted sense on the part of social workers that building on the feelings and wishes of those served is essentially sound. On the other hand, many situations arise in which other considerations seem paramount. Just how determining should self-determination be? "Hard-to-reach" individuals, families, groups, and neighborhoods[1] throw up the question with force. They are not articulating requests for service. Under one concept of self-determination, we should leave them alone. The "hard-core family" on public assistance should receive the regular allowance to which it is legally entitled and nothing more, according to this position. The gang of teenagers creating aggressive mayhem should likewise be left to go its self-chosen way. Further illustrations could be multiplied, but it is more important to move on to the somewhat philosophic question rooted in and around the great idea of self-determination.

It seems helpful to proceed – evolutionary fashion – from the simple to the complex. I shall start with a kind of one-celled notion and develop the theme into a complex organism of values.

Reprinted by permission of the National Association of Social Workers, New York, and the author from *Social Work*, v: 3–8, 1960.

1 / Social work has no general term for the people it serves. *Client, group,* and *community* are commonly used. *Clientele* is perhaps an approach to generalization. In the "human relations field" there seems to be a growing use of the term *client system.* In this paper the term *client* will include individuals, families, groups, and communities.

SELF-DETERMINATION NO. 1

The heart and extent of this concept is that we as social workers should help people to do what they want to do and not stimulate them to go beyond their wishes. Self-determination is the supreme value, and it maintains its top position in any hierarchy of values, including those in which there are conflicts. For the worker the situation is pure and clear: help the people served to do what they want to do. There is little or no conflict between the values of the client and the worker. The latter's function is entirely devoted to providing the means and opportunities for the fulfillment of the desires of the client.

This position is clear and internally consistent as long as self-determination is maintained as the king value, with all others subservient to it. The working and meditating hours of the worker are relieved of the tearing-apart kinds of conflict which beset devotees of other concepts of self-determination. But "Self-determination No. 1" is a simple soul who, if he ever existed, would not be helpfully related either to the practice of his profession or to the real world. There may be workers who sound as though they belong in this club, but usually one finds that questions bring forth many qualifications ("It depends," and so forth), so that the simple and pure notion of self-determination is soon lost. Essentially, however, this concept is basic and should not perish. Rather, it needs a special kind of company and context.

SELF-DETERMINATION NO. 2

Suppose we help a person do what he wants to do today, but tomorrow he wants the opposite. How do we know what he wants? By what he says? He may have been saying it for years without ever really acting on what he says. Ambivalence turns one straight path into at least two, going in different – sometimes opposite – directions. When a part of the client expresses a feeling and seems to reach a decision, the worker would be derelict if he moved quickly in this direction without devoting time, understanding, and skill to assessing whether this feeling and decision are in fact what the client wants, uncomplicated by other and even contrary wants.

Illustrations are common. A woman is so angry at her husband that she says she wants a divorce; as the situation unfolds, however, she shows much positive feeling and need for the husband, particularly if the worker is skilful in accepting her hostile feelings. A certain gang of girls made nasty remarks about a settlement house and everybody in it. They threw rocks at the windows, and unfortunately their aim was pretty good. Months later, after the worker had dealt with the girls and had come to know them well, she was convinced that the original hostile behavior was the method they used to ask for help from the agency, without being able to put their need into words. Behavior was their language.

"Self-determination No. 2," then, recognizes ambivalence and non-verbal communication, and adds the dimensions of time and the worker's professional qualifications, so that the eventual decisions have increased stability, depth, and clarity resulting from some working through of conflicting feelings.

It is not always possible or even desirable to eliminate all conflict or ambivalence. Many situations have built-in and all-but-unresolvable conflicts. The client dealing with a chronically ill relative is doomed to mixed feelings. The unmarried mother is appropriately expected to be in conflict about the decision as to whether to keep or give up her baby. There is no satisfactory answer in the sense that it completely eliminates the appeal of the contrary decision or that no regrets will later be felt. People and life are not like that. But the contribution of the worker is around a new perspective on tense and mixed feelings. In assessing what the client wants and in helping him to achieve it, the aim is to take into full account the varieties of ambivalence and changes over time.

SELF-DETERMINATION NO. 3

Reality in its multitudinous forms enters the self-determination picture. It can be biological, as in principles of health. It can be economic, as related to a balanced budget (even installment buying requires that the payments be met). It can be legal, as in obeying laws. There are other forms of reality, but the essential point is the stubborn quality of it, which sets up rules and expectations not controlled by our clients, but which must be met by them. These factors narrow substantially the range of reasonable choices open to the client – and to us all. A man may want his public assistance allowance trebled and may be able to make a good case for the increase, but he is not the one who should or can make this decision. The same line of reasoning goes for bad health practices, illegal behavior, spending well beyond one's income, and the like. A frequent problem faced by social workers is that many of those we serve have so weak a grasp on reality that they become enmeshed in its retaliations, and the client thereby loses the opportunity to express his self-determination in matters appropriate for it.

Reality has a fixed and final sound which can distort social work diagnosis and functions. The assumption is too often made that the client meets role expectations, that he "adapts," "adjusts," to his physical and cultural setting. The latter is presumed to be right, or rigid, something that does not lend itself to planned change. This is a strange position in a world full of dramatic and large-scale social, economic, and political change. C. Wright Mills in *The Sociological Imagination* makes the effective point that "nowadays men often feel that their private lives are a series of traps." These are large-scale societal changes which individuals do not understand or control. The writer pleads for "sociological imagination," which grasps the connection between the inner life of the individual and the larger framework of society.

This orientation does not give the client of a public assistance agency the right to decide on the amount of his allowance, but it does suggest that various social aspects of his situation might be examined and changed. Perhaps the agency should offer larger amounts; perhaps he can be helped to become self-supporting; perhaps there is a need for new economic institutions which will employ him. A crucial criterion for social change is whether it will increase the opportunities for appropriate self-determination for many people.

Returning to the original point about reality: the kind of exercise of self-determination that disregards reality is full of fantasy – it is unhealthy and self-defeating. A good part of the function of the worker may be to help the client distinguish what is fixed and stubborn from what is open to his decision. Skill in diagnosis inevitably involves the sorting out of what is relatively fixed from what is relatively changeable. Wise strategy of helping people to change is based on concentrating on what is most flexible. The client may still decide to flout reality (as all of us do at times), but then at least he will be better prepared for the consequences. It may well be that we can do our best work at the stage when the wallop of reality has been felt. There are great learning opportunities in such crises.

SELF-DETERMINATION NO. 4

Almost always, other people are involved in the self-determination of the client. His sense of responsibility may encompass them in varying degrees. There are instances in which parents abandon their children, husbands desert their wives, the gang beats up an innocent victim just to express feelings. At the other extreme is the person who allows himself to be exploited by others so that he is not making for himself the kinds of decisions that are the right of every human being.

Self-determination is enmeshed in a complex network of social relationships which move the notion far from the simple level on which each client does what he wants to do, yields to his own impulses. Even Robinson Crusoe was not completely alone psychologically or culturally. The problem then is to find some principles that will offer guidelines out of this maze. One might be that the exercise of self-determination by one person should have minimium inconsistency with such exercise by others. This is a kind of equivalent to the golden rule and Kant's categorical imperative. It does not eliminate all conflicts – not necessarily a desirable goal – but it does provide a helpful framework and even rather specific guidance. As a homely illustration, it is not rare for a club of adolescent boys to plan an affair involving a girls' club without much consultation of the wishes of the latter. The group worker can easily make the suggestion to ask the girls about some idea that is being argued. A large area of potential contribution by social workers is embedded in this simple technique of consulting people who may be affected by a decision. How many times, in how many kinds of relationships, is this step omitted!

At the other extreme, with the person who is being exploited, the principle is rather different. The worker needs to diagnose carefully the areas in which legitimate self-determination is violated and then try to reinforce the client and influence the environment so that he may become able to enjoy the rights to which he is entitled.

With "Self-determination No. 4" we are in the midst of a question that has burned hot throughout much of human history. Egoism versus altruism is a kind of statement of it – a misleading one, I believe. Altruism asks for a kind of selfishness which seems unrealistic and unsound. Some of the worst acts of egoism have been perpetrated under the guise of altruism. The sense of selfhood is too deep, strong, pervasive, and instinctive to build on its elimination. More hopeful is the approach which recognizes and respects the drive toward selfhood in all of us, striving to help people understand how each can achieve identity only as he respects the same drive in others.

Many therapists have been so intrigued by the methods and orientation of their professions that they have overlooked the social dimension of self-determination. Individual dynamics are so intricate and fascinating that there is the temptation to regard them as all of significant reality. Perhaps subtly, the therapist is beguiled into an acceptance of what the client says about his social setting as being all that is important for the therapist to understand about it. The culture that has impregnated the client may be lost, as may be the impact of the client on the people he intimately affects. In just these areas social work has paid a price – the weakening of the "social" in its calling – for an otherwise fruitful dependence on psychiatry. It is a strange kind of ethic that elevates the desires of the client above those to whom he is socially related. The "unseen audience" should not be victimized by therapy. Along with being an object of transference and other kinds of feelings, the therapist ought to be a kind of social conscience which helps the client relate his self-determination to all of those with whom he has relationships. To do anything else would contribute to social degeneration.

SELF-DETERMINATION NO. 5

Here we come close to the center of the human enterprise – to what, one may hope, distinguishes us from animals and from blind followers of instinct. A useful handle, much discussed in social work and elsewhere, is the process of decision-making. The infant when hungry "decides" to cry. It is a simple, instinctive reaction. A mature decision, at the other pole, is guided by rationality and intelligence. The learning of the ability to make the latter kind of decision is regarded by some as more important than the benefits which may accrue from any specific act of decision. Learning how to approach problems rationally is thereby elevated to the position of one of the most prized skills.

A whole flood of implications flows from "Self-determination No. 5." One is the growing concern about the probable consequences for oneself and for others from any given decision or action. Another is the need to attain sufficient perspective so that unconscious distortions and urges are kept at a minimum. Still another is the generation of a more or less conscious method for dealing with problems. In addition, there is the more thoughtful examination of previously assumed values. The list could be elaborated.

The content of intelligent decision-making has been given considerable attention by John Dewey and many others. The current human relations movement, with its ideologies and activities, is devoted to this end. In grand terms, it is the application of the scientific method to human affairs.

The social work client may be ready in only modest and varying degrees to participate on these more rarified levels of human expression. Yet his self-determination takes on profundity only as he moves toward them. Each client needs our best diagnosis in terms of where he is and how far he can go, but the direction of change supported by the worker should be firmly derived from rationality. This may sound strange to those who strive so hard to understand all the perplexing irrationalities in people. But what is often overlooked is that the attempt to understand irrationality is essentially rational. Whatever concepts or constructs we may use to explain instinct-based behavior, they represent the struggles of intelligence to bring experience into some sort of order. The direction is clear.

The theme of freedom runs through this orchestration of the elements of self-determination. If one takes a pure and completely consistent deterministic position, self-determination is an illusion; it is simply acting in accord with controlling forces which may or may not be understood. In the Marxian context – *i.e.*, the idea that history is economically determined, especially in terms of class – the behavior of many of us would have to be considered a current and potent example of determinism; although that point of view leaves open the choice to join with the class that will presumably be victorious.

Social work is based on the assumption that people are free to make significant choices and that they can be helped to make better ones. But the attempt to use freedom to make decisions that are contrary to reality or largely irrational is self-defeating. Confusion rather than creativity flows from the disregard of facts and reason. Only as one takes account of the relevant factors does true freedom operate in decision making. Yielding to unexamined impulses is more a surrender to instinctive drives than the expression of mature self-determination.

This is not to claim that we are predominantly rational. Social work has dealt too much with raw ids to make this error. The orientation is rather to the effect that the forces within and outside of us should be recognized and scrutinized with whatever rational capabilities we have. To help in this process is a major function of the social worker. Insofar as this help is successful, the worker is enabling the client to reach toward "Self-determination No. 5" – a pretty high level of social functioning.

SELF-DETERMINATION NO. 6

The subtitle of this paper, "King or Citizen in the Realm of Values," raises the question of hierarchy or priority. It is hoped that what has been said makes clear that self-determination is *not* king, or a supreme value. The various qualifications and contexts are meant to show that the mere act or desire to act according to one's wishes is neither a final nor a complete basis for a professional point of view. Assuming this position, are we left in a kind of "it depends" vagueness as to which values rise above others in specific situations and in general? I think not. Value problems cannot be reduced to the simplicity or specificity of administrative charts which show clearly who is above whom, but there are meaningful patterns and points of reference.

Most basically, the supreme social work value is human worth, an enormous idea, probably the greatest discovery in human history. Perhaps it suffers from too frequent mention in social work without sufficient elaboration of its rich meanings. It is based only moderately on what people are; much more on what they can be. It applies not only to those immediately before the social worker, but also to every human being on this earth (we may yet need an interplanetary concept). The specific content of the human worth idea evolves with history. It has many facets: legal and civil rights, standard of living, freedom to develop potentialities, intellectual and artistic interests, and others.

With this supreme value, self determination then becomes modified. If what the client wants will result in the exploitation of others or the degradation of himself, the worker should try to help him change his desires.

The steps suggested in this paper are meant to be criteria for judgments about self-determination which will help to place it appropriately in a hierarchy of values in any given situation. It seems more useful to approach the hierarchy question in this way (human worth at the top and self-determination subject to a set of criteria) than to attempt a rigid blueprint or chart. All this leads to the definite position that self-determination is *not* the king value, is not supreme in the realm of values.

CONCLUSION

While self-determination is not supreme, it is supremely important. Only through the rich utilization of this concept can we fully honor the human-worth value. This is in line with the best in democratic traditions. As we study and diagnose each situation, our concern should be for maximizing the choices for the people we serve, subject to the framework suggested above. Even with young children, there are appropriate matters about which they should be helped to make decisions. In an even more extreme example, the man in prison has many conditions imposed on him, but he might be helped to make his own decisions about jobs in the prison, recreation, what to do after he is released, and other matters. The point is that the value system of social work requires this maximization of self-determination.

In addition to its values, the methods of social work themselves require great stress on self-determination. People can be and are manipulated, but constructive changes which take root inside the person, group, or community usually need to be based on participation and consent. The Supreme Court decision on desegregation attempts to manipulate the environment – to eliminate by force the practice of discrimination in schools. It does not pretend to change the feelings of the prejudiced. Some have concluded that therefore this historic decision is useless or harmful. I do not agree, and think that over the long pull the lessening of discriminatory practices can and does lessen prejudice. In the legal and perhaps other power-packed arenas, it is often necessary to override self-determination of some people for the sake of human worth. The alternative would be to wait for complete agreement, an impossible political goal on most issues.

In social action, then, social work adapts its concept of self-determination to the realities of the process of political change; but the great bulk of social work practice has internal change as its goal. Here we find that imposing, telling, or giving orders do not work well. Only as the client is thoroughly involved and comes to accept on deepening levels the process of change can our methods be effective in relation to our goals. We may not be able to produce research-based proof (although there is some) for this position, but it is supported by so much practical experience on the part of so many of us that we fully accept and act on it.

There is a deeper and weightier support for self-determination: its existence and potency is a fact. Social workers and other professionals may enable, stimulate, impose, and even use force, but what the client feels, thinks, and values is ultimately his private affair and more within his control than that of the professional. The delinquent can be forcibly placed in a training school, but he cannot be forced to change his notions of the kind of life he wants to lead. For this the inner boy must be involved, must decide to re-examine himself and to change. This is a very important reason for emphasizing so much the significance of the relationship with the worker. Through it our boy learns to trust and have confidence in the worker so that he is ready to share some of his precious inward self with a view toward changing it. Only the boy himself can make this decision. Without his consent we can probably modify his outward behavior; with it there is the opportunity for changes in inward values, an essential and basic purpose of social work.

16

Responsibility, self-determination, and authority in casework protection of older persons

Protection of older persons is a matter of increasing concern to the community at large, to social work as a profession, to social agencies, and to the social work practitioner. Inevitably, whatever philosophy social work has about its responsibility for protection of the aging will provide the foundation for casework protective service to the older person.

The Community Service Society of New York is currently engaged in a study of the mentally deteriorated or disturbed older person as part of its larger program of research in the field of social and health services for the aging. Dr. Margaret Blenkner, director of the study, has drawn attention to the fact that, although social work is logically the profession to assume a major responsibility for the protection of the aged person who lacks relatives able to do so, it has seldom taken this responsibility.[1]

Investigation of the literature and a preliminary review of the cases in our study have led the writer to believe that a re-examination of the concepts of responsibility, self-determination, and authority as they apply in social work is basic to an understanding of protection of older persons. Hence, this paper will be concerned with the idea of protection in relation to these concepts as fundamental to casework practice with the aging. The paper is presented from the perspective of the writer's five years' study of the aging and their problems, first as supervisor of research interviewing in the larger program, and more recently as project associate in the protective care study.[2] The first phase of this study, for which the writer

Reprinted by permission of the Family Service Association of America, New York, from *Social Casework*, XLII: 258–66, May-June 1961.

1 / Margaret Blenkner, *Proposal for a Study of the Social Work Component in Protective Care of the Mentally Deteriorated or Disturbed Older Person*, Community Service Society, New York, 1958, p. 3. (Mimeographed)

2 / It is the writer's good fortune to have worked with Ollie Randall in the pre-

was primarily responsible, was directed toward (1) "review, analysis and distillation of pertinent principles, concepts and questions contained in documents and published literature" and (2) "consultation with knowledgeable persons regarding the soundness of formulations arrived at."[3] It is hoped that, despite their controversial nature, the formulations presented will help to clarify issues and stimulate expression of differing viewpoints. The next phase of the study involves intensive content analysis of research and service records of a sample of both applicants and non-applicants to the Community Service Society who have been identified as having a protective problem.

BACKGROUND

Blenkner has estimated on the basis of previous research that, at a minimum, between 5 and 10 per cent of the non-institutionalized urban aged may be in need of protection of some kind. In numbers, this represents approximately one to two million of our aged, many of whom are undoubtedly cared for by relatives and other sources, but of whom a sizeable although unknown number are not.[4]

The problem concerning protection of these uncared-for older persons may be outlined in the following series of questions: Who is to take responsibility for an adult unable to take responsibility for himself when he has no relative or close associate able and willing to do so? What is the responsibility of the social work profession, the social agency, and the social worker in relation to the client who lacks or loses the capacity for self-determination in a crucial area of his functioning? Does assumption of responsibility by agency and worker under such circumstances require direction of the client and control of his affairs, even possible intervention by initiation of necessary legal proceedings? Can the social agency and social worker in good conscience carry out social work treatment in such situations unless they are willing to exercise authority? Is the basic social work question regarding authority, "Is the use of authority sound?" or is it, "What makes for the sound use of authority?" What is the meaning of authority in social work?

These questions are significant for the social work profession and are

liminary thinking-through of issues pertinent to the study and to have had, as a member of the advisory committee to the Project on Guardianship and Protective Services of the National Council on the Aging (formerly the National Committee on Aging of the National Social Welfare Assembly), the benefit of Virginia Lehmann's lucid thinking.

3 / Margaret Blenkner, *op. cit.* p. 8.
4 / *Ibid.*, p. 5.

especially pertinent to aging persons and social agencies serving them. Aging is likely to bring most people to some diminished functioning and increased dependency at rates that vary within the different aspects of the personality and organism. Thus, in the aging process, there is always the potential of an individual's becoming unable to care for himself or to exercise adequate judgment for fundamental self-direction. Such inability may never eventuate, but it is a vivid reality for many. The younger adult who lacks capacity for judgment for adequate self-care is likely to have relatives who assume responsibility or can be helped to do so. This is less true for many older adults who have outlived responsible relatives or associates.

Because of the potentiality of breakdown in the aging client, it would appear that there is inherent within every social agency serving the aging a specific protective obligation, whatever the agency's major service. This obligation requires definition by the agency, and implies readiness by agency and worker to assume some degree of responsibility and, indeed, to use some degree of authority, should there not exist a responsible relative or associate of the individual willing and able to do so.

Protection of the aging in the field of social work is complicated by the special characteristics and needs of the aging person. Services and facilities available for protection are limited and ambiguous. The biological and psychological aspects of aging create the need for participation of the medical and psychiatric professions in the protective problem. Fiduciary relationships, such as guardianship, and other legal protections for individual rights create complicated issues that call for the participation of the legal profession.

The providing of a full range of protective services is extremely complicated, technically difficult, and financially costly. They can run the gamut of simple supporting services of a protective nature to guardianship and initiation of commitment proceedings. The civic and professional problem of intervention in a person's management of his own affairs – whether, when, and how to intervene – must also be resolved. It is important for the profession of social work and the community as well to have awareness not only of the obligation to the aging client in need of protection but of the complicated issues and difficulties in providing protective services.

PROTECTION

Protection as a concept is pervasive in social work. It is the very nature of social work to guard, to defend. Social work promotes the social growth of both individual and community. It protects by preventing harm to the individual, and by serving as a bulwark to the community against the social disintegration of its members. Social work both enables and protects.

Protection is both a qualitative and a quantitative concept. The type and quantity of protection will depend on the nature and degree of client incapacity, as well as on the function of the social agency. Need for protective action applies to clients regardless of age. The term "protection" is pertinent to any group of persons who present certain similar identifiable characteristics. Protection may be related to children, the so-called "hardcore" multiproblem dependent families, the aging, or any similarly identified grouping of clients. A specialized body of protective practice tends to develop in relation to such groups, which requires adaptation of methods in relation to the identifiable idiosyncrasies of the particular group, and adaptation and development of resources. A small but growing body of literature related to protection of the aging is to be noted. Garrettson, McCann, and Hemmy, among others, have made important contributions, as has the American Public Welfare Association.[5]

Mention should be made that the elderly person, as an adult and in contrast to the child, has passed into full exercise of his civil and personal rights. Protection of the aging person, thus, has a special character to be considered when authoritative action is taken affecting him and his rights. A comparative consideration of protection in different fields within social work – both as to the differences and similarities in the intrinsic nature of each particular population and as to the casework treatment methods that have been evolved – offers an intriguing area for exploration for the mutual enrichment of work with all groups having problems in protection.

The elderly person needing special protective consideration is likely to show signs of some mental disturbance through unusual, bizarre, difficult, offensive, or self-neglecting behavior, sometimes of a harmless or sometimes of a dangerous nature. He may or may not be aware of his limitations. Elderly folk with benign though troublesome symptoms frequently remain in the community, and many more would do so were there some degree of protective supervision.

Social work protection to the aging person logically consists of use of professional expertise, which includes sound psychosocial diagnosis and

5 / Jane Garretson, "The Family Agency and Protective Services to the Aged Client," United Charities of Chicago, 1956. (Mimeographed)

Charles W. McCann, "Guardians of the Aged," *Grass Roots Private Welfare*, Alfred deGrazia (ed.), New York University Press, New York, 1957, pp. 225–229.

Mary L. Hemmy and Marcella S. Farrar, "Protective Series for Older People," SOCIAL CASEWORK, Vol. XLII, No. 1 (1961), pp. 16–20.

American Public Welfare Association, *Essentials of Public Welfare Services for Older People – Services for the Senile Aged*, American Public Welfare Assn., Chicago, Nov. 29, 1955.

evaluation of the client's functioning in his social situation, and the use of treatment processes and methods which are adapted to the aging person and his special characteristics; development and use of ancillary supporting services; collaboration in the individual case with medical, psychiatric, and legal representatives.

What gives social work protective services for the older person their special character? First, the way in which mental disorganization can occur in the older person calls for special knowledge and judgment. An aging client may have adequate functioning and complete capacity for self-determination in some areas, and a range of inadequate functioning and incapacity for self-determination in other areas.

Next, the possibility of mental breakdown and incapacity for self-determination at some point creates the extraordinarily delicate problem for the social agency and social worker of when and how to take the initiative, step in, intervene, take responsibility, act. To do so presumes some use of authority. When the client agrees to the agency's intervention, or responds positively to the influence of the agency and worker to act in a particular way, the ultimate decision is the client's. The problem is slippery in those circumstances where the client, even though incapable of adequate judgment and self-care or potentially harmful to himself or others, is unwilling to accede to agency initiative or lacks the capacity to do so. Such situations are likely to present emergencies, requiring rapid action if the client is to be protected from harm. The social agency is faced with a need to develop techniques and procedures that permit fulfilment of the social protective obligation and yet afford to the client, worker, and agency the legal safeguards that this kind of intervention necessitates.

PROTECTIVE TERMINOLOGY

The term "protection" in its various ramifications in social work bears examination. "Protection" and "protective" are used in many ways in social work. Phrases such as "protective care," "protective services," "being in need of protection," "having a protective problem" are commonly used. A client who properly belongs in a nursing home because of severe physical disability may be said to need a "protective setting." Or the hard-core multiproblem family may be said to need "protective care." A mentally ill person may be described as one who needs the "protection" of a hospital. A very old person, simply suffering from the normal infirmities of aging, may be said to need a "semi-protective living arrangement."

How can the older person with a protective problem be identified and differentiated from the older person who has no such problem? Such identification represents a basic diagnostic problem that must provide the background for treatment choices. Such identification is necessary so that estimates can be made of how many of these persons there are likely to be in a community. Further, elderly persons with a protective problem need to be classified in some way to show the degree of seriousness of the protective problem and other qualities, not only for diagnosis and treatment, but for research purposes as well.

In the Community Service Society, in early attempts to define "protective care," it was found necessary first to set up a definition that would identify the "person with a protective problem," irrespective of whether or not the problem was under control at a given time. In other words, the conditions and the behavior that make necessary some degree of supervision and control of a person and his affairs by someone other than himself had to be specified. Not until then could there be a consideration of how the supervision and control were or could be provided, and a delineation of the extent to which the persons thus identified did or did not present a problem of protective care to the community.

The following working definition of the "person with a protective problem" was arrived at:

A protective problem occurs when an individual has a mental disorder which results in or is associated with:

1 His limitation in functioning and self-management being manifested by his being only marginally capable or completely incapable of caring for his personal physical needs, and/or performing the activities necessary in daily living, and/or planning and making decisions, and/or handling his finances, and/or

2 His being dangerous to himself and/or others, and/or

3 His manifesting such obnoxious or disturbed conduct that it offends and brings him into conflict with the mores of the community.

The person whose incapacity is solely due to physical disability is excluded. Persons with mental and physical disabilities, which are frequently associated, are included.

Definition of the services or care that such persons require, or more properly the *social work component* of these services or care, is seen as the outcome of the study, not its starting point. Nevertheless, some structuring of the concepts is required in order to analyze them and communicate with others regarding them.

The following definitions of "protective services" in a narrow sense and in a broad sense are suggested.[6]

1 Protective service in the *narrow sense* is: (a) that which is based di-

6 / These definitions from Virginia Lehmann are based on notes of a discussion with her.

rectly upon legal authority, or which calls legal authority into play; or
(b) that which is based upon legally sanctioned procedures.
2 Protective service in the *broad sense* includes: (a) a continuum of
services, all those needed by elderly people who are not able, unassisted,
to care for themselves (such as counseling, nursing, housekeeping, medical
care, and so on); or (b) the readiness to call into play those actions
described under protective services in the narrow sense.

Thus, presumably, the use of protective services in the *narrow* sense
would pertain in regard to elderly persons with severe manifestations of
senile breakdown. Social work activity would be based directly upon calling into play legal authority and procedures. It could be thought of as
legally based protective action. Presumably, protective services in the
broad sense would pertain in regard to elderly persons who manifest a
range from mild to severe degree of senile breakdown, and consequently
require for their protection a range and variety of services, from those of
a simple supporting nature to those of more complex nature, such as
guardianship or initiation of commitment proceedings. Social work activity would be based upon professional expertise, including the likelihood of
some use of professional authority, with readiness to call upon legal
authority and procedures.

Neota Larson, chief of the Welfare Branch of the Bureau of Old-Age
and Survivors Insurance, which, like the Bureau of Public Assistance, has
been extensively involved in the protective needs of older persons has
suggested the following groupings of services needed by them:[7]
1 Preventive measures, such as golden age programs;
2 Supportive measures (much like those indicated under 2(a) in definitions given above);
3 Protective services, "where someone else must be given the authority
to act in the individual's behalf completely or in respect to some phase of
his life," (much like those suggested under 1(a) and 1(b) in definitions
above).

"Protective care" is another term that may warrant some consideration. At the beginning of the Community Service Society study, "protective care" was used as an over-all term that, as now seen, included services
plus facilities and, at times, the problem and the person as well. Lehmann
has suggested that "protective care" be used to refer to *facilities* as distinct from the more intangible term "services." She would restrict its use

7 / Neota Larson, "Protective Services for Older People." Paper presented at
Biennial Round Table Conference of the American Public Welfare Association, Dec.
5, 1959. Bureau of Old-Age and Survivors Insurance, Washington, D.C. (Mimeographed)

to such resources as nursing and boarding homes and institutions for the aged, which provide literally for the direct care of the person.

The foregoing discussion represents, not an arbitrary investment in particular definitions for universal use, but an attempt to indicate the desirability of working on those basic notions in protection of the aging that need a common terminology, and to offer some illustrations for possible consideration. Clarification and agreement as to the meaning of some basic terms would be a genuine aid to practice. Although social workers in the field of aging suffer from the disadvantage that concepts and practices are not jelled, they could profit by this state of affairs to settle on a uniform use of some basic terms.

RESPONSIBILITY

Social work, philosophically speaking, accepts a generalized protective responsibility toward the individual and society. Such responsibility presumes capacity, strength, and authority for performance.

The potential inability to care for the self which is germinal in the aging process, and the consequent specific obligation of the social agency to serve the aging protectively, create the need for the agency to define its policy as to what kind and degree of responsibility for protection it carries and what role it will assume in serving the older person in the event of his breakdown.

The exceptional requirements for a genuine protective service understandably are strong deterrents to the social agency in moving toward assumption of a full protective role. The social agency is faced with deciding whether it wishes to or must go beyond the minimum service of recognition of the client's need and the responsible transfer to another source which will provide the protection.

The attitude of most social agencies toward providing protective services has usually been determined and limited by the genuine administrative and service complexities – by the costliness in professional time, money, and special resources required by protective situations; by the intricacies and expense of guardianship and other fiduciary relationships; by reluctance to become involved in possible commitment proceedings in an authoritative role, and conceivably in a lawsuit.

Beyond the genuine practical difficulties of providing a protective service, much of the reluctance of many social agencies to become so engaged may be due to their interpretation of that aspect of social work's value system which is concerned with self-determination, and to their wish not to invade client rights.

However, it is essential to distinguish between what constitutes *invasion* of rights and what constitutes *preservation* of rights. Protection has as its aim the preservation and not the invasion or destruction of rights. Rigid adherence by the social agency and worker to the concept of client self-determination when client capacity for self-determination is seriously lacking may unwittingly become abnegation of service. If they fail to assume the responsibility for facing the attendant problems of their client at the critical point of his inability to care for himself properly, the result may be a denial, however unintentional, of a painful and difficult aspect of need. The issue becomes, not *whether* to take responsibility to act protectively – in the social work sense – but *when, how, to what degree,* and *with what safeguards* to client, worker, and agency.

Can we speculate that the deterioration potential in aging, because of its disturbing reminder that we are all heir to it, may serve as a deterrent to social work initiative in this important area of human need? Does denial of the aging process per se unknowingly find its expression in social work through denial of service?

Failure by an agency to define its policy and practice concerning the nature and limits of its protective responsibility is likely to transfer the burden of definition to the front line practitioner and create a serious predicament for him.

Usually, client participation and self-responsibility are primary worker goals, even with clients who may have only minimal capacity for self-direction in essential areas of living. However, when an older person is no longer capable of self-direction in some crucial part of his life, the social agency and social worker may be forced into a different caliber of relationship with him. In some measure, a shift from a client self-determining kind of social work practice to one entailing use of authority becomes necessary.

SELF-DETERMINATION

The right to self-determination and freedom of choice is deeply rooted in the cultural and professional being of the social worker, and is essential to his own psychic needs as a human being. Humanitarian ideals, faith in the worth and dignity of the individual, and self-determination are values that are embedded in the culture and democratic structure of American society, which social work reflects.

On the other hand, that the concept of self-determination is not an absolute, nor indeed the most basic consideration in a democracy, has been recognized by society as well as by social work. Each individual's freedom is limited by innumerable social and psychological controls which are essential if many individuals are to live with each other in an operating society. These include not only external controls, but the built-in controls within the structure of the individual's personality, representing the accumulated force of parental and societal influence, which have become familiar through psychoanalytic exposition. On the question of self-determination in relation to social work, the articles by Bernstein and by Biestek are of special interest.[8]

In social work, self-determination as a value has been translated into the methods by which help is given. The goal of the modern sophisticated helper is somehow to motivate, to engage the will, to enable or to release individuals or groups, so that they may think and act for their own benefit and improvement and in harmony with their social situations. The professional helper of today has arduously learned by self-discipline, hard won self-knowledge, technical training and experience, how *not* to impose his will to satisfy his own personal needs. He gains satisfaction in identifying with the self-fulfilment of individual and group clientele. The social worker's own personal and professional values concerning individual rights and self-determination have been fortified by the technical developments in social work methods which emphasize both the client's right to decide and the effectiveness of his self-directed behavior.

It is quite understandable that any seeming negation of the principle of self-determination in social work practice represents a formidable force to be dealt with. Unconscious as well as conscious attitudes become mobilized to resist what is a seeming regression to authoritarian practice. Such resistance becomes emphasized when an authoritative action by the social worker or agency is also foreseen as leading to an individual's loss of his freedom through commitment to a mental institution, however necessary this may be. Any activity by social agency or social worker leading to commitment, whether voluntary or involuntary, cannot help but provoke anxiety when they participate in this most serious experience.

AUTHORITY

Authority, like responsibility, is intrinsic in the nature of social agencies and of social work as a profession. It derives from their assumption of a welfare role that is accepted as valid by the state and the community, to which they are accountable.

In the consummation of social work's purposes, awareness and use of

8 / Saul Bernstein, "Self-Determination: King or Citizen in the Realm of Values," *Social Work*, Vol. v, No. 1 (1960), pp. 3–8.

Felix P. Biestek, "The Principle of Client Self-Determination," SOCIAL CASE-WORK, Vol. XXXII, No. 9 (1951), pp. 369–375.

self-determination have in no way precluded the use of authority. Social agencies and social workers have probably functioned all along, consciously or unconsciously, with the use of authority in some form and to some degree, whether with mild subtle influence or with more assertive action.

Some well-intentioned unconscious misuse of authority has probably occurred in social work. A fine line of distinction needs to be made between the authoritative action which is genuinely protecting of an individual and that which is taken primarily to facilitate the administration of an agency's program.[9]

Authority is a complex concept which has challenged the thought of numerous writers, and is coming under increasing scrutiny in social work. Greenwood identifies authority as one of the essential elements characteristic of a profession. The de Schweinitzes refer to "inherent authority" (experience and learning leading to judgment which less experienced and learned persons will follow) as contrasted with "constituted authority" (the power to act). Taylor delineates the social control function in casework wherein "the case-worker–client relationship is almost inevitably charged with some elements of power, open or subtle." Studt states that there are authority factors of a social and psychological nature in casework, and that the casework process emerges as a "particular, highly skilled form of the exercise of influence."[10] It can be observed that the climate of social work has become increasingly conducive to accepting the validity of the authority concept in practice.

"PROFESSIONAL AUTHORITY" AND "USE OF AUTHORITY"

Professional authority, as generally conceived, can be taken to mean *the power to influence* that inheres in the social work profession, in the social

9 / Ollie Randall, in oral communication with the writer, has drawn attention to a question that can be raised about the too-enveloping nature of the authority sometimes assumed over the person and the property of the aged of an institution.

10 / Ernest Greenwood, "Attributes of a Profession," *Social Work*, Vol. II, No. 3 (1957), p. 45; Elizabeth and Karl de Schweinitz, "The Place of Authority in the Protective Function of the Public Welfare Agency," *Bulletin*, Child Welfare League of America, Vol. XXV, no. 7 (1946), pp. 1–6; Robert K. Taylor, "The Social Control Function in Casework," SOCIAL CASEWORK, Vol. XXXIX, No. 1 (1958), p. 18; Elliot Studt, "An Outline for Study of Social Authority Factors in Casework," SOCIAL CASEWORK, Vol. XXXV, No. 6 (1954), p. 233.

Additional pertinent articles published subsequent to the presentation of this paper: Samuel Mencher, "The Concept of Authority and Social Casework," *Casework Papers, 1960*, Family Service Association of America, New York, 1960, pp. 126–133; Irving Weisman and Jacob Chwast, "Control and Values in Social Work Treatment," SOCIAL CASEWORK, Vol. XLI, No. 9 (1960), pp. 451–456.

agency and the social worker, by virtue of professional knowledge, ethics, and competence – influence that is used to affect the individual and the community to act to achieve betterment. Professional authority is constantly operational in every aspect of social work. It is the breath of the profession.

Professional social work authority is usually carefully differentiated from legal authority, as was indicated in the preceding article.

The power of the social worker and social agency to affect the client's behavior, attitudes, and circumstances has long been recognized. In turn, controls have been developed, that can be tightened, to help agency and worker achieve client good rather than injury, however unintentional. These controls are professional ethics, knowledge, training, supervision, and consultation.

The same controls are the profession's assurance to client and community that there will be no arbitrary use of authority. These controls, combined with clear agency definition as to policy and practice in protective service to the aging, and collaboration with the legal resources and the medical and psychiatric diagnostic resources in a community, should afford safeguards against improper authoritative acts.

The delineation of the legal controls and safeguards within which the social agency and worker may and should act, as compared with those applicable to the ordinary citizen, becomes very important. The profession may face the anomaly of having professional responsibility and greater moral authority than the ordinary citizen has to act in an emergency lacking an individual's consent, without necessarily any greater legal authority to do so. A legal status has yet to be accorded the social work profession, an achievement that would reinforce the professional authority within social work. Indeed, this lack of legal status may play a part in holding back assumption of protective responsibilities in social work which require authoritative action.

Use of authority, or the authoritative act, represents a means by which social agency and social worker affect and influence the client. It connotes intervening, power in the sense of ability to do (rather than to dominate), acting, taking initiative or responsibility.

It is essential to relate the use of authority to the intent, to the purpose of the action taken, and to distinguish between that which is "authoritarian" and that which is "authoritative." If the intent is a capricious robbing of rights, the action is *authoritarian*. If the intent is to guard the worth and dignity of an individual who lacks the capacity to assert his rights, the action is *authoritative* and the use of authority is protective and humanitarian.

Social work is altruistic in that the client's interest is paramount. The same altruistic component exists when authority is used in a client's behalf, with or without client consent. The controlling, coercive aspect of authority in social work represents only the means which may be needed to achieve protection of the individual and of society.

The technical means by which a social agency and worker exercise authority through influence upon a client are part of professional equipment, and are not necessarily explained to the client, nor is their use necessarily dependent upon his permission. For instance, when a caseworker fosters and controls the casework relationship, how this is done is not usually a matter for consultation with the client even though the ultimate goal may be the client's self-direction.

Intervention in a client's affairs may arise from a decision by agency and worker, and not necessarily from client request. For instance, when action is initiated by the agency and worker toward involuntary commitment, the origin of the action is within the agency and worker.

It is suggested that the concept of professional authority be recognized as including not only the idea of *influence* but of *intervention*. Intervention in this context refers to the social agency's and social worker's taking responsibility and acting for the client when, according to expert professional judgment, this is considered necessary and there are no desirable alternatives. Such intervention may range from an uninvited and unwanted home visit by the social worker to action leading to involuntary commitment. When client consent is not obtained, legal safeguards are essential. This use of authority is likely to be rarely used by most social agencies, but it needs to be specified as an authentic expression of professional social work authority. Assumption of such responsibility represents acceptance by the profession of social work of the ultimate obligation which inheres in the fulfilment of its social purposes.

The elucidation here of the social worker's protective role with the older person and the possible need to act authoritatively in no way minimizes the great difficulty in performing the role and deciding about the critical point at which professional authority should be used which goes beyond influence to intervention. Sound psychosocial diagnostic evaluation and expertise are a *sine qua non* for the protective action that calls for use of authority involving intervention in a client's life.

It is to be emphasized that guardianship and involuntary commitment, which present stumbling blocks to the social agency, are achievable by court action only, and are not accomplished by the act of the agency or social worker. The latter can only utilize concern for the worth, dignity, and fundamental rights of the individual to see that adequate social judgment is combined with medical and psychiatric judgment to provide the court with a sound basis for legal judgment and action.

In the performance of agency service for older persons, legal aspects especially related to commitment and to fiduciary relationships, such as guardianship and power of attorney, pertain. These, it would seem, require availability of legal consultation in individual case situations, in much the same way as agencies provide psychiatric consultation to staff in cases presenting serious psychiatric problems.

Finally, it is necessary for social work to develop specific safeguards, perhaps in conjunction with the medical and legal professions, so that sound methods can be evolved for protecting not only the client but the agency and staff worker when necessary authoritative steps have to be taken for the welfare of the client. Some such safeguards could consist of joint legal, medical, and social work consultation and decision case by case, and would provide a basis for reliable accountability in the case situation. Also, there is need for exploration of the feasibility of "malpractice" insurance. It is to be hoped that these safeguards would free the agency, and in turn the practitioner, to be imaginative and ingenious in developing techniques for helping the older person in the community.

IRVING WEISMAN
JACOB CHWAST, PH.D.

17

Control and values in social work treatment

Social work treatment, whether casework or group work, is one of society's alternative ways of exercising social control of persons who manifest deviant behavior, although such services are not usually regarded in this way. Society uses other control methods such as reward and approval, open criticism, corporal punishment, and enforcement of segregation. These forms of control are clearly recognizable, which is not true of control through treatment. A treatment service, the purpose of which is to enhance an individual's social functioning, nevertheless contains an element of control. This article will present, in a simplified form, some of the complex interrelationships between treatment and the control elements inherent in the treatment situation.

In this paper, the term "control" will be used to include the entire range of pressures, both external and internal, that lead the individual to function in adaptive ways. External or social controls consist of both formal sanctions governing human actions, as embodied in laws, and less obvious informal sanctions. The informal sanctions are transmitted by parental and cultural approval and disapproval.

The survival of any society is dependent on a system of organization that enables its members to carry out certain tasks. A system of social organization must therefore produce in individuals a pattern of behavior which, in broad terms, conforms with the standards sanctioned by the total group. Individuals, from one generation to another, who are reared in a particular social system therefore come to regard the existing practices as natural and right, since these are the customs and ways of their parents and ancestors. Moral, ethical, and spiritual values become

Reprinted by permission of the Family Service Association of America, New York, from *Social Casework*, XLI: 451–6, November 1960.

attached to the customs and, in consequence, are considered sacred and inviolable.[1]

In both the theory of social psychology, with its concept of socialization, and the theory of psychiatry, with its concept of growth and development, there is recognition that the society and culture to which the individual belongs play a major part in shaping his behavior and personality. There is also agreement that the individual incorporates the beliefs and attitudes of his culture by use of certain psychological mechanisms. For example, Gillin and Gillin observe that through the use of the mechanism of identification, a psychoanalytic concept, the child absorbs not only the norms and values of the parent but also those of the society.[2] Fenichel notes: "Originally the child certainly had the wish to do the things the parents do; his aim was an identification with the parents' activities ... The standards and ideals of the parents are an essential part of their personality. If children want to identify themselves with the parents, they also want to identify with their standards and ideals."[3] The net effect of this process of identification is to bring about socially acceptable behavior on the part of the child.

CONTROL IN SOCIAL WORK TREATMENT

Social work agencies that provide various types of treatment services generally deal with individuals whose behavior deviates in some way from society's expectations. These individuals have some difficulty, either psychologically or interpersonally, in functioning in their milieu. The goal of treatment, in a democratic society, clearly is not that of helping such individuals achieve conformity for the sake of conformity. Rather, the goal is to help them make some modifications in their patterns of living, primarily in the area of their particular problem of social dysfunctioning. The areas of dysfunctioning that become the focus of treatment are those in which the consequences of the individual's behavior are damaging to himself or to others. The above definition of the treatment goal is somewhat narrower than others that are sometimes offered. Whether treatment goals are defined narrowly or broadly, they always involve normative concepts and, therefore, some element of social control. This is true even when social control factors are not made explicit in the formulation of

1 / Robert E. Lee Faris, *Social Disorganization*, Ronald Press, New York, 1948, p. 18.

2 / J. L. Gillin and J. P. Gillin, *Cultural Sociology*, Macmillan Co., New York, 1948.

3 / Otto Fenichel, M.D., *The Psychoanalytic Theory of Neurosis*, W. W. Norton & Co., New York, 1945, p. 102.

treatment objectives. For example, certain control elements are implicit in Hamilton's listing of objectives: preventing social breakdown, conserving strength, restoring social functioning, making life experience more comfortable and compensating, creating opportunities for growth and development, and increased self-direction and social contribution.[4]

The social control function in casework has been elucidated by Taylor, who discusses the control implicit in such goals as strengthening family life, building wholesome community life, improving interpersonal relationships, and so forth. He points out that such verbs as "mould," "restore," "shape," "better," "improve," "help," "encourage," "assist," "develop," "relieve," "solve," and "resolve" are used repeatedly in agency reports. He states: "By its very institutional structure and function, the casework agency is normative, evaluative, and judgmental."[5]

A corollary to the premise stated above is that the social worker, in his interactions with clients in a treatment relationship, inevitably functions as a social control agent whether he intends to do so or not. A particularly thorny problem that arises is whether the worker is aware of the degree to which he reflects, both implicitly and explicitly the norms and standards of his own culture and social class.

Social workers, as well as other persons in the helping professions, tend to subscribe to types of behavior, and to think of them as universal standards. It would be more appropriate, however, to regard these so-called "universals" with skepticism, since they are not absolutes. For example, Harris observes that in our society we implicitly accept certain concepts of the rights of man and of his place in the universe but that these concepts do not obtain in all cultures.[6] Social workers, from their knowledge and personal experience, are likely to have certain concepts about the feelings of parents toward their children, expecting the parents to be tender toward their offspring and protective of the young. These assumptions may not apply equally in this society or in others, since the family serves a number of social, economic, and biological functions in addition to child rearing. These functions are weighted differently by different groups but we tend to expect the family to meet the needs of the individual for companionship and self-fulfilment while it serves basic social, economic, and biological functions.

As indicated earlier, if members of a particular society are to live to-

4 / Gordon Hamilton, *Theory and Practice of Social Casework*, 2nd ed. rev., Columbia University Press, New York, 1951, p. 239.

5 / Robert K. Taylor, "The Social Control Function in Casework," SOCIAL CASEWORK, Vol. XXXIX, No. 1 (1958), pp. 17–21.

6 / Dale B. Harris, "Values and Standards in Educational Activities. 1. Parent Education and Personal Values," SOCIAL CASEWORK, Vol. XXXIX, No. 2–3 (1958), pp. 159–167.

gether with some cohesion and unity, even when the society permits considerable individual differences and sub-group variations, some degree of conformity is demanded of its members. All societies, obviously, make some allowance for such variations and differences. To maintain cohesion, however, each society develops a system of social control; the controls serve to encourage approved patterns of behavior among the members and also to deal with violators. Greenwood points out that social work treatment is "... concerned with action and change; it therefore belongs among the controlling agencies of society ... social workers, by virtue of their technical knowledge and community-sanctioned status, possess a form of power which they exercise to reach certain ends." He notes that the aim of the practitioner is unlike that of the social scientist, whose aim is to describe the social world accurately. He states that the "practitioner's chief end is the effective *control* of that world, and to this all knowledge is subordinated."[7]

It seems clear that the control element in social work practice is fundamentally related to its professional value system which embodies certain concepts of individual and community well-being. The question of professional values, of course, raises a number of philosophical issues that cannot be dealt with here. It should be remembered, however, that values represent idealized objectives of human behavior, and that controls, whether exerted by society or by the individual, represent ways of enforcing these values. Thus, a value is the abstract ideal of what is expected of the individual while a control is a social or psychological process by which the ideal is achieved and enforced.

The use of control, as a method of treatment, has generally been frowned upon by the helping professions. Such avoidance of control may in part be a reaction to damage, real or assumed, that has been suffered by clients, or by therapists themselves, at the hands of domineering fathers, castrating mothers, stern teachers, brutal policemen, or punitive judges. Unhappily, this reaction has tended to divert the attention of social workers from this phenomenon and only recently has there been an effort to study objectively the place of social and personal controls in the treatment process. Another unfortunate effect of such reaction was the creation of an artificial antipodality between treatment and control measures. In consequence, the potential, and sometimes crucial, usefulness of various controls for certain clients was often unrecognized and the social worker was thereby robbed of a tool which, if properly used, could be effective in furthering the aims of treatment.

7 / Ernest Greenwood, "Social Science and Social Work: A Theory of Their Relationship," *Social Service Review*, Vol. XXIX, No. 1 (1955), pp. 24–25.

RELATIONSHIP BETWEEN INNER AND OUTER CONTROLS

The informal controls, obviously, have great power in influencing the behavior of the individual, particularly in his early years when he is absorbing standards from the significant adults in his life. As the standards become internalized, they form an enduring inner self-control system. Even in later years, the process of identification and internalization continues. It would seem that the formal controls, expressed in legal sanctions, are generally less effective in modifying behavior; such sanctions appear to be less powerful in producing long-term positive results. This statement should not be taken to mean, however, that there is not a need for externally imposed controls for certain individuals at particular times, or even for many individuals at some time in their lives.

The need for external controls through probation or institutionalization is being increasingly recognized by agencies dealing with persons with character disorders and other types of personality disturbances whose behavior creates danger to themselves or others. Attempts to treat such individuals without the support of some formal control have been relatively unsuccessful. Even in the treatment of other types of clients, the need to set firm, clear demands is often indicated, since such firmness may constitute an ego-supportive experience.[8] Often a crucial treatment problem, in any setting, is to find a way of working with a client within a framework of personal and social controls and still allow room for spontaneity and creativity.

The following brief reports, based on cases treated in various settings, may serve to illustrate the types of control used in the treatment relationship.

John, a gang member, mentioned with obvious discomfort that trouble was brewing on his block. He said that a "rumble" was scheduled over the weekend. The worker, observing the boy's distress in the face of real danger, suggested that he stay close to home. He also told John that he would take necessary steps to alert the appropriate authorities to try to prevent the clash. Although such advice and activity on behalf of the client may not technically be "control," the worker was clearly directive and his action was based on social values. In this instance, the worker offered physical protection to the client and also endeavored to relieve anxiety.

On a visit to the furnished room of Mrs. C, whose adolescent son

8 / Jacob Chwast, "The Significance of Control in the Treatment of the Antisocial Person," *Archives of Criminal Psychodynamics*, Vol. II, No. 4 (1957); Dale G. Hardman, "Authority in Casework – A Bread-and-Butter Theory," *NPPA Journal*, Vol. v, No. 3 (1959), pp. 249–255; Calvin F. Settlage, "The Value of Limits in Child Rearing," *Children*, Vol. v, No. 5 (1958), pp. 175–178.

Morton was home for a three-day visit from his foster-care placement, the worker saw only one bed. It was quite evident that Mrs. C and the boy were sharing the bed without being aware of or concerned about the inappropriateness of this arrangement. The worker diplomatically suggested that other sleeping arrangements might be more comfortable and thereupon helped Mrs. C to obtain a cot temporarily. This kind of intervention obviously does not deal with the basic problem but it nevertheless is educational. Such direct action by the worker is based on clinical understanding and social values.

Arlene, aged 4½, clouted Mary with a block in the nursery school. As the teacher comforted Mary, Arlene hit George with the same block and then, becoming even more excited, dumped all the toys from the shelf. The worker, who happened to pass by, took Arlene by the hand and led her from the scene to a nearby office, where she soon quieted down sufficiently to return to the group. Arlene's acting-out behavior continued, which heightened her anxiety and led to further assaults. When control was asserted, both her anxiety and aggression abated.

Jane, a well-developed girl of 15 from an underprivileged background, was having difficulty both at home and at school. She truanted from school and stayed out late, often not returning home until three or four in the morning. She associated with friends of whom her family disapproved. Finally, after she had stayed out all night, her father took her to court where she was adjudged delinquent and placed on probation. The probation officer found her defensive, uncommunicative, and suspicious. During the course of the contact, it became apparent that Jane's difficulty with her parents and other authority figures was of long standing. The probation officer structured the probationary relationship with her; he informed her in a non-punitive manner that she could not be permitted to stay out all night. He further explained that such conduct was dangerous and that he felt concerned for her welfare. He pointed out that such actions on her part would necessitate a court hearing, which most probably would be followed by a remand to a detention home. Subsequently, Jane stayed out overnight without permission. This was reported to the probation officer who brought her into court and, in her presence, recommended detention. When the probation officer visited Jane at the shelter, she became communicative for the first time. She told him she was not angry for he had "leveled" with her and told her exactly what would happen. After this experience, Jane entered into a sustained treatment relationship.

VALUE CONFLICTS

In applying controls, the worker must exercise considerable caution. There is risk that the worker, under the guise of promoting necessary adaptations in certain areas of the client's functioning, may attempt to enforce the standards and values of the dominant social group. He may, as a result, intrude into areas of functioning that do not present problems to the client or that they are not indicative of possible damaging consequence to the client or others in his milieu. Such intrusion may have the effect of making the treatment relationship an instrument of social control rather than a helping tool; the client's problems may thereby be added to, rather than unraveled.

The imposition of certain dominant cultural values is likely to result in a serious lack of communication and rapport between the worker and client, in the establishment of treatment goals inappropriate to the client's needs, and in a treatment approach that contains a strong element of pressure on the client to conform to a particular pattern of behavior. The worker, for example, may unconsciously impose his own middle-class values on the client in relation to education, job selection, courting, and so forth. He may proceed on the assumption that these values are "universals" and are, therefore, equally appropriate for the client and for himself. The following case illustrates this point.

Henry, a 16-year-old delinquent of normal intelligence, came from an underprivileged family and neighborhood. During the course of treatment, he raised the question about quitting school to obtain a job as a shipping clerk in a small factory. Henry's plan evoked, in the middle-class worker, considerable concern, because the boy's academic record showed clearly that he had capacity for a higher level of education. The worker believed that a more appropriate vocational goal would lie in the direction of a skilled occupation, such as that of a dental mechanic or a draughtsman. It seemed to him that for the boy to enter a less skilled type of employment would be a tragic waste of potential capacity. Henry, however, was not interested in entering into a long-range educational program, especially since neither his family nor his friends gave him any encouragement along these lines. His father, a longshoreman, with irregular work, had to feed four other children. Also, Henry's mother complained about lack of money. The family expected a boy of 16 to go to work, and their expectation was no different from that of the neighborhood.

It is clear that a conflict in value systems existed between the worker and the client. Although the full implications of the conflict could only be understood by careful analysis of the case, which will not be attempted here, it is obvious that such a conflict created a problem in treatment. The problem might have been avoided if the worker had adhered more closely to the original aim of treatment – to check the boy's delinquent tendencies.

If he had been in conflict about leaving school, further exploration of his feelings about the step would, of course, have been appropriate. Henry, however, considered the contemplated job entirely compatible with his personal and social expectations and viewed it as a source of immediate satisfaction. An unskilled vocation was not ego-alien to the boy even though it was to the worker. The worker's value-laden perception of the boy's potentialities and of an appropriate vocational choice gave rise to difficulties in treatment. Such difficulties often arise when the worker and the client, because of different cultural backgrounds and social experiences, do not share the same set of aspirations and goals.

The social worker's middle-class orientation may become conspicuously evident when he deals with problems of aggressiveness and sexuality. To a lesser degree, it may be evident when he deals with such matters as social behavior, patterns of family living, privacy, personal hygiene and appearance, recreational outlets, and education and vocational aspirations. Also, a client's attitude toward his own or another person's possessions and property may be at variance from that of the worker.

In setting goals for treatment, the worker should endeavor to evaluate the appropriateness of his value-laden concepts of desirable behavior and adequate social functioning. If the worker makes the error of considering his own values "universals," his treatment efforts are not likely to succeed. The worker should endeavor to understand the client's values, recognizing that relatively few standards can be validly applied to all members of society. Failure to recognize relative personal and cultural patterns, in fact, can only defeat the purpose of helping persons to attain self-fulfilment in a democratic sense. Also, it may produce unanticipated negative consequences in the treatment process, including new conflicts, increased tension, heightened resistance and, perhaps, a withdrawal from the relationship.

A treatment relationship that does not take into account the client's value system may become a form of coercion and pressure. The coercive element is most likely to appear when the worker deals with persons who do not readily share his own aspirations and whose experiences in day-by-day living are different in character. We do not mean to suggest that social workers must give up their personal and professional values, but only that they recognize that the client's values must also be considered if treatment is to be planned sensibly. Without such consideration, there can be little empathy with the client and little chance of effective treatment.

Another problem in treatment stems from the fact that social workers at times are so permissive and nonjudgmental that they may seem to the client not to stand for anything. When treatment proceeds on this basis, the worker does not provide the client with a sound basis for identification. He may also fail to demonstrate his concern for the client and to offer him the protective care that he may need. This kind of approach is probably the result of the worker's wish to avoid playing an undesirably dominating role. It is not our purpose, here, to appraise the value of a directive or nondirective approach in relation to various treatment situations. We should like to note, however, that the worker must come to accept his role as an enabling person, willing to take responsibility to help the client achieve both self-fulfilment and self-control. There would seem little question, therefore, that the social worker should make clear to the client, at points consonant with the developing relationship, that he sub-scribes to these principles of a democratic society. Among other things, the worker must make clear that he stands for the rights of others, for lawful procedures, and solutions by reason and justice rather than by force or trickery. While standing for these values, he must endeavor not to put burdens on the client that will threaten the treatment relationship and create barriers to its forward movement.

The worker should ask himself whether he is trying to make the client a "nice person" – one who is honest, orderly, punctual, industrious, and reliable. Although these values are unquestionably desirable for promoting the welfare of society as a whole – and perhaps of the particular client – he must ask what meaning they have for the client. Are these values meaningful to the client at this time and in his own milieu? Also, to what extent must the client modify these values? Can the worker and his agency accept such modifications? May the demands placed upon the client be tantamount to expecting him to relinquish his subgroup identification? If modifications cannot be made in line with the client's perceptions and needs, treatment success will be diminished.

VALUE AND CONTROLS AS THEY INFLUENCE TREATMENT

It must be quite clear by now that, in the implicit and explicit use of values, social workers are essentially imposing controls on the client. In treatment, we must continually ask ourselves whether the client can be, or should be, helped to incorporate certain values into his own functioning. If we expect him to develop inner controls, the values cannot be alien to him. We know, psychodynamically, that social approval is an important factor in the in-corporation of values. Social approval includes the worker's approval, which can be a powerful dynamic when experienced by the client.

In social treatment, there is a crucial need to select an appropriate value focus from a wide range of possibilities. This selection can have real meaning only if it is made on the basis of differential diagnosis. The latter must take into account personal and social data, including a delineation of areas of difficulty and potential or overt danger to the client or to others.

This kind of value focus and its implementation in the treatment process may provide the worker with a foundation for helping clients build healthy internal controls. Such controls, when based on both the client's values and the values implicit in our own social structure, permit a real expression of an individual's potentialities in our democratic society.

LLOYD E. OHLIN
HERMAN PIVEN
DONNELL M. PAPPENFORT

18

Major dilemmas of the social worker in probation and parole

When a field of service strives towards professionalization of its training requirements and its practice, two basic problems of general significance occur: (1) those charged with the responsibility for professional education must maintain a close integration between preparation and practice; (2) educators and practitioners alike must create conditions in the field which will make professional behavior possible.

The integration of preparation and practice must be maintained if changing needs of field workers are to be met by appropriate educational revision, consistent with professional goals:

The function of a profession in society and the demands implicit in its practice determine the objectives of education for that profession. The responsibilities which its practitioners must assume designate the content of knowledge and skill to be attained. They determine also the character of the educational experience which students must have to become the kinds of

Reprinted by permission of the National Council on Crime and Delinquency and the authors from *National Probation and Parole Journal*, July 1956, pp. 211–25.

This article draws on a portion of interdisciplinary research which has been carried out under a three-year grant by the Russell Sage Foundation to the Center for Education and Research in Corrections at the University of Chicago. It reflects the collective efforts of the staff of the Center. The authors wish to acknowledge their great indebtedness to the contribution of the late Frank T. Flynn, formerly Professor of the School of Social Service Administration, University of Chicago, and Associate Director of the Center for Education and Research in Corrections. Space limitations have compelled a very general treatment of the problems discussed in this article. These limitations have also prevented a full citation of the supporting evidence drawn from the literature, case analyses, and field interviews. Detailed treatment of these and other problems in the field of corrections will be presented in a book now being prepared for publication.

people required both for competent service and to contribute to the ongoing development of the profession in a changing social order.[1]

This is not difficult to sustain when professionalization of the field of service has gained general acceptance. In such a case, the existing body of theory, principles, and methods will provide appropriate responses for the majority of problems encountered in the field; situations of practice will have been standardized and the roles of practitioners clearly defined. It is then relatively easy to control or modify the content of educational experience to train persons adjusted to the work realities of the field.

The situation is far more difficult when there is no general agreement on appropriate professional functions in the field. This usually occurs where the claim to control over professional education by one group is met by equally strong claims from competing groups who envision different training requirements. In such a case, different precepts and techniques of practice compete for recognition, and the work settings and orientations undergo constant change. Under these conditions the practitioners' need for theoretical, conceptual, and technical support from the centers of professional education is most acute. However, it is also at this point in the struggle for professional recognition that the schools of professional education are least well equipped to provide this support in the form of integration of the service needs of the emerging field of practice into the generic educational curriculum. This problem can be solved only through the coordinated efforts of educators, practitioners, and research workers in an impartial assessment of the problems and needs of the field service and an objective reconstruction of the educational curriculum to meet these needs.

The second major problem involved in the professionalization of a new field of service relates to the organizational arrangement and systems of expectations within which the emerging professional practitioner must carry on his work. The need for reorganization, as well as the amount of conflict and resistance encountered, is likely to be at a maximum when an established system of professional education and practice extends its professional mandate to lay claim to a new field of service. An effort is then made to reorganize the new field in the image of allied services where the profession is generally accepted. This movement focuses the resulting struggle of competing groups on such basic problems as definition of the objectives of the field of service, standards of recruitment, methods of job

1 / Charlotte Towle, "The General Objectives of Professional Education," *Social Service Review*, December, 1951, p. 427.

performance, redefinition of administrative and practitioner roles, and reorganization of the expectations of other agencies and the general public as to the nature of the service to be provided. Conflict develops on these points precisely because the professional cannot work effectively in a setting which does not give him adequate freedom to implement his professional skills and knowledge. In the transition period the professional is faced with special dilemmas and problems that make it extremely difficult for him to work effectively and to retain a professional identification with other members of the profession who are unaware of or relatively unconcerned about his position. The problem is further complicated by the fact that the professional knowledge and skills of the practitioner have not been adjusted to the requirements of the new work setting. Consequently, though the need for reorganization of the work setting to provide greater professional freedom is evident, there is no clear-cut understanding of the form and direction which such reorganization should take. A pertinent example of this problem is the situation of the psychiatrist and other therapists in correctional institutions. Although they have achieved general public acceptance, they feel severely hampered in their work because the custodial and administrative staff as well as clients, have not properly defined their roles and granted them the power and freedom necessary to function professionally.

SOCIAL WORK EDUCATION FOR PROBATION AND PAROLE

Since World War II the social work profession has increasingly become a source of recruitment for probation and parole field services. This occupational expansion takes place at a time when social work education is built on a generic program applicable to all social work settings, subject only to specific on-the-job training. The special requirements of correctional work are a dramatic challenge to this program. Practitioners and social work educators interested in the correctional field have pressed for broadening the system of generic social work education to incorporate theoretical knowledge and methodological skills which would prepare practitioners to handle the problems of serving the offender client in the correctional agency setting. They are convinced that social work training provides the best available professional preparation for this work.

It [probation] is rather a *process of treatment* aimed at effecting a readjustment within the community setting, of the attitudes, habits, and capabilities of the offender. If this is the goal of probation, then casework becomes the best method for achieving this goal, since the sole aim and purpose of casework is to strengthen the individual's ability to "regulate his own life" in society.[2]

This concern that social work educators and practitioners have in the professional development of the correctional field has raised many questions. Is probation and parole social work? Does social work education as presently constituted adequately prepare practitioners for the correctional field? Can the theoretical and methodological requirements for correctional work be successfully incorporated into generic social work education?

All these questions call for more detailed exploration than has thus far occurred.

One of the functions of research, under such circumstances, is to inform the educator and the field administrator of the empirical problem of implementing the professional position. It seeks to describe the conflicts and limitations which beset the practitioner and to highlight the discrepancy between what is taught in the schools and what is demanded in practice. The results of such research should provide the basis for the rational development and strengthening of educational programs and a core of knowledge and understanding for the professional reorganization of the field of work itself. This article is an attempt to outline the major dilemmas in which the social worker often finds himself as he tries to carry out his professional obligations as a social worker while fulfilling his job obligations as a probation-parole officer.

The professional in any field is more than the possessor of certain knowledge, skills, and techniques for doing his job. He is identified with a professional which constitutes for him a subculture. This subculture defines for its members the purposes, aspirations, and obligations of the profession as a whole and makes a meaningful pattern of the complex experiences of the occupational life.

Professional education as a re-educative process has to fulfill a task that is essentially equivalent to a change in culture. Since the individual's attitudes have been formed through his dependence on relationships and through his response to authority pressures within the family and other organized groups,

2 / Ben Meeker, "Probation Is Casework," *Federal Probation*, June, 1948, p. 52. Cf. Arthur E. Fink, *The Field of Social Work*, New York, Henry Holt, 1942, pp. 213–261; Frank T. Flynn, "Probation and Individualised Justice," *Federal Probation*, June, 1950, pp. 70–76; Elliot Studt, "Casework in the Correctional Field," *Federal Probation*, September, 1954, pp. 19–26; *Training Personnel for Work with Juvenile Delinquents*, U.S. Department of Health, Education, and Welfare, Children's Bureau Publication No. 348, Washington, D.C., 1954.

Kurt Lewin holds that one of the outstanding needs for bringing about acceptance in re-education is the establishment of an "in-group," that is, a group in which the members experience a sense of belonging.[3]

Insofar as the practitioner is a professional man he has internalized this subculture, drawing from it the roots of his professional "identity" – his professional "self." The significance of this identification is dramatically experienced by many social workers in the correctional field. Correctional work is generally conceived by the larger profession of social work as a marginal activity[4] and it receives neither the recognition and status nor the educational and organizational support accorded to other fields of service in the profession. Consequently, correctional practitioners often feel that they are alienated from and not accepted by the general profession. This results in a confusion of professional identification which inhibits the continuity and progress of their personal careers and retards the general professionalization and development of correctional services.

The social worker, because of his practical concern with human development, has become especially aware of the fact that he is a man with a mission as well as a technical expert.[5] The social work school deliberately instills in its graduates a set of expectations about the role of the worker in relation to his client, agency, and community. It has consciously organized its curriculum to produce graduates who are oriented to the needs of traditional agency settings (best illustrated by the private family agency and the outpatient psychiatric clinic). These expectations are not always fulfilled in the correctional setting and the discrepancy between expectation and actuality is a measure of the "reality shock" experienced by the new worker. His reaction to the dilemmas in which he is placed has profound consequences for himself, his clients, the probation-parole service, and the wider field of social work.

THE PROBATION-PAROLE SETTING

The probation-parole occupation has undergone continuous change with the entrance of the social worker representing a significant turning point in its professional development. The social work recruit comes to an

3 / Charlotte Towle, "The Contribution of Education for Social Casework to Practice," Cora Kasius, ed., *Principles and Techniques in Social Casework*, New York, Family Service Association of America, 1950, p. 262.

4 / Cf. U.S. Bureau of Labor Statistics, *Social Worker in 1950*, New York, American Association of Social Workers, 1952, p. 23.

5 / "Competencies expected of social workers were grouped into three categories: (1) Perceptual and Conceptual Knowledge; (2) Skills, Methods, Processes, and Procedures; (3) Personal Professional Qualities. Attitudes permeated all three. The

agency in which many clients have not voluntarily sought casework service, are not "motivated for treatment," and are limited by lack of capacity even if they could be motivated. In addition, other occupational and interest groups and occasionally general public opinion view him with watchful suspicion, even hostility. Like other public institutions in a democratic society, his agency has organized its directives and structure partly in response to the pressures and counterpressures of public opinion. The nature of the clientele and agency organization poses for him many serious theoretical and practical problems which make his adjustment and the exercise of his professional competence far more problematic than he had been led to expect during his educational and field work training experience.

The social worker often finds the agency organized in terms of presocial work theories of probation and parole. From the point of view of work orientations, two types of probation-parole workers have dominated the field. The "punitive officer" is the guardian of the middle-class community morality; he attempts to coerce the offender into conforming by means of threats and punishment and his emphasis is on control, protecting the community *against* the offender, and systematic suspicion of those under supervision. The "protective agent," on the other hand, vacillates between protecting the offender *and* protecting the community. His tools are direct assistance, lecturing, and praise and blame. He is recognized by his ambivalent emotional involvement with the offender and others in the community as he shifts back and forth in taking sides with one against the other.

A third type, the "welfare worker," is entering correctional work with increasing frequency. His ultimate work goal is the improved welfare of the client, a condition achieved by helping him in his individual adjustment, within limits imposed by the client's capacity. He feels that the only genuine guarantee of community protection lies in the client's personal adjustment since external conformity will only be temporary and in the long run may make a successful adjustment more difficult. Emotional neutrality permeates his relationships. The diagnostic categories and treatment skills which he employs stem from an objective and theoretically based assessment of the client's situation, needs, and capacities. His primary identification is with the social work profession.

The three types of workers are often found as colleagues in the same

first two of these categories have been referred to graphically as 'must know' and 'must do' items. Perhaps the third should be designated as the 'must be and must feel' category." Ernest V. Hollis and Alice L. Taylor, *Social Work Education in the United States,* New York, American Association of Social Workers, 1952, p. 27.

organization, particularly during the period of emerging agency professionalization. Their differing work orientations frequently generate conflict and impose limits on the extent to which any of these work patterns can achieve full expression.

OCCUPATIONAL DILEMMAS

Three conditions structure the occupational dilemmas of the social worker:[6] (1) the nature of the clientele, (2) agency organization, and (3) community expectations.

The client

By virtue of the control which traditional casework agencies exert over their intake policies, the profession is able to insist on the fulfillment of certain norms which are sometimes inapplicable or opposed to the requirements of probation-parole practice. The model in social casework presumes that the individual applicant selects an agency,[7] asks to become its client for service,[8] defines the service appropriately,[9] and is acceptable to the agency on the basis of his motivation and capacity for treatment.[10] With the possible exception of the last of these criteria, the probationer or parolee appears to be excluded from generic casework consideration as a client. The ramifications of this disparity between social work norms and correctional practice are manifold. The social worker in corrections feels that he has not been sufficiently prepared to deal with clients who are unmotivated, who lack capacity for treatment, or who do not require his help. His expectations for providing helpful service are frustrated by clients who refuse help or fail to acknowledge the existence of problems which require help of the kind the practitioner feels professionally equipped to offer. In addition, he is confronted by a work load which does not allow him enough time to concentrate on trying to overcome these difficulties and render

6 / A complete study of probation-parole requires analysis of problems encountered by the "punitive officer" and the "protective agent" as well as the "welfare worker" as represented by persons recruited from the field of social work. In this article only the problems and dilemmas of social workers will be considered. It should be noted, however, that each of the other types of workers faces equally serious and consequential problems in their work adjustment.

7 / Helen L. Witmer, *Social Work – An Analysis of a Social Institution*, New York, Rinehart, 1942, pp. 179–180.

8 / Swithun Bowers, "The Nature and Definition of Social Casework," *Principles and Techniques in Social Casework, op. cit.*, p. 108.

9 / *Ibid.*, p. 11.

10 / Delwin K. Anderson and Frank Kiesler, "Helping Toward Help: The Intake Interview," *Social Casework*, February, 1954, p. 72.

appropriate casework service. The basic problem is that his academic training had not given him the skills and guides to action for converting a relationship of control and authority into one of consent and treatment.

The social worker desires a warm, neutral, and nonjudgmental relationship with his client.[11] He recognizes, however, that the client regards him as a participant in the punitive and condemning system of apprehension, judgment, and correction. He knows that the offender is compelled to come to him as a condition of probation or parole and often approaches him with hostility and an interest in concealing facts and feelings. The social worker knows that his authority is real. For example, both he and the client know that the actual decision on revocation usually is the worker's, even though the formal authority is lodged elsewhere. His profession tells him that this is "an initial obstacle to be worked through," but it does not teach or tell him what to do. This is a major though not an insuperable barrier for the recruit who has no specific training to apply.

Failing to find guidance from the social work profession in dealing with this problem, the social work practitioner sometimes turns to older workers or supervisors in the probation and parole system itself. Since many of these persons do not share a common theoretical and conceptual background of training with the social work recruit, the advice he receives sharpens rather than resolves his dilemma. To meet his own need to overcome client hostility toward him as an authoritarian figure in order to establish conditions requisite to treatment, and at the same time to satisfy the pressures of the community (and, in some agencies, the pressures of his superiors) for client conformity, he frequently attempts to play two roles. On the one hand, he tries to offer a caseworker's sympathetic understanding and help; on the other, he is the agent of law and respectability, attempting to explain one function as separate from the other. Because he has no clear conception of how or when to integrate control and treatment functions, and lacks knowledge of the skills by which they might be made mutually supportive, his attempt to play two roles is frequently unsuccessful.

Because humans tend to react to any one phase of an agency experience in terms of the total self and in terms of a totality of needs, it may not be a simple matter to render services clearly distinguished one from another. An agency may conveniently divide itself into two sets of services and proffer them like

11 / Cf. Charlotte Towle, "Social Case Work in Modern Society," *Social Service Review*, June, 1946, pp. 168–169, for the casework model of this relationship and the treatment process.

two different commodities. But a man has not two separate sides to his head or to his heart.[12]

This makes his dilemma clear, but it does not resolve it.

The social work recruit brings with him a model of treatment purpose and process from the classroom, casework literature, and field placement experience. He grants the possibility of incorporating the "wise use of authority,"[13] but in work situation where the anticipated traditional process does not unfold he feels bewildered and betrayed because he has never been taught techniques appropriate to other than nonauthoritarian and nonjudgmental relationships.[14]

The social caseworker in probation and parole also experiences difficulty in classifying the problems represented in his caseload. He finds many clients with whom he would have difficulty establishing a treatment relationship even under ideal working conditions because of personality structures and lack of capacities, and because of the paucity of available knowledge and techniques. Many of the types of cases which he encounters in his agency experience have not been included in the theoretical and methodological training with case materials received during his educational preparation. Although he usually learns to classify his caseload and provide service for many who need and can use it, the probation-parole officer trained in casework first goes through the painful process of rebuff, dismay, and experimentation. He often finds it necessary to seek guidance from sources other than social work itself, sources which deal with his specific clients and problems.[15]

The difficulties which the social worker encounters with his caseload are further complicated by lack of familiarity with the criminal and delinquent subcultures from which most offenders emerge. Social casework

12 / Charlotte Towle, *Common Human Needs*, Chicago, University of Chicago Press, 1945, p. 61.

13 / Elliot Studt, "An Outline for Study of Social Authority Factors in Casework," *Social Casework*, June, 1954, pp. 231–238.

14 / In the article by Charlotte Towle, "Social Case Work in Modern Society," *op. cit.*, it is noted that some clients "become confused, anxious and frustrated" in the neutral casework relationship and that it is then advisable "to be supportive – i.e., ... to use authority, meet dependency, impose demands, and convey moral judgments in a sustaining way so that the individual may become more self-determining, or at least, less self-destructive in his behavior." The social worker points out, however, that the school has not shown him when or how to do this.

15 / In one study, all but one of the social work officers in the probation and parole agency gave as his first reading choice either the NPPA JOURNAL or *Federal Probation*, in preference to social work journals. This is an indication of the partial alienation from the social work profession which practitioners trained in social work frequently experience under the pressure of solving their immediate work problems.

emphasizes the importance of identifying the social environment with which the client is interacting in order to understand how he perceives and feels about his situation and how he may be helped. This requires knowledge and familiarity with the cultural and social backgrounds from which offenders come, a familiarity which the officer does not usually bring from his own background and knowledge which his formal education does not specifically give him.[16]

Agency Organization

Democratic administration has been defined as the art of compromise through which divergent and contradictory social forces modify one another and reach a final expression simultaneously reflecting the wishes of all but those of no group completely.[17] Because the probation-parole agency must adapt itself to the threat of powerful and antagonistic groups in its environment,[18] it occasionally represents an extreme case of the generalization that every organization displays a discrepancy between its stated purposes and the objective consequences of the actions of its functionaries.

The failures of probation and parole are more spectacular than those in most other professions, and newsmen have the occupational motive of "good copy" to encourage them to scrutinize correctional practice and organize critical public opinion around a dramatically destructive episode. Elected judges, legislators, and other public officials have a vested interest in being on the popular side of a crisis, and occupational groups whose interests are inherently in opposition to client-centered probation and parole supervision are able to use periods of public excitement to further their own purposes. Consequently the administrator is under pressure to anticipate possible criticism and to organize the agency and its policies in self-protection. The problem is frequently intensified for the social work administrator who feels a professional obligation to expand his program and recruit social work officers, thus requiring support from important officials and citizens not only to protect the agency but to aid in its development.

The accommodation to external threat is expressed in an emphasis on

16 / Cf. Otto Pollak, "Cultural Dynamics in Casework," *Social Casework*, July, 1953, pp. 279–284; Melitta Schmideberg and Jack Sokol, "The Function of Contact in Psychotherapy with Offenders," *Social Casework*, November, 1953, p. 386; and Elliot Studt, "Casework in the Correctional Field," *op. cit.*, p. 25.

17 / Reinhard Bendix, "Bureaucracy: The Problem and Its Setting," *American Sociological Review*, October, 1947, pp. 493–507.

18 / Cf. Philip Selznick, "An Approach to a Theory of Bureaucracy," *American Sociological Review*, February, 1943, pp. 47–54.

public relations revealed not only in positive educational campaigns, but also in organization of the agency and the development of policies on client supervision and the worker's role in the community.

During this transitional period, however, when the agency is striving for public acceptance of its work through increased professionalization of staff and operation, the interests of the administrator and the caseworker tend to diverge. The caseworker often perceives the public relations interest of the agency as a compromise with enforcement concepts promoted by other occupational groups in the community. He frequently feels that the agency's treatment objectives are being sacrificed for agency protection. He feels that he is under pressure to make nonprofessional decisions on his cases. This divergence of interests between the agency-centered administrator and the client-centered caseworker is illustrated below by problems arising in (1) the area of supervising the caseworker, (2) the rules for supervision of clients, and (3) informal policies about agency-community conflicts.

1 In the eyes of the social work profession, supervision by personnel skilled in imparting knowledge and techniques and in helping workers to recognize and profit by their errors without ego-destructiveness is mandatory for client welfare and workers' professional growth. The emphasis on agency protection in probation and parole, however, often results in promoting men who are successful in public relations rather than skilled in casework supervision. Also, when agencies are in a period of transition, the protection of morale and seniority leads to promotion of older employees trained in fields other than social work. Under these conditions, the social worker feels that the central focus of these supervisors is to prevent him from acting in ways which might embarrass the agency. He feels that treatment problems not involving the possibility of public condemnation are of secondary concern, and that aiding his professional growth very seldom becomes a work function. The limitations imposed by the supervisor oriented to public relations, and the consequent variance in understanding the subtleties of casework, pose for the social worker many problems which penetrate a large number of his daily activities. He has been taught to expect supervision of a learning-helping nature; when this source of support and professional guidance is absent, he feels that he has lost one of the main links to his professional identity and competent professional performance.

2 The "rules of client supervision" are an inheritance from an earlier phase of probation-parole when control over the client was more openly advocated. For the social work administrator, however, they are functional, since they are a formal expression of community expectations concerning

control of offenders which can be used as a defense against public criticism that the agency "coddles" its clients, or enforced to achieve other administrative ends with clients and workers. The "rules" sometimes are extended by informal policies and official requirements into a structure unacceptable to the social worker because he cannot interpret it as reasonable and necessary for his client. If a client must, by virtue of court order, parole decision, or informal agency requirement, abstain from drinking or observe a curfew, neither the worker nor the client can escape the realization that these are restrictions from which other adults are formally immune. The effect of this is to deny the client participation in normal activities and to reinforce his conception that he is somehow different *in kind* from other persons in the community. For the worker it reinforces the conception that the agency and the community regard his goals, methods, and clients as different *in kind* from those of other social agencies. The caseworker further feels that the "rules" may prevent individualization according to his client's needs.

3 Agency policy controlling the agent-community system of relationships also has important consequences for the casework task. The degree of emphasis on public relations varies greatly from one agency to another. An urban agency may generally achieve more autonomy than a rural one; in districts of similar population density, community pressure increases from federal to state to county levels of jurisdiction. Two extremes of agency structure exist – the relatively "autonomous" agency and the "restricted" agency.

(a) In the "autonomous" agency the social worker has far greater freedom to reject the control function and to pursue the treatment objectives of casework. For example, he makes definite recommendations for disposition, which are followed with few exceptions, and he feels free to circumvent court or parole board directives which he regards as opposed to his client's welfare. He is in a position to reject pressure from finance companies and to persuade the judge to remit court costs and restitution. He contacts clients as seldom or as often as casework needs and caseload requirements dictate and will usually arrange appointments before making home visits. He feels free to inform clients explicitly that their drinking, sex habits, hours, driving, purchases, etc., are of concern to him only when they constitute casework problems. He frequently feels the obligation to inform the client of discriminatory practices by certain employers and may even encourage him to conceal his criminal record in approaching them for employment.

It is within the "autonomous" agency that the social caseworker feels he can act most consistently with the professional directives received in his academic training. He feels he can confine his role essentially to the treatment function and permit other agencies to discharge the control function as they do with other citizens in the community. In short, he seeks to structure the performance of his work and the organization of his work relationships according to the model of social casework in traditional agency settings.

(b) In the "restricted" agency this freedom to pursue the treatment orientation and to reject the control function as a significant part of the worker's role is impossible to achieve. The social worker in the "restricted" agency encounters many points of conflict in fulfilling agency policy and maintaining a service-treatment relationship in the interests of the client – each of which is a professional norm. A uniform policy of mandatory home visits, for example, prevents individualization according to client needs. Other agency policies forbid undertaking treatment with clients whose problems may require occasional "acting out" as a prerequisite to eventual adjustment, a situation the worker has been trained to anticipate and accept as appropriate to casework. More importantly, the social worker often feels that he is forced to emphasize immediate client conformity to unrealistic standards; e.g., early curfew, abstention from drinking, from sexual relationships, etc. He frequently feels that such action keeps the client from being integrated into his own legitimate groups, prevents the client from viewing him as a treatment resource, and denies the worker the opportunity to move beyond the question of conformity in interviews. He thus has difficulty in "motivating" the unmotivated or strengthening a client's weak capacities. When he also feels compelled by agency policy to make unexpected night visits, to look in bars and pool-rooms, to check on clients at work – in short, to practice "surveillance" – the problem is intensified. One social worker reported: "My God! My clients won't talk to me; they don't even want to see me. They pull the curtains when I drive up to the house."

Community Expectations
As generally portrayed in social work education, the "community" is composed of heterogeneous individuals who share certain basic values and interests. Problems of casework clients involving other people are seen as personal problems of the client, and alternative solutions are explored in the counseling relationship to aid the client's decision. The worker-client relationship is conceived as private and confidential, and the only responsibility of the worker is his client's welfare. For example, it would be unusual for a businessman to request the cooperation of a family, medical, or psychiatric social agency in persuading a client to pay a debt, and it would

be regarded as clearly improper for a caseworker of such an agency to accept this responsibility.

The social worker in corrections, however, soon recognizes that the community consists of a number of interest groups with varying and conflicting demands upon him and the offender client. He finds that many officials and citizens have a negative attitude toward his client and that this is reciprocated by the client. His task is not only to alter both conceptions, but to deal with the problems raised by these conflicts of ideas and interests during the conduct of the case. He finds himself subjected to various pressures to act in ways which violate his own conception of the proper role and function of a social worker. He feels that his profession has not provided him with realistic conceptions of the "community," expectations of the pressures he will encounter, or prescriptions for appropriate action.

The probation-parole worker feels, for example, that the police pursue enforcement objectives without sufficient regard for the consequences of their actions on the offender's adjustment.[19] Such acts as indiscriminate arrest on suspicion are perceived by the worker as not only impeding the client's adjustment but re-enforcing the offender's conception of himself as a person apart from and rejected by the community. The worker experiences widespread pressure by the police and other official functionaries to define his role as that of an enforcement officer who should use control measures to restrict the client's freedom and coercion to punish him for wrongdoing. When he attempts to resist these pressures, he finds probation and parole interpreted as leniency and himself identified as a "sob-sister." Recognizing that police, prosecutors, judges, and others are often guided by values and objectives different from those which he considers primary, he is uncertain as to how to proceed, especially at those points where he is required to commit what he feels are gross violations of professional norms. An illustration is often found in the use made of the worker's presentence report, where the judge not only may dispose of cases on grounds other than treatability and humanitarian equality,[20] but also may violate confidentiality by making the report public. Powerless to prevent police and others from pursuing their own interests in the client in ways which he defines as interference with the treatment and adjustment of the client, yet requiring their cooperation in his daily work, he feels untrained to deal satisfactorily with either the client or the officials.

19 / Other major interest groups frequently mentioned with varying degrees of similar criticism by workers are lawyers, judges, finance companies, bonding companies, used-car companies, and institutional personnel. Cf. U.S. Department of Justice, *Attorney General's Survey of Release Procedures*, Vol. IV, *Parole*, Washington, D.C., 1939, pp. 220–221.

20/*Ibid.*, Vol. II, *Probation*, pp. 470–471.

Social workers have tended to adjust to this situation in a variety of ways. Some have expended considerable effort in seeking to educate and influence officials and citizens to understand the rehabilitative approach of the worker, the nature of the client-worker relationship, and casework methods for effecting client adjustment. Others resort to evasions, sentimental appeals, and "slanted" or safe reports. Still other workers have sought to withdraw in some measure from the norms of client service and confidentiality, accounting for apparent norm violations as limitations of the setting.

A final group of problems experienced by social workers in corrections relates to their identification with the profession. Since community officials and citizens with whom he frequently deals, as well as his own supervisor in many instances, are not social workers, the officer is usually restrained from employing the diagnostic and treatment vocabulary he has been trained to use. This limitation frequently creates anxiety in the worker, who fears the hazards of daily communication and the loss of familiarity with the technical tools of his profession. Probably more important is the difficulty experienced in maintaining a professional identification with other social workers. Not infrequently social agencies look with suspicion and distrust on the probation officer who seeks collateral information from their records. The stereotyped image maintained by social workers in traditional welfare agencies concerning the nature of casework practice in corrections often leads them to share the general community conception of the probation-parole worker as a law enforcement agent. This lack of understanding and acceptance of his position and problems by social work colleagues and educators contributes to a process of professional alienation, thus promoting further anxiety in the worker as to his professional identification.

RESPONSES OF THE SOCIAL WORKER

As a result of these barriers to professional practice in probation-parole, as conceived in traditional social casework terms, many social workers leave the field. Some give up social work entirely, disillusioned and convinced that both social work as a discipline and corrections as an area of practice are without genuine reward or meaning. Some return to more traditional casework settings, convinced that it is not possible, at least for them, to operate professionally in probation-parole work. Others remain in corrections, unhappy with their most recent job experience, but feeling committed to this specialty because of an awareness of casework needs in the field, because of the nature of the contacts and experience they have acquired, and because of a genuine conviction that the necessary knowledge and structure can be created for professional casework in this setting. As to the social workers who remain in corrections, five general types of adjustment have been distinguished, varying principally with the length of time the officer has worked, the nature of the agency organization, and the character of community conditions.

1 One type of adjustment is found in the relatively "autonomous" agency directed by a social work oriented administrator. The worker feels that the agency is moving toward increased professionalization and that he is able to function significantly as a professional in spite of the obstacles. He identifies himself primarily as a social worker but hastens to point out major differences between ideas and practices of the larger profession and those of the correctional field.

2 In the "restricted" agency, the worker is often harried and bewildered by demands made upon him by clients, supervisors, officials of other agencies, and the community at large for "unprofessional" behavior. He gradually accepts the "protective" definition at various important points and explicitly identifies himself as a probation-parole officer divorced from the field of social work.

3 Also found in the "restricted" agency is the worker who completely rejects what he regards as "anti-professional" demands and seeks to come to terms with these pressures by manipulation and evasion. Since the extent to which he can achieve this by himself is limited and because the effort – itself a violation of social work norms – tends to isolate him from the agency in which he works, he blames both the profession and the agency for his predicament. He derives his ultimate justification for evasion from the social work ideology of client service, however, and therefore retains a professional identity – albeit an alienated one – and he hopes to transfer to a correctional agency where the climate will be more conducive to treatment efforts.

4 Quite commonly the recent recruit to the field of corrections operates as a marginal and ambivalent worker. He experiments with various "new methods and techniques," including client coercion, in attempting to solve his work problems. Seriously disturbed by the "reality shock" of his first contact with correctional work, he already feels disenchanted with social work. The career patterns in the field suggest that he will continue experimenting for a while and will eventually resolve his conflicts by becoming one of the other types.

5 Finally, the social worker may accept the protective measures of the "restricted" agency as more or less natural and necessary for probation-parole work, trying to give service and treatment to clients as fully as pos-

sible within the given framework. He sees himself as a special kind of social worker and explains the imposed restrictions on clients as "necessary reality," identifying the client's difficulties in accepting these restrictions as a lack of capacity to adjust "to society."

CONCLUSION

The problems of the social worker in probation and parole have been related to the generic education he receives and to the special circumstances he faces in an area of practice where his caseload differs from that of more traditional settings, where powerful community forces oppose his ideals, and in which his agency attempts to protect itself by demanding of him decisions which seem unprofessional to him.[21] His responses to the unexpected and painful dilemmas include withdrawal to another setting, experimental-evasive-manipulative tactics, and alienation from his professional identification. These symptoms indicate a lag between social work education and the requirements of probation-parole practice.

If social work is to retain probation-parole as an area of application, it will have to participate in the solution of three problems, each demanding revision of social work preparation for the field: (1) community expectations about probation and parole must be modified to allow the professional sufficient freedom to pursue treatment interests; (2) he must be given the knowledge and skills which will enable him to do constructive work when alternatives are limited by public opinion and agency organization; (3) the practitioner must be provided with the knowledge required for work with his particular clientele.

1 Amelioration of the problem of agency organization is an extremely complicated matter requiring modification of both training and practice. Special attention must be given to ways of integrating probation-parole activities with those of other agencies which also are charged with responsibilities for offenders' conduct but which have different values and objectives. Administrators must realize that policies and organizational devices have consequences which go beyond their intended purposes. They must develop more understanding of the conflicts which caseworkers encounter

21 / Since this paper has taken a "problem" focus, it has necessarily neglected the many points at which the social worker in corrections is able to operate professionally in terms of the mandate he receives in his educational preparation. A comprehensive occupational analysis would reveal that casework in this field is consistent with that carried out in more traditional social work settings for a major part of the casework problems which the social worker encounters. A more detailed publication of the research material prepared by the Center for Education and Research in Corrections will make it possible to demonstrate this point.

in pursuing treatment objectives and make realistic attempts to clarify the professional caseworker's role in a correctional setting. Administrator and worker alike must take into account the fact that the specialized functions of each can lead to divergent interests and objectives, and become alert to ways in which these conflicts may be minimized.

Administrators will be unable to solve these problems without the co-operation of specialists in public administration, social work education, and research. Probation-parole organizational problems which appear unique actually may be identical in kind with those in other settings.[22] Both corrections and social work have a research obligation to examine the question by studying agency settings and actual work. If it is true that apparently unique probation-parole difficulties are only special instances of generic work problems, careful modification within the generic curriculum could benefit both probation-parole and the larger area of social work practice. If social work education is to fulfil its obligation to its graduates in the field, it will have to adjust to the need for refinement of administrative training.

2 Discovering and teaching to students treatment skills which are effective in a situation where alternatives are circumscribed goes beyond the value statements common in probation-parole literature which state that this can or must be done or which merely rationalize present difficulties. Graduates must be trained in the why, when, and how of such methods, just as today they are equipped with experience in techniques appropriate to other settings. If techniques can be developed, generic education could more adequately train graduates to serve clients within the relatively narrow frameworks of various settings, particularly public agencies.[23] With the development of techniques that work, it may be possible to legitimize control approaches with a rationale of greater significance than "the worker must accept the limitations of the agency." Today there are points at which a worker cannot pursue the welfare of his client and accept the agency at the same time.

3 The worker needs training in dealing with certain types of clientele, especially the "unmotivated client" and the client with "limited capacity." Although these problems are amplified in the correctional caseload, they are found more generally and therefore are of interest to practitioners in various settings. In addition, the probation-parole worker, at some point

22 / Earl Bogdanoff and Arnold J. Glass, *The Sociology of the Public Worker in an Urban Area*, unpublished M.A. thesis, Department of Sociology, University of Chicago, 1954; Charlotte G. Babcock, "Social Work as Work," *Social Casework*, December, 1953, pp. 415–442.

23 / Cf. Studt, "An Outline for Study of Social Authority Factors in Casework," *op. cit.*

in his preparation, must acquire information specific to his field – e.g., knowledge of the criminal subculture.

The problems of agency organization and casework method for situations of limited alternatives are related in that progress in solving one will reduce the difficulties of the other. Both merit objective and evaluative research, the results of which may be used directly to broaden generic theory and method and to advance administrative reorganization of the field. This research work must be supported by organized pressure from professional groups in the field to promote the development of treatment orientations in correctional settings, with full recognition of the public commitment to work within a framework of varying degrees of control.

The challenge to professional education comes at a time of transition, which in itself sharpens many dilemmas. The transition will last a long time, but it will be less painful if the social work profession reaffirms its identification with workers in corrections and provides them with the support which pioneering merits.

PART V
The use of authority in social work practice

INTRODUCTION

The central thrust in the seven articles included in this section is how authority in social work practice can be used in a helpful and positive way for individual clients and groups and as a part of professional activity. To illustrate this theme, articles are chosen to represent a variety of settings and problem situations relevant to social work practice. The choice made here does not by any means exhaust settings and problems in social work practice, but rather tends to indicate a range of social work practice where authority is inherent either in the social agency or in the professional worker. Broadly speaking, two groups of social agencies are covered in the seven articles; agencies whose services are geared to deviance, prevention, and rehabilitation, and agencies that are primarily oriented to the task of providing adequate levels of social participation and integration. Social agencies charged with the task of ensuring adequate income support and maintenance are excluded from our selection mainly because no articles relevant to the purpose of this book could be located. This is a significant omission insofar as improvement of social work practice is concerned.

It is hoped that the reader will attempt to relate each of the seven articles to theoretical knowledge and understanding of authority, that is, to evaluate social work practice, especially the use of authority in social work, in the light of theory, and to establish functional linkages between social science theories and concepts and social work practice.

The criterion used in selecting each article was its significant contribution to "practice wisdom" in social work. In social work a large reservoir of "practice wisdom" exists. Because of the youth of social work as a profession and its basic orientation as an "artistic profession" this reservoir of knowledge remains as the most singularly important source and body of knowledge. Social workers have an obligation both to use creatively the "practice wisdom" of other social workers and to contribute to the total body of knowledge.

One of the interesting features of these articles is the presentation of case material drawn from individual authors' experience. Five of the seven articles include case illustrations, making the author's point more alive. Without the case material from practice it would have been difficult, if not impossible, to demonstrate the actual use of authority in professional practice.

As stated before, each of the seven articles makes a significant contribution to positive and helpful use of authority in social work practice and is written by a practitioner with professional experience. Yelaja's article on the use of authority in child protective service can serve as a central frame of reference for other articles in terms of its conceptual analysis and understanding of authority and its integration with social work practice in the area of child protective service. In his article, Yelaja develops an hypothesis for further exploration, which can be stated as follows. The assumption is made that authority as an integral part of child protective service has a potential for positive use in helping neglectful parents improve the care of their children. Its effective use, however, depends upon the extent to which the social worker understands the meaning of authority vested in him. It is therefore hypothesized that the effectiveness of authority in reaching out to an unmotivated or resistive client is greater if the social worker can communicate through feeling and empathy and can appreciate the fact that his authority may remain ineffective until clients have sensed a genuine concern for their welfare. In developing this hypothesis, Yelaja has drawn heavily from Barnard's theory of authority.

Meyerowitz's article on the use of authority in child placement and Miller's article on the use of rational authority in the adolescent group are based on Fromm's conception of rational authority, which has its source in professional competence requiring constant scrutiny and criticism by those who are subjected to its use. Both Meyerowitz and Miller emphasize that (rational) authority can be helpful to clients and must be considered as an integral part of social work treatment, although the central purpose of treatment differs in child placement and in the adolescent group with behavioural problems.

Redl and Wineman deal with the use of authority and permission in working with emotionally disturbed children within an institutional setting. "Permission" and "authoritative verbot" are considered as techniques in helping emotionally disturbed children. With the help of case illustration, they rather successfully demonstrate how these two techniques, if simultaneously applied in therapeutic situations, especially superficial behaviour manifestations that are clearly not acceptable within "normal standards of behaviour," can be useful in helping emotionally disturbed children. Their techniques provide a useful and practical approach to those social workers who are interested in "behaviour modification" treatment technology.

The three other articles by Orchard, Knisely, and Fink reiterate the basic theme on positive use of authority in social work practice, but they illustrate this theme through a variety of social work practice settings, which include correctional services, rehabilitation of criminals, mental health and counselling services and supervision.

Although the subject of authority has received increasing attention in social work literature, at least five general areas seem to be inadequately covered in the literature. First, there appears to be little or no exploration of the impact of organizational structure on the use of authority, especially social agencies with a highly bureaucratic structure where organizational authority is concentrated at the top. An examination of how concentrated organizational authority will affect the use of authority by a social worker in the helping process would be a significant contribution to the literature. Second, the question as to whether the use of authority in social work practice does in fact pose ethical problems and issues for individual social workers generally seems to remain unanswered. There is a popular assumption or myth about authority being in conflict with professional values, but the social work literature is sadly lacking in documentation of specific ethical problems experienced by social workers in practice. As a result there is a mystery surrounding the ethical behaviour of social workers who carry a "legitimized authority role" in their practice. Third, the place of authority in private social work practice is not dealt with in the literature. When professional social work is practised under private auspices, the legitimation and sanctioning systems of authority take an altogether different form and perhaps meaning for both the professional worker and the clients. An analysis of authority factors in the worker-client relationship under private auspices would be a significant contribution to the social work literature. Fourth, social workers are increasingly interested in the "behaviour-modification" approach to treatment in recent years, but the social work literature on behaviour modification has hardly considered the role of authority in treatment programmes aimed at modifying behaviour of clients. The field of correctional services has experimented with operant conditioning, peer-group reinforcement, etc., as specific types of behaviour-modification programmes. It would be interesting to consider how the use of authority can facilitate the behaviour-modification programmes. The Redl and Wineman article seems to point up exciting potential for building a reservoir of practice knowledge and skills in the use of authority within the context of the "behaviour-modification" approach to treatment. Finally, the use of authority in family therapy appears to be neglected in social work literature. Authority plays a crucial role in sound family functioning and indeed many familial problems can be directly traced to the breakdown of the authority system and patterns in family life. Yet, in the treatment of troubled families, authority has received inadequate consideration and emphasis. Articles based on practice experience of the use of authority in family therapy would be significant contributions to the social work literature.

19
The concept of authority and its
use in child protective service

Authority – its legitimate place in the worker-client relationship and its use as an enabling factor in the helping process – has been a subject of some controversy in the professional literature of the past. Social case-workers, especially those in authoritarian agencies, have wrestled with this issue in an effort to resolve what seems to be a dilemma. A quick review of the professional literature on the subject of authority and its use in social work practice would, however, indicate a shift of emphasis. Although we have settled the basic controversy of whether social casework based on authority is an integral part of social work practice, the efforts now seem to be directed increasingly toward the development of a better understanding of how authority can be used as a dynamic in a growth-inducing experience for a client who is resistant to help and comes involuntarily to a social agency.[1]

The Editor of *Social Casework*, summarizing this trend, observed:

... current writers are stressing that an authoritative relationship, which always has in it negative connotations for the client, can be used constructively in offering him certain services, and that the protective role can in time be modified, permitting the development of a dynamic and positive relationship through which the client can develop emotionally ... It seems to close the debate as to whether casework can be practiced in an authoritative setting. The question now is how the client, in any setting, can be understood, helped, supported, and "reached" emotionally.[2]

Reprinted by permission of the Child Welfare League of America, New York, from *Child Welfare*, XLIV: 514–22, November 1965.

1 / See, for instance, the institute on "Authority and Choice in Protective Service," CWLA Eastern Regional Conference, Philadelphia, May 1965.

2 / "Casework and Authority," Editorial Notes, *Social Casework*, XXXV (1954), 258.

In keeping with the contemporary trends of thinking, this paper[3] is presented with two objectives. First, it seeks to clarify in depth the concept of authority from interdisciplinary standpoints. Second, it attempts to discuss some of the problems underlying the use of authority in child protective service.

AUTHORITY IN THE HELPING PROCESS

The central theme of this paper is based on the premise that authority as a power of communication can be used as a dynamic in the helping process, depending upon the degree to which the caseworker understands the meaning of authority and also the degree to which neglectful parents are willing to identify the positive aspects of authority for enhancing their parental motivation. The *Social Casework* Editorial Note has emphasized some of the positive aspects of authority, recognizing that authority has a greater potential of producing negative feelings, but that these can also be utilized in the helping process.[4] The professional literature of the past is replete with the discussion of this aspect of authority, but very little emphasis seems to have been placed on viewing authority in light of its positive and benevolent elements.

CHILD PROTECTIVE SERVICE

I shall discuss child protective service as background for discussion of the concept of authority. In the social agencies offering service to neglectful parents, one finds certain distinctive characteristics in the helping process that differentiate it from that used by "voluntary-client" agencies. Although most social agencies are structured to offer services to clients who come to the agency of their own initiative to seek help for their problems – individual or social – the nature of neglect makes it obvious that the parent who has been neglecting his child does not request the service of his own volition, but that the request for service comes from someone else. Protective service to children is, therefore, initiated by the agency, and, unlike service from other social agencies, it cannot be withdrawn when the parent refuses or is unable to use the agency's help. The agency is obligated to continue work with the parents as long as conditions of neglect persist, although in some instances casework service might be terminated because

3 / Adapted from *Authority as a Dynamic in Casework with Neglectful Parents: Historical and Present Perspectives of the Issue*, thesis submitted in partial fulfillment for Advanced Curriculum Certificate (Philadelphia: School of Social Work, University of Pennsylvania, 1964).
4 / "Casework and Authority," *loc. cit.*

of the parents' refusal to cooperate. In such instances, however, the agency would evaluate the situation to determine the need for court intervention.

Protective services for children are established under state laws.[5] Even though in some states responsibility for protecting children is delegated to private social agencies, it still remains primarily the responsibility of the state, and most of the state governments have enacted laws covering this. Since the basis of social service to parents neglecting their children is within the framework of the law, it therefore carries with it community sanction and a range of normative values governing an acceptable standard of child care. These standards of child care have changed from time to time and are subject to further modifications. Agencies providing protective service, however, operate on a given set of standards, and the parents' motivation for improvement in child care is measured against these standards, which continue to serve as guidelines throughout the casework service.

Although the authority of child protective agencies emanates from law and carries with it the inherent threat of separation of children from parents when conditions of child neglect persist, the very fact that the protective caseworker is willing to help the parents without invoking legal action and that the community accepts that parents have a right to an appropriate service before they are adjudged neglectful diminishes the importance of legal authority. It becomes obvious that the concept of authority has a range of meanings of which an examination would be worthwhile. Such an attempt is exceedingly important to the understanding of how authority can be used most helpfully in developing impaired parental capacities and strengths.

RANGES OF MEANING

What are the various dimensions of authority? What is the range of its meaning, and how can these be understood in the context of the worker-client relationship and social work practice in child protective service? In our attempts to define authority, some dependence on sociologists, psychologists, and behavioral scientists seems to be justified and, to some extent, necessary because of their extensive work on the subject. A note of caution is necessary, however, when applying their knowledge and findings to social work practice. It must be remembered that most of these social scientists have studied authority with a bureaucratic model as back-

5 / For example, in Pennsylvania the County Institution District Act of 1937 and the County Code Act of 1955 establish the legal base for county responsibility for protective and other child welfare services.

ground; the findings may not always fit into the social work model based on democratic values.

POWER IN AUTHORITY

Authority, as defined by Parsons, "is an institutionally recognized right to influence the action of others, regardless of their immediate personal attitudes to the direction of influence. It is exercised by the incumbent of an office or other socially defined status ..."[6] Another useful definition of authority derived from sociological analysis is given by Lasswell and Kaplan, who offer a series of definitions of significant concepts such as influence, power, and authority.[7] Power is only one of the operative values on which authority relations are based, but it is one of the most important ones. According to these two authors:

Authority is thus the expected and legitimate possession of power. We say "expected" because the actual power structure does not necessarily coincide with that described in the political formula; and "legitimate" because the formula is the source and basis of legitimacy. To say that a person has authority is to say not that he actually has power but that the political formula assigns him power, ... and regard[s] his exercise of it as just and proper.[8]

Mencher, however, prefers to define authority as "the power to induce changes in, or to exert control over, the behavior of another. Its influence is dependent upon how it is perceived or accepted by those to whom it is directed."[9]

Although power is one important ingredient of authority, it alone does not always reach the desired objectives of authority. Power is the actual ability to control, which may or may not be a right based on a particular position, and it may result from such diverse factors as prestige, physical coercion, persuasion, and class. As Merton points out, "... positions in the class, power, and prestige hierarchies contribute to the potential for interpersonal influence, but do not determine the extent to which influence actually occurs."[10] "Thus, authority is the *potentiality* to influence based

6 / Talcott Parsons, *Essays in Sociological Theory* (rev. ed.; New York: The Free Press of Glencoe, 1954), p. 76.
7 / Harold D. Lasswell and Abraham Kaplan, *Power and Society* (New Haven, Conn.: Yale University Press, 1950), pp. 131–133.
8 / *Ibid.*, p. 133.
9 / Samuel Mencher, "The Concept of Authority and Social Casework," *Casework Papers, 1960* (New York: Family Service Association, 1960), p. 127.
10 / Robert K. Merton, *Social Theory and Social Structure* (rev. ed.; New York: The Free Press of Glencoe, 1957), p. 419.

on a position, whereas [the] power is the actual ability of influence based on a number of factors including, of course, organizational position."[11]

Implicit in all of these definitions is the important thesis that authority becomes meaningful and its power felt only when it is accepted by those on whom it is exercised. Friedrich[12] and Barnard[13] describe authority as a character and quality of communications rather than of persons. Friedrich says that "when we speak of the authority of a person, we are using a shorthand expression to indicate that he possesses the capacity to issue authoritative communications."[14] Seen in the perspective of formal administrative organization, "authority," says Barnard, "involves two aspects: first, the subjective, the personal, the *accepting* of a communication as authoritative, ... and, second, the objective aspect – the character in the communication by virtue of which it is accepted ..."[15] The essence of the definition provided by Barnard seems to be that "authority ... lies with the persons to whom it is addressed, and does not reside in 'persons of authority.' "[16] It is the willingness to be influenced, whatever the origin of the willingness, that determines authority as power.

AUTHORITY FROM THE LAW

What are the implications of the above analysis on the worker-client relationship in a social casework setting such as a child protective service? The protective caseworker derives his authority from the law that authorizes the agency to protect neglected and abused children. The power to act is thus embedded in the very nature of the role of the protective caseworker. His authority, however, in terms of legitimate power to act and to influence the behavior of the client in the sense of helping neglectful parents will not find really meaningful expression unless the client accepts this authority. The authority of the agency and the protective caseworker becomes effective with parents only when the neglectful parents yield to their need for help. The acceptance of the authority, then, depends upon the nature of authority as represented by the protective caseworker and as perceived by the neglectful parents.

11 / W. G. Bennis and N. Berkowitz, M. Affinito, and M. Malone, "Authority, Power and the Ability to Influence," *Human Relations*, XI, No. 2 (1958), 144.

12 / Carl J. Friedrich, ed., *Authority* (Cambridge, Mass.: Harvard University Press, 1958), pp. 28–48.

13 / Chester I. Barnard, *The Functions of the Executive* (8th ed.; Cambridge, Mass.: Harvard University Press, 1950), p. 172.

14 / Friedrich, *op. cit.*, p. 36.

15 / Barnard, *op. cit.*, p. 163.

16 / *Ibid.*

An analysis of authority factors in protective social casework reveals both sociolegal and psychological aspects. As observed by Studt:

Every casework relationship starts with a formal authority relationship. The caseworker is unknown to the client, but is brought together with him by reason of the caseworker's position in an agency to which has been delegated the community's power to help. In each case, and in any social agency, the formal authority relationship must become a relationship of psychological authority if the client is to be helped.[17]

The formal and legal aspects of authority inherent in the role of child protective service remain, but their influence is not so strong as the psychological authority. Studt further observes:

It may be said that, in the casework relationship, whenever the psychological aspects of the authority relation develop strongly, the formal social authority aspects, although still present and effective, become secondary; and the casework process emerges as a particular, highly skilled form of the exercise of influence.[18]

PSYCHOLOGICAL AUTHORITY

The concept of psychological authority that is the main plank of the worker-client relationship in social casework has been studied at greater length by Tufts.[19] Fromm's definition of psychological authority "as an interpersonal relation in which one person looks upon another as somebody superior to him,"[20] however, comes nearer to professional authority that is based on the superior knowledge and skills of the worker. The distinction between legal authority and psychological authority is clear-cut – legal authority is a formal power that has been legitimized in the institution structure of the society, but "authority, in its psychological aspects, is an interpersonal relation in which one person (or group) exercises influence over the social behavior of another person (or group) who does not fully accept the reasoning that relates values to actions, but in which both parties know that this influence is being exercised; its intent is known, and hence recognized for what it is."[21]

17 / Elliot Studt, "An Outline for Study of Social Authority Factors in Casework," *Social Casework*, xxxv (1954), 233.
18 / *Ibid.*
19 / Edith M. Tufts, "Psychological Authority: An Operational Definition for Social Work," *Social Work Papers*, viii (1961), 1–8.
20 / Erich Fromm, *Escape from Freedom* (New York: Farrar and Rinehart, 1941), p. 164.
21 / Tufts, *op cit.*, p. 8.

This leads to an important distinction between "authoritative" and "authoritarian" that seems to be significant for understanding the meaning of authority. The distinction between the two may be based upon their basic purposes. Wasser says: "It is essential to relate the use of authority to the intent, to the purpose of action taken ..."[22] Szurek defines an authoritative role as non-coercive authority derived from superior skill and competence for the benefit of the person being helped; this differs from the authoritarian role in which coercive power is used by a person who, for his own ends, seeks to dominate the one being helped.[23]

RATIONAL AND IRRATIONAL AUTHORITY

The distinction between rational and irrational authority might open up still another aspect of the meaning of authority. Fromm, for instance, distinguishes between the dictatorial irrational authority and the rational authority that has its source in competence. He says that the person who functions competently within authority "need not intimidate ... [others] nor arouse their admiration by magic qualities."[24] He further says that "authority not only permits but requires constant scrutiny and criticism."[25] It seems that the ingredients of power and force in authority become less significant in rational authority. Along these lines, Miller says:

What I propose is the exercise of *rational* authority. By rational authority, I mean that which is authoritative through reason, not through force or fashion. The teacher ideally represents rational authority ... not when he says, "This is so because I say so (or because everybody says so)," but "This is so for the following reasons which you may examine."[26]

De Schweinitz and de Schweinitz, discussing the place of authority in the protective function of the public welfare agency, make a further distinction between constituted and inherent authority. Constituted authority is an authority of the office and carries a status symbol, but inherent authority emanates from personal qualities of the individual. It is "the authority of experience and learning, leading to judgments which less

22 / Edna Wasser, "Responsibility, Self-Determination, and Authority in Casework Protection of Older Persons," *Social Casework*, XLII (1961), 265.
23 / S. A. Szurek, "Emotional Factors in the Use of Authority," in Ethel L. Ginsburg, ed., *Public Health Is People* (New York: Commonwealth Fund, 1950), pp. 212–213.
24 / Erich Fromm, *Man for Himself — An Inquiry into the Psychology of Ethics* (New York: Holt, Rinehart, and Winston, 1947), p. 9.
25 / *Ibid.*
26 / Joseph S. Miller, "The Use of Rational Authority in the Adolescent Group," *Journal of Jewish Communal Service*, XXXII (1956), 272.

experienced, less learned persons are willing to follow ... without any compulsion to do so."[27]

The implications of the discussion on the concept of authority from an interdisciplinary standpoint for child protective service could be summarized briefly. Authority is a power to act in behalf of neglected children. It carries with it a range of negative feelings for the parents, who may continue to resist as long as they see only one dimension of authority involving the threat and danger of the removal of children. The reaction of parents is likely to be more positive, however, if they can sense the concern of the caseworker and are able to empathize with the caseworker's feelings of respect and his strong impulse to help despite the parents' resistance. The possibility of an unlimited growth potential in terms of enhancement of parental motivation for better child care is increased when the caseworker's authority finds an optimum balance between the agency's expectations and an appreciation of the parents' improvement, though this is often slow. In the ultimate analysis we see that authority as a power of communication has its source of effectiveness in the client and not the caseworker.

CLIENT CHOICE

The issue of authority and choice has fomented a good deal of agitation and critical thinking, since it involves the very basic concept and principle of social casework process. There seems to be a conflict between an authority-based, agency-initiated service and the range of client choice necessary in a growth-inducing experience. Although it is true that the range of choice offered to neglectful parents is limited, and that it does not provide the same range of choice given to a voluntary client in a non-authoritative social agency setting, there is still some freedom of choice that can be used as a dynamic to release growth potential. Commenting on freedom and authority, Moss states:

Throughout the authoritative service, parental freedom is limited in only one way: parents are not free to abuse or neglect their children. The parents have no choice in dealing with the cultural-legal principle of safeguarding children's rights to grow and develop. The parents do, however, have vast free-

27 / Elizabeth and Karl de Schweinitz, "The Place of Authority in the Protective Function of the Public Welfare Agency," CHILD WELFARE, XLIII (1964), 286; reprinted from [Child Welfare League of America] *Bulletin*, xxv, No. 7 (1946), 1. Quoted from Porter R. Lee, "Changes in Social Thought and Standards Which Affect the Family," in *Proceedings of the National Conference of Social Work* (Chicago: University of Chicago Press, 1923), p. 289.

dom. They may choose not to see the agency worker; they may cooperate superficially with the worker, but not change their behavior; they may risk court action with the expectation that their children will remain at home; they may try to improve their children's care.[28]

Inherent in this protective role is one choice that is constant – to be or not to be. The protective caseworker can certainly use this choice as a real dynamic in terms of clarifying to neglectful parents the nature of choice and possible consequences of either of the choices they are prepared to make.

The skill of the social caseworker in an authoritative setting such as child protective service depends on being able to help clients use the limits imposed by agency structure and social demands. As Pray observes:

... social casework is the art of helping individuals to find and use satisfying and constructive human relationships, and these relationships always involve a constant adjustment of personal needs and wants to the limits imposed by others and by the social whole. Social caseworkers have to work within those limits, just as the clients must do.[29]

The point that is, therefore, of crucial significance in offering a meaningful choice to neglectful parents lies in the ability of the worker to represent the social force that is behind his constituted authority.

The parents yield to their own need for help only when they have sufficiently tested the strength of the worker. In every helping process, a moment is reached when one choice becomes a reality. Speaking about this ultimate single nature of choice, Faatz says:

No matter what the service, no matter how it begins, whether voluntarily or otherwise, no matter how much or how little external pressure has been exerted upon the person to get him to the source of help, there is but one crucial moment of time that matters, and this is the moment in which the self chooses between growth or refusal of growth, life or the negation of life; when the organism, in short, chooses to live and turns its energies from the negative fight against what is, to the vibrant immediacy of what it can do, no matter. This is the moment in time that occurs in every process of help, irrespective of difference of function.[30]

The dynamic of the choice in working with neglectful parents depends

28 / Sidney Z. Moss, "Authority – An Enabling Factor in Casework with Neglectful Parents," CHILD WELFARE, XLII (1963), 387.

29 / Kenneth L. M. Pray, "Casework Paves the Way in Preparation for Freedom," in *Social Work in a Revolutionary Age* (Philadelphia: University of Pennsylvania Press, 1949), p. 214.

30 / Anita J. Faatz, *The Nature of Choice in Casework Process* (Chapel Hill: University of North Carolina Press, 1953), p. 53.

upon the ability of the worker and his disciplined awareness of the professional self. "If caseworkers truly incorporate this concept into themselves as a genuine part of the professional self in helping, then an unrealized potential for helping opens up."[31]

GROWTH POTENTIAL

How the use of meaningful choice within the framework of the limits of authority can act as a dynamic in releasing growth potential can be further illustrated with the help of the following case material:

The Brownlees, a young couple, were referred to the agency because of the neglect of their two children, Annetta, 2 years, and Quinn, 4 months. The children were frequently left without supervision. Quinn, born prematurely, never received medical followup and treatment. The children were ill-clad and appeared dirty and undernourished. At the time the family came to the agency's attention, the father had left the mother and the two babies under the care of the maternal grandmother, who was also a client of the agency.

The mother, mentally limited and too immature to handle the care of two babies, welcomed the agency's intervention as a source of relief. The father, chronically unemployed, vacillated between periods of total dependence and rejection of his responsibility toward the family. Although no evidence of marital conflict was visible, the parents were simply refusing to shoulder responsibility.

The caseworker, holding the mother primarily responsible for the prevailing neglect of the children, told Mrs. Brownlee that she would either have to take the children for medical examination, apply for assistance, etc., or face court action. After some initial resistance to authority, the mother began to organize her strength. The baby was examined, and regular appointments at the district health clinic were kept. Her application for assistance was granted, and she moved to a separate household, although with great hesitancy about being totally self-dependent. Seeing the change in the family, the father was reunited and, with the help of the caseworker, joined a vocational training program. The caseworker supported the family's progress by exploring community resources for household furniture and surplus food.

In a series of joint and separate interviews the caseworker helped the young couple with budgeting, planning a routine for the children, etc., and thoroughly tested their motivation for handling parental responsibility and also supported them in their growth experience. The case was closed after a year and a half, when the parents demonstrated a greater independence.

31 / Ibid.

The protective caseworker's desire to help must find a spontaneous expression in order to bring about a growth-inducing experience. Very often the worker finds himself in a state of despair, especially when he encounters resistance from the neglecting parents to acceptance of his authority. He is likely to interpret this resistance as defiance and nonacceptance of his inherent and constituted authority. But, if he fails to recognize the struggle within the client himself in finding a place within the client-worker relationship, and if he does not help him yield to his own need as a parent, his authority and role may remain separate. Taft makes a pertinent observation in this context:

Basic to a relationship such as this with clients of a protective service, is the caseworker's conviction that her client really wants something better for himself ... It takes into account the resistance that can be centered around change ... The caseworker knows that it is just this resistance that helps her client to find her own strength. She also knows that the same strength which is used in fighting ... authority ... can also be used in the rebuilding of relationships that have been broken, and in the creation of a truer balance within the family itself.[32]

AMBIVALENCE

Usually the beginning phase in protective social casework is marked with intense feelings on the part of both the parents and the worker, since the worker has approached the parents when they did not want him. Because they know that he represents "authority," their reaction often tends to be negative and hostile. Even the most skillful and experienced worker often goes through this beginning of the social casework process with neglectful parents with some degree of awkwardness and uncertainty about himself.

The negative feelings might be so intense that the parents may refuse to see the worker, or even when they do cooperate, they may be unable to face the reality of their neglect and the predicament of their children. Although some parents may be so fearful and mistrustful of becoming dependent that they see authority as a power struggle in which they must either capitulate or rebel, other parents may welcome the authority and having the worker take over responsibility for the care of their children. Understanding and accepting these ambivalent feelings of the parents in order to help them resolve these feelings and move toward responsibility

32 / Jessie Taft, ed., *Counselling and Protective Service as Family Case Work: A Functional Approach* (Philadelphia: Philadelphia School of Social Work, 1946), p. 160.

for their children is indeed a challenging and rewarding part of the case-worker's job.

It is the strength of authority that burdens and threatens not only the parents but the worker as well. Discussing the inherent feelings of fear about authority in the caseworker, Meyerowitz writes: "He may fear the power it entails and the danger of its misuse, and be resentful towards parent and agency for throwing this burden on him."[33] The struggle of the caseworker in coming to grips with the meaning and use of authority has a built-in danger of overidentification with either positive or negative feelings of authority. For instance, "He may expect parents to be moti-vated just because he approaches them with authority. He may view authority as the coercive means of controlling parents or accelerating their movement."[34] The protective caseworker can resolve his struggle by con-scious understanding of his own feelings and his professional role. Hard-man makes a pertinent observation in this context:

The degree to which a worker can be helpful to a client with authority conflict is a function of (1) *the degree to which the worker understands and accepts his own feelings around authority, and* (2) *the skill with which he uses his dele-gated authority.*[35]

The basic skills on which the caseworker's authority is based are his internalization of the meaning of authority, his disciplined concern, and his understanding of the social and psychological factors in parenthood. The authority of the caseworker can find meaningful expression in the helping process only when he understands what it means to give help and to take help.

HELP FROM THE CLIENT

The foregoing discussion may seem to suggest that the caseworker's skill-ful use of authority is the sole determining factor in the helping process with neglectful parents. There is, however, another dimension that is of crucial significance in deciding to what extent the neglectful parents will use the help. This is, in large measure, dependent upon their perception of the caseworker's authority. The caseworker in the constructive use of his authority must be aware of the limits of his authority as determined by the client's perception. Barnard introduces the term "zone of indiffer-

33 / Hilda Meyerowitz, "Use of Authority in Child Placement," *Jewish Social Service Quarterly*, XXXI (1955), 328.
34 / Moss, *op. cit.*, p. 390.
35 / Dale G. Hardman, "Authority in Casework – a Bread-and-Butter Theory," *National Probation and Parole Association Journal*, V (1959), 253.

ence" to identify the area within which each individual is willing to accept controls without conscious questioning.[36] It seems then if authority is an essential element in the treatment plan, the caseworker's greatest chance of success lies in broadening the client's "zone of indifference" rather than threatening the total relationship through expecting too much of the client before he is ready to accept authority. In this context Mencher observes:

Authority is a tenuous phenomenon, and the total casework relationship can be threatened when the worker makes demands that are out of keeping with the client's expectation and that result in the client's denying authority.[37]

AUTHORITY AS A DYNAMIC

Although authority is necessary in providing protective service to children, it is not sufficient. The dynamic in a protective agency is the skill of the caseworker as he carries his role. His disciplined self-awareness and his understanding and sensitivity toward parents are the bases of an integration of professional helping and agency authority. Authority, it seems, can be a real dynamic in the helping process with neglectful parents only when the protective caseworker recognizes the strength and limits of his authority and helps the parents yield to their own need to have something better for themselves and for their children.

The following case material is presented to emphasize how authority can act as a dynamic in helping neglectful parents find a new meaning in parenthood under most hopeless and depressing conditions.

Thomas, a 7-year-old child, was reported to the agency when the school teacher noticed severe burns on his hand. According to the school's information, the father inflicted the burns as a disciplinary measure. Thomas, both physically and mentally retarded, was not toilet trained and appeared uncared for. Investigation revealed parental rejection of the boy. The parents denied physical abuse, but expressed concern about the tremendous problems in handling the child, who often wet his bed, could hardly speak coherently, and was uncontrollable.

In a series of joint interviews, the caseworker explored the feelings of the parents about Thomas and their ability to respond to the child's needs. The father revealed his extreme sense of insecurity and loss of control when Thomas repeated "abnormal behavior." The mother acknowledged that Thomas was not safe and that she would like him to be placed.

The agency finally petitioned the court, requesting the placement of Thomas.

36 / Barnard, *op. cit.*, pp. 168–169.
37 / Mencher, *op. cit.*, p. 136.

Prior to the court hearing, Thomas was sheltered at the agency. Most of his behavioral problems almost disappeared as soon as he left the home environment. The neuropsychiatric examination held at the juvenile court indicated mental retardation, but latent potential for growth under good institution care. The psychiatric examination of the parents revealed low intelligence, but lack of any psychosis or mental disturbance. As a result of the court hearing, Thomas was committed to institution placement.

During the time of Thomas' separation from the home, the parents kept regular appointments to see him and were delighted to watch his slow, but steady, physical and emotional growth. Both parents evidently accepted placement of the child as mutually beneficial and involved themselves with plans for the child's future.

The above case is a poignant expression of how authority can be helpful without being coercive and punitive. It is inconceivable that the parents would have accepted the responsibility for their emotional rejection of Thomas and could have participated in this planning of future care without the support of an authority imbued with firmness and respect for parental motivation for change despite the parents' initial rejection of the child.

CONCLUSION

Authority as an integral part of child protective service has a potential for positive use in helping neglectful parents improve the care of their children. Its effective use, however, depends upon the extent to which the protective caseworker understands the meaning of the authority invested in him. Authority can be viewed as a power of communication and not merely as a springboard of action. The possibility of its effectiveness in reaching out to an unmotivated or resistive client is greater if the caseworker can communicate through empathy and can appreciate the fact that his authority may remain ineffective until the neglectful parents have sensed his genuine concern for themselves and their children.

HILDA MEYEROWITZ

20

Use of authority in child placement

In the last few years intensive casework treatment has become an essential part of foster home care. It is hard to determine whether the children we are accepting for placement today are actually more disturbed than those we placed formerly or whether we have become more alert to the various expressions of emotional difficulties. Formerly the aggressive, defiant, acting out child got attention as foster parents complained and requested replacements. There was little time and attention given to the withdrawn, seemingly conforming child who was no burden to the foster parents. To-day we recognize the underlying disturbance in both kinds of behavior and treatment becomes an essential part of meeting the needs of children in placement. We also are more attuned to the parents' ambivalence and conflicts around separation from their children and more ready to extend help to them. We no longer believe that foster parents can truly take the place of the child's own family. We understand more clearly children's feelings about their own families, their conflicts and loyalties, their frequent confusion around identification with two sets of parental figures. This awareness of children's needs has made us scrutinize and evaluate the traditional way of functioning in child placement.

We have looked at the developments in related settings, have tried to learn from family counseling and child guidance clinics. While we have learned a great deal from them, child placement has a setting peculiarly different in its complexity which requires that we find our own methods of work, using selectively the knowledge and advances of other fields. Inherent in child placement is the transfer of some of the parental rights, the fact that someone other than the parent carries the adult responsibility

Reprinted with permission from *Journal of Jewish Communal Service*, XXXI: 327–34, 1955.

for the child. This transfer of rights and responsibilities may be affected through court commitment to the agency or through private agreement. In either case it invests the agency with an authority that becomes an integral factor of the treatment situation. The treatment also has to encompass the child's life situation which the agency provides and partly controls. It also needs to consider the balance of the relationship between three groups of participants – parents, child and foster parents. Moreover, our treatment is not limited to the controlled interview situation but flows from the everyday living experience of the people involved.

Placement begins with the parent turning over some of his parental responsibility to the agency. While inner and outer forces may make it essential for the parent to accept placement, and while there may be some relief, the turning over of some of these rights heightens the feeling of loss, of inadequacy, and failure. Unless the parent can be helped to resolve some of his feelings and to relate somewhat positively to the authority vested in the agency, he will not be able to support the child in his move towards placement and in the later acceptance of it.

It is the strength of this authority which burdens and threatens not only the parent but also the worker who has to represent it. Our profession upholds strongly the right of the individual of self determination and freedom of choice. From this deep basic conviction may stem a negative reaction towards authority on the part of the worker. He may fear the power it entails and the danger of its misuse, and be resentful towards parent and agency for throwing this burden on him. Yet, authority is part of our living reality which we have accepted as part of our democratic society. We become resentful and rejecting of it only when it is misused as, for instance, in a dictatorial setting. Eric Fromm in "Man for Himself" distinguishes between the dictatorial irrational authority and the rational authority that has its source in competence. He describes that the person who functions competently within authority may not intimidate others nor arouse their admiration by magic quality. He further says authority not only permits but requires constant scrutiny and criticism.

To represent rational authority competently requires not only maturity but the worker's resolution of his own conflict around parental figures who have represented or are still representing authority to him. Most placement workers can identify with the child. Unless the worker can also understand and accept adult figures in the child's life, he will not be able to extend help to establish the balance necessary for the triangular relationship. Agencies recognizing that not every worker will have this maturity have set up a structure to safeguard the balance of the relationship between parents, foster parents and children around parental visiting, medical care, schooling, etc. With such a structure there is the danger that the worker who has not resolved his conflicts will use the structure without richness but as a crutch or rigidly and punitively.

In the structure of supervision, the supervisor represents the authority of the agency. This may reactivate the worker's unresolved conflicts around parental figures. The skillful supervisor will help the worker to become conscious of this. Together they will evaluate the meaning and process of this experience and relate it to the worker's feelings toward the client, so that the worker can handle his authoritative role with a minimum of conflict and a freedom to assert or yield according to the needs of the situation.

In an agency like the Jewish Family and Children's Bureau in Baltimore, that has cared for about 47 children annually in foster care, there is flexibility and closeness to administration, both of which encourage experimentation. I shall attempt to describe some of our processes and thinking.

We have found that the newly admitted disturbed children are frequently not ready to accept foster parents. They need a great deal of professional help before they are ready to establish meaningful relationships with adults. Our disturbed children have often lived with emotionally upset parents or other adults and bring their disturbed attitudes and expectations into new situations. The anxiety producing separation may even heighten the conflict. If these disturbed children are placed in the usual type of foster homes, the foster parents will react according to their own needs. While this may be helpful in some cases, in others it may intensify the child's problems. For the foster mother this may create a situation of tension which may bring forth rejection of the child.

We have found it helpful, therefore, to place the disturbed child, especially the one just coming into placement, in a setting that to some degree can be controlled professionally. We use for this purpose a study home in which we have an experienced foster mother, who can serve about 3–4 children at one time. Her attitude is warm, but with little emotional involvement, and she has a tolerance for various expressions of children's behavior. She has established a certain routine which gives children security, but she is flexible to the worker's directions. She functions as a semi-professional who accepts the worker's intense activities. She shares with the worker her observations of the children's reactions and her way of handling them, accepting that these reactions will be handled by the worker in terms of their deeper meaning and content. She has a similar attitude towards parents to whom the worker remains closely related. During this placement the parents experience separation and the yielding of some of their rights, but they are not yet faced with as competitive a situation as they would be with a regular foster family.

In this somewhat protected, yet by no means wholly sheltered environment, the worker tries to get the impact of the child's feelings. He plays a very active role in the child's living experience and uses his authority to make decisions which were formerly made by the parents. This precipitates expression of feelings and opens avenues for projecting onto the worker feelings the child carries towards parental figures. The worker is aware of the child's adjustment to the reality situation — foster home, school, relationships with peers — which he can modify to some extent. In treatment he will need to be attuned to the ego strength of the child and be selective in terms of interpretation, time, etc. Children, in order to grow up wholesomely, need an adult to assume certain responsibilities until such time as the child develops knowledge, judgment, and maturity to assume responsibility for his own decisions. While the worker assumes this responsibility at first, his role changes as the child becomes ready to relate more freely to other adults. At that point the foster mother will be helped to take on more responsibility so that the child can be prepared for more normal demands of living. To the degree to which the child can relate, greater demands are made upon him.

The case of Irwin, an exceedingly frightened boy, will illustrate the worker's use of authority and the treatment process in this setting.*

Irwin, 12 years old, born out of wedlock, was referred to us after he had taken his grandmother to the hospital. In the year prior to this, his indulgent, severely retarded mother and weak ineffectual grandfather had died. He blamed his grandmother, whose lack of interest and neglect he felt caused the deaths of his grandfather and mother. His picture of authority was confused; he was afraid of being whipped, afraid of neglect, illness and death. He regressed. His games and phantasies centered around funeral parlors and his goal was to become a mortician. With all his fear and distortion, the child had a hold on reality and could reach out for protection. The worker, who had been in court with him and placed him in the study home, became the central parental figure on whom the child was encouraged to project his feelings.

Because of the family health history, a number of medical examinations were necessary immediately. There could be no choice about this but the worker let the child express his terror that these examinations could cause his death. In light of Irwin's fear, vaccinations and tonsillectomy were postponed. The worker interpreted the medical care as the attempt to protect and preserve the child's health. Irwin, realizing that he was not neglected and feeling the

*Case material by Mr. Daniel C. Goodman.

worker's deep concern, began to trust him. He began to talk more readily and freely about the mother's and grandfather's death, still maintaining that they were caused by the grandmother. The reasons for these deaths were interpreted to him in the light of their real causes and with his guilt and fears somewhat relieved, he could first hint at and later discuss his death wishes towards the mother and grandfather. As the worker discussed these wishes as natural and without any magic, he became less fearful and guilty. The symptomatic picture in the foster home changed and he related more readily to the foster mother yet he seemed all too conforming for a child capable of such strong negative impulses. The worker became somewhat more demanding of him, encouraging him towards greater participation in the foster home, emphasizing more strongly his authority. An outburst came in relation to a visit to the grandmother who meanwhile had been placed in a very good Old Age Home. Irwin was impressed when he saw this but disturbed when his psychotic grandmother had only a stream of complaints for him. He left confused, his guilt somewhat alleviated yet very hurt by the grandmother's lack of interest in him. He was so ambivalent about visiting, that the worker made the decision that Irwin would not return for another few weeks. At first that brought forth relief, but with encouragement he could let himself get very hostile at the worker. The worker remained gentle, acceptant of him and "alive." Following this the child seemed relaxed, feeling protected by this strong authority and more ready to express his negative feelings.

A good deal of further work needed to be done with the child. He needed to be given an experience that emphasized the protective elements in authority. He also needed a controlled relationship in which his hostile impulses would be accepted. After he had been helped to re-evaluate the power of his death wishes, he became more accepting of himself and freer in his self-expression. Having worked this through in relation to the worker, he could relate to other adults with greater security. He could begin to engage himself in thinking and planning for the move towards a long time foster home. Again our understanding of the child made it possible for the agency to select more carefully the regular foster home and to prepare the new foster parents. While there was regression before and after the replacement, the worker's knowledge of the child, the depth of the relationship formerly established, facilitated a faster resolution and a more direct handling of the problem.

In talking about treatment in child care agencies, we also have to consider the group of children who have needed to relate to a succession of parental figures due to many replacements and who have experienced many changing relationships with workers in the agency. They are far harder to reach. Their protective mechanism of withdrawal, evasion or acting out and disregarding authority seems to call for a treatment situation of far greater permissiveness through which they can gradually come to a reorganization. This permissiveness cannot be carried by the child placement worker who needs to carry the authority for certain realistic demands in the life situation. We therefore have found it necessary to refer these children to a psychiatrist for treatment. The treatment in these cases is similar to that in a child guidance clinic.

For the child in treatment with a psychiatrist, the worker's role has to be refocused. While supporting the child in his ambivalence and conflicts around treatment, the worker will assume responsibility for integrating the treatment process and goal with the casework foster parents and parents. Again the decision to initiate psychiatric treatment is an authoritative one. While we may not go further than helping the child towards the recognition of his own unhappiness and a willingness to explore whether someone can help him towards a more satisfying life, we have to work more decisively with foster parents. Where foster parents have feelings of failure, especially in a long time home, the fears of what the child may reveal, the anxieties around the child's possible increased difficulties, need to be dealt with. All of this may serve to bring out the foster parents' own conflict and possible emotional disturbance. The worker can deal with this as it relates to the child. Where the foster parent is too deeply disturbed to respond to this kind of help, we may question the wholesomeness of the setting for the child, or we may help the foster parent to accept help for himself either through family counseling or clinical treatment.

We find that with children more carefully selected for a specific placement, we have less need to enter into "treatment situations" with foster parents. Unless the relationship is of many years standing where the child has truly found a home for himself, we will consider replacement rather than getting involved into treatment of deeply neurotic patterns or encouraging foster parents to get treatment for themselves in order to be more helpful to the child. The burden of treatment begun on this basis is just too much to carry for the child and agency.

Our emphasis on treatment with the child's parent is entirely different. We know that some of them are too sick to involve themselves and we may never do more than help the parent accept placement with the minimum of guilt and the smallest degree of "interference." With other parents the prognosis is better. Treatment with reunion of the family as a goal may be possible.

Most parents who come to us are not ready for treatment; they have at that point reached the conclusion, or the community has reached it for them, that nothing but placement can be the solution. While the difficulties more often than not are projected on the child, it is with a sense of their own failure and inadequacy that the parents yield some of their rights and responsibilities to the authority of the agency. While there may be relief that someone else will carry the burden, there is also fear of what the change will mean. Will the child be taken over completely? Will I lose my child's love? To what end will the agency use its authority? All this is heightened if the child is committed by the court and there is the additional question as to whether the child will ever be returned to the own family.

In our identification with the child we are perhaps too often less perceptive, less concerned with the parents' feelings than with those of foster parents and child. Too often we have used our authority in setting up a structure that would hopefully enable the child to relate to a substitute family. As we recognize the power of familial ties between parent and child – even if negatively expressed – we search for the parents' strength, the reasons for their failure and with it develop a greater understanding and skill in helping them. Yet we seem to have stopped somewhere in the middle. We still have not removed some of the barriers we have set up on the basis of our belief in substitute families. The structure of placement, the many restrictions imposed upon parents require scrutiny and far greater relatedness to the individual situation. Is it essential to have all the limits established seemingly for the benefit of the child but in effect appearing punitive to the parent? Are they in the long run a help or a barrier towards the child's reunion with the own family? Is it possible that we expect the parent to pay too high a price in order to preserve the foster home placement? Do we generally use measures which should be used selectively only?

We have struggled with these questions, felt the burden of authority most keenly in relation to parents. At the same time we have been concerned to provide an experience of a constructive authority that may help parents to get engaged with us.

In the beginning the threat of authority can overwhelm the parent and often is exaggerated in anticipation of the unknown. Our identification with parents, our respect for their feelings, our sharing of observations of the children, our encouragement of parents' participation in important decisions help to break down some of the totality of this threat. While there can be no denial of the areas of responsibility that the parents need to give up, the emphasis must be on the responsibilities that they can continue to carry. At first parents may want to focus on the child only and keep themselves out. The worker will accept this as their need to reaffirm their roles as parents and respond to it. They in turn will usually respond to the worker's true knowledge of the child, his concern for him and his acceptance of the child's behavior with all his difficulties. The worker will encourage the parents to discuss their reactions towards visiting the child in a new strange setting and to what they see in the foster home. As they find the new authority different from their anticipation, accepting and honest, they often gradually give up some of their defenses and move into a deeper involvement with the worker.

The beginning phase is often most crucial in terms of the authority and I should like to illustrate what happens in this phase of placement by the case of Mrs. Meyer.

Mrs. Meyer, a mother of three children, each of them from a different father, had been known to many agencies in the city. The children were referred to us for placement on the basis of a neglect commitment. There had been two stormy court sessions, and prior to, as well as after, commitment Mrs. Meyer refused to work with two protective agencies which offered to help her care more adequately for the children. She was defiant, provocative, and refused to bring the children to the agency except when threatened with contempt of court action. In her interview with the worker, she was exceedingly hostile and sarcastic. She challenged the worker's need to see her as he was going to take the children anyhow. The worker tried to focus on the help the children would need from her in their preparation for placement. She seemed startled but unbelieving. He then proceeded to tell her that he would like them to know that their grandmother was too sick to care for them and that Mrs. Meyer needed to go to work. Mrs. Meyer's amazement was obvious. She had not expected anyone to be concerned about her children's feelings towards her. She agreed with the explanation but was unwilling to share it with the children. When the worker gave the children that interpretation in her presence, she watched suspiciously and then relaxed.

While Mrs. Meyer would not admit to it, she actually prepared the children for placement so that they could move into it fairly relaxed. She seemed to sense that we were not just taking her children away and that we would not forget all about her. The worker reviewed her privileges and responsibilities. He shared information about the foster home and assured Mrs. Meyer that her son would continue at the same parochial school she had selected for him. When Mrs. Meyer brought the children on the day of placement, she made it quite clear in her hostile, challenging manner that while she would come to the agency to discuss the children, she was not going to talk about herself. She does not need help. In leaving, she stopped and wondered about the children's clothing, how would one know what they needed and what fitted them. The worker asked for her suggestions and the sizes she thought right and promised to use them in shopping.

After placement, Mrs. Meyer came to the office without an appointment. She brought some of the children's clothing she had ironed. The record continues, "I had commented earlier that separation from the children was very hard on her, and Mrs. Meyer had said nothing so that I dropped it at that point. Now Mrs. Meyer said that she had not thought it would be that hard. When I asked her whether she wanted to tell me what it was like, Mrs. Meyer said it was hard with them in the home but without them it was much worse. She had no purpose anymore, no reason to live. There is no more ironing to do, no more washing, no more kids to yell at. She proceeded to tell about her experiences, her attempt to provide a home through marriage, her failure at it. As I recognized the hardships of her life, the lack of satisfaction in it, she responded hostilely but then broke down crying profusely, saying how much she missed her older boy, repeating it over and over again almost in a hysterical manner.

"In the midst of crying, Mrs. Meyer jumped towards the door saying she does not want to talk anymore. I said that sometimes it helps to talk about a situation and get it off one's chest, no matter how much it hurts. Mrs. Meyer then sat down and talked about Aaron. He is everything to her, anything he wanted that she could possibly get him, she got for him. He always got his way and he was the 'boss' in the family. I commented that Aaron was only a little boy, seven years old. Could he really be the boss? Maybe he could not take the responsibility for being the man in the family. Maybe he needs to be the little boy for a long time. Mrs. Meyer cried, saying she wants her baby back. I responded that it was not the intent of the agency to keep the child in care. We did want her to have her children back, but before that could be accomplished, she would need to make some changes and we were here to help.

"Mrs. Meyer picked this up immediately, saying nobody could help her. She had tried in the past and all she had gotten was a slap on the other cheek. She talked about the experiences with some other agencies. I suggested that this may be different, perhaps she has something to work towards – getting the children home. When they were home with her, there was always conflict in that she could not care for them adequately. I wondered whether there was something she could do by herself so that she could have the children home. Mrs. Meyer responded, 'you mean getting a job and working steadily.' I thought that that might be one area to begin with and wondered whether it would help to talk things over and do them differently. She felt you can't help a person who is emotionally as mixed up as she is. I maintained that I thought she could be helped. I had seen other people helped, people with emotional problems who really wanted help. Mrs. Meyer sort of bickered with me, yet not quite so hopelessly." A beginning had been made but Mrs. Meyer could not trust the sincerity of the worker's interest. She needed to test him in asserting herself as mother. We let her do this by vetoing the child's having dental work accomplished because of her fear of anesthesia.

This mother, while still vacillating in her trust of agency and constantly challenging our activities, seems to be moving towards accepting help and deciding whether she can make the emotional investment in order to have her children or at least her oldest son returned to her. The realization that forces in the community required certain adjustments from her forced her to move into a situation in which she needed to have to be related to an agency or lose all contact with her children. Authority is used in this beginning in order to engage the client and not to threaten and keep her away from the agency. Mrs. Meyer can respond to our acceptance of her as a mother and she can begin through the mutual concern for the children, though still fighting her own involvement. Parents like her are the ones who easily threaten foster parents as they don't want to permit their child to take roots in a foster home. From our experiences so far, it seems that with all this mother's shortcomings, the children may be better off with their mother, especially when they are older and can take more responsibility for themselves.

In summarizing I should like to say that too often we have left too much to the foster mother, hoping that the impact of the new living situation would help the child to a resolution of his conflicts. In this process we have become greatly identified with the foster parents who carried the major burden, always being afraid that the foster mother may request replacement. Constantly faced with a shortage of foster homes, wanting to avoid the trauma of additional moves for the child, we put emphasis on maintaining the *status quo*. We used our authority to help the child to comply and to limit any "interference" with our plan. This interference came mostly from the child's own family, and because we were so identified with our plan, we easily lost sight of the strengths that the parents expressed through their actions. While philosophically we accepted as our goal the child's return to his own family, our attitudes towards parents, our lack of identification with them made us use our authority in a way that made parents feel pushed out, rejected and unwanted. In the course of the years we lost many parents or saw them continue their negative patterns expressing their disturbance and guilt. We moved in a vicious cycle realizing the child's reactions and disturbances in relation to this.

With the agency's intensive involvement with the child, children could express freely the depth of their conflict. When we began to realize the deep meaning parents have for their children, we tried to evaluate diagnostically the parents' responsiveness and look critically at our methods and skills in helping them. We are faced with a particularly complicated situation in that the parent does not come for treatment to the agency, yet he has to be related to it throughout the time the child is in placement. He can begin to get engaged by being related to his child through the worker who knows and helps his child. On the strength of this relationship with the awareness that his child is being helped, not blamed, he may gain an experience meaningful enough so that he can risk his own engagement with the goal of being a better parent to his child. If we can see placement as a means of helping child and parent to a better adjustment, the foster home placement being a plan towards that goal, we will find ways of using our authority as a constructive, positive force in helping people deal more adequately with realities in their life situations.

FRITZ REDL
DAVID WINEMAN

21

Authority and permission in working with
emotionally disturbed children

It may puzzle the reader to find these two techniques listed under the
same heading, since they obviously seem to belong at opposite ends of the
same line. Open permission as an encourager of behavior seems to be
the exact reverse of "authoritative Verbot," by which we mean a sharp
and clear statement that this piece of behavior is intolerable. For the practitioner who undergoes training in the daily practice of survival with disturbed children, either one of the two techniques certainly deserves a
section of its own, and their technical ramifications are enormous. For the
purpose of describing their potentials in such an abbreviated list as this
one is meant to be, they might well be handled in the same section.

When we refer to "permission" here, we do not mean the larger issue of
a policy of "permissiveness," its clinical advantages and limitations, which
we discuss in other places. We use the term here to refer to a specific act
on the side of the adult which is meant to influence surface behavior only
right here and now. The use which this technique of "permission" can
be given falls into three categories:
1 We sometimes openly "permit" in order to *start a piece of behavior*
which we want and which might otherwise have been blocked, or at least
in order *to take the sting of anxiety or guilt* out of it. This use of permission
is well known. It may be openly verbal, or implied in the adult's attitude
or general policy. In arts and crafts, a child, for instance, may have hesita-
tions about getting to work on a wood gun he planned to make, because
of the fear that the inadequate results might draw criticism from the group
leader. By openly encouraging and "permitting" enthusiastic experimen-

Reprinted with permission from Fritz Redl and David Wineman, *Controls from
Within* (Glencoe, Ill.: The Free Press), 1952, pp. 217–25. The original title of this
chapter was "Permission and 'Authoritative Verbot.' "

tation without too much worry about whether materials are wasted or not, the group leader gets the youngster going full force, and allows him to enjoy his exploit without the compunctions of perfectionist guilt or shame. 2 The technique of "permitting" can, however, also be used for the opposite end, a fact which seems to be less well known. By "permitting" something openly, we sometimes really stop it faster than by any other technique. This effect is usually limited to the case where a piece of behavior was meant to irritate, antagonize, or try out the adult, or to express an attitude of rebellious defiance. If permitted openly, such an exploit loses all its attraction to the child, and the activity is stopped right away, with none of the accompanying "frustration-aggression" which would have been tied to a more direct form of limitation. In the beginning, for instance, we could often watch the youngsters "surreptitiously" picking something up that belonged to the adult, just waiting for a response of fury and a Verbot. Instead, when we could afford that, we made it clear that we didn't mind at all: "You can try out that lighter, as long as you just watch out that you don't break it." The youngster would soon lose interest and put it back where it belonged.

3 The most fascinating use of permission as a technique of control, however, is made when it is applied not to stop an activity we couldn't prevent except by extreme means anyway, but to "take the triumphant rebellious sting" out of it, and through that *keep it on a manageable level*. In this way, the technique does not bring about absolute stoppage of the behavior, but decontaminates it of its negativistic sideline, and at the same time keeps it within tolerable limits. To use a crude illustration: a youngster may be engaged in a milder form of name calling or some semi-aggressive "horse-play" directed toward the adult. By humorously permitting a certain level of it, or even entering into it up to a certain point in mock action, the "triumphant sting" is taken out of it, and it soon peters out without swelling up to the intensity it would have reached had it been left alone, and without one's having to wrestle with the secondary by-products of sharper interference forms.

During the evening program tonight, we were doing some finger painting and water colors. Bill was rambling around and, in a rather subtle way, trying to lure Andy out of the activity. But the latter was quite fascinated by the effects he was getting with his water colors and so was quite impervious to Bill's seductive wiles. I suggested to Bill that I would be glad to help him mix his colors and that the other guys were getting a lot of fun out of working with the paints. Why didn't he come over? But, no, he didn't want to and so the pattern dragged on for about another fifteen minutes or so, with Bill finally making open overtures to Andy: "Hey, Andy, let's go out and shake some cherries off the tree," or "Hey, Andy, c'mon let's go out and sell some flowers to that old lady next door and make us some money." But Andy adamantly stuck to the painting and ignored Bill, partly now getting some sadistic gratification out of thwarting him. Bill, in final desperation, began to chase around the living room and jump off and onto the couch and then, crouching up on the fireplace mantle, jumped from there onto a nearby lounge chair, giggling and whooping. He now began to displace against me the aggression meant for Andy because of the latter's ignoring of him. This behavior was against house rules which discourage the use of the living room for such activities but I felt at this moment that an open command to stop would play even more into Bill's hands. So I walked from the dining room, where we were doing the painting, into the living room and said, "Oh boy, look at the stunt man. I guess you found yourself something to do, didn't you?" This was rather unexpected, for Bill had thought I would interfere, perhaps even chase him. But he went along with me and said, "Hey, Barbara, catch me" and jumped from the mantle into my arms. I held him for a minute and he brushed my cheeks with his open hand in a mock slap, saying "Hi ya, mammy," and then leaped down to the floor, now appearing to have had a mood change for the better. The others still being absorbed in their painting, I danced a little jig with Bill and then he had the idea of turning the record player on to listen to some of their new records. I went back to the finger and water color painters in the next room. (Entry: 5/13/47, Barbara Smith) *

This evening the group had, as a program innovation, a "picnic supper" in my apartment. It was the first time they had ever been there, and they were quite boisterous and excited, but still in a somewhat positive way. The minute they hit the place they were all over it like a blitz. They got into every conceivable nook and cranny; they examined my closets, the bathroom, my wardrobe. They had to use my hair tonics and handle my shaving equipment. They poured over my desk, every drawer of which they yanked open and shut and went through like a horde of frantic termites. They breezed through my pipe collection and carried it triumphantly like battle trophies into the living room. They were touching, feeling, smelling, in a mad outpouring of tactile and other sensory investigations of every single item that could be dislodged and moved. My attitude was one of deliberate *carte blanche*, realizing that I had made a mistake in having them in that early in the game to begin with, and now wouldn't stand a chance to prevent serious collective aggression against my domicile if I took a restraining approach. And, of course, I didn't want to have this visit end up in a scene of group bouncing, either. The funny thing

*Entry refers to the date of the social worker's activity and the worker's name.

is, this very desperate effort of mine to "permit" and even enjoy what was going on anyway seemed to have a really restraining effect. They handled literally dozens of fragile and breakable items – little jade elephants out of a collection I have and curio pieces of china and glass. My guitar and accordion changed hands dozens of times without any one ever deliberately mishandling them. Nothing was broken during the whole evening. Yet these same children had, during the previous thirteen days at Pioneer House, destroyed ninety per cent of the toys and other equipment. I am now convinced that real damage would have been done had I been frightened by our previous experiences and tried to lock up or protect my possessions with open effort. Had I tried any one of the other ranges of interference techniques, the evening would have ended in disciplinary mayhem with tantrums being thrown all over the place. Not that I want to pretend, in retrospect, that the idea itself of bringing them to my house that early in the game was too well timed. (Entry: 12/14/46, Fritz Redl)

It is important, of course, to remain realistic about the possibilities and limitations of this technique of "stoppage or decontamination through permission." It can, as the examples show, be a great help, but, of course, there are limits to its use. It must never be applied in too open contrast with what we really are able to "accept," and its too liberal application might easily be confused by the children with actual permissiveness or total license, or might be interpreted as a sign of weakness, fear, or disinterest on our side.

By the technique of "*authoritative Verbot*" we mean exactly what the term implies. We simply say "NO," and we say it in such a way that it is clear that we mean it and we don't soften it up by arguing, explaining, or what not. We simply imply: "This has got to be stopped. We can't have it. That's all there is to it, and right now we don't care whether you understand or like it at all. It's got to be stopped, that's all." We said: we *imply*. If we would say all this explicitly it would take away from the very nature of the technique suggested here. Of course, not all our "No's" are of this nature. Some of them really belong in the section of "signal interference": while the spoken word is only a short "No," the total context of the situation is so clear that everybody knows or has just shortly ago discussed all the reasons why such behavior is unacceptable anyway. Then, the "No" only serves as a signal reminder of a larger policy that has already been worked out. In the present item, we really go one step beyond that. We seriously suggest that occasionally a simple clear "Verbot" of behavior, the reasons for which may be far beyond what can be explained or got across right now, may do a great deal of good. We have often been amazed at how it works. For, even in cases where youngsters are engaged in openly adult-defying conduct, if that adult suddenly comes out with a clear-cut limitation demand, it may take the youngster so much by surprise or assuage his own beginning unconscious anxiety about his exploit so well that he actually does stop, even though we wouldn't have believed it possible. The "hygiene" of saying "No" is an important issue, of course. Such "authoritative Verbot" must be free of hostility, anxiety, or anger on the side of the adult. It must happen in a basic atmosphere of acceptedness and tolerance, as an exceptional rather than a usual gesture.

It is sometimes accompanied by changes in gesture, physiognomy, or tone of voice. Occasionally, it makes a great difference from which "status source" the "No" is issued. Thus, we would find that, in moments when the group leader who was involved with the children in an aggressive scene could not have stopped them any more except by sharper interference techniques, the "overgroup representative," executive director or director, appearing freshly on the scene, could still stop things by nothing stronger than a clear-cut "No, that doesn't go, stop it." A planned manipulation of hierarchy and role distribution in our interference tactics was one of the most important items in our stock in trade at camp as well as at the Home. Whatever the details might be, we soon learned that we could save ourselves some of the much more conflict-producing interferences if we learned how to predict when whose "No" would be most effective.

Among the cases in which the use of this technique seemed most effective were the following:

1 If the youngsters were engaged in their misbehavior not so much because of uncontrollable impulsivity or pathology, but more because of the temporary "excitement" engendered, and because of a lack of reality-awareness or the feebleness of their value danger signals from within. In those cases a clear "No" seemed to snap them back to a previous state of control which they would have been capable of had not the addition of the excitational stimulation been present.

2 If the youngsters were just about to go farther than they really would have wanted to, so that they actually were pleased by or began to ask for a stoppage by the adult. Our "No" then saved them guilt feelings, anxieties, or loss of face.

3 If, in spite of the impulsive and pathology-conditioned mayhem, by some miracle the basic relationship to the present adult was still intact, so that signals coming from him would still be meaningful and challenge them toward unconscious cooperation.

4 If the "No" was surrounded by a situation whose impact was clear

enough in itself (like the danger in station wagon traffic misbehavior) and had often been handled more explicitly before.

5 If the youngster's behavior needed to be stopped, while the issue itself was much too complicated to be taken up at the moment, and the youngsters were dimly aware of this. An example of this was given occasionally when our youngsters were engaged in some of their naïve and basically harmless sexual excitation, which would lead to sex language being bandied about gleefully – and, for a change, without aggressive intent – or to hopping around in the nude in a small child's enjoyment of narcissistic exhibitionism. Sometimes outside circumstances made it necessary to curb such activity, even when it was not possible to explain why. Once, for instance, the youngsters had to be stopped from exhibiting themselves gleefully at the window to innocent passers-by, enjoying the mild shock or curiosity reactions thus produced. The whole mood in which it happened was relatively harmless, but we thought we had reasons of a community relationship nature to interfere. Short of using heavy interference means, which we didn't want to for clinical reasons well understood by the psychoanalytically trained educator, all that would be left would be arguing. But how would we argue with them? Any appeal to decency or morals would, at that stage of the game, have been wasted effort – you can't appeal to something that isn't there. To threaten them with what these people would do to them or that they might call the police would only stir up their already overdeveloped antagonism against "those people" and "the police," who represent law and order to them, a hatred which we did not want to stir up. And to impress them with the fact that these people might not find such behavior nice or might object to it would have been just grist for their mill – that was exactly what they wanted to begin with. We were pleasantly surprised, therefore, when we noticed that the youngsters gave up their activity when we simply said: "Stop that, we can't let you act that way." The clarity of our interference signal, coinciding with a vague notion that somewhere there was more to it which we couldn't or wouldn't raise at that moment, sufficed to bring the scene to an end.

It is clear, of course, that "Verbot" would have no power once excitement had trespassed a certain degree, where clearly traumatically derived pathology was rampant, or where a total loss of reality relatedness had already occurred.

As I came into the housemother's quarters tonight, I was confronted with Danny hitting viciously at Larry, while the housemother was trying to pull him away but unsuccessfully so because of his bulk. Danny was yelling at her:

"Keep your hands off me, you dirty whore. I'll kill the bastard." "Oh, oh, what's the matter in here, off the beam again Danny?" I asked, and he, for the first time aware of my presence in the room, dropped his attack on Larry and said, "Goddamit Fritz, every time I wanna talk to Emmy private this mother-fucker has to butt in, etc., etc." After being permitted to ventilate his gripes for about fifteen minutes, he calmed down, and then I played checkers with Larry out in the living room while the housemother talked quietly with Danny about his clothing, which was what he wanted to do in the first place. (Entry: 4/14/47, Fritz Redl)

At 12:15 A.M., I got a call from the housemother that the kids were rioting and running all over the place clad only in shorts. This behavior included sallies out into the really frigid snow-covered Second Boulevard to fill pails with snow so they could make snowballs to throw from inside at passing traffic. The total staff was alerted but nothing seemed to work, and so I dressed hurriedly and tore down by way of frozen and deserted Hamilton Avenue to the Home. When I got there, they were acting according to specifications over the telephone and Joe, Andy, and Danny especially were "higher than kites." Joel (counselor) by this time had corralled Sam, with whom he has an excel-lent relationship, and was half talking, half protectively holding him so that he wouldn't get into any more mischief. Emily (housemother) was trying to calm Larry, who was absolutely manic with excitement but who was not daring enough to get into active participation and was screaming as though he were beside himself. When I parked my car and started on the double to-ward the house, Joe and Andy, who at that precise moment were dashing out to the sidewalk to get more snow both yelled, practically in unison, "Oh, oh, there's Fritz," and tore up into the house, not forgetting to bolt the door against me in their mad dash, so that Emily had to let me in. The boys were now upstairs dashing around. I went up there, bumped into by Andy in the dark as I entered. I grabbed him unceremoniously while I bellowed out to all others within earshot: "I want you in bed right now." Thank God, the magic of hierarchy worked, and there was a rustling as they all tore out of their hiding places and into bed. I marched Andy in, and stayed around for another full hour. Aside from a few upsets in the two rooms which were quickly handled, they dropped off to sleep without much trouble. (Entry: 1/15/47, Fritz Redl)

Pearl Bruce and I were co-counselors today and, after school, tried to interest the boys in some active games indoors since it was freezing cold outside. They were in a wild and primitive mood, however, and our program efforts fell seriously short of reaching any mark. Soon, Andy and Joe began sexual teasing of Pearl and me and got really quite mean about it. Andy lashed out at Pearl viciously when she sharply told him that she did not want him to jump up and hit at her breasts. In one of these exchanges between Pearl and Andy, Dave (Executive Director) who was making systematic fifteen-minute inspection tours of the house because of the wild mood of the boys, walked in on the situation and sharply ordered Andy to keep his hands off Pearl. He dropped them immediately and then began a whining attack on Pearl and me, "Aw, they never let us kids do nothin'." Finally, he went downstairs to Dave's office to talk to him. (Entry: 2/5/47, Vera Kare)

There is one more issue, however, which we had better emphasize in order to be sure to avoid a severe misunderstanding: we are talking only about the occasional trick of getting kids to stop something by simply forbidding it, and thus, so to speak, "swaying them off their feet" temporarily, without having to use interference techniques as drastic as the original situation seemed to suggest. This is very different from, and has nothing to do with, a policy of solving life problems by "authoritative Verbot," instead of involving the children in an understanding of what is going on, creating self-participative insight into the reasons why their behavior cannot be tolerated, or even by direct appeal and reasoning of all sorts. We would strongly oppose any such policy of autocratic restrictions, firmly believing in the intrinsic value of cooperative planning, challenge to value sensitivity and insight, symptom tolerance, and, of course, democratic group leadership. In fact, we are convinced that the nondamaging use of the occasional "authoritative Verbot" is possible only if the rest of the lives of the children is built on the other policies just mentioned as far as their disturbance degree allows. We consider "authoritative Verbot" as an interim interference stopgap only, and want it clearly understood as such. It must be followed and surrounded by a wide range of other techniques.

JOSEPH S. MILLER, M.D.

22

The use of rational authority
in the adolescent group

In our time we have seen some very important changes in authority manifestation which I want to discuss later, for it is necessary that our views
and our practices keep in touch with the forces which move people. First,
I want to state my thesis.

I am going to talk about adolescent groups dominated by an autocratic
indigenous leader and bent on destructiveness. The villain of my piece,
albeit a gentle and well-meaning one, is the professional leader's so-called
permissiveness, alongside which the destructive trend can thrive. My hero
is the exercise of rational authority by the professional leader. In this
statement, I want to develop why rational authority, rather than non-
authority, can be an effective instrument, how it can be applied and what
is likely to happen as a result.

Coming to group work through a discipline different from yours, I will
feel more comfortable if you allow me to set forth some premises and
definitions on which my statement rests, and I beg you to bear with me if
these are elementary to you. Let me start with the group work agency
itself. I have nothing to say about the agency that aims only to provide
play and educational facilities. Besides teachers, it needs custodians of its
properties and its enrollees, but it need not waste money to employ professional workers. If the agency counts on interesting programs to improve
the well-being of its members, I recommend the addition of recreational
aides and entertainers.

Where, however, the agency uses professional social workers, I must

Reprinted with permission from *Journal of Jewish Communal Service*, XXXII:
268–74, 1956.
Presented at the Annual Meeting of the National Conference of Jewish Communal
Service, Atlantic City, N.J., May 23, 1955.

assume a much deeper interest in the social welfare of its clients. I assume it is engaging professionals to observe, to understand and to *influence* the behavior and relating processes of its constituents. Why observe and try to understand, if not to treat?

To those who argue that the group work agency is not a treatment facility, I say that every contact of the professional worker is treatment. We are here to discuss whether it is good or bad treatment and whether therapeutic opportunities are being missed.

To those who argue that the group work agency is short-staffed and therefore cannot indulge in treatment, I say all the more reason to make the limited contacts more meaningful. What can possibly be more important to the agency and the worker?

When you get a grasp of the endless array of negative influences on the lives of some of our youngsters – I mean in their families, their over-crowded schools and delinquent neighborhoods – you will regard your impact on them more seriously. Can you think back on your own youth and recall some person who gave you a significant nudge for which you will always be grateful?

Coming to group work from the field of individual therapy, I was amazed and thrilled to see the marked and rapid effect group work might have. It is odd for me to be saying this to you, but I feel that many group workers are unaware of what a vital therapeutic instrument group work can be.

Well, treatment for what and toward what? Agencies, of course, have among their membership hysterics, obsessives and all other diagnostic categories. At the Educational Alliance, unless we needed a more specific psychiatric diagnosis, we preferred a view which would serve as well for those who, never in their lives, get near any formal diagnosis or therapy.

This view is that the human being tends to grow unless arrested or diverted by some internal or external destructive process. When we speak of destructiveness in an individual or group we do not mean only delin-quency, assaultiveness, or suicide; we mean laziness, apathy and indiffer-ence as well. When we speak of health, we do not mean only a cessation of the destructive manifestation; we mean growth. And growth means not necessarily learning to make an ashtray in ceramics class, or learning to dance, or becoming orderly at meetings. All these attainments are amply present in many destructive people. By growth, we mean movement in the direction of finding oneself as a separate and unique being – similar to his fellows and his family, yet relatively free of their irrational holds on him. As such the individual tends to look on the world and on life with interest and wonder.

Perhaps you notice that I have put our goal in terms of the individual. This is not just a prejudice I brought from individual therapy. I am interested in group work to help the individual to grow. In our time we have too often seen individuals regimented to put forward the group.

What I say here applies to people but especially to adolescents; and perhaps this is a good place to mention the features which make this so.

First, as the trite expression goes, adolescence is that period between childhood and adulthood. This is not just a truism; it is a fact of profound significance because the change-over does not occur simply and completely in one leap. In the individual the wish to become an adult may appear before the corresponding physical maturation and the necessary know-how. Then we have a youngster afraid he will not be able to make the change. Or, the physical maturation may burst upon one who does not know what it is all about. Within the group there are many embarrassments arising when one youngster fails to mature as fast as his confreres.

Second, in the adolescent period, both dependency and rebelliousness reappear. In my opinion this situation calls for the presence of a clear and forceful adult who will provide a structure and limits in which the youngster can find himself and grow. Needless to say, it is better if the adult be knowledgeable and not a know-it-all.

Third, since we are group workers, it is important to note that the adolescent has a greater need for the group than one has at any time in his life, before or after. I think this fact should make us less fearful of losing clients because of our forwardness or directness.

Fourth, with adolescents, treatment needs to be more active and direct. This is so in group work as well as in individual therapy. When the treatment is direct and active, the adolescent can be very responsive. This underscores the value of the significant, though limited, nudge the professional leader can give.

Now to come to the main issue. Most of my statement here derives from my experience as psychiatric consultant at the Educational Alliance, located in New York's lower East Side, which most of you know is a delinquent or near-delinquent neighborhood. The groups concerned in this discussion were presented to the seminar because of some destructive activity such as gross disorderliness, stealing and fighting. Each group had an average of 9 boys or girls.

From the presentation, it was easy to gather that the group was led along its destructive path by an indigenous leader who might or might not also be the elected leader. Usually the group of 8 or 9 included 1 or 2 assistants to the leader. These would not necessarily be warm friends with the leader or in accord with him in his destructive pursuits. Rather, they might be considered to prefer the role of lieutenant to that of challenger. The remaining 6 members were generally less active followers and might include some potentially constructive youngsters.

If I have given the impression that the group would be a wholesome one if only its destructive leader vanished, I did not intend this. Nor is it true that the followers were simply unwilling prisoners of the leader. I see them rather as confused – not knowing where they are or where to go – but perhaps they were attracted by the force and glamor of the leader and the group.

It is, however, true that the leader was exerting autocratic authority on his fellows. One could see that he made decisions for the group without really sounding out the others. Simple examples of this are getting the club to admit or bar certain new members, getting the club to expend its money for this purpose or that, or getting the club to take a certain position in relation to the agency. In clubs which have not begun to use parliamentary procedure, the leader and his assistants give the impression that decisions were reached somewhere, somehow, between meetings. In clubs which use parliamentary procedure, there is a more obvious straining apparent. There must be a vote, but the leader and his assistants make unfavorable discussion and voting unpopular.

We are accustomed to think of authoritarian authority on youngsters being superimposed from above or outside. But in these groups it comes from within.

I want to repeat that the reports to the seminar on these groups always contained some refreshing rumblings of a constructive nature. As one looked at the followers one saw some constructive potential which for the greater part gave way to an apathetic decision to follow the leader. For example, the healthy side of a boy might lead him to question a certain action the leader is advocating. He would be drowned out in shouts not just to the point where he was intimidated, but to the point where his unhealthy side took over and made him believe his question was after all stupid. In other words, his constructive rumblings were weak in conviction.

Next, our interest (at the seminar) turned to the staff worker. What was he doing in the face of the above? If I may speak of him as a composite and be allowed to oversimplify, I would say he was a superb observer of interactions within the group and of individuals' assets and deficits, but his actions were not consistent with these observations.

Why should this be so – a worker making brilliant, penetrating observations and then not acting on them? In the workers I know, it was certainly not because of lack of interest or lack of courage.

For one thing, modern psychiatry was born in the Victorian period when authoritarianism was at a peak. The psychiatric lessons learned then were of the evils of the cruel parent and the harsh schoolmaster. Think of the novels of that period. Remember the fiercely authoritarian schools the heroes of boys' books attended. Anyway, I think social workers do not want to be authoritarian; they want to be nice and do good. So they shy away from *any* kind of authority.

But there is a more important difficulty. I said earlier that the villain in this piece is permissiveness. Of course, I do not mean the permissiveness Freud recommended. Freud taught that patients in psychoanalysis needed to be allowed to reveal themselves, regardless of what they were, and needed the supportive patience of the therapist when they went through the rough periods of change. More recently, for many, the word "permissive" has come to mean "passive." I think many workers in our fields believe that the patient or client in a destructive mess will see out of the corner of his eye that the therapist or worker permits his destructiveness and is not angry at him for it, and, seeing this, he will give up being bad. What the patient more often feels in such instances is that the therapist does not understand or does not care, or the situation must be hopeless.

At any rate, to the extent that our composite worker passively watched and permitted the destructive process to exist, to that extent it continued or even flourished. To the extent that he failed to heed and support the positive rumblings in the group, to that extent the potentially constructive members learned to ignore their healthier impulses; and to the extent that the worker failed to challenge the leader, to that extent he unwittingly re-enforced the notion that the leader is not to be challenged. In short, what happens in such instances is that the destructive process goes on, the individuals involved, sometimes even the worker, becomes apathetic and the glimmers that life can be better subside.

Where does this sort of permissiveness come from? Are the schools teaching it? Is it our own timidity? Is it the pendulum swing away from authoritarianism? Is it an influence of Non-Directive Counselling? Is it a "gift" from Progressive Education?

Let me interrupt the discussion of our destructively-led group to define the different modes to which the word "authority" has been attached. First, *authoritarian* authority refers to the force of irrational superiority. It may be backed by physical force, threats, or an irrational connotation of father, king or policeman, and it is embodied in such a figure. I have already offered the autocratic indigenous leader of our groups as one example. Another is the totalitarian dictator of our time.

But, if you think the totalitarian dictator derives his power through sheer force, you need only recall the abundant use of propaganda which told the people what and how to think and eventually succeeded in making many feel not simply that they *must* follow the leader, but that they *want* to. This propaganda did not gain credence by having its leader's stamp of approval. Often it was anonymous or invisible. In our own society, this *invisible* authority is represented currently by a tremendous pressure to conform, not just in dress or manners but even in thinking.

If a few decades ago, the authority picture in youngsters' lives was one in which the parent forbade the daughter's use of lipstick and the schoolmaster slapped his ruler across the boy's knuckles, the picture we commonly see today is different. Now the youth says, "I need a leather jacket. Everybody's got one except me"; and the parent, far from exerting any kind of authority, bemoans his powerlessness saying, "I can't do a thing with him." I shouldn't fail to mention a goodly number of parents who even help their children pick up the invisible signals and help supply "what you're supposed to have."

The so-called permissiveness I described should more properly be called "non-authority." To what I have already said about it, I will add only that in present-day group work, the professional leader's use of it amounts to abdication before the destructive autocratic leader and the pervasive invisible authority.

Of course, I am not recommending a return to authoritarian authority or suggesting that the professional leader meet the autocratic leader with more of the same. What I propose is the exercise of *rational* authority. By rational authority, I mean that which is authoritative through reason, not through force or fashion. The teacher ideally represents rational authority not when he says, "This you must do," but when he says, "This is so." And not when he says, "This is so because I say so (or because everybody says so)," but "This is so for the following reasons which you may examine."

In our field of group work we may formulate our use of rational authority as follows: "I am a man. I have lived and seen things and I know something of life. I have studied and practiced in the field of interpersonal relations. I have an interest but not an axe to grind. I have watched you for some time and this is what I see. I am making myself heard and watching your reactions but not compelling your obedience."

Now let us pick up our discussion of the group at a point where the autocratic leader is moving the group in a destructive direction; the remainder of the group's membership is flashing a few constructive glimmers but for the greater part is following the leader's destructive course; the professional leader is standing by permissively; and all this is taking place in an atmosphere of irrational, invisible authority.

From this point on, the worker is using rational authority. How? Mainly as commentator. He observes what goes on and makes the most significant and pertinent comments on it – not on the ostensible issues presented by the youngsters but on the dynamic issues seen by the professional worker. For example, he might say during a club meeting, "I notice that Pete (the autocratic leader) wants to get his buddies from down the street initiated into the club, even without a vote. I have the impression a few of you don't want those boys. But none of you has said anything." The comment is not on the pros and cons of the prospective members, but on the interchange between the autocratic leader and the passive followers. We advise the leaders of our groups in all ages to offer an evaluation at least once a year, again an evaluation mainly of dynamic focus.

At the Educational Alliance we have had a few instances of stealing, furniture slashing and the like. I learned very early in my contact there that, when the worker thought Johnny did it, then Johnny *did* it, even though the worker could not prove it. When the worker dealt with this in a non-authoritative way, there was no progress. If the worker said, "We want to find out what you had to do with this," Johnny would dodge and deny endlessly. But if the worker used his hunch as rationally authoritative and said, "Johnny, we know you stole the phonograph records. We know you long enough to know that you have some nervous trouble which makes you do such things and we're here to help you arrange treatment for it," Johnny usually admitted his misdeed and engaged the worker on the issue of treatment.

If I have suggested that this kind of treatment makes everything all right in one easy lesson, please forgive me. Just like individuals, groups have resistance too.

First there was the resistance of the indigenous leader who would resort to every conceivable sabotage of the worker's efforts. He might bring the group to decisions outside of regular meetings, i.e., in the absence of the worker, he might absent himself or call off meetings.

More important was the resistance of the oppressed followers. If they were simply oppressed, they would welcome the professional leader's interference and join it. They eventually did, but before that, they were fearful of the autocratic leader, uncertain of the worker, and unclear themselves. Over all they were attracted to the power and glamor of their leader. Repeatedly they would rise to assert their loyalty to him and criticize the worker's interference. Only if the worker persisted bravely, brought more evidence forward, and followed up the defensive tactics, would defection in the ranks of the followers occur.

At such times a confusion would appear in the membership. The group would become disorganized and dissolution would appear imminent. None of our groups actually disbanded but I believe such a development certainly could follow.

As the reconstructive process continued (here I am using a composite group rather than a specific one to list the sequence of reactions), there was an emergence of allies to the worker and then the emergence of a new club leader. If this seems unnatural – that the follower replaces the leader who in turn may become a follower – it really isn't. Organized on bully lines, Johnny is the natural leader, but, when the lines of organization change, the leadership changes, too.

I do not mean to say that only the leadership changes, the destructive tendency is interrupted, and then all is quiet. In the destructive mold things were locked, but in the constructive reorganization things are open. So problems become more apparent. There is movement.

Such movement may attract the deposed autocratic leader to return as a member with a different kind of interest. With things open, youngsters find themselves and may very well change to different groups more to their liking. Some might quit the agency. I repeat our goal in group work is the freedom in which one can find himself and grow. Again I state it in terms of the individual and certainly not in terms of agency statistics.

Until now, I have omitted a subject which is not specifically germane to the thesis of this paper. Yet it is so close and it crops up so often in discussions that I cannot overlook it. I refer to the setting of limits.

In my opinion it is necessary and desirable to set limits. The principles involved are the following:

1 When an activity (or inactivity) is diagnosed as destructive it should be interrupted – this for the good of the offending individual as well as the group and the agency.

2 While workers and administrators may disagree on the line of limitation, we all recognize that life has limits. Agency doors have to be closed some time at night. It may as well be a definite time. If a gang of boys is allowed to demolish the furniture and terrorize the rest of the membership, the agency will become a den for a gang instead of an agency for the community.

3 Limits are not just a painful, necessary reality. I believe limits provide a good setting for one to grow in – contrary to some currently popular notions of Progressive Education.

4 It is helpful in our work and in accord with our rational pursuit to an-

nounce the reason for setting a limit. For example, we say, "You can't steal because, in the interest of your health and ours, we interrupt whatever unhealthy activity we see." Or a small child, innocently exploring or playing with a lamp, will be asked to desist because we cannot afford to have it broken. Or a group may be singing in good spirit and fun and be asked to stop because the worker has a headache and cannot stand the singing.

Through all I have said here runs the thought of the professional worker as example to his clients. Of course, I do not mean this in any petty sense but in the sense described, that the adolescent is floundering on the issue: Shall I see myself and my fellows as each is? Shall I face life with interest and responsibility? Shall I step up and be a man? To the adolescent the best answer to the question, Can life be faced? is the presence of one who faces it.

I am aware that the most domineering, most manipulative people have claimed their authority to be rational. How, then, can we place so much faith in the prescription of rational authority? For one thing, any half professional worker can see through such claims made by possessive mothers, would-be dictators and the like. For another thing, workers are supposed to know something about themselves. Also, it is assumed that every agency provides a certain amount of check through seminars and supervision. Nevertheless, each of us is capable of some such unwitting manipulation, and this is a valid objection to the approach recommended here. It is an objection to be aware of, but if the worker and the agency can afford to make mistakes and admit them, it does not amount to a weighty objection. Despite it, I believe that the exercise of rational authority by the professional worker provides the best approach to many destructive tangles in the adolescent group.

HAROLD ESTERSON

23

The professional leader's use of
rational authority: comment

As a discussant to Dr. Miller's paper, I will address my remarks in two directions. First, I should like to show how the conceptions suggested by Dr. Miller apply to work with individuals. Secondly, how certain feelings and factors in interpersonal therapeutic situations interfere with the use of rational authority by the therapist, caseworker or group worker.

First, I would like to tell you how I think about the group, and how I think about the individual. Then, how both group and individual seem rather inseparable to me when I think along dynamic or therapeutic lines. When an individual walks into my office he brings with him a host of others. These others, as well as the patient or member or client, have been subject to specific cultural influences. The extent to which this individual has taken up with the culture, and conformed to it, is a matter of professional determination, soon to be explored with the individual. What I mean to say is that a person never appears in isolation. It seems to me one needs to view this individual as a member of one or another group. This group may be a social one, or a familial one. In any case, we know that he has had experience with the primary group, the family. The exploration in the early as well as later stages of contact will deal with the ways and means this individual has interacted with members of his family. Frequently, the individual has disconnected himself from his family physically, or in some defensive way, and he will talk about groups other than the familial one.

One such person told me that she had a great deal of concern and

Reprinted with permission from *Journal of Jewish Communal Service*, XXXII: 275–9, 1956.

When this paper was originally given, the writer was Consultant Psychologist and Director of Counselling Services at the Educational Alliance, N.Y.C.

anxiety about a group of friends. Discussion with her revealed her anxiety lest these friends, this social group, turn out to be just like her family group. She felt that the familial climate did not lend itself to emotional growth. The kind of group a person selects depends largely upon his past experiences with other groups. Certain individuals may feel more comfortable in a group which has an authoritarian leader. In many instances, the history of the person reveals that the authority figure in that person's family was of the authoritarian variety. Certainly, there are other factors which attract an individual to a specific group other than the person's experiences with authority figures. For example, in some groups, feelings of physical ugliness is a factor which not only attracts members to a group but also binds them together. When I suggest that some people are more comfortable in groups led by authoritarians, I mean to say that they experience a minimum of anxiety. A situation which is familiar and known tends to produce less anxiety than one which is strange. If one has had frequent experience with authoritarians, one knows already how to integrate with that other person. To take up with a more rational authority requires a new integration and hence a different use of one's self. To state it differently, one needs to re-do one's inner climate in order to deal with an outer climate, foreign and strange.

For example, if you take an individual with an authoritarian background, and view him in a different kind of environment, governed by different authority (principles), he will twist and squirm, manipulate and provoke, in order to re-establish for himself that authority which suits his inner life. I might add that when these individuals fail at re-establishing the known, they begin to view the different authority as some queer specimen or some intriguing person. When this occurs, one can be fairly certain that some new experience has become available to that individual.

The individual, and that includes all of us, living with a typically defined authority, and here I include all the varieties suggested by Dr. Miller, not only lives with that authority, but also incorporates within himself the ways in which he has reacted to the authority as well as the authority himself. Hence, when this individual becomes an authority, he may subject others to the same kind of treatment that he was subject to. Frequently, if the nature of the person of the authority figure did not suit him, he will develop reactions against this form of authority, and assume behavior different or opposite from the behavior of his authority figure. However, if one digs further, one is liable to find the very qualities within the person which he so disliked in the authority figure with whom he had lived.

What I am getting at is the fact that the battle which we frequently see raging within the club rages within each individual. All the elements of personality noticed within the group are found within the individual himself. The struggle within the group between the authoritarian and the rational authority may be the same struggle that rages within each individual within that group. As suggested by the previous speaker, the job of the professional is to interfere in this battle or conflict, and lend a hand in supporting the more rational elements within the group. In doing this he supports all those reasonable and human elements within each member.

I believe these observations were implicit in Dr. Miller's previous presentation.

In the examination of an individual who is a member of a group, it would be extremely important to know where this individual fits in the group. Does he side more with the authoritarian elements, or does he show some rebelliousness towards them? Does he belong to a group which abhors intimacy and finds it disgusting or is the group one which encourages closeness and openness of exchange? Is this group devoted to maintaining forms of behavior which are useless in day to day operations, or are they flexible and ready for change? Are they preoccupied with what others think, or are they genuinely interested in their own welfare and pursue the avenues which would bring them satisfaction?

Most of the disturbed youngsters I have seen in group work agencies play distinct roles within their groups. Often they are either the scapegoats or the jokers. The assuming of such a role not only says something about the individual in question, but also suggests some diagnosis of the club.

One of the main points made by Dr. Miller which applies to work with individuals seems to be his conception of "the significant nudge." This idea has importance in working with individuals of all ages, but is specifically germane in working with adolescent individuals. For the adolescent, there are new physical urges, as well as anxieties about the future. In adolescence, he or she begins to think about the future and about such things as career and marriage. Behavior in relation to the opposite sex manifests itself in movements to and away. Preoccupation with the body is frequently observed. For the young lady, her figure, her attractiveness, her charm, her sexual appeal, are all of great concern to her. Ideas of having children may enter consciousness and bring with them various anxieties. For the young man, there comes a concern about his physical appearance and physical strength. Concern with being like everyone else becomes prominent as well as concern about being attractive to the opposite sex. Being independent becomes a matter of great urgency. Some adolescents push more vigorously towards becoming independent, while others are more confused about being children and adults at alternate times. Some are confused by parental and school attitudes. Many adolescents complain that when it suits adults, they ask them to be adult. On other occasions it suits the adult to see the adolescent as a child, and on such occasions the adolescent may become quite upset, and frequently discouraged.

Status and belonging are other factors which influence the adolescent's behavior. In this period of his life he begins to come to grips with various values. He begins to question parental values, and in some instances defies familial customs, and values. He feels that his values and the values of the group are much more profound and genuine than those suggested by his family. He may become more alert to the fact that in his family there is a difference between what is taught and what is practiced. In cases where religion is an issue, he may openly suggest that his father and/or mother are hypocritical. Many of these conflicts are part of the *sturm und drang* of adolescence.

In other situations it may very well be that the adolescent has a point. His point of criticism, however, may be linked up with deep problems of defiance and dependency while in other instances the adolescent may be more perceptive and have more integrity than the parental figures. It is precisely here that the rational authority, the keen professional, makes his entrance. If all the facts suggest that the youngster has strivings in the direction of living a more reasonable and a more satisfying life than his parents', then the significant nudge is of the greatest value, and may put the youngster on a track which will lead him in the direction he seeks. In my experience with adolescents, I have noted that one has great difficulty in getting them to reveal what they are interested in for the future. They are greatly shocked and surprised to find that you, the rational authority, agree with what they have to say. They will then admit that for a long time they thought themselves crazy because they harbored such ideas. The feeling that one is crazy because one wants to live differently from one's parents seems to be derived from irrational criticisms directed at the ideas which the youngster had suggested.

Even in those cases where the rebelliousness and defiance has an admixture of pathology, one needs to be careful to pull out those aspects of the youngster's rebellion and defiance which have some health to them. Let me briefly illustrate this point. A former patient of mine defied her family when she was 17 years old. She and her family lived in Poland, and she had the distinct impression that to remain in Poland would eventually lead to destruction by the Nazis. She married early against her family's wishes, and left the country. Her family was subsequently killed. The defiance actually and literally saved her life. Around this period she also had a strong interest in helping delinquent children, something her family strongly opposed. In her middle thirties she recovered this desire, and returned to school in an effort to achieve her goal. This was a person whose perceptions of what was going on were undoubtedly clearer than those of her parents.

Recently I saw a 16 year old boy referred by the group work staff of the Alliance. The main complaint of staff was that he instigated fights and was always the center of some destructiveness. Fortunately for him, the staff was rather sensitive to the kind of person he was, and referred him for diagnosis. This youngster was psychopathic-like, and in part he agreed to see me in order to get me to tell his father that it was all right for him to drive a car. Beneath this, however, there was an apparent dissatisfaction with the way his family lived. He was quite intense when he spoke of the fact that his family does not make much money, but yet pretends to be as well off as other relatives. They pay much higher rentals than they really can afford. In fact, this youngster had made an excellent diagnosis of the parental trouble. His problem, of course, was that he was exactly the same way. He talked with great pride about how he was friendly with a fellow who was the son of an outstanding member of the community.

As indicated above, the adolescent has many paths to take, and many decisions to make about his direction. The strong feelings of insufficiency or inadequacy about achieving particular goals may lead the adolescent to some provocative social behavior geared in part to express his dissatisfaction and hopelessness, and in part to calling society's attention to the fact that he is deeply troubled. This latter aspect, and usually the former too, may be completely unconscious for him. To recognize the various troubles that the individual is having, and to deal with them rationally may save the individual a great deal of pain as well as hopelessness. For him to know that some other human being is aware of what he is living through is very encouraging. He no longer needs to shoulder the burden alone, and may then be able to take up in a direction which is more useful to him.

In some instances, the significant nudge may not show results until some years have passed. In other words, the nudge and its therapeutic value may not be immediately visible. The fact that someone has recognized the trouble may be sufficient for the youngster to give the matter further thought. Group workers are in a particularly unique position to give any of these youngsters the push that they need. After all, the adolescent gathers with his friends in the agency for social and personal purposes. His group is quite different from the school group which has a specific learning purpose. At the same time, they know that the staff people are social workers, whose job it is to be interested in them. In a society which is as impersonal as ours, and which has schools large and overcrowded, the personal understanding of the adolescent yields large and productive benefits. Certainly, group workers who have contact with adolescents meet with these problems in their daily practice. We do not have sufficient data to know how well we succeed in being the rational authority proposed by Dr. Miller. We do know, from other work, that frequently our role of rational authority is somehow met with interference. I presume that when I lose my role of rational authority, something in me or in the relationship between me and the individual has gone astray. This phenomenon is frequently termed counter-transference. The counter-transference can be examined from two vantage points: the horizontal and the vertical. I can explore what there is in my own background which prompts me to respond in a non-rational and a non-therapeutic way, and I can look for elements in the relationship between myself and the other person which may push me in some useless direction. Undoubtedly, explorations of both directions are extremely important. Here I merely wish to state some common occurrences which make for counter-transference. Perhaps later others will comment more about it.

In one sense, the individual worker has a softer touch than the group worker. The individual therapist works in the confines of his own office, and at best he and his supervisor become aware of his failures. This is not the case in group work. You are working out in the open, where your usefulness to the membership can be viewed by all. That includes the Board of Directors. I think that another important area which frequently troubles the worker, and leads him into ways he deplores, is the lack of clarity of his role. The caseworker and therapist know that the job is to understand the client. He trusts that with the understanding there will accrue therapeutic benefits. The group worker, on the other hand, has been frequently burdened by over-emphasis on program. Program has not been measured by the intrinsic values it has to the members, but too often on the basis of how it looks. If many members turn out for a dance and the dance is orderly, things are said to go well. As a result, the group worker frequently has to take great pains to see that things are neat and orderly. Simple provocations at those rather hectic moments may lead the worker to lose his temper or perhaps behave in a way which he later regrets.

In addition, the group worker is not in a unilateral relationship but rather in a multilateral situation. He needs to have a relationship with every member of the group. This exposes almost every aspect of the group worker's personality. In essence, more of you is required than in the individual relationship. Again in the one to one situation, when dealing with a provocative, destructive youngster, one can easily ask the youngster to leave, or at worst, physically escort him to the door. This is not so easy when one has ten or twelve youngsters in a group. These adolescents are extremely well trained in provocation and can scatter to the four winds or the four stairwells of the agency if it suits them.

Generally, it seems to me that one's own attitudes towards authority, one's own hostility, one's own need to prove, one's own narcissism, etc., are factors which enter into the counter-transference situation. The extent to which we ourselves have worked out our own adolescence, to that extent are we able to deal effectively with the behavior of stormy adolescents. In any case, it always seems worthwhile to examine one's own reactions, not only from the point of view of becoming more effective, but also using the situation to learn more about the group or the other person. I have frequently found that my own reactions yield great diagnostic truths about the person or group with which I am dealing.

For example, to experience fear or boredom when I am with another person can frequently mean that this is precisely what the person means to communicate, and how he behaves with others. To live with my reaction leads me to some more severe counter-transference. To use my reactions as clues to understanding what the other person is doing seems beneficial and fruitful for all concerned.

BERNICE ORCHARD

24
The use of authority in supervision

The use of authority is frightening to many social workers, yet whether we like it or not, authority is an important component in public welfare programs as well as in other social work programs. In public assistance clients must meet eligibility requirements, must follow agency policies concerning verifications, reporting income and others. Public welfare caseworkers must determine that eligibility requirements have been met, must follow agency policies concerning eligibility and budgeting. Supervisors, among other duties, must see that the caseworkers under their supervision follow agency policies and do not make costly mistakes in determining eligibility and budgeting.

All of this involves the extensive use of authority. It is important that this authority be used constructively, which is not possible when one is afraid of it or conversely enjoys excessively the feeling of power that it brings.

Caseworkers tend to deny that authority is a component in casework practice. They stress the concepts of individualization and self-determination, both of which are very important concepts, but a client or a caseworker or a supervisor can be self-determining only within certain boundaries: first, the boundary of community law and order; second, the boundary of agency policies and, in a public agency, the laws under which the agency operates.

Two kinds of authority are generally recognized: the authority of competence and constituted authority.[1] The authority of competence comes

Reprinted with permission of the American Public Welfare Association, Chicago, from *Public Welfare*, XXIII: 32–40, 61–2, January 1965.
1 / Studt, Elliott, "An Outline for the Study of Social Authority Factors in Casework," *Social Casework*, Family Service Association of America, 44 East 23rd Street, New York, New York, June 1954, pp. 231–238.

from one's knowledge, experience and skill. A social worker who is assigned to supervise other social workers presumably has been given this position because he has greater knowledge, experience and skill in social work than the persons supervised. This greater knowledge, experience and skill is in social work, not in all areas. The supervisee may be a much better gardener than the supervisor or a much more skillful tennis player.

Constituted authority is the authority which is inherent in the position. The position of supervisor gives the supervisor certain authority over his supervisees: the authority to determine whether work is satisfactorily completed, the authority to evaluate the work of the supervisee for salary raises and promotions. The position of supervisor carries agency authority whether one has the authority of competence or not but certainly the supervisor can carry his role more adequately when he also has the authority of competence. The supervisor needs to be able to accept his authority with awareness of his attitudes toward it and their effect on his use of it.

ATTITUDES TOWARD AUTHORITY

How do one's attitudes toward authority develop? Initially they stem from the parent-child relationship but modifications usually occur as one is influenced by persons in authority outside the home as one grows up. The baby or small child has to be dependent because he cannot meet his own needs. His dependence brings about submission to his parents who seem to him to be all-powerful. The small child also has a desire for independence, a desire to act out natural impulses which parents are trying to teach him to control, which brings about resentment of the authority of the parents. This is often referred to as the dependency-authority conflict.[2]

How or whether the child resolves the dependency authority conflict depends to a considerable extent on the kind of authority to which he is subjected. In "ideal" situations in "normal" middle class American families, the child gradually takes over voluntarily the standards of loving parents and learns to control his own behavior in accordance with their expectations and to accept constituted authority without much conflict. If parents have been very strict and severe he may accept their controls through fear but also feel anger and resentment followed by guilt, which may interfere with his own acceptance and use of authority as an adult. The child who has had too little control from parents or inconsistent control will have trouble learning to control his own behavior and as an adult

2 / Towle, Charlotte, *The Learner in Education for the Professions*, The University of Chicago Press, 5750 Ellis Avenue, Chicago, Illinois, 1954.

may resent and rebel against authority and have difficulty exercising it constructively when it is part of his responsibility.

USE AUTHORITY CONSTRUCTIVELY

What should be the supervisor's attitude toward authority so that he can use it constructively? He needs to accept the fact that the supervisory role includes authority. He needs to have the ability to be firm when necessary, to have patience, to have a sincere desire for supervisees to succeed and progress. He should have no need to deprive, hurt or retaliate, no need for power over others. In carrying out his administrative authority the supervisor is carrying out the policies and regulations of the agency, not exercising personal authority. His authority of competence is used for the benefit of the client, the supervisee and the agency.

THE SUPERVISOR'S RESPONSIBILITIES

Customarily the process of supervision is divided into two components: education and administration. Charlotte Towle adds a third which she calls "helping,"[3] or perhaps enabling is a more descriptive word. It means enabling the supervisee to do his work to the very best of his ability thus increasing his own satisfaction from his work as well as benefiting the client and the agency. The enabling component permeates the supervisory process through the supervisor-supervisee relationship. The supervisor's attitude toward and use of authority is an important factor in the supervisor-supervisee relationship.

Administration has been defined by Berkovitz[4] as an enabling and directing process. In a social agency this means creating favorable conditions for carrying out the agency program of service to clients. The supervisor has an important role in agency administration. He must: 1) see that the agency policies and procedures are carried out by his supervisees; 2) see that work is done in accordance with agency standards and the agency time schedule; 3) recognize the supervisees' particular skills and use them for the benefit of the program, if possible; 4) control the work pressures on the supervisees so that they do not become too great a strain (in view of the size of caseloads in many public welfare agencies this is

3 / Towle, Charlotte, "The Role of Supervision in the Union of Cause and Function in Social Work," *Social Service Review*, The University of Chicago Press, 5750 Ellis Avenue, Chicago, Illinois, December 1962, pp. 396–407.

4 / Berkovitz, Sidney, "The Administrative Process in Supervision," *Social Casework*, Family Service Association of America, 44 East 23rd Street, New York, New York, December 1952, pp. 419–423.

often an impossible task); 5) see that conference, dictation and other schedules are maintained so that the work of others is not impeded; 6) help workers understand the reasons for policies and procedures; 7) serve as a channel of communication between the caseworker and the director and board, especially a channel through which the caseworker can make suggestions about policy: how current policies affect clients, desirable new policies, policies that should be changed or discarded; 8) evaluate the supervisor's work in accordance with agency standards.

Within the educational component of supervision the supervisor's responsibilities are to impart knowledge to the supervisee so that he will 1) understand the purposes and goals of the agency program; 2) develop understanding of the psychological, social, cultural and economic factors which affect clients' behavior, and apply his knowledge in his work with clients; 3) understand and apply casework concepts; 4) carry over learning from one case situation to another, seeing similarities and differences; 5) understand how his own feelings and prejudices may interfere with his work at times.

In some agencies or at some times the administrative component of supervision may need to be emphasized more than the educational component while in others the educational component may be emphasized more than the administrative component but both are important. In public welfare traditionally the administrative aspects have been emphasized but the present concern about rehabilitative casework services should increase the importance of the educational functions of supervision.

THE IMPLICATIONS OF ENABLING

As stated above, the enabling component of supervision comes about mainly, though not entirely, through the supervisor-supervisee relationship. The relationship is a configuration made up of many factors, some contributed by the supervisor, some by the supervisee. It is not static but is constantly changing, again depending on many variables. Each needs to accept his own role and that of the other. The supervisor needs to accept his role as teacher, enabler, checker and to accept the authority inherent in it. The supervisee needs to accept his role as a person not yet competent to practice independently, as a learner and a subordinate but hopefully a learning, growing person who is continually attaining greater competence and ability to function with increasing independence. He needs to accept the authority of the supervisor without great dependence and loss of initiative.

In addition to authority, the supervisor-supervisee relationship has equally important ingredients. As in all relationships acceptance is a basic factor. Acceptance should be mutual. The supervisor accepts the supervisee as a capable but not perfect person who will make some mistakes and have some prejudices but who is sincerely interested in providing good services to his clients. Occasionally the supervisee may turn out not to be this kind of person but, in view of the careful selection process used by most agencies in the employment of staff, the supervisor is justified in this initial expectation. The supervisee accepts the supervisor as a competent person who has the ability and interest in helping him learn and who has the authority to expect acceptable work, to make suggestions and corrections. The supervisee should feel the security of acceptance which will not be withdrawn because of occasional errors of judgment in evaluating situations.

Trust is another mutual ingredient of the supervisor-supervisee relationship. The supervisor trusts the worker to grow and develop, to be responsible about carrying out assigned work, to follow agency policies and procedures but he does not expect him to be perfect. The supervisee trusts the supervisor to give him information as needed, and to be interested in helping him grow and develop on the job but not necessarily to know or give him all the answers.

UNDERSTANDING LEARNING PATTERNS

The supervisor needs to understand the worker's learning patterns, prejudices and reactions to new situations because these affect his work. Some persons react to authority figures with subserviance and dependence, some with resistance. Some persons in a new situation seem to learn very quickly but do not retain the new learning; some start slowly and hesitantly but when they have the security of adequate knowledge move ahead rapidly and confidently. Others appear to resist new learning when they are testing it out before incorporating it. These are but a few of the patterns which supervisors should recognize and understand so that they can differentiate between learning patterns and learning problems, between conflicts and prejudices which a supervisee can modify when he becomes aware of them and personality problems which may prevent success as a social worker.

Some dependence is inherent in the role of the supervisee just as some authority is inherent in the role of the supervisor. Partly this comes from the lack of knowledge, experience and skill of the supervisee. As his knowledge, experience and skill increase the dependence should diminish.

Whether this happens depends to some extent on the supervisor's attitude toward authority and dependency. He should be able to accept the normal dependence of a new worker and give freely the information and knowledge which the new worker needs but he should not need to keep him dependent because the dependency itself is gratifying to the supervisor. As the supervisee gains in competence the supervisor should encourage him to function with greater independence so that he will continue to grow and develop.

Identification is a frequent ingredient of the supervisor-supervisee relationship. The supervisee wants to be a professional person like the supervisor, to model his professional performance after that of the supervisor. This makes it imperative that the supervisor provide a desirable professional image. At the same time the supervisor should encourage the supervisee to develop techniques that are natural to him because he is a separate person who should maintain his own identity as a professional person and not become a carbon copy of the supervisor. An insecure supervisor may feel that the supervisee's performance reflects his skill as a supervisor to such an extent that he does not permit the supervisee freedom to develop in his own way. The supervisee's success or failure is not necessarily the success or failure of the supervisor.

Ambivalence is bound to be present to some degree in the supervisor-supervisee relationship because it is present in any relationship which includes authority and dependence. The supervisee will resent the supervisor's authority at times and the supervisor will be annoyed at the supervisee at times. Since individuals learn and work best in a positive climate it is hoped that positive feelings will predominate but realistic acceptance of negative feelings when they occur should avoid a detrimental effect on the relationship.

SUPERVISORY METHODS

The supervisor uses his authority of competence and his constituted authority constantly in his day-to-day work with supervisees. In much of the interaction he does not recognize his use of authority or think of it as such. When he is faced with dealing with a worker's inadequate performance he recognizes this as a time to use his authority but often feels uncertain and hesitant. He wishes to be fair and to approach the worker in a way which will help him to be able to improve. There are principles which he can follow which may increase his own security that he is handling the situation fairly and with objectivity.

1 The supervisor focuses on the inadequate aspects of the supervisee's work but not on his total performance and he is careful not to imply that because the work is inadequate in some areas, the supervisee is an inadequate person.

2 The supervisor does not give negative criticism until he can see a repetition of the same error several times or until he observes a pattern of problems in certain areas. He wants to be sure that this is not a single incident which will be corrected quickly by the supervisee. Simple mistakes may be given back to the supervisee for correction without spoken or implied criticism but a repeated pattern of careless work will need to be discussed with the supervisee.

3 When the caseworker wishes to carry out a casework plan which seems unwise to the supervisor he needs to consider whether the client will be damaged if the caseworker is permitted to carry out his plan. If the supervisor decides that the caseworker's plan will not harm the client, even though another plan might be more helpful, he may permit the worker to go ahead with his plan with the idea that the caseworker may learn more quickly from his mistake than from being urged to follow a different plan which is not his own. Awareness of the supervisee's learning pattern is important here. Some people learn more readily from their own mistakes than any other way while others are devastated by making a mistake. If the caseworker's plan will, in the supervisor's considered opinion, really be damaging to the client, he will, of course, need to insist gently but firmly that it not be carried out.

4 The supervisor needs to consider before discussing unsatisfactory work with a supervisee whether the supervisee has too much to do, because his lack of production, careless work or frequent errors may come from too much pressure. It is helpful if the supervisor knows how his supervisees react to stress. Some persons work best when they feel pushed while others become anxious, disorganized or immobilized. Perhaps the worker needs help in setting priorities or in organizing his work.

5 The supervisor ought to ask himself whether he has frustrated the supervisee by not giving him enough help or by keeping too tight controls when the worker is ready to take more initiative and become more independent. He may need to find out from the supervisee whether his methods of supervision are meeting the supervisee's needs. The problem may be due to a lack of understanding or communication between them.

6 Does the supervisee have the knowledge that he needs to do the work that is expected of him? Because there is so much to be done public welfare workers often are pushed into carrying a too heavy work load too

soon. Their lack of necessary knowledge adds to the feeling of pressure and creates frustration which may affect attitudes toward work as well as amount accomplished.

7 The supervisor will want to find out, if possible, whether the supervisee is experiencing heavy outside pressures such as family problems or health problems which may be affecting his work. If the outside pressures are temporary it may be possible to ease the job pressures a little until the supervisee can attain a balance again. If the outside pressures are prolonged the supervisor may be able to suggest resources which will help the supervisee cope with them.

To sum up, when the supervisor sees a pattern of poor work in certain areas or certain reactions which interfere with a worker's performance he looks first for realistic causative factors and deals realistically with any that he finds. Often pointing out an unproductive or erroneous pattern to a worker in a matter-of-fact, non-punitive way means that the worker is able to correct the pattern himself and without feelings of inadequacy.

UNDERSTANDING THE CASEWORKER

The supervisor needs to keep in mind that social work makes heavy demands on its practitioners.[5,6] They deal with troubled people with serious problems and needs. Many are people whose standards and values are very different from the social worker's standards and values. Some clients behave in ways which social workers have been brought up to abhor. New workers without graduate social work education often do not have knowledge of human behavior, cultural patterns or economic conditions which make it easy for them to have understanding and sympathy for some clients. Meeting a constant barrage of problems and needs is very wearing, especially when the resources available really do not meet the needs. Social workers have to find ways of protecting themselves against these constant assaults on their feelings. At times work may suffer from the emotional pressures of the job just as it may from volume. Supervisors can help supervisees find healthy ways of dealing with their feelings so that they do not handle their frustrations by being punitive toward their clients. Just recognizing the frustrations and showing understanding of

5 / Babcock, Charlotte G., "Social Work as Work," *Social Casework*, Family Service Association of America, 44 East 23rd Street, New York, New York, December 1953, 415–422.

6 / Schour, Esther, "Helping Social Workers Handle Work Stress," *Social Casework*, Family Service Association of America, 44 East 23rd Street, New York, New York, December 1953, pp. 423–428.

the feelings may relieve the pressure so that the worker can mobilize his energy to give service to his clients.

Occasionally a supervisee shows a pattern of resistance or emotional blocking which interferes seriously with his work. The resistance or blocking may manifest itself in any of a variety of ways:

1 The supervisee has an intellectual understanding of human behavior and casework theory which he can discuss knowingly with the supervisor but is not able to use when confronted by a client. This is also a stage of learning – when one knows much more than he can apply in practice and so the supervisor needs to make sure that the pattern persists over a period of time and continues to interfere with the supervisee's relationship to clients before identifying it as emotional blocking. Perhaps this person needs professional help, perhaps he could function in some areas of social work not requiring intensive treatment relationships or perhaps he should not be in social work.

2 The supervisee avoids certain pertinent topics in discussion with clients, changes the subject as the client is about to bring out meaningful material, asks inappropriate questions, is unable to work with certain kinds of problems or kinds of behavior. This may be due to inexperience but if prolonged usually indicates difficulty in handling feelings, fear of his own or clients' feelings or similarity to some difficult situation or relationship in the supervisee's life. For instance, a divorced woman may be angry at men and judges harshly her male clients or she may have difficulty only with those whose behavior is similar to that of her former husband. More often, however, the emotion which is aroused is related to something which occurred much earlier in the worker's life and has been repressed and "forgotten." The repression is threatened and painful feelings may be stirred up against which the worker unconsciously protects himself by not hearing what the client says or by not following an obvious lead given by the client.

3 The supervisee agrees in conference to carry out certain treatment plans but doesn't do it. It may be that he does not understand the plan well well enough to execute it and further discussion will clarify it for him. If it happens repeatedly or always in the same types of situation, the supervisor will conclude that the supervisee is blocked by his own feelings which may be related to the client or the situation or may be related to the supervisee's feelings about authority and/or his relationship to the supervisor.

4 The supervisee retains strong prejudices after knowledge and experience in social work should have modified them and has such rigid standards

and values that he is unable to understand clients' behavior and to work with those whose behavior violates his standards. Actually some behavior exhibited by clients threatens his maintenance of his own standards and values and so he has to erect rigid defenses against the feelings which are aroused. This kind of person should not continue in social work because it is too hard on him emotionally – to say nothing of the effect his lack of understanding and punitive attitudes may have on the agency's clients.

The resistance and emotional blocking most commonly encountered is that which is brought about by a reactivation of the worker's conflicts or repressions by particular kinds of behavior or case situations.

After the supervisor clearly identifies the pattern and rules out realistic factors which might be affecting the supervisee's performance, he points out the pattern to the supervisee as he sees it in specific cases. "In this and this and this case you stopped the client just as he was about to tell you something important." "In A, B and C cases it seems to me you were bothered by clients' expressions of hostility." "Have you thought about how much alike Mrs. X, Mrs. Y and Mrs. Z are and that you reacted much the same way to each?" The supervisee's first reaction may be to deny that there is any validity to the supervisor's observations, in which case the supervisor does not insist on his point of view but may suggest that the supervisee think it over. The supervisee frequently returns saying that he has decided the supervisor was right. In some instances, it may be necessary for the supervisor to point out the pattern when he sees it again. Often bringing the pattern to the supervisee's attention means that he can change it, perhaps not immediately, but gradually. It is not important to the supervisor why the supervisee is disturbed by the particular situation because the supervisor does not engage in a treatment relationship with the supervisee. If the pattern persists and continues to interfere with the supervisee's work the supervisor may suggest that he seek treatment elsewhere.

CONCLUSION

There is a great deal of authority inherent in the supervisor's role – both the authority of competence and the constituted authority derived from the responsibilities of the position. It is important that supervisors recognize and accept this authority so that they can use it constructively. They need to understand their own feelings about it, their possible reluctance to accept it, their fear of it, or their pleasure in the feeling of power that it brings, to mention the extreme reactions. Authority can be a constructive

and helpful component of the supervisor-supervisee relationship. It provides structure and support. Through his authority of competence the
supervisor enables the worker to learn the work he is expected to carry
out, to learn to understand the persons with whom he is working, to learn
the methods which are most effective in meeting clients' needs. Through
his constituted authority he facilitates the worker's use of agency policy
and procedures. Through the evaluation process – both day-by-day and
formal periodic evaluations he enables the worker to recognize his
strengths and weaknesses and helps him grow and develop to his maximum
potential.

SALLY KNISELY

25

Authority: a factor in the casework relationship
with trial visit patients

In our casework program with mentally ill patients outside the confines of a hospital, we have as a part of our setting certain procedures of a constructively authoritative nature. However, every mentally ill patient probably suffers in one way or another because of his real and distorted fear of authority. In our trial visit program, both the real and the distorted authority, from the patient's point of view, are often symbolized by the caseworker. Within this program it becomes an important objective of the caseworker to begin to establish a relationship with a patient by helping him sense the real and constructive authority that exists in the caseworker as opposed to the exaggerated and distorted sense of authority he invests in her. Even under these circumstances, a relationship can be established in most cases.

As the term implies, "trial visit" is a trial release, an extended visit granted by the hospital to the patient because he is well enough to go home while remaining under hospital jurisdiction. It is recognized, however, that a patient is not well enough to take the tremendous step from hospital life to family and community adjustment without having to face many problems. Therefore, he may be assisted with these problems through the trial visit casework program.

Preparation for release on trial visit is carried out in one of two ways. In some cases, the interpretation to the patient of the trial visit program is made by the hospital caseworker. The patient is then released, and his first contact with the Regional Office casework program takes place when the caseworker contacts him after he has arrived at home. In other instances, the Regional Office caseworker who will work with the patient

Reprinted with permission of the author and the National Association of Social Workers from the *Journal of Psychiatric Social Work*, XXIV: 36–41, October 1954.

during his trial visit goes out to the hospital to meet him before he is released and interprets the trial visit program to him. In whichever way the patient is prepared for release, his trial visit is originally granted for a period of three months. If he gets along quite well during those three months, as reported to the hospital by the caseworker in the community, the hospital ordinarily extends the trial visit for additional three-month periods until a year has elapsed, at which time the patient is discharged from the hospital. If during this year life at home becomes too much for him at any time, he can return to the hospital of his own volition, or his family has the responsibility to return him.

AUTHORITATIVE ASPECTS OF THE TRIAL VISIT PROGRAM

The authoritative quality of certain casework procedures has special significance in this program and must be seen from the patient's point of view. Consider the position of a patient when his trial visit is about to begin. Before he leaves the hospital, his trial visit status is discussed with him either by the hospital caseworker or by the Regional Office caseworker. In either case, aspects of the trial visit interpretation may be forgotten once the patient is outside the hospital. This is true not only because of the patient's mental illness and his thoughts about returning home, which are uppermost in his mind, but because the trial visit concept is one he cannot grasp until it has begun to be an actual experience for him. Once on trial visit status, and returned to his family, he leaves behind him much of the realistic and distorted authoritative qualities he may have associated with the hospital. Yet, certain realistic aspects of the hospital authority are still present. Technically, he is a hospital patient during his entire year of trial visits, and various tasks delegated to the social worker can be labeled "authoritative" although these can be used constructively with the patient.

First of these authoritative procedures is sending the original appointment letter to the patient after he arrives at home. This letter, carrying the authority of the agency, represents the beginning of a "constructive authoritative" role with him. It is also a going out to him, and a way of offering something which he needs but may not want. It is an effort to help him with the many problems he may be closely harboring within himself and hesitating to share with anyone, for fear of rehospitalization.

Secondly, the authority invested in the social worker's position can be used helpfully in seeing the patient's close relatives while he is at home. A casework program of this kind cannot help the patient unless the other significant members of his family are seen. For example, the mother may be a very disturbed person herself, and this the caseworker needs to know. The son's mental illness is often uppermost in the mother's mind, a real threat to her adequacy; she may, therefore, react punitively toward him, or she may take such an overprotective attitude that she prevents him from taking progressively healthy steps on his own initiative. Or, because of his unusual behavior, she needs sympathy and understanding in order to lessen the household tension and make both of them more comfortable.

The three-month social service reports to the hospital, on which the hospital bases its decision as to whether or not to extend the patient's trial visit, is a further authoritative step in helping the patient. Through these reports constructive use of authority for the patient's welfare is exercised. This is true whether the patient is adjusting well, or has become so disturbed that he, his family, and the worker are discussing the patient's possible return to the hospital.

The worker is frequently able to sense from a patient's conversation and behavior that he is beyond making decisions for himself. Such a patient may have become so confused and disoriented, or perhaps delusional, or his destructive impulses may be so overwhelming, that he cannot any longer be responsible for making decisions. He is then desperately seeking someone to assist him, someone he can depend on at that moment. I am reminded of a woman who had been out of the hospital on trial visit only ten days, and who came in as soon as she received my appointment letter, although I was a complete stranger to her. She was severely depressed, trembling, sobbing, and disheveled. Stumblingly, she spoke of blood, her fear of razor blades, and her attempt at suicide the previous day. Her coming without waiting for the date of our appointment was a good indication of her need to place herself within a stronger, surer authority because of her own overwhelming loss of control. Kindly authority is most helpful to such a seriously disturbed and troubled patient.

But from the point of view of another patient, this letter might mean the stirring of anxious thoughts and the activation of fears. Repeatedly, the receipt of a letter on official Veterans Administration stationery arouses in the patient all his real and distorted fear of authority. At first he keeps his appointments not because he is requesting or expecting help of any kind, but because he is suspicious and afraid of some "authority" if he does not respond – some authority in the Veterans Administration vaguely involving the caseworker with his possible rehospitalization.

Most of these patients on trial visit status receive disability compensation. This money is usually placed in the care of the hospital manager while the patient is hospitalized, and a certain monthly allotment is sent for his expenses while he is at home on trial visit. The worker has authoritative responsibility to help a patient with the use of his trial visit allowance and to see that his budgetary needs are adequately covered by this money.

The worker's authority is further helpful to a patient whenever the consultation of the Regional Office staff psychiatrist is sought. This is true whether the worker speaks with the psychiatrist directly or indirectly requests that the patient be seen by the psychiatrist.

Patients attribute to the case worker the ultimate authority to return them to the hospital. The worker does, in fact, possess some authority but only in so far as she reports on adjustment and arranges for psychiatric examination; all of which may ultimately lead to a medical decision that the patient requires rehospitalization.

In each of these instances of the worker's helpful authority, whether it is seeing the patient's relatives, writing the hospital reports, using the psychiatric consultant, or discussing these procedures with him, the patient in some degree distorts this useful authority because of his own mental illness and his past experiences with authority. The crucial question, then, is how to establish a relationship with a mentally ill patient in an "authoritative" casework program outside the hospital confines, when the patient does not seek help on his own initiative and does not want the help we know he needs. Under these circumstances, much depends on the manner in which trial visit status is interpreted to him.

INTERPRETING TRIAL VISIT[1]

I cannot know the exact meaning to each patient of my "authority" when I first see him; for these feelings within him are as individual as each of his other problems. I can observe, however, his rigid, mechanical, timid movements, his anxious face and frightened eyes – his severely withdrawn approach. Or I can see his surly, arrogant, masterful manner, his belittling and ridiculing approach to me. Or perhaps he shouts and complains and defies – another approach. But a theme of fear runs through all three – the fear of my connection with the hospital. Because of this fear of authority, a further explanation of why I want to see him and of his trial visit status is too complicated, too far above him, and he would comprehend little of it. And even if I made such an explanation and he did take out of it certain ideas, this would do little to help establish a relationship with him – to help him as a person relate to me as a person. I find it much more success-

1 / Editor's note: The first person form is here used to convey more fully the give-and-take between worker and patient.

ful to make the most simple verbal explanation possible. In my first interviews, therefore, I say only as much as the patient seems to be requesting to know at a time. I may never mention the term "trial visit," which he knows, until the patient is more comfortable with me. Through my use of the most simple words and a very informal approach – friendly gestures, the offering of a cigarette – the patient begins to feel or sense, something of me as a person in this new, unknown trial visit experience.

Generally, in the first interview as he hesitantly sits across from me, I take the initiative. I begin by asking him in a quiet voice if he knows why I wrote him. He may recall his social service preparation at the hospital and hesitantly say, "I knew somebody would get in touch with me." If he can say this much, I know he has made some tie-up between his release on trial visit from the hospital and the reason he is coming to me. For it is important that he understand the tie-up even though I do not talk at length of "trial visit" as such. Because he understands it, however, it also means that he is fearful of what I will do to him, and this we must try to work out together as the relationship develops. If he can say nothing of his hospital preparation for trial visit, I may ask him if he remembers talking to a social worker before he left the hospital. He may respond with some such phrase as, "She said I'd be home for three months," or, "She said you'd get me my money." Some reference to money or compensation is frequently made by patients, and it is one way they test out the "authority" of the trial visit caseworker. If a patient is a little more free to bring out his opposition to trial visit, he may say, "I haven't got anything more to do with the hospital – I'm home now!" He may ignore my question about the hospital caseworker and say, "Can you get a job for me? I got to go to work." He may be so withdrawn and fearful that he does not answer at all. There are a considerable number of patients in this program who are too ill to take much, if any, part verbally in the interview situation. These severely withdrawn, mute patients have long since removed themselves as far as possible from any situation involving authority. My aim is to minimize the overpowering authority they expect in me; and to attempt to establish a relationship wherein such a patient will sense understanding, kindliness, and respect in whatever way I can convey it. This can only be done by the skillful handling of silence in these interviews.

On the other hand, the patient's fear may take the form of an aggressive, hostile outburst against the hospital and against me. Whether he remembers anything that was told him at the hospital about trial visit, whether his comment is about money, employment, a statement in opposition to trial visit, or whether he brings up another of many topics, I pick up whatever simple phrase or sentence he mentions, and continue talking to him with sincerity, calmness, and respect. The topic itself is generally secondary so far as establishing a relationship to him is concerned. Whether he is able to disguise it or not, foremost in his mind are thoughts such as, "What kind of a person is she?"; "What is she going to do to me?"; "How can I somehow manage to please her, or show her that I am getting along O.K. so she will not send me back to the hospital?"

Months later, when our relationship is a stronger one, the patient himself sometimes tells me these early thoughts about me. To alleviate his fears a little, if possible, I make a simple explanation to him of who I am and why I am seeing him. I may say that the hospital let me know he is at home and has asked me to find out how he is feeling. Often a patient will say in response, "Oh, I'm fine." I accept this comment. I tell him I am really glad he is. If he does not seem too anxious and fearful, I may follow this by asking him what he has been doing since he came home. This makes him a little more anxious because he does not know whether I will approve of how he has spent his time. Perhaps he responds with, "Oh, not much," or, "I go for a walk now and then," or, "I've just been taking it easy," or, "Oh, I know I have to get a job." Each reply says a great deal in terms of how the patient is testing me: Do I expect him to be doing "something" in particular? Is going for a walk an adequate adjustment for an "adult" man? Do I expect him to go to work immediately? My acceptance of his words does not necessarily lessen his anxiety a great deal, for he knows inside himself that he has not told me much of anything about how he is getting along. He has no more reason, therefore, fully to believe my words of acceptance and reassurance. This is why it takes more than conversation between us, and the patient needs to "feel" his way along with me, to "feel" something of how I treat him, in order for our relationship to begin to develop.

My first several interviews with a patient are apt to be quite short. However, in each of these short successive interviews, the patient and I talk simply together as well as we can about the topic he has formerly mentioned. If he has forgotten the topic since our last interview (he may, because of his confusion, fear, and anxiety), I ask in some informal manner if we were not talking about so and so. Or I may say that the last time we saw each other, he told me such and such. This helps him get started, as well as makes him realize that he pays no penalty for forgetting, and the "we" also helps to establish the relationship. Each succeeding interview not only carries the discussion a tiny bit further, but allows him to feel his way along, to sense what I am like, and to realize that nothing harmful is happening to him.

In making a further appointment after an interview, I try to interpret a little more of the trial visit program and do it in such a way that it promotes the developing relationship if possible. I may ask him when I am going to see him again. He may look puzzled, dismayed, or frightened, or may even say, "Do I have to come back?" I then explain quietly that I do want to see him and that the hospital has asked me to continue seeing him, but I, too, would really like to know how he is getting along. He may then ask how long he has to continue coming. I then explain that he is ordinarily expected to continue seeing me for a year and during this time I will be reporting to the hospital regarding his progress. By the look on his face I can see that this is hard for him and I often say, "I know it's pretty hard to come here, isn't it?" or a similar sympathetic mark.

In our interviews I try to ask as few direct questions as possible so that a patient does not feel I am prying or probing into his life. But when it is unavoidable, either to clarify something he has vaguely stated or to help him bring out something I know he wants to reveal, I pose a question. However, I always preface my question by some such phrase as, "Let me ask you, if I may, did you mean so and so?" In this manner I am letting him know I am really trying to understand what he is saying or thinking. I am also giving him implied permission not to answer if he does not choose and I am, therefore, not imposing my "authority" on him.

By the time I have seen a patient several times, he generally mentions some family member. This may be his mother, in connection with his hospital custody papers, or regarding how she gives him his trial visit allowance money, her encouragement for him to get employment, etc. I take this as my cue to bring up the possibility of seeing his mother. But this is also another test in the relationship between us; for even though he may have mentioned his mother in criticism, the fact that I want to see her makes the patient immediately anxious about me again. Whether he can verbally question why I want to see her or not, he begins to wonder about me. He thinks I do not accept his story as he has related it. He thinks I distrust something he said, and now I am going to check on him and how he is really getting along. If he is too fearful to ask the question so obviously on his mind, I take this up with him by saying quietly, "You wonder why I want to see her." I recognize with him that in one sense it is like checking up on him. I add that I understand that his mother is also really interested in his remaining at home, and if I can talk with her perhaps I can help her understand the difficulty about his money, or her requesting him to go to work, etc. I do not believe that this explanation eases his anxiety to a great extent. However, I do not demand to see his mother nor will I see her without his knowledge. In an unusual case, I may see the mother against the patient's wishes. If he becomes quite anxious, I ordinarily state I will not see her until we have talked it over again. Actually, we may discuss it several times before he is agreeable. Meanwhile, he has had the realization, the feeling, that I have not done something which he has not been ready for me to do. This again helps to develop the relationship between us.

I will have had several interviews with him, and probably seen his parents, by the time I am ready to send the hospital the first three-month report on his adjustment. Discussing this report with the patient is another point where my realistic authority needs to be explained as carefully and as sympathetically as possible. It is also a further step in interpreting his trial visit status to him, but at the same time it makes the establishing of the relationship difficult because it brings into sharp focus for him all his distorted fears of authority and my connection with the hospital. I explain as simply as I can, perhaps in several interviews, that I will soon be letting the hospital know how he is getting along so that they can take action with regard to continuing his trial visit. Whether the patient can express it verbally or not, his fear shows up immediately through his reactions. I may then state for him that I know he is worried lest he will have to go back to the hospital. I may tell him that as I see it, he seems to be getting along quite well, and enumerate several things he has told me he is doing every day, stating that these are some of the things that I will tell the hospital. If he cannot take part in this discussion, I say something to the effect that I know this is difficult for him but I want him to know what I am doing so that he will know what he can count on in me. If I feel that the patient's anxiety has not been diminished by any of our discussion, I may suggest something to the effect that I know we have not known each other very long, and maybe he will have to try to trust me just a little. However, after he has actually received a letter from the hospital extending his trial visit, he has a little more confidence in me. He is not quite so fearful that I am trying to rehospitalize him. Therefore, the relationship between us becomes a little stronger.

In working with any one of these mentally ill patients, his suspicious attitude, the fear and anxiety he feels, his process of testing my "authority," may continue many months, as many patients have subsequently confirmed. In the beginning, the patient comes for his appointments to report to me, to comply with what he assumes are the requirements, to placate, or to prove to me that he is well enough so that I will not "send him back." Therefore, the process of interpreting to him in whatever simple ways I can what his trial visit means, must be repeated many times – especially his distorted fear of my authority to rehospitalize him. But as time goes by and he experiences the reality that he is not sent back, he becomes a little more free and begins to see his interviews with me in a little different light.

The point in his trial visit at which he has gained enough security with me so that he knows I am not sending him back to the hospital varies with each patient depending on his own illness, his past experiences with authority figures, and how able I have been in conveying to him my sincere interest in helping him get along outside the hospital. The patient himself will begin to indicate this difference in our relationship by his more relaxed manner with me, his discussion of deeper problems, and perhaps his request to see me more frequently. It is at this point that he no longer fears my "authority" and sees in our relationship something of positive value for himself. This is also the point beyond which I no longer need to interpret to him the meaning of his trial visit status.

In summary it is to be noted that our trial visit casework program has constructively authoritative aspects. Even though these mentally ill trial visit patients are fearful of the caseworker's real and distorted authority in the beginning and do not seek casework help on their own initiative, a positive relationship can be established. Relationship with these patients is established through the slow and careful interpretation to them of their trial visit status and simple, friendly discussions of their experience during the first three months they are out of the hospital. Most patients, once the relationship is sufficiently secure, are more free to discuss various problems pertaining to their daily adjustment, and they are then increasingly able to profit from the case work help offered to them.

ARTHUR E. FINK

26
Authority in the correctional process

As one starting point in a discussion of authority in relation to the correctional services it may be useful for us to consider the all-pervasive place of authority throughout our lives. Certainly, if we reflect upon it a bit we can recall how early we begin to become aware of authority in its many manifestations. We may encounter this early in our family situations, especially in relation to our parents – the limitations that are imposed and our struggles against what we are obliged to do and the prohibitions about what not to do. These rules may not make very much sense to us, nor are we overly enthusiastic about respecting them, but little by little and each of us in our own way makes some kind of working accommodation to them. We have met authority and we will never be without it as long as we live.

AUTHORITY IN THE SCHOOL AND COMMUNITY

Then our little world of the family opens to a larger world of the school and the community and we experience authority as it is expressed by other persons and imposed by other rules. Certainly the teacher and the principal, with all of their professed willingness to help us, seem to resemble our parents and to have a liberal assortment of prohibitions, commands, and regulations with which some of us begin to have trouble. Sometimes, some students have so much trouble that it seems necessary for school officials to take restraining action or, in aggravated situations, to disassociate such youngsters from the school system. Regardless of what action the school takes, all students have experienced its authority and some have come into uncomfortable conflict with it.

From *Federal Probation*, xxv: 34–40, September 1961.

COMING TO TERMS WITH AUTHORITY

In the larger community, of which the school is only one part, the adolescent – we will assume for the purposes of our discussion he, or she, is that far along – meets many more rules, limits, injunctions, indeed laws. Here, again, there will be varying adaptations to these demands, and not unrelated to the degree of success achieved in earlier encounters with authority. In some instances these earlier difficulties may be so unresolved that action may have to be taken by an agency known as the juvenile court. The man, or woman, who presides over this court, insists he wants to help and this sounds just like what some other people have said; in fact, the judge is painfully reminiscent of those other authority figures – parents, teacher, principal – and he seems to have even stricter rules than they had.

With all due respect to parents, teachers, and principals, it may be observed that perhaps for the first time the youngster has had to come to grips with authority, that literally and actually he is face to face with authority as he and the judge look at each other. In all likelihood the judge knows something about him already, for another person who looks familiar and who is in the same room, has prepared some material which, too, sounds familiar. One of the large tasks of the judge will be to set in motion the process by which this youngster can begin to get help in coming to terms with authority, as he, the judge, acts on behalf of and as an agent of the community and as he, at the same time, acts for the welfare of the boy. Nor are these purposes contradictory; rather they are integral aspects of the very service for which the court was created and for which it continues to exist.

Let us assume the judge, having examined the material the probation officer has prepared and making his own analysis of the youngster and the difficulties he is having, decides to place the boy on probation. Here, again, the boy faces authority – authority of the community, of the court, of the judge, and now the authority of the probation officer. Like the judge, the probation officer has a service: Primarily serving the community but also serving the offender as to conduce to his welfare. As he begins to work with the boy the probation officer may encounter considerable resistance. This may take the form of silence or mumbled and unintelligible replies; or resentment and sullenness; or a blaming of his troubles on other people; or an aggressive hostility expressed against the court, the judge, and the probation officer. The disciplined probation officer will recognize and understand these various manifestations, seeing them as some of the many ways in which human beings in trouble try to keep from having to face their own part in their difficulties. The probation officer who not only represents authority, but *is* authority, must get past this shielding front, and must help the boy to begin to take hold of what he can do about himself.

Not infrequently as the boy begins to open up and to permit communication between himself and the probation officer he may press for a relaxing of the authority which the probation officer is exercising. To some people it may seem to make good sense to ease up on the use of authority – after all this boy has had a hard time at home and at school, other people have been too strict with him, and besides that he is only a boy as yet. To other people it may seem very important to bear down on this boy; to let him feel the full force of society, and to teach him a lesson this early. The competent probation officer may see it differently. As he gets to know the boy he becomes aware that while there has been authority in the family and in the school the boy has managed, by one means or another, to avoid coming to terms with it. Perhaps there has been too much strictness, or not enough, or a too erratic use of it. The probation officer's job will be to take this boy as he is, where he now is, and to help him with the reality of the struggle he is now having with authority.

This help which the probation officer offers the boy around authority is ineffective when presented in lecture form. It takes on meaning when it is handled with respect to specific items, such as the conditions of probation. For an apparently simple example I will quote from an actual record.

For the time being, he would be obliged to observe a 10 p.m. curfew and attend school daily. Carl balked at this. He was 16 and didn't want to go to school. We talked about this, Carl complaining that he wanted to work and I pointed out that I wondered if he would really be satisfied with that and wondering, too, if he could really be self-supporting. The factor most impressive to Carl, however, was learning that although at 16 he had a legal right to stop school, in the eyes of the law he was still a minor and could not leave home without his parents' permission ... Carl looked most unhappy and fumed for awhile. I suggested he think about that seriously and commented we could talk about these things at his next interview. The remainder of the time was spent preparing Carl for his Mental Hygiene Clinic examination. Carl did not like the idea at all ... I explained why we felt a psychiatric examination was important and made arrangements for a later interview with him. He left the office in a very disgruntled frame of mind.

Carl came in on time for his next appointment. I was greatly encouraged by this interview because for the first time Carl was really able to talk back, almost to the point of arguing. True, everything he put out was negative and hostile, but it does show he can be reached. He even shed a few tears which he didn't try too hard to hide this time. We talked in spurts for well over an hour and Carl did not appear ready to bolt as on previous occasions.

He was angry about his Mental Hygiene Clinic examination because I thought he was "crazy." As we struggled with this and finally cleared it up we got to talking about "trust." Carl did not even trust his mother, why trust the court?

There are a number of comments that can be made about these fragments of interviews with Carl that bear on our discussion of authority. For one, authority can be dealt with most effectively, especially with an adolescent who heretofore has not come to terms with it, in small bits. To tackle authority in all of its manifold aspects and in its totality would be overwhelming for Carl – indeed would be meaningless. To relate it to such tangible requirements as school and a curfew provides him with something he can handle, or can refuse to handle. He can then know what he is doing and can be held to his part in it by his probation officer.

TAKING ON RESPONSIBILITY

This leads to another aspect of authority – namely, the responsibility which the individual carries in relation to it. The imposition of authority from above or from the outside is not effective of itself alone. It is only as the individual who encounters authority takes some responsibility for what that authority means to him or does to him that any beneficent action follows. As long as Carl can keep himself untouched – really untouched inside of himself – by any authority so long can he continue to resist the demands of society and go his own way. However, when authority impacts upon him in small, but not unmeaningful, areas of his living, then he must come face to face with it and carry the responsibility for dealing with it negatively or positively. If he deals with it negatively he can still keep it outside of himself and respond to it destructively; if positively, he begins to internalize it and lets it begin to operate constructively in his life.

THE STRUGGLE WITH LIMITS

Another aspect of authority relates to the struggle that all of us, including the offender, have around limits. We push against limits and yet we would be terrified without them. They are essential to growth, to change, and to all aspects of living. Many years ago Kenneth Pray remarked about the need for such limits.

These limitations are not only ineradicable facts of life to which ... we are bound to adjust ... they are, in fact, the very bases upon which we discover our own capacities, for we must have something to struggle against in order to find ourselves, to achieve selfhood with all its satisfactions. Without these limits we are lost in a tidal wave of surging impulses, none of which is better or more satisfying than any other.

It is the probation officer's job to understand this and to work with the delinquent in his struggle with limits for by so doing he, the probation officer, is enabled to offer the constructive possibilities of authority.

NECESSITY FOR CHANGE FROM WITHIN

Let us assume that Carl and his probation officer are working together satisfactorily and let us take up with Bill who has made such little use of probation that the judge has felt obliged to revoke probation and place Bill in a training school. The judge has no illusions about the training school, he will not expect miracles, but he does hope the more controlled setting of the training school will provide Bill with the opportunity to settle down a bit, to take a look at himself, and with the help of a trained worker to take steps toward bringing about some change within himself. Bill may not have learned yet to live within limits; nor to have come to terms with authority; and he has probably managed to hold off any genuine change within himself. He may resent the rules of the institution and may start out breaking as many of them as he can. He may defy authority as it is embodied in the person of the superintendent and members of the staff. These are all matters with which he and his worker will need to do something about.

At the one extreme the response of the institution may be to bring the full force of its total power to bear upon Bill and to flatten or crush him. The other extreme would be based upon feeling sorry for Bill and all his misfortunes and to cushion the impact of the institution upon him. It is here suggested that neither of these extreme measures is likely to prove useful. In the one instance Bill's unresolved struggle with authority may be sharpened and intensified still further. In the other – the easing up – it would be a disservice to Bill because it would be relieving him of his own share of responsibility for the situation in which he finds himself. There is a useful service somewhere in between the two.

Bill needs to feel the power and the authority of the institution as something that can be used helpfully in relation to his problems. As mentioned earlier this is not gotten over to Bill via the lecture method, but around specific situations as they arise and as Bill handles them and as he can talk things over with his worker. In this process undoubtedly Bill will make mistakes, but with the help of the worker he can learn from those mistakes. If he is overprotected he does not have the opportunity to test himself against the reality in which he is and hence can gain no benefit from the experience. Throughout all of this – this mean between two extremes – it is essential that change shall come about in Bill. This is something that Bill must do and be responsible for; it is not something that another person, not even the worker, can do for him.

AUTHORITY AND THE MAN IN PRISON

As we did with Carl let us do with Bill – let us move on to another kind of situation in which we can examine authority in relation to the correctional process. Let us assume we are dealing with an adult offender who has been on probation, whose probation has been revoked, and who is now in prison. Many of the foregoing remarks also apply to the man in prison. Perhaps they apply in greater degree by reason of not having been worked out earlier in life: The struggle with limits; coming to terms with authority; taking on responsibility for one's self; and the necessity for genuine change.

One of the hardest jobs the prisoner has is to get himself *into* prison. To the layman this must sound like double-talk; of course the man has gotten himself in. However, a closer examination of these words – or perhaps more strictly speaking what is behind the words – reveals there is such a thing as being in prison physically and another thing which is being in prison psychologically. In the latter sense this means facing what it is that has gotten him there; not merely the act or the acts for which he was tried, convicted, and sentenced but essentially the kind of person he is that has gotten him to this pass. From the start it will be the worker's job to help the inmate face all of that. Many, if not most prisoners, may feel that they have been sent to prison unjustly. It is not uncommon for the inmate to insist it was someone else who committed the offense; or that the other person got off with a light sentence; or if he was the only one involved that he wasn't given a fair trial; or that he drew a "bum rap." There are an infinite number of ways of denying one's involvement of being in prison, and it is frequently in this kind of situation that the worker must start. His first job may be to help the prisoner to face the real fact that he is in prison, that he has gotten himself there. This will be necessary before the worker can help the prisoner get something out of the prison experience, and ultimately to be ready to get himself out of prison, able to stand on his own feet, and taking responsibility for himself.

Some prisoners may express their disinclination to face being in prison by open defiance of the prison's rules. This aggressive behavior may be a way of a prisoner denying he is in prison. True, he knows his body is behind walls and in a cell, but he is unwilling to face his real self in his predicament. A competent worker recognizes what is going on within the prisoner, recognizes as an employee of the prison that rules must be obeyed, and sees the prisoner's responses as offering an opportunity to look at himself, to struggle with limits, to come to terms with authority, and to bring about some change within himself.

Another prisoner may, right from the beginning, bend all his efforts to getting out by legal recourse. Again, the skillful worker will see this as a way of not facing being in prison. Here, the worker's efforts will be directed to helping the prisoner to express, largely by words and feelings, his responsibility for himself and his part in being where he is. It will not be until the prisoner can be helped to get past this point that he can begin to use what prison has to offer and really prepare himself for release.

Another way of getting out is by escape, and understandable to the layman as this desire may be it still has meaning to the prison worker as a refusal to face one's self and the situation one has brought about. Nor do prisoners customarily discuss their intentions with staff workers, but on at least one occasion this happened. After bringing this to the attention of the appropriate prison official the worker recorded his account of the experience. A portion of this is excerpted here for the purpose of illustrating some of the points of our discussion.

I asked him how he was feeling now about being here and about wanting to be out on the "street." Was he still thinking about escaping? He did not look at me; instead he stared at his hands, looking very dejected. He said he still thinks about it; he cannot help but think about it. Every night he thinks about his family and how much he feels his place is with them. The agonizing slowness of time makes him want to scream sometimes at night. He would feel better if he could do this, but he is afraid they will send him to state hospital if he does. He feels his life is being wasted in here. His rightful place is with his wife and child. He thinks about getting out a lot. I told him I knew that getting out was important to him, and I wanted to see him get out, but not by means of escape. I wondered if he knew what escaping would mean to his wife. What would she think about it? He said he has never really asked her directly, but he knows she would disapprove. He told me he thinks he is going to try to be with her for their anniversary. I wondered if he were successful in getting out, how long did he think he could stay out. He knows what he would face when he came back (if he came back alive), then how about the next anniversary, and the next one, and the next one, and the ones after that. How long could he expect his wife to wait for him if he received additional time?

Despite having access to a hacksaw this prisoner did not escape nor try to escape; the prison officials took the situation in hand and nothing happened. The important consideration for us here was that a worker could help the prisoner to face something of himself; could help him to take some responsibility for himself; could help him in his struggle with authority; could help him to be "in" prison so that he, the prisoner, could in time really get himself "into" prison, and then to begin working toward bringing about the kind of change within himself that would enable him to move toward getting himself out of prison. The getting "out" here means only getting his body out, but within that body, or person, enough inner change happening so that he could take responsibility for himself, and for what he thinks and does so as to keep him a self-respecting and useful citizen – useful to himself and to other people too. Incidentally, this particular prisoner did serve out his minimum term, had his difficulties in prison, but was deemed ready for parole supervision and was eventually released. He may not have been a new man at the time of his discharge, but he was certainly a changed man because he had used the prison experience to do something different about himself than had been true previously.

Another way that a prisoner may have of not facing himself and his situation is to want to escape from it by way of self-annihilation. The worker records, later, the following incident with the same prisoner.

Another long silence followed and then he remarked that if he were man enough, or had courage enough, he would take his own life. I inquired if he really felt it took a man to do that. He nodded. I said that if he really wanted to solve all of *his* troubles, that would be the easy way to go about it. It did not take courage.

It is to be hoped that these several excerpts will give substance to the points about helping the offender in his struggle with authority. Obviously, this is not done by the lecture method nor by telling the prisoner what he ought to do. He knows what he ought to do. The help consists of working understandingly with the prisoner, enabling him to get certain things out of his system, and confronting him with his own share of responsibility for what he is and what he does. It consists in helping him to make decisions about himself. He has to make them; another person, no matter how gifted, cannot make them for him.

What has just been said about the man in prison is just as true of the woman in prison. Here in North Carolina we have become familiar with some of the constructive possibilities of working with women offenders after they are committed to Women's Prison. Each year students from the School of Social Work have carried on their field work training under the supervision of a qualified staff at Women's Prison. All of the points that have just been discussed, about the offender, are very real in the working experience of these students – the struggle with limits; the coming to terms with authority; the necessity for inner change; and the taking on of responsibility for one's self. Not infrequently it is around this last point that students have the hardest time. As they work with women prisoners they become increasingly aware of the tendency on the part of the prisoner to put the blame on someone else or something else. One of the hardest jobs the student has (assuming she has learned it to the same degree within herself) is to help the prisoner to admit to herself the share she has in her own difficulties. It is quite understandable that the student may have genuine feeling for the predicament the prisoner is in, especially if there are children in the home outside. However, the student learns, and usually the hard way, that it is no service to the prisoner to get caught up in her – the prisoner's – difficulties and to overlook the necessity to help her face her own responsibility. It is only as the prisoner can be helped to come to this – to really get herself into prison – that she can begin to use the opportunity prison offers and thus move step by step toward ultimately getting herself out of prison.

AUTHORITY AND THE MAN ON PAROLE

Now let us look at the last of the situations in which as professional workers in the correctional field we are engaged, namely, parole. Again, we will have to make some assumptions. The man who is on parole has encountered authority in its many forms from his early life onward. More recently he has been in prison, and the judgment has been made that he is ready to leave the institution and to make a go of it on parole. No more than any other person can he avoid the demands that will be made upon him as he tries to live and work in a kind of modified liberty. Indeed, by reason of all that he has gone through – the behavior that got him to a court and then to prison, and the person that he is – he may have a more difficult time working out his salvation than other persons.

The parolee finds that even though he is out of prison there are rules to go by. Many of these seem restricting and even though he may have learned something from the prison experience these restrictions may prove irksome if not at times downright frustrating. As with all of us the struggle goes on interminably – the struggle between the inner and the outer. The rules are explicit – about working, supporting one's dependents, the kind of company one keeps, the limitations on travel, etc. Does one conform to these requirements only as they are insisted upon by the parole officer with all the force of the law which he embodies; or does the parolee act upon the basis of some change within himself that has been going on for some time? I am willing to suggest that it may make a great deal of difference as to how the parole officer goes about his job with the parolee.

The way the parole officer works will depend to a great extent upon his convictions about people– his respect for them as human beings, with all of their shortcomings; his appreciation of the uniqueness of each person with whom he is working; his belief in the capacity of people to change; and his conviction that true change must come from within. As he works on these premises he can approach each of his parolees as individuals who have difficulties of a serious nature and who need help in getting themselves straightened out – and that he has the skill to help. He, too, must believe in the rules, and must realize that his helping is within the bounds set by the rules.

Suppose we take a simple, and not unusual situation which is taken from the actual record.

Much of Jim's troubles come from his not having found himself and in not being sure of what he wants. This was particularly true about his job. He was also aware that he needed to find companionship and affection. He remarked, "I guess I want what I have never had." He seemed to see the point when I said most of his trouble was in his own attitude toward people, his unwillingness to trust himself and others enough to give them friendship. We talked of ways of solving the problem constructively and of his other choice of escaping from his troubles as he had before into vagabondage and crime.

An examination of this excerpt reflects a willingness on the part of the parole officer to talk things over with his parolee. There was a back and forth quality about this intercommunication. The parole officer was giving Jim the chance to talk over some of his difficulties and enabling Jim by what he was saying and doing to come to decisions about himself. He was quite willing to have Jim engage himself in his own problems and to hazard some of his – Jim's – own solutions.

Several months later Jim brings Marie to his conference, and his parole officer records some of the interview as follows:

Jim then reminded me that he had mentioned Marie to me as the girl with whom he was going and added that her mother objected strenuously to him. Marie smiled and nodded agreement. It quickly became apparent that they were in love and Jim said they hoped to be married. However, the chances for it did not look so good because of her mother's opposition and Marie was only 19. I said it must seem pretty tough if they were fond of each other, and wanted marriage but found the way blocked. What did they propose to do? Jim said they would have to wait until Marie was 21 unless her mother changed her mind. He added, "Of course, we could always go over the state line." I asked him what he thought of this last remark as a solution. Jim replied it would be a risk since he was on parole. I agreed, saying I too thought it would be a great risk. He might get away with it but if he didn't he would have a lot of time ahead of him.

Here, again, the parole officer could involve Jim in his own thinking and consequences. It might appear to many people – uninformed people – that the simplest thing would be to impress upon Jim what he could do and what he could not do. This we all know as the ordering and forbidding technique, but we also have doubts about the lasting effect of decisions made along that line in contrast to the value of decisions made by the individual in a self-responsible way. This requires of the individual – Jim – that he face up to himself, that he recognize the limits within which he has to operate, that he be fully aware of the authority that surrounds him, and that he make his own decision upon the basis of change that has taken place within him – and that he carry responsibility for the decision he has made. These are the identical points that have been stressed throughout these pages – and are as applicable to the man on parole as to any of the other persons about whom these remarks have been made.

CONCLUSION

In conclusion I refer again to Kenneth Pray. It will be recalled that earlier I quoted some of his remarks about limitations. Written in the middle 1940's the wisdom in them is as firm today as yesterday. Referring to freedom Mr. Pray insisted it was a relative term when he said:

There is no absolute freedom anywhere in this world and there ought not to be. None of us has absolute individual freedom; none of us believes in it; none of us would know what to do with it if we had it. Some structure of authority, defining and enforcing the necessary limits upon individual personal responsibility and conduct, as a condition of social cooperation, is an indispensable basis of any kind of life in any society. Such authority is essential in the prison; it is essential in the outside community.

... Within these essential limits of social cooperation, freedom for every individual to make his own choices and judgments, to take responsibility for his own life, is not only an invaluable right of personality, it is an inevitable and immutable fact of life. Every individual will ultimately take and use that freedom whether we like it or not. That is to say, in the last analysis every individual will behave as he himself wants to behave, for his own reason, to attain his own ends ... We may of course, while he is within our immediate influence, get him to behave outwardly the way we want him to behave – sometimes under practically physical compulsion; for a somewhat longer time, perhaps, through fear of painful consequences of acting otherwise; for a still longer time, probably, through hope of ultimate reward such as an earlier release from confinement. But when he leaves our sphere of power – and all prisoners will ultimately do so – he will act as he himself, deep down inside, wants to act.

Several times it was remarked that the method of lecture or admonition was not especially effective in helping the offender to deal with himself or the difficulty he is in. Yet for many people it seems so natural to tell others what they ought to do or not to do, and then to assume that others will do what they are told simply because they are told. And when it comes to working with the offender who has not yet come to terms with authority it seems to make even more sense to tell him what to do or even to direct his life for him. I am moved to observe that such an approach if not downright harmful is of limited usefulness or of no use at all, because it is based upon a misleading notion of human behavior. The worker in the correctional field is likely to be far more effective if he can engage the offender in the process of doing something about himself. Basic to this process is the quality of the relationship between the helper and the helped whereby the one enables the other to express ideas and feelings and even actions – and to which the helper responds in such a way as to increase the opportunity for the offender to take an additional responsibility for himself.

Thus as we bring to a close our discussion of authority in the correctional process it is essential that we be convinced of its usefulness; indeed of its indispensability. We need to value it – as much for the worker in corrections as for the person being helped. But we need to see, also, the other aspects as they are related to the use of authority, namely, the use of limits, self-responsibility, and inner change. By our understanding of these and our skillful use of them we thereby offer to the offender the opportunity to realize more fully his own capacity as a human being to live satisfyingly and constructively.